THE
EDUCATION
OF AN
ARMY

THE
EDUCATION
OF AN
ARMY

British Military Thought, 1815–1940

JAY LUVAAS

THE UNIVERSITY OF CHICAGO PRESS

CASSELL & COMPANY LTD
35 Red Lion Square, London wc1
Melbourne, Sydney, Toronto
Johannesburg, Auckland

First published in Great Britain March 1965
First edition, second impression November 1970

I.S.B.N. 0 304 93726 6

Printed in the United States of America by
The University of Chicago Press
and bound in Great Britain
870

To Frances and Donald Hampson

IN GRATITUDE

PREFACE

A few years ago, while investigating the impact of the American Civil War upon European military thought, I became acquainted with the work of several prominent English military historians and theorists. Reading some of the books of Henderson, Fuller, and Liddell Hart merely whet my appetite for more, and at the same time I became aware of other interesting figures lurking about in the shadows—Burgoyne, MacDougall, Maurice, and Hamley, soldiers prominent in their day whose names now crop up more often in antiquarian catalogues than the military histories. I had read enough of Wilkinson to be impressed by his grasp of the past and insight into the problems of his own day, and the didactic history that so many European soldiers had written about the Civil War raised suspicions that perhaps there was more to Napier than meets the eye.

The desire to learn more about these men, coupled with the lack of any history of British military thought after the Napoleonic wars, led to the decision to undertake the present work. Originally it was my intention to write about ten representative individuals, and to complete the group portrait I chose Repington, who seemed to offer the clearest picture of the pre-1914 army and its problems. But during one of many long sessions with the service journals, an article written in 1831 popped out in much the same way as a solitary Grade-A bluebook commands attention when it follows a column of dreary and tired examination papers. The author, once identified, provided a fresh contrast to the personality and

opinions of Napier, and in this way Mitchell, although unknown and of no special significance, worked his way into
the book. Many others might also have been included—
Douglas, the Chesney brothers, Maude, Maguire, and Callwell, to name only a few. The subjects treated here are not all
necessarily the most important, but I have found them
interesting and I believe that they best represent the issues
and the attitudes that have shaped modern military thought
in Britain.

The purpose of this book is to determine when, if ever,
and under what conditions the pen has been mightier than
the sword, by investigating the nature and extent of the
influence that various military writers—historians, theorists
and journalists—have exerted upon British military theory,
doctrine, and policy from 1815 to 1940. The method followed has been to depict each subject against a backdrop of
contemporary issues and personalities, using continuing
problems like the nature of the reserve forces and the role of
the army in Imperial Defense to link the figures together and
suggest the drift of British military thought. My hope is,
naturally, to awaken interest in one or more of the personalities, several of whom deserve a good biographer; to suggest
areas where further research would pay dividends; and to
make some contribution to the history of British military
thought during this, the most fruitful and revolutionary period
in military history and one of the most significant in the
history of England and the British Empire. If readers should
come away with a better idea of the potential role and contributions of the military analyst, soldier or civilian, so much
the better.

Many have contributed to this volume, and in a variety of
ways. Certainly without the constant financial support of the
President and Faculty Council of Allegheny College and a
generous grant-in-aid from the Social Science Research
Council, it would have been impossible to have made the
necessary research trips to England. Weekly visits to the
Cleveland Public Library were in part subsidized by a grant
from the Allegheny Student Government.

I am also indebted to a number of libraries and librarians.
In England, Mr. D. W. King, Librarian, the War Office, whose
vast knowledge of the British army during this period is
matched only by his hospitality to visiting scholars, went to

considerable trouble to answer all queries and to suggest elusive sources that otherwise would have gone unnoticed. Mr. J. S. Richie and Dr. Rae were good enough to assemble all pertinent manuscripts in the National Library of Scotland so that they might be scanned in the short time available. Similarly Brigadier R. G. Thurburn and Mrs. Westland placed every facility of the Army Museum's Ogilby Trust at my disposal, while Lieutenant Colonel E. E. N. Sandeman, Librarian, Royal Engineers Corps Library, and Captain J. H. Bickell, Curator, R. E. Museum, went to unnecessary lengths to make my stay at Chatham enjoyable as well as profitable. Brigadier John Stephenson, who probably has done more to enliven the Royal United Service Institution than any other individual in the history of that organization, provided guidance and enthusiasm at a crucial stage, and made the Wolseley papers available at some inconvenience: to him I owe special thanks for overlooking the fact that I was not an officer in Her Majesty's Service. Sitting on top of one of the finest collections of military literature in North America, Mr. John Spurr, librarian of the Royal Military College of Canada, and Mr. Jack Martin, his able assistant, extended many personal favors and made available several items not located elsewhere. And finally I have to thank Mr. P. M. Benjamin, librarian of Allegheny College, for his willing co-operation, and the courteous and ever-helpful staff of the Cleveland Public Library.

I wish also to thank the following individuals: Professor Kenneth Bourne, who allowed me to use many of his own notes; Professor Michael Howard, who first pointed the way to the Spenser Wilkinson papers and made available a complete bibliography of Wilkinson's writings; Mrs. George Shield, who helped to locate several manuscript collections; Professors R. A. Preston, D. M. Schurman, and C. P. Stacey, each of whom has enriched the book with his own specialized knowledge; Professor Theodore Ropp, who continues to give guidance and inspiration; Mr. Joseph Hopkins and Mr. Wilbor Kraft, who read the entire manuscript and made a number of helpful suggestions; Mr. Ralph K. Bennett and Lieutenant David Kuhnert, former students whose research papers have added to my knowledge of Maurice's significance and the "Wolseley Ring"; Miss Kim Brooks, who typed most of the manuscript, and Miss Jean Stewart, Mrs. Pauline

Seeley, and Mrs. Marie Watson, who helped with the final chapters.

I wish especially to acknowledge my debt to several who are personally involved with the book. Miss Victoria Wilkinson made available those of her father's letters which remain in the possession of the family. I owe her many thanks for her hospitality as well as for permission to quote from the family letters. Major General J. F. C. Fuller has answered all queries and volunteered some documents not readily available elsewhere. To him I am also indebted for permission to quote from his letters to Liddell Hart, and since these reveal that he is intolerant of fools and often critical of Americans, I feel that I have double cause to be grateful for his help and hospitality. Finally, at the risk of compromising my last chapter, I gladly acknowledge my great debt to Captain and Mrs. B. H. Liddell Hart, whose generous hospitality during the course of two summers made it possible for me to stay in England long enough to complete my research. Giving unlimited access to his vast files, Liddell Hart invited debate, respected dissent, and was too much the historian to interfere with the working habits or opinions of another. I have tried to repay the debt I owe him by demonstrating the same concern for truth and a similar passion for accuracy.

I wish also to thank Liddell Hart for permission to quote passages from *Thoughts on War, Great Captains Unveiled, The Tanks;* Miss Nancy Scammell for permission to use the correspondence of her father, the late Colonel J. M. Scammell; and General Sir Frederick Pile for permission to quote from his letters to Liddell Hart. I should like further to acknowledge the following: Ardant du Picq, *Battle Studies* (Military Service Company [The Stackpole Company]), General Mellenthin, *Panzer Battles* (Cassell and Company, Ltd.); Colonel Repington, *Vestigia* (Houghton Mifflin Company); Sir Ian Hamilton, *Listening for the Drums* (Faber and Faber, Ltd.); Spenser Wilkinson, *Thirty Five Years* (Constable and Company, Ltd.) Major-General J. F. C. Fuller, *Armoured Warfare* (Eyre and Spottiswoode); *Memoirs of an Unconventional Soldier* (Ivor Nicholson and Watson, Ltd.); *Foundations of the Science of War* (Hutchinson and Company, Ltd.). I am indebted to Dr. Lawrence S. Kubie and the *Archives of General Psychiatry* for permission to quote from his article, "The

Eagle and the Ostrich," and to Captain Victor Gondos, editor of *Military Affairs*, for permission to use my earlier article on the first British official historians and J. M. Scammell, "Spenser Wilkinson and the Defense of Britain."

I am also grateful to Dr. Richard L. Pearse for directing me to the work of Dr. Kubie; to Mr. D. Armour Hillstrom, who gave support and comfort in another vital area; to Professor Richard Hutcheson, who helped me to see some of the philosophical implications in Fuller's writings; and to my parents, who shared the burden—but not the responsibility—of reading proofs.

And finally, I should like to thank my wife for her patience and assistance while facing handicaps similar to those that deprived poor Mrs. Napier of her free time.

CONTENTS

THE
EDUCATION
OF AN
ARMY

I THE ARMY IN DECAY
1815–54

GOOD fortune, wrote Frederick the Great, is often more fatal than adversity, an observation that found confirmation in Napoleon's victory over his successors at Jena. The record of the British army from Waterloo to the Crimea offers additional proof that past performance may indeed undermine progress. Basking in the glow of the victories in Spain and at Waterloo, the British army dozed and enjoyed its laurels while the nation forged ahead into the industrial age.

The army suffered from neglect. With the end of occupation in France came inevitable reductions and retrenchment. Parliament shunned military questions, allowed the militia to disintegrate, viewed every request from the army with a "cold and thrifty" eye, and would not vote money enough even to give every deserving soldier a good conduct medal. The reformers who attacked abuses in the army usually failed to provide means for correcting them, while the commons was so absorbed in its struggle with the crown over control of the army that it neglected to overhaul the cumbersome military machinery that distributed responsibilities and administrative duties among thirteen different offices. There were some in Parliament who objected even to the formation of the United Service Club as being "likely to foster the military spirit and the professional pride of officers to the peril of the State." [1]

The army suffered still more from failure to solve its own

[1] The Hon. J. W. Fortescue, *A History of the British Army* (London, 1899–1930), XI, 47. Most of the material for this brief introduction is

problems. The rank and file contined to endure inadequate
and monotonous food, congested and unhealthy barracks, and
extravagant, uncomfortable uniforms; most recruits were
illiterate and eventually became addicted to drink, a threat to
discipline that was held in check only by the lash, and this
harsh punishment produced in turn an outcry from the social
reformers. The leadership was uneven and uninspired. Promotion was by purchase, except in the artillery and engineers,
which brought high rank to many incompetents and provided
little stimulus for others to study their profession. Army
officers were the worst paid of all public officials (the pay of
superior officers had not increased since 1714), vacancies in a
shrinking army were depressingly few, and the typical regimental officer spent two-thirds of his time in garrisons
overseas, where ability to maintain discipline and provide
care for the troops was of greater practical value than
knowledge of military history or theory. Besides, there were
few libraries available: the officer might, if he wished, read
the newly established *United Service Journal,* his only link
with what was going on elsewhere in the army, but in most
respects his horizons were limited to the activities of his
regiment. Indeed, the British army of this period was not so
much an army as a conglomeration of detachments scattered
over the empire. There were 440 military stations in Ireland
alone.

With no disposition to change, for even the Duke of
Wellington "opposed every project for the major reforms of
military administration" advanced during his lifetime,[2] the
army found itself facing pressing new problems. Steam was
revolutionizing transportation, the telegraph transformed
communications. The advent of rifled weapons made conventional tactics obsolete. The increased size of the empire added
to the burden of the army until there were barely enough
troops, according to Wellington, "to relieve the sentries on
duty in different parts of the world." The shift from mercan-
tilism to free trade, the growth of cities and the subsequent
decline in rural population, and the clamor for reform in the

drawn from this and Vol. XIII of Fortescue's monumental history, Lieutenant Colonel J. S. Omond, *Parliament and the Army 1642–1904* (Cambridge, 1933), and Cecil Woodham-Smith, *The Reason Why* (London,
1955).

[2] Michael Howard, "Wellington and the British Army," in Howard
(ed.), *Wellingtonian Studies* (Aldershot, 1959), p. 89.

1830's all had an impact upon the nature of the army, while revived fear of an invasion by the French in the following decades stimulated interest in the reserve forces and enlivened the debate between advocates of a larger army and those who would build new fortifications to protect arsenals and dockyards.

Three soldiers who survived the Napoleonic Wars to become famous military writers form the subjects of the first three chapters. Napier represents the conventional point of view; his writings illustrate the pride of every British soldier in the exploits of the Peninsular War and the general reluctance to adjust to the new requirements of the industrial age. Mitchell exposes many of the weaknesses in the British military system long before they become evident during the Crimean War. And finally Burgoyne, a remarkable old gentleman, records the demise of the Peninsular army and the resurrection of a military body better equipped to meet the challenge of a new age. These are not necessarily the most important military writers of their day, but together they present a faithful picture of the problems and issues that concerned thinking soldiers in the generations following Waterloo.

1

THE PENINSULAR TRADITION

Major General Sir William Napier

A CHANCE remark first directed Napier to writing history. Probably the notion occurred to him early in 1823 when, during one of his habitual walks, he disclosed to his companion, Lord Langdon, the shortcomings in a recent publication about the Peninsular War. Impressed by Napier's evident mastery of the subject, Langdon urged the young officer to write a history of his own.

Napier hesitated. His meager literary reputation and his rank of colonel on half pay lacked stature enough to command the attention of military readers, but the suggestion grew. His attempts to find expression with canvas and clay had failed to absorb a restless energy. Lingering doubts finally were overcome by his wife's persistent encouragement and his own intense desire to enhance the memory and reputation of his former chief, Sir John Moore, whose exploits in the Peninsula in 1809 had been eclipsed by the subsequent campaigns of the Duke of Wellington.

Napier plunged to the task and began his *History of the War in the Peninsula,* which was to consume the next sixteen years and ultimately place him in the front rank of military writers, an influential figure in his own time and a revered historian to succeeding generations.

The name Napier already was indelibly associated with the struggle against the French in the Iberian Peninsula during the Napoleonic Wars. Charles, the eldest of the three brothers, temporarily had commanded a regiment under Moore at Corunna, where he was wounded and taken prisoner. Exchanged in 1810, he was wounded again at Busaco. Charles returned to England after the Battle of Fuentes d'Onoro in 1811 and saw no further action in the Peninsula. He later became a well-known military reformer and commander in India.

George, the second brother, was also wounded at Corunna. He was shot again in the combat of Redinha in April, 1811, and in January the following year lost an arm leading the storming party into the breach at Ciudad Rodrigo. By 1814 he was back on active service, this time to command the 52d at the Battle of Orthez. George remained in the army until 1838, when he was appointed governor of the Cape of Good Hope. If his later life was to be less distinguished than those of his brothers, it was also a great deal less turbulent.[1]

William Francis Patrick Napier, the third of five sons of Colonel the Honorable George and Lady Sarah Napier, was born on December 17, 1785. His boyhood was spent in Ireland, where his father was comptroller of army accounts. Napier attended grammar school as a day pupil in a small town near Dublin and devoted his free hours to exploring ancient history with Plutarch and the nearby fields with a poacher known as "Scully the tailor." Details of Napier's early days are lacking, but manifestly he owed more to his mother's influence and his own interest in books than to any formal instruction. His teacher, his sister attests, was a pedagogue "totally unfitted" to cope with a boy of imagination and high spirits; but extensive reading in history, travel, and poetry contributed directly to Napier's mastery of the language and days spent in the fresh air with the village vagabond helped him to develop an unusually powerful physique.[2]

Napier's military education was more complete. Entering

---

[1] A brief sketch of the careers of each of the Napier brothers is found in The Hon. Sir John W. Fortescue, *The Last Post* (London, 1934), pp. 174–217. Sir Charles Napier is treated in T. R. E. Holmes, *Four Famous Soldiers: Sir Charles Napier, Hodson of Hodson's Horse, Sir William Napier, Sir Herbert Edwardes* (London, 1889), pp. 1–170.

[2] Details of Napier's career are taken from H. A. Bruce (ed.), *Life of General Sir William Napier, K.C.B., Author of "History of the Peninsular War"* (London, 1864). Bruce, Napier's son-in-law, was responsible for revising the manuscript written by Major General Sir Patrick Mac-Dougall, who had married another of Napier's daughters. MacDougall, "for private reasons," did not want to be identified as the author (see chap. iv). Additional material on Napier may also be found in Holmes, *Four Famous Soldiers*, pp. 227–59; and J. W. Fortescue, *Historical and Military Essays* (London, 1928), pp. 219–35.

the army in 1800, at the age of fourteen, he held commissions successively in the Royal Irish Artillery, the 62d Infantry of the Line, and the Royal Horse Guards. In 1803 Sir John Moore invited him to join one of the three regiments forming the experimental brigade at Shorncliffe, and Napier left the Blues and the pleasures of London society for the less remunerative but more rewarding life as subaltern in the 52d. He subsequently became captain in the 43d, another of Moore's regiments, and the next two years were happily spent mastering the details of drill and tactics and studying military history, particularly the campaigns of Napoleon. Napier was not the most popular officer at Shorncliffe but he was easily among the most envied, for he was one of those individuals who, seemingly without effort, excels at everything. Tall, handsome, and powerful, he was a successful company commander, a first-rate athlete, an accomplished artist, and noted for a remarkable memory.

Napier first saw active service in the 1807 expedition to Copenhagen. The following year he accompanied his regiment to the Peninsula, where he spent six years compaigning under Moore and Wellington. He marched, barefooted, with Moore's army on the retreat to Corunna in 1809. In 1810 he was twice wounded, first in the combat of the Coa after his company won distinction for a desperate rear-guard stand, and again at Cazal Noval, where he earned the brevet rank of major. A bullet in the spine received here did not prevent his fighting at Fuentes d'Onoro in 1811, after which he was sent home to recuperate from a severe fever. Napier returned to Spain in 1812. Although twice again forced to return to England on sick leave he still managed to participate in the battles of Salamanca, Vitoria, the Nivelle, and Orthez. A veteran of some thirty engagements by the time he left the Peninsula in 1814, William Napier was admired throughout the army as much for his personal bravery as his tactical skill.

Understandably, Napier had lost much of his zeal for soldiering. The boy who had entered the army "lightly and without consideration" had grown disenchanted from years of hard campaigning; by 1811 he was writing his mother that he felt "condemned to a profession I dislike by religion, honour, and necessity." Marriage in 1812 to a niece of Charles James Fox, the Whig statesman, made Napier all the more anxious about a career which seemed to offer slender reward, and more than once during the campaigns of 1813 and 1814 he was strongly tempted to leave the army. Weary of destruction and endless fighting, his health had also become a matter of real concern.[3] In 1815, now a lieutenant-colonel, he spent four months at the Senior Department of the Royal Military College at Farnham—the predecessor of the present Staff College, Camberley—but Napoleon's unexpected return from Elba interrupted his studies and he was crossing the Channel to rejoin Wellington when Waterloo was fought. Napier remained with the army of occupation in France until 1819, at which time he returned to England and retired on half pay. Unable to lead an idle life, he turned his thoughts first to painting and sculpture, and ultimately, when these failed to give lasting satisfaction, he took up the pen.

Napier's first publication was an article on Jomini's *Traité des grandes opérations militaires* which he wrote in 1821 for the *Edinburgh Review*.[4] Although well known on the continent, the famous Swiss theorist was ignored by English critics until the appearance of Napier's review.[5] Napier was generous in his praise. Jomini, he wrote, had produced "unquestionably one of the most profound, original, and interesting" works in military literature, a sharp contrast to the usual run of "fatiguing memoirs" cluttered with "embarrassing and unprofitable details." Instead of commencing with a statement of maxims carefully supported with selected battles and campaigns, Jomini had analyzed the major campaigns of the past seventy years and by a process of induction had arrived at the fundamental principles of war. One great governing principle in particular had emerged: the need to operate with the mass of an army against the decisive point. The chief merit of Jomini's work, according to Napier, lay in his detailed examination of this principle and its influence upon modern war.[6]

---

[3] Bruce, *Napier*, I, 73–74, 144.

[4] "Traité des grandes opérations militaires, contenant l'histoire critique des campagnes de Frédéric II., comparées à cellas L'Empereur Napoleon; avec un Recueil des Principes généraux de l'art de la guerre," *Edinburgh Review*, XXXV (1821), 377–409. Napier is identified as the author, in Bruce, *Napier*, I, 225.

[5] "The Theory of War," *The United Service and Naval and Military Magazine*, 1857: I, 160 (cited hereafter as *United Service Magazine*, although the title varies from 1841 to 1890).

[6] Napier, "Traité des grandes opérations militaires," pp. 379–81.

Napier agreed with most of Jomini's principles. Reviewing the various lines of maneuver illustrated by the campaigns of Frederick and Napoleon, Napier showed a decided preference for a strategy of simple and interior lines in which an army is concentrated in a central position vis-à-vis an extended enemy, rather than operating in two or more widely separated columns. In the Peninsula Moore and Wellington had repeatedly maneuvered from a central position against superior but divided French forces, and Napier was convinced that if the commander were to exercise effective personal control, the army must remain intact.

He was more cautious than Jomini, however, in reducing the subject of tactics to fundamental principles. Too much, he insisted, depended upon terrain, morale, the skill of the generals, and chance. Of one thing Napier was sure: "that general who can operate with the largest mass upon the most decisive point, must be successful," and the best way to achieve this was by an oblique order that would bring the bulk of one army across the line or flank of another. In modern times the best exponent of this technique, "the perfection of the art," had been Frederick the Great, who had often concentrated superior numbers and firepower where it could be decisive by advancing his army in echelon. Wellington's victory at Salamanca was another "beautiful application" of this principle.

Napier found little to criticize in Jomini. He believed that the Swiss theorist "holds an exact discipline rather too cheap," and he was not sure that Jomini altogether understood Wellington's tactics—a criticism repeated twenty-five years later by a committee of Royal Engineers who likewise claimed that Jomini was "generally misinformed, uncandid, and biassed" in his treatment of the British army and its commanders.[7]

Napier's learned analysis of Jomini's theories reveals that already he was a diligent student of war. It also exposes the unbounded admiration he felt for Moore and his earnest desire to "rescue" the reputation of the hero of Corunna "from the harpy claws that would tear and deface it." [8] Meanwhile

[7] *Ibid.*, pp. 338, 400–401, 404–5; *Aide-Memoire to the Military Sciences. Framed from the Contributions of Officers of the Different Services, and Edited by a Committee of the Corps of Royal Engineers in Dublin* (London, 1846–52), I, 1.

[8] Napier, "Traité des grandes opérations militaires," p. 396.

his interest in the Peninsular War was further sharpened by an interview with Soult, one of Napoleon's marshals, during which the two discussed the former's campaigns against Wellington. With a promising start in literature, the reputation of a friend to rebuild, and a growing interest in recent military history, Napier was ripe for the suggestion that he enlist his talents for a history of the war in the Peninsula.

His first step was to consult Wellington, who gave him some official correspondence and the portfolio of King Joseph's letters captured in 1813 at Vitoria. But the Duke, although willing to answer any questions, withheld his private papers, partially because he intended to write "a plain didactic history" of his own, but also because he wished to protect the reputations of those who had served under him. Napier also tried to obtain the Orders of Movement in the custody of Sir George Murray, Wellington's quartermaster-general, but Murray likewise refused to give up the papers because he, too, planned to write a history of the campaigns.

Napier next journeyed to Paris, where he had better success. Soult gladly offered his own papers and used his influence to make available "an immense mass of official correspondence." Day after day Napier labored in the *Bureau de la Guerre* copying documents. He even was given access to the muster rolls of the French armies in the Peninsula—not the yellow-bound documents fabricated to conceal the cost of the war from the French people, but the true returns bound in green for the private information of the emperor. In Paris Napier also consulted numerous high-ranking officers who had served in Spain and Portugal, and at least twice he talked with Jomini, who was full of promises but "who told me a great deal of of interesting matter relative to everything but Spain." [9]

Back in England, Napier collected correspondence and journals from many British officers, while to others he sent detailed queries for information on obscure or disputed points. His wife, who gave him all the time eight children would allow, provided indispensable assistance when she broke the code of King Joseph's correspondence, an accomplishment that Wellington vowed would have been worth twenty-thousand pounds to him at the time. Wellington

[9] Bruce, *Napier*, I, 243, 248, 254.

himself provided invaluable information to such an extent that Napier confessed that the early chapters of his first volume "may be almost said to have been written under his dictation." [10]

The *History of the War in the Peninsula* took sixteen years to complete. Five years of research, correspondence, and hard writing went into the first volume alone, which Napier rewrote five times before sending it to the printer. Much of the time he was handicapped by sickness and severe pain from the bullet lodged near his spine, and there were days when he could write only by lying on his back. Often he despaired that he would not live to complete the task. There were also frequent distractions; after publication of the first volume in 1828 Napier was continually harassed in a war of pamphlets waged with officers whom his criticism offended. His combative nature, as well as his obvious qualifications, caused expectation to stand "everywhere on tiptoe," and each volume when it appeared tarnished the reputation of some prominent officer. The uproar provoked by the publication of the first volume "was like the 'breathing of the west wind' when compared with that which followed the publication of the second," while according to a review in the *United Service Journal,* succeeding volumes were awaited with "trouble and anguish from the Horse Guards even to the remote garrison of Sidney." Truth, Napier discovered to his sorrow, was indeed "offensive to many." [11]

The *History* was not an immediate success. Public opinion in 1828 was not prepared for a book which, as stated in the *Times,* "assailed the still dominant policy of Toryism, and conceded infinitely more credit to Napoleon, to his system, and to the French army, than the still rabid anti-Gallic feelings of the country would pardon." Indeed, the publisher lost so heavily on the first volume that he was unwilling to handle the others except at a greatly reduced commitment, and Napier was forced to print the remaining volumes at his own expense.[12] But soldiers, to judge from the comments in

[10] *Ibid.,* pp. 259–68; II, 457–59.
[11] *Ibid.,* I, 401, 537; *United Service Magazine,* 1829, No. 2, 469; 1834, No. 3, 86–87.
[12] John Murray, the publisher, had paid 1,000 guineas for the copyright of Vol. I and had signed an option to take future volumes at the same price. He lost over half of his investment on the first volume, a loss further aggravated by the strong public reaction to the severity of

the *United Service Journal,* recognized the intrinsic merit of
the work even when they disagreed, as many of them did, with
the political and military opinions of the author; and gradually the book fought its way to public favor because of the
eloquent and vigorous manner in which Napier had com-
memorated the deeds of Wellington's great army. By the time
the last volume was published in 1840, Napier's fame as the
greatest military historian England had produced was secure.[13]

Napier's *History,* which a modern authority has described
as "the finest military history in English and perhaps in any
language," [14] represents a rich mixture of personal experience
and insight into the nature of war combined with exhaustive
research and heroic prose. His powerful narrative of the
battles and sieges gratified those who had participated as
much as it delighted the generations that followed.

Not that Napier was without flaws as an historian. His
basic approach reinforced a natural inclination for hero
worship. "It is the business of the historian," he claimed,

who has no other claim to attention than the clearness and ability
with which he calls into relief the actions and motives of others,
to bring the exploits of the hero into broad day-light, to show them
in all their beauty of detail as well as in their grandeurs of
proportion, otherwise they will be passed unheeded. . . . The
multitude must be told where to stop and wonder, and to make
them do so the historian must have recourse to all the power of
words. . . .[15]

Napier treated Moore as a warm friend rather than an
objective critic. Another of his heroes was Marshal Soult, who

Napier's criticisms and by a letter from Washington Irving in Spain
reporting inaccuracies and a strong French bias. Murray refused to
print Vol. II on the same terms and he suggested that Napier find another publisher. Samuel Smiles, *A Publisher and His Friends: Memoir
and Correspondence of the Late John Murray with an Account of the
Origins and Progress of the House, 1768–1843* (London, 1891), II,
284–86.

13 *United Service Magazine,* 1829, No. 2, 481, 626–27; 1830, No. 1,
202; 1831, No. 2, 62. H. Morse Stephens, "Napier," *Encyclopaedia Britannica* (9th ed.; Chicago, 1892), XVII, 186–87. The *Times,* February 14,
1860, is quoted in Bruce, *Napier,* II, 1–2.

14 G. P. Gooch, *History and Historians in the Nineteenth Century,*
(New York, 1949), p. 305.

15 "The Despatches of Field-Marshal the Duke of Wellington," *London
and Westminster Review,* XXVIII (1838), 407.

had befriended his brother Charles after Corunna, and he admired Wellington as "a great soldier, a great statesman, and withal an honest man." But his foremost hero was Napoleon himself, "the greatest man" in history, "the most wonderful commander, the most sagacious politican." [16]

Mistaking the man himself for the ideals Napoleon expressed in public, Napier often allowed historical judgment to succumb to partisan feelings. This was true also of those whom he disliked, men such as Generals Thomas Picton and Robert Craufurd and especially Marshal William Beresford. Described by a friend as "one of the most vehement of men," [17] Napier became downright virulent in his treatment of Beresford, who retaliated by inspiring a series of lengthy *Strictures* refuting Napier's *History*. The battle of the books raged bitterly, with many of those who basically agreed with Napier becoming incensed by his undue severity. Modern historians have taken a more charitable view of Beresford.[18]

Sir John Fortescue has attributed Napier's lack of restraint to the gnawing pain caused by the bullet lodged near his spine. "When sitting at his table in comparative ease and comfort," Fortescue observed, Napier wrote in an ordinary hand, but on those days when tormented by his old wound he employed a more vertical and peculiar style, and most of the scathing criticisms—and brilliant passages—appear on the original manuscript in what Fortescue has described as Napier's fighting script. [19]

At best this is a partial explanation, and it does not excuse the "bitter unmeasured censures" of Tory ministers that

---

[16] Napier, *History of the War in the Peninsula and in the South of France from* A.D. *1807 to 1814* (new ed.; New York, 1890), I, 233, 336n., 478; V, 219–20; "The Despatches of Field-Marshal the Duke of Wellington," p. 372; Bruce, *Napier*, II, 24–25, 200.

[17] *Ibid.*, I, 448.

[18] Sir Charles Oman, *Wellington's Army 1809–1814* (London, 1912), pp. 36, 147; Oman, *A History of the Peninsular War* (Oxford, 1902–30), IV, 265–67. For the views of Napier's contemporaries, all of them more favorably disposed toward Beresford than Napier, see reviews in the *United Service Magazine*, 1834; No. 3, 83–99, 1831; No. 2, 37–55. Napier's answers to the various *Strictures* are found in appendices to the *History*, V, 297–351. According to Sir John Fortescue, Napier's criticisms of Beresford's conduct at Albuera, however severe, "pale before the scathing judgment which was passed upon it in his most intimate correspondence by Wellington" (*A History of the British Army* [London, 1899–1930], VIII, 210).

[19] Fortescue, *Historical and Military Essays*, pp. 226–30.

forced an admiring son-in-law to concede that in his political prejudice Napier violated "the dignity and high judicial functions of the historian." Napier was a lifelong Whig. His *History* was as much dominated by political doctrine as the writings of the Whig historians Macaulay and Hallam, and "he could never look with unprejudiced eyes" upon Tories like Castlereagh and Canning, who had guided England safely through the Napoleonic Wars yet were in Napier's judgment, "ignorant of every military principle, and . . . too arrogant to ask advice of professional men." [20]

Hero worship, political (and national) prejudice, and personal vendettas naturally discolor Napier's *History,* but rarely do these faults destroy the value of his narrative. His was essentially a military history, written in the first place for professional students. As far as most soldiers were concerned, his grasp of the material, his imagination and ability to describe an action vividly and in authentic detail more than compensated for the blemishes caused by excessive partiality. One writer expressed the wish that the maps (which Napier himself drew) had been on a larger scale, another complained that Napier had "sacrificed to the general grand effect all minor and apparently trifling things," and there were those who believed that their services or regiments had been slighted, but most of Wellington's old soldiers evidently looked upon the *History* as a faithful and stirring record of their struggles against Napoleon. How the Duke himself reacted is unknown for certain. One source quotes him as saying: "Napier may be somewhat radical, but, by G————, his History is the only one which tells truth as to the events of the Peninsular war." Another has stated that Wellington "upon principle, refused to read Napier's work" because he had no desire to quarrel with the historian, and that in self defence against "supercilious criticism" as well as "patronizing approval" he decided to publish his most important and secret despatches.[21]

The most eloquent tribute perhaps came from Napier's intimate friend, General Sir James Shaw Kennedy, who testified:

[20] Bruce, *Napier,* I, 65, 68; II, 33; Oman, *History,* I, ix; IV, 67; Napier, *History,* II, 302–3; 330–31; III, 193 ff.
[21] "The War Game of Prussia," *United Service Magazine,* 1831, No. 1, 75–76; 1844, No. 3, 280; Bruce, *Napier,* II, 37–38; Smiles, *A Publisher and His Friends,* II, 286–87.

Some of the circumstances stated by Sir W. Napier . . . I supposed were only known to myself. . . . The astounding extent of
authentic information contained in his great History will be an
increasing wonder in proportion as time affords more opportunities for testing it. In depth of thought, eloquence, and military
skill and knowledge, it is altogether unrivalled by any other
military work in our language; and that feature which will always
carry with it the highest commendation is the uncompromising
truthfulness with which it is written, although most of those who
took an active share in the war were still alive when the work was
published.[22]

Frequently some veteran would pounce upon Napier's account, in which case Napier would take great pains either to
defend his version or else, if convincing new evidence were
produced, to publish a correction for eventual incorporation
into a new edition.[23] When Oman and Fortescue rewrote the
history of the Peninsular War in the following century, the
number of factual errors in Napier that they uncovered was
relatively small. Most of their corrections concerned questions
of interpretation or judgment rather than historical accuracy.

From the first, Napier's *History* completely dominated the
field. Sir George Murray, who had hoped to write the definitive
history of Wellington's campaigns, realized the futility of
competing with Napier and gave up the attempt "in despair,"
and no rival appeared until the works of Oman and Fortescue.
When the British regimental histories were compiled in the
1830's by order of the Horse Guards most of the volumes,
according to Oman, were "nothing more than copious extracts
from Napier, eked out with reprints of the formal reports
taken from the *London Gazette.*" Indeed, sections from Napier
invaded many of the books written after 1830, when fading
memories were reinforced by unacknowledged passages from
the *History*, and most of the campaign studies which appeared in England as late as the turn of the century consisted
"of little more than an analysis of Napier, with some supplementary comments hazarded." [24]

[22] Kennedy, *Notes on the Battle of Waterloo: With a Brief Memoir of
His Life and Services and Plan for the Defence of Canada* (London,
1865), pp. 11–12.
[23] See, for example, Napier's letters in the *United Service Magazine,*
1833, No. 2, 542; 1840, No. 2, 250–51, 442; 1840, No. 3, 257. See also
Bruce, *Napier,* I, 445.
[24] Stephens, "Napier," XVII, 186; Oman, *Wellington's Army,* pp. 18–
38 *passim.*

Napier's *History* is significant, however, for another reason, one which often has been neglected. To his contemporaries Napier was more than England's foremost military historian; he was also widely esteemed as a military writer. Although not a theorist in the same sense as Jomini ("Theorising," one officer explained, "never has been the characteristic of Englishmen; it is held, perhaps, in too great disrepute" [25]) his personal experience and profound knowledge of war enabled him to speak with authority upon any military subject. A fellow military historian and critic, Major John Mitchell once challenged his readers to name "the modern continental writer who can be placed even by the side, much less above Napier. . . . Napier has his faults, no doubt . . . but he is, nevertheless, the first military writer of his day. . . ." [26] From the appearance of the first volume until the Crimean War no military writer was as often quoted as Napier; certainly none was more authoritative.

How good was British cavalry; how useful the bayonet? Could the army afford to dispense with corporal punishment, and what was the secret of good discipline? As ancient Greeks had turned to Homer for guidance on a variety of subjects, so those interested in these and similar issues consulted the epic work of their own day to see what Napier had to say about the Peninsular army and its practices. So great was Napier's prestige as a military writer that on at least one occasion he was offered a virtual blank check to write a book on "the Philosophy of War," a task which he shrank from because of the insurmountable difficulties involved.

Napier's reasons for refusing to attempt such a work when he was approached for a second time suggest that had he written a book on war it might well have rivaled Clausewitz's *On War* in scope and imagination, if not in influence. "The Philosophy of War," he wrote in 1848,

is to me a phrase of extensive signification. It involves a preliminary investigation of the human mind as to why men engage in warfare at all. Then would come the distinctions between religious wars, civil wars, wars of aggression and aggrandisement, wars of defence, wars of folly, and wars of necessity. Then the

[25] "The Regeneration of the Army," *United Service Magazine*, 1849, No. 1, 1.

[26] J. M. (Major John Mitchell) to the Editor, *United Service Magazine*, 1831, No. 3, 250. For the career of Mitchell, see below, chap. ii.

progress of the art! its varying phrases in different degrees of civilization, how far it can be carried on by barbarous nations, how far it depends upon civil institutions and the progress of the sciences; how much it depends on such extraneous matters, and how much upon original genius in a general. And all reasoning on these points must, to carry weight, be supported by illustrations taken from history and experience. What an overwhelming labour! Can any man treat it satisfactorily? There is no work on the "Philosophy of War," I believe, in any language. [Evidently Napier had not yet read Clausewitz.] . . . I believe the greatest genius would shrink from it, as beyond the power of man to treat with accuracy and authority. Bacon, who has considered all things belonging to philosophy, has not touched upon it. . . . I do not think it can be done, and at all events I feel that I cannot do it in a way satisfactory to myself and the reading world; and I have long make a resolution never to publish my views on any subject I do not thoroughly understand, or at least think I understand.[27]

How Napier would have dealt with these and other similar problems in a general treatise must remain a matter of conjecture. Certainly his slanted view of civil-military relationships and his intense partisan spirit would have imposed practical limitations upon any study of a theoretical or philosophical nature. Napier's *History* does indicate, however, how he might have pursued some of the more obvious aspects of war such as strategy, tactics, and command, subjects that he did "thoroughly understand."

Characteristic of Napier's military thought is his faith in the accepted principles of strategy, which to him were nearly synonymous with the maxims of Napoleon and Jomini. "The Emperor's views, opinions, and actions will," he predicted, ". . . go down with a wonderful authority to posterity," and he had a healthy respect for Jomini's "profound knowledge of the theory of war." [28] Napier's basic precepts, if random observations deserve to be called such, may be thus summarized: menace your enemy's flanks, protect your own, and always be ready to concentrate all arms against a portion of the enemy's army or the weakest segment of his line. Avoid double lines of operation whenever possible, beware of flank marches within reach of an enemy, and never abandon one line of communication before establishing another. Because a

[27] Bruce, *Napier*, II, 278.
[28] Napier, *History*, I, 276; II, 220.

skilful offensive is usually the best defense, an army must always be in condition to fight. Above all keep the objective firmly in view and disregard those "minor events and inconveniences" which, if permitted, will obstruct execution of the soundest of military plans.[29] Although Napier occasionally would hazard a generalization on the futility of defending a long river line or the secrets of mountain warfare he never felt qualified to formulate strategical precepts of his own. "How," he inquired of a friend, "can a man who has never commanded an army in the field dare to dogmatise on such a subject? A great and successful commander may do so safely, no other person can." [30]

In his tactical observations, Napier found little fault with the performance of British infantry in the Peninsula. Manifestly he preferred the line to the column. The French assault formation, usually a column varying from twelve to twenty-four ranks in depth, may have succeeded against other continental armies,

but against the British it must always fail, because the English infantry is sufficiently firm, intelligent, and well disciplined to wait calmly in lines for the adverse masses, and sufficiently bold to close upon them with the bayonet. The column is undoubtedly excellent for all movements short of the actual charge, but as the Macedonian phalanx was unable to resist the open formation of the Roman legion, so will the close column be unequal to sustain the fire and charge of a good line, aided by artillery. The natural repugnance of men to trample on their own dead and wounded, the cries and groans of the latter, and the whistling of the cannon-shots as they tear open the ranks, produce the greatest disorder, especially in the centre of attacking columns, which, blinded by smoke, unsteadfast of footing, and bewildered by words of command coming from a multitude of officers crowded together, can neither see what is taking place, nor make any effort to advance or retreat without increasing the confusion.

Conceding that "well-managed columns are the very soul of military operations," Napier nonetheless preferred the two-rank line. At Redinha in 1811,

[29] This passage is summarized, much of it in Napier's own words, from scattered observations in the *History*, I, 177–78, 245; II, 323, 363, 409–11, 448; III, 72, 91, 121, 166, 266; IV, 75, 78, 90, 209–10, 455.

[30] See *ibid.*, II, 54, 61, 69, 266, 360; III, 58; IV, 330, 427; Bruce, *Napier*, II, 278.

. . . thirty thousand men, forming three gorgeous lines of battle, were stretched across the plain, bending on a gentle curve, and moving majestically onwards, while horsemen and guns, springing forward simultaneously from the centre and from the left wing, charged under a general volley from the French battalions.

And again, at Albuera, "the fire of the enemy's columns alone destroyed two-thirds of . . . [the] British troops; the fire of their lines would have swept away all!" [31]

These passages are not merely descriptions of British actions in the Peninsula; they also express unlimited confidence in the "thin red line," and nowhere in Napier's *History* is there any suggestion that linear tactics had become outmoded. Nor was there any reason why Napier should have thought otherwise: the arms issued in the British army at this time were of the same model and in many cases the same vintage as those provided in 1800, while the revised drill book varied only in minor detail from the regulations prescribing the training of the Peninsular army. Major General Sir Henry Torrens' *Field Exercise and Evolutions of the Army,* published in 1824, rested on the fundamental principles introduced by Sir David Dundas some thirty years before and represented an attempt to re-establish uniformity rather than to bring tactical doctrine up to date.[32]

One other aspect of Napier's tactical observations upon infantry deserves notice. The value of intrenchments had not yet become an issue, but because fieldworks had been used in the Peninsula and Wellington's army was reputedly saved in 1810 by the famed lines of Torres Vedras, Napier occasionally did comment upon the subject. "Against rude commanders and undisciplined soldiers lines may avail, seldom against accomplished generals, never when the assailants are the better soldiers. . . ." Marlborough broke through all the

[31] Napier, *History,* I, 183–84; III, 50, 109.
[32] One officer wrote in disgust in 1834 that "every infantry officer commanding a company knows to his cost that the stocks, from age and rottenness, split with the concussion after firing. . . . Through a *nominal motive* of economy, the soldier is supplied with arms that have been in store (very often) upwards of thirty years: the woodwork shrunk and rotten, the iron-work of an inferior quality . . ." ("Improved Musket and Bayonet," *United Service Magazine,* 1834, No. 3, 546–48). As late as 1845 it was observed that the system of Dundas "remains in use almost unchanged" ("Observations upon Infantry Drill," *United Service Magazine,* 1845, No. 3, 97–106).

French lines in Flanders; and if Wellington succeeded at Torras Vedras, it was perhaps because his lines were not attacked. Like most professional soldiers of his day, Napier maintained that intrenchments only taught soldiers to consider themselves inferior to their enemies. He did not, however, criticize the use of intrenchments as a pivot of maneuver, and in his view the real strength of the lines of Torres Vedras lay in the fact that Wellington's regular troops were stationed behind the lines, "completely disposable and unfettered by the works." Napier insisted that an army must preserve its mobility.[33]

Napier displayed less confidence in British artillery and cavalry, neither of which had played a very significant part in Wellington's operations.[34] Indeed he rarely discussed artillery, and his casual comments suggest that the most useful function of artillery was to lend moral support to attacking infantry.[35]

As for the cavalry, Napier's *History* provoked a lively controversy over the relative values of British and French cavalry and of the future of cavalry against infantry. "But how vain," Napier wrote, "how fruitless to match the sword with the musket—to send the charging horseman against the steadfast veteran." The cavalry combat at La Serna in 1812 illustrated a solid "military truth, that cavalry alone are not able to cope with veteran infantry save by surprise," for it offered "a frightful spectacle of the power of the musket, that queen of weapons."[36] These words naturally offended many former cavalrymen who felt that they had not been given their fair share of the credit for Wellington's victories, and Napier's *History* raised anew the question of armament and tactics best suited to British cavalry. Most of the old "sabres" who rushed into print on this occasion found fault with Napier's judgment if not his accuracy in his treatment of cavalry actions in the Peninsula.[37] One writer, identified only as

33 Napier, *History*, V, 24–25; II, 420–21.
34 See Oman, *Wellington's Army*, pp. 94–114. According to Oman, the Peninsular army was deficient in both arms during the early years, but even after the artillery and cavalry had become proportionately strong, say by 1811, Wellington continued to rely primarily upon his infantry to win battles. Almost never did he employ either arm in those massed formations characteristic of Napoleonic tactics.
35 Napier, *History*, IV, 128, 313.
36 *Ibid.*, III, 260; IV, 65.
37 This controversy appears to have commenced in 1831, with the

"Elian," supported Napier by asking his critics just when, if at all, the British cavalry—"all chosen men in point of personal appearance, and, with the advantage of superior horses"— had in fact acquired any moral ascendancy over the French cavalry? According to Elian, the answer was "never." (It is perhaps pertinent to point out that "Elian" was a favorite pen name of Napier himself.[38]) It is also pertinent that Napier's *History* is not mentioned in the foremost British work on cavalry at the time of the Crimean War. Captain Lewis Edward Nolan, "a celebrity in cavalry circles," skirted the Peninsular War as much as possible in his *Cavalry: Its History and Tactics*, preferring instead the more fruitful— and encouraging—campaigns of Frederick and Napoleon. When he does mention the Peninsular War, he utilizes a French source, the *Guerre de la Péninsule* of General Foy, which contained many remarks flattering to cavalry.[39]

But if Napier's predilection for infantry alienated some who represented the other arms, all British soldiers could agree wholeheartedly with his estimation of those who had fought in the Peninsula. Here the English had indeed demonstrated that they were a military race, possessing "all the most valuable military qualities in as high, and many in a much higher degree than any other nation." Despite wretched equipment, inferior numbers, and inadequate peacetime training, Wellington's men had persevered and eventually had

---

publication of the third volume of the *History.* For a sampling of the literature on the subject, see the following unsigned articles: "The British Cavalry on the Peninsula," *United Service Magazine,* 1831, No. 1, 305–10; 1831, No. 2, 59–65; 1832, No. 1, 57–63, 457–64; 1832, No. 2, 336–42; "Actions of the British Cavalry," *ibid.,* 1831, No. 2, 357–63, 552–30; "Light Cavalry in the Field," *ibid.,* 1831, No. 1, 512–15; "Lancers and Light Dragoons," *ibid.,* 1831, No. 2, 69–76; "Distribution of Light Cavalry and Infantry in the Field," *ibid.,* pp. 205–9; "Yeomanry Cavalry: With Remarks on the Revised Cavalry Movements," *ibid.,* pp. 210–14. Mitchell's criticisms of Napier are discussed in chap. ii.

[38] "Elian," "Colonel Napier and His Cavalry Critics," *United Service Magazine,* 1833, No. 2, 257. For the use of Élian as a pen name, see Bruce, *Napier,* I, 389.

[39] Nolan, *Cavalry: Its History and Tactics* (3d ed.; London, 1869), *passim.* Nolan's theories are summarized briefly in Cecil Woodham-Smith, *The Reason Why* (London, 1955), pp. 172–73. Nolan was one of the first killed in the famed charge of the Light Brigade. Foy's secret admiration for British infantry is noted in Oman, *Wellington's Army,* pp. 19–20. A half century later, military writers still commented on the inadequacies of Napier's treatment of cavalry operations in the Peninsula. See General Sir Evelyn Wood, *Achievements of Cavalry* (London, 1897), pp. 59–60.

defeated armies on the Continent: "six years of uninterrupted success had engrafted on their natural strength and fierceness a confidence which rendered them invincible." This was due in part to the gifted leadership of Wellington, but basically it represented a triumph of English institutions and character.[40]

The real secret of British success in the Peninsula, according to Napier, lay in the superior discipline of Wellington's army. "When completely disciplined,—*and three years are required to accomplish this,*" the British soldier is "observant, and quick to comprehend his orders, full of resources under difficulties, calm and resolute in danger, and more than usually obedient and careful of his officers in moment of imminent peril." It was a stern code of discipline, together with superior tactics, that made the British infantry the most formidable in Europe and encouraged Napier to state that "in the number of soldiers, rather than of men, the English general had the advantage." [41]

Three years! Napier maintained that three years would suffice to produce a disciplined, effective soldier, and in this respect he was far ahead of his time. For not until 1871 was the principle of short service—six years with the colors and another six with the reserve—adopted, and then the primary motivating force was to provide the army with effective reserves. Soldiers were willing to accept short service after 1871 because the Prussians had demonstrated that it could be done, yet here we find the historian of the Peninsular War asserting that their own experience proved that three years sufficed to produce a soldier equal if not superior to Napoleon's veterans. Whether Napier would have supported another feature of the Cardwell Reforms, the linking together of regiments with separate interests and traditions, is a different matter. He took great pride in his own regiment, believing that "a moral force will always bear upon the execution of orders under regimental control which it is in vain to look for elsewhere." [42]

[40] Napier, *History*, II, 181; V, 209, 214.
[41] *Ibid.*, I, 20–21; II, 366–67; IV, 449. Italics mine.
[42] *Ibid.*, IV, 250. Sir Charles Dilke quoted Napier to support his contention in 1888 that the length of service should be reduced to correspond with the practice in the Continental armies (*The British Army* [London, 1888], pp. 172–73). Most British military writers, however, have ignored Napier's judgment on this point.

"War tries the strength of the military frame-work; it is in peace the frame-work itself must be formed. . . ." Time and again Napier cried out against the inadequate or total lack of peacetime military preparations in England. If Wellington was forced to ignore the rules of siegecraft at Badajoz, it was

> Because the English ministers, so ready to plunge into war, were quite ignorant of its exigencies; because the English people are warlike without being military, and under the pretence of maintaining a liberty which they do not possess, oppose in peace all useful martial establishments. . . . In the beginning of each war, England has to seek in blood for the knowledge necessary to insure success.[43]

Had those in charge of the administration of the British army after 1830 paid as much attention to these and many similar remarks as they did to Napier's stirring descriptions of battles and sieges, perhaps the force sent to the Crimea in 1854 would not have had to pay such an outrageous price during the operations against Sebastopol.

Napier's faith in the supremacy of the British regular and his dislike for the Spanish allies closed his eyes to the potentialities of what Clausewitz called "a people's war," a struggle that has a "kind of nebulous vapory essence" which never condenses into a solid body where it can be reached and defeated by an invading army. Clausewitz contended that "small detachments" of regular soldiers were necessary to encourage the masses in a national rising, but Napier claimed that the English alone had won the War of Spanish Independence. Spanish and Portuguese guerrilla bands may have harassed the enemy, but never had they seriously affected the progress of the French. A force without strong leadership and strict discipline could not compete with regular soldiers: "it was the disciplined battalions of Valley Forge, not the volunteers of Lexington, that established American independence," and without English gold, men, and leadership the war in Spain against Napoleon would have been lost. Clausewitz maintained that a people's war could be effective under specific conditions (all of which prevailed in Spain), but his reflections on the subject were "more a feeling-out of the truth than an objective analysis, because the subject has as yet

[43] *Ibid.*, III, 403; IV, 106. See also *ibid.*, III, 90–91.

really been too little in evidence and has been too little treated by those who have long observed it with their own eyes." Napier, on the other hand, could see no wisdom in studying the operations of the Spanish *Partidas:* such irregulars were to be valued "as their degree of organization approaches that of regular troops," and their operations in the Peninsula had been little more than a succession of surprises and massacres offering "little instruction, and no pleasure" to the military reader.[44] Jomini was another who could derive no pleasure from his recollection of that "spontaneous movement" against the French armies in Spain. Granted a people's war "presents something grand and generous which commands admiration, the consequences of it are so terrible that, for the sake of humanity, we should desire never to witness it [again]." Like Napier, Jomini contended that popular risings could succeed only with the assistance of regular disciplined armies.[45]

Significantly, Clausewitz, Jomini, and Napier each regarded war as an art rather than a science, although Clausewitz believed that war most properly belonged to the province of social existence. Of the three Jomini placed the greatest emphasis upon the need to observe basic principles, particularly in the realm of strategy. Tactics were less subject to fixed laws because "a thousand other things frequently are the controlling elements." Here the "metaphysics of war"—passion, and the military qualities alike of generals and of the armies they lead—"will ever have an influence upon its results." This did not prevent, however,

the existence of good maxims of war which, with equal chances, will be able to procure victory; and if it be true that these theories could not teach with a mathematical precision what it would be suitable to do in every possible case, it is certain at least that they will always point out the faults that are to be avoided. . . . such maxims would thus become, in the hands of generals commanding brave troops, more or less certain pledges of success. . . . Good theories founded upon principles, justified by events, and joined to discussed military history, will be . . . the

[44] Karl von Clausewitz, *On War* (Washington, D.C., 1950), pp. 457–62; Napier, *History,* III, 17, 144–45. Further observations on the subject of guerrilla warfare are found in *ibid.,* I, 43–44, 172, 388, 415; II, 71, 128–29, 208; III, 269, 424.

[45] Baron de Jomini, *Summary of the Art of War, or, a New Analytical Compend of the Principle Combinations of Strategy, of Grand Tactics and of Military Policy* (New York, 1854), pp. 42–43.

true school for generals. If these means do not form great men, who are always formed by themselves when circumstances favor them, they will at least make generals sufficiently skillful to hold the second rank among the great captains.

Clausewitz held the opposite view, contending that emphasis upon precepts and rules led to the neglect of those intangible forces and effects so basic to war.[46]

Napier belongs somewhere between the two. Clearly he recognized the validity of fundamental rules. Jomini listed him among that growing school of military historians who were attempting to develop the relationship between military events and the established principles of the art of war.[47] Napier usually judged individual generals (particularly, one is tempted to add, those for whom he felt no affection) by their adherence to accepted principles. Thus the initial assault at San Sebastian failed because the rules of siege warfare were neglected. Suchet deserved a similar fate in his operations in June 1813, because his dispositions "were vicious in principle," and the fact that some succeeded even when they deviated from established rules proved only that "success in war, like charity in religion, covers a multitude of sins."[48]

On the other hand, because so much in war depended upon what Napier chose to call "accidental circumstances" and what Clausewitz meant by "friction," censure is justified only when it can be demonstrated that an unsuccessful general had "violated the received maxims and established principles." Napier had campaigned long enough to appreciate that war, "however adorned by splendid strokes of skill, is commonly a series of errors and accidents," and that even the most gifted generals "do but grope in the dark." "Practice and study may make a good general as far as the handling of troops and the designing of a campaign" are concerned, but more is required than professional skill to produce a great general. "Genius begins where rules end": the greatness of

[46] *Ibid.*, pp. 327, 329; Clausewitz, *On War*, pp. 71, 84–86. The theories of Jomini and Clausewitz are discussed in Edward Mead Earle (ed.), *Makers of Modern Strategy: Military Thought from Machiavelli to Hitler* (Princeton, N.J., 1943), pp. 77–113.

[47] Jomini, *Summary of the Art of War*, pp. 20–21.

[48] Napier, *History*, IV, 342. "There is no operation in war so certain as a modern siege, provided the rules of the art are strictly followed. . . . [W]hen no succoring army is nigh, the time necessary to reduce any place may be calculated with great exactness" *ibid.*, III, 224, 404. See also *ibid.*, IV, 329; V, 149.

Napoleon and Wellington lies in the fact that they were not sticklers for rigid adherence to a system but knew when "to strike without regard to rules." The best way for an officer to learn from military history, therefore, was to investigate such instances, and if Wellington's campaigns were to serve as special models in future continental wars, it was largely "because he modified and reconciled the great principles of art with the peculiar difficulties" that always confronted those in command of British armies.[49]

Save for a handful of irate cavalrymen and an occasional critic of the stagnant state of the army before the Crimean War, most British soldiers could accept the fundamental assumptions behind Napier's treatment of tactics and strategy. One prominent exception was Sir George Murray, Wellington's former right-hand man, who once had refused Napier access to his papers because he had hoped himself to write the definitive history of the war. There was evidently bad blood between the two, for Napier accused Sir George of deliberately placing obstacles in his way even to the extent of influencing his publisher to withdraw support for the second and succeeding volumes. Now Sir George attacked "the very superficial character of . . . Napier's military opinions, or strategical doctrines," and he cautioned "those readers who have not themselves a knowledge of military affairs . . . against relying implicitly upon our military historian's professional opinions." But Sir George's rockets produced no effect beyond drawing a lively return fire: Napier's position as a military writer was too formidable to be shaken by a few reckless assaults, even after some of his weak spots as a historian had been exposed.[50]

---

[49] *Ibid.*, I, iv, 59; II, 190; III, 86–87, 105, 406; IV, 405; V, 54, 152, 216–17.

[50] "History of the War in the Peninsula, by Lieut.-Colonel W. F. P. Napier," *Quarterly Review*, LVII (1836), 510, 529. Sir George accused Napier of being partial to the French, unfair to the Spaniards, and of distorting facts as well as characters and motives of individuals, but most of his criticisms were of the work as "a treatise upon military science" (*ibid.*, LVI [1836], 437 ff.). Napier's emnity toward Sir George is revealed in his "Reply to the Third Article in the Quarterly Review on Colonel Napier's History of the Peninsular War," *London and Westminster Review* XXVI (1837), 543. Sir George is identified as the author of the unsigned articles in the *Quarterly Review* in Samuel Smiles, *A Publisher and His Friends*, II, 284. According to Smiles, Sir George had nothing to do with the decision of John Murray to discourage publication of Napier's second volume; the firm simply had suffered too heavy a financial loss on the first volume to justify publishing the rest on the same terms.

With the appearance of the final volume of the *History*, Napier drew the curtain on one phase of his career. Frequently asked to write biographies of Napoleon and Wellington, he always refused because the necessary papers were not available. "Depend upon it," he confided to a friend, "Waterloo has a long story of treachery and secret politics attached to it which will not be made known in our days, if ever. . . . I could not write at ease under the impression that I was writing in the dark." [51] Besides, he was growing old and somewhat infirm, and he feared that he would no longer feel strong enough to make extended research trips. He did take time from his *History* to produce a pamphlet, "Observations Illustrating Sir John Moore's Campaigns," and he took Sir John's brother severely to task for writing a biography that failed to do justice to the famous general. He also managed a parting shot at Colonel John Gurwood, editor of the first series of the *Wellington Despatches*,[52] before leaving the field for the more recent campaigns of his brother in India.

In 1841, the year after the final volume of his *History* was published, William Napier was promoted to major general and subsequently sent to Guernsey as lieutenant-governor. Here he spent five of the most stormy years of his life trying to reform abuses tolerated by the dominant clique. He saw to it that a new and beneficent constitution was adopted and a Royal Commission appointed to inquire into the civil and criminal laws of the island. He also reorganized the militia and devised a system of defense to meet the supposed threat of a French invasion. Despite these accomplishments, however, Napier had neither the disposition nor the patience to cope with the conservative opposition at Guernsey and a cautious government at home. When his term of office expired in 1847, he returned to England and submitted his resignation. He spent his remaining years revising the *History*, defending his brother's actions in India, and contributing letters to the *Times* on a variety of subjects, military and political.[53]

Napier wrote the history of Sir Charles Napier's conquest of

[51] Bruce, *Napier*, II, 47–48.

[52] *Ibid.*, I, 413; Napier, "The Life of Lieutenant-General Sir John Moore, K. B. by his brother, James Carrick Moore," *Edinburgh Review*, LIX (1834), 1–29; "The Despatches of Field-Marshal the Duke of Wellington," *London and Westminster Review*, XXVIII (1838), 367–436.

[53] Bruce, *Napier*, II, 81–131 *passim;* Holmes, *Four Famous Soldiers*, pp. 251–52.

Scinde while still at Guernsey, and for the same reason he had first undertaken to write about the war in the Peninsula—to vindicate the fame of a personal hero. Sir Charles' campaigns and the ensuing controversies with James Outram and the directors of the East India Company had "excited a keen interest" in England. Instead of receiving unanimous praise and expressions of gratitude from his countrymen, Sir Charles found himself frequently accused of provoking an unnecessary war to further his own selfish interests, while his wise and beneficial administration of the conquered territory was compromised by a truculent spirit which, inflamed by ill health, made new enemies in Parliament and in the press. By this time William's powerful and intemperate pen had silenced most critics of the *History*, who had discovered that it was far better to allow errors and harsh judgments to slip by unchallenged than to become involved in a nasty public controversy. He was free to rush with his customary ferocity to his brother's defense. In 1845 he completed *The Conquest of Scinde,* a brilliantly written narrative which "often strayed into untruth and unfairness." Not content merely to demonstrate that the charges against his brother were false and malicious, he also greatly exaggerated the significance of Sir Charles' military accomplishments.[54] Six years later appeared *The History of General Sir Charles Napier's Administration of Scinde,* a work described by Carlyle as "one which every living Englishman would be the better for reading." This was followed in 1857 by the first two volumes of *The Life and Opinions of General Sir Charles James Napier.* By this time the partisan in Napier had clearly won out over the historian: his "passionate fraternal love upset the balance of his judgment, and insensibly corroded his love of truth. He was grossly, often ludicrously, unjust to almost everybody who opposed his brother." Even an admirer questioned "whether any other writer, posing as a grave historian, was ever responsible for so many and such cruel calumnies." [55]

[54] The battle of Meeane is a case in point. According to Fortescue, Charles, who supplied William with all of his material, "never realised what manner of battle he had fought," and that while the battle "remains a brilliant little episode in the conquest of India," it was "hardly unique, as William Napier would have us believe" (*The Last Post,* pp. 192–94). See also Holmes, *Four Famous Soldiers,* p. 84 n.

[55] *Ibid.,* p. 169 n. For Napier's defense of his brother, see *ibid.,* pp. 252–57.

The last ten years of his life were spent as a secluded invalid. Unable to walk out of doors, Napier's sole source of amusement was the occasional visitor who came to discuss some topic of current interest. His principal occupation continued to be the establishment of his brother's fame on a durable basis, but now and again he would send "some trumpet-like letter to stir men's spirits" for publication in the *Times* or else communicate his views on national defense to acquaintances still active in public life.

Of primary concern to Napier, and indeed to most English-men, was the growing fear of an invasion by the French after the entente existing between the two countries since the early 1830's had been disrupted ten years later by divergent policies in Egypt and Spain. Lord Palmerston had stressed the possibilities of such an invasion in 1845, when he urged reforms to strengthen the militia. Two years later the Prince de Joinville contributed to the general alarm by calling attention to the inadequacies in Britain's defenses. The army estimates of 1847 represented an early attempt to improve the situation, but threatening sounds from across the Channel made most Englishmen acutely aware of the seriousness of the problem and the need to find a quick solution. The journals of the period contain numerous letters, articles, and editorials calling attention to the peril of a French invasion and debating the various ways this might be thwarted. When a French admiral testified before a committee of the national assembly that it would be easy to land 70,000 men because the English "have nothing organized for an attack," a great naval review was held in Spithead to demonstrate England's naval might "in an unmistakable manner." [56]

Having served as lieutenant-governor on an island a scant thirty miles from the French coast, Napier was more sensitive than most to an invasion threat. He submitted detailed plans for the defense of the Channel Islands to the Home Office, the Horse Guards, and the Duke of Wellington. Guernsey, he stated, could be defended "by a few works well placed" to force the enemy "to assail the island in a given quarter, where the whole island force could meet his disembarkation with advantage. . . ." No landing could be prevented on Jersey,

[56] "The French Navy and the Designs of France," *United Service Magazine*, 1853, No. 2, 164–68; 1853, No. 3, 119: Fortescue, *History of the British Army*, XIII, 9–13; Lieutenant Colonel C. Cooper King, *The Story of the British Army* (London, 1897), p. 241.

but Alderney, the key to British naval supremacy in the Channel, could "easily be made impregnable; it cannot be blockaded, and it offers means for a large war harbour." Wellington, however, was unimpressed. "Though in all his communications . . . he has never hinted that he thought my views were weak or ill-founded," Napier confessed privately, "The Duke has never shown a disposition to act on any plan emanating from me." [57] Later Napier modified his views, insisting that while adequate fortifications could still defend Alderney, the remaining islands "must fall to France whenever she chooses to annex them. . . . steam gives her such an *expeditious* force that she can throw ten or twelve thousand men into either in a few hours. . . ." Ireland too was indefensible. Aside from a "coup-de-main against London," Napier believed England to be fairly secure against a large-scale invasion. The sensitive area between Dover and Portland could be defended once railroad lines were constructed to facilitate the shipment of troops. To protect London he would fortify in advance all possible avenues of approach and garrison these with volunteers in time of emergency. He also recommended the construction of intrenched camps to shelter the regular forces as they retreated before an enemy advancing from the coast. Thus men—the volunteers and the regular army—and not fortifications would form "the true defence of the country." [58]

Public response to the invasion scare was more evident still in 1859, when hundreds of Volunteer Rifle Corps were formed. "Fiery meetings were held all over the country at which militant patriots let off steam against the French." Some 160,000 eventually joined the volunteers, an organization that had been created primarily to aid in the defense of England against invasion rather than to provide replacements for battalions of the regular army, and there was considerable speculation about the relative merits of such troops and the best way they could be trained and employed.[59]

Napier participated in this public debate by bombarding his friends and the *Times* with letters of advice for the use of the

57 Bruce, *Napier*, II, 248–50, 333.
58 "Notes on the Defence of the Country" is reprinted as Appendix IV in Bruce, *Napier*, II, 516–22. Similar sentiments are expressed in his correspondence with Shaw Kennedy; see *ibid.*, II, 329–32.
59 F. W. Hurst, *The Six Panics and Other Essays* (London, 1913), p. 37; Fortescue, *History of the British Army*, XIII, 527–33.

volunteers against Britain's traditional enemy. He had long advocated the formation of such units as "the surest auxiliary defence that we could have," and in his view the introduction of the rifle had further enhanced their value. Previously they would have had to stand up and fight at close range to be effective, which meant that they would have been forced to adopt much of the regular drill. But the rifle had rendered many intricate maneuvers unnecessary. Instead of being "mere mimics" of the regular infantry, the volunteers should now be used as irregular riflemen. Armed with the new long-range rifles—"and we ought to have a million of them at least in different stores ready for the occasion"—and supported with the new Armstrong field piece, "said to be of sure stroke at two miles' distance," the volunteers of 1859 could harass enemy columns "and yet . . . be too far off for the enemy to detach flanking parties against them." Volunteers should be guided by their "individual intelligence" rather than the evolutions of the barrack square: above all they should be adept at light-infantry work. Napier even compiled special instructions for the training of volunteers, which he sent to a son-in-law engaged in the formation of a volunteer corps. The underlying principle is explained thus:

> If you spread skirmishers out and merely skirmish to your front according to parade teaching, you do away with half their personal intelligence and half their rapidity, and parade rules are not always applicable to fighting ground. My notion therefore was not to break down all formality of movement and formation, for they are a good beginning, and awaken the men's minds to their business; my object is to go beyond them. . . . What you have to do is to . . . entice the enemy to spread out, having for yourself the power of suddenly concentrating in the most rapid manner; that is, you gain the speed of irregularity and yet divest it of confusion.

With volunteers armed and trained for service as light infantry, Napier was convinced that England could be successfully defended against any invader. True, the French also possessed rifles and long-range artillery,

> and it would be a fair fight between the riflemen on each side; but the heavily loaded Frenchmen would soon tire, and the main column must halt to rally them again. Thus the long-ranging arms, pushing the volunteers into their natural career, have quadrupled their power; and all former points of weakness being swept away,

they will be a real support to the regular troops, instead of a drain and a burden.[60]

The startling feature about Napier's recommendations for the Volunteer Corps is that he placed such emphasis upon use of the rifle, for probably no two people in England were more reluctant to see the Minié rifle replace the old smoothbore musket than Charles and William Napier. The new weapon had been selected in 1851, after extensive trials had demonstrated that it was 20 per cent superior to the old musket at 100 yards, 37½ per cent at 200, and 48 per cent at 400 yards. Wellington accepted the new weapon, "stipulating only that it should not be called a rifle lest the whole of the infantry should clamour to be clothed in green," but a number of old soldiers still preferred the percussion musket. The secretary of state for war, Lord Panmure, stated that the old weapon was "better than all the inventions that could be discovered," and Sir Charles Napier fairly scoffed at the idea of the Minié being more valuable than the musket. "I fought in 'The Bush' in America," he recalled, and

so thick it was, that we could hardly pierce its denseness; my regiment was opposed to Kentucky *riflemen*. We had *muskets,* and we beat them. We had *red coats*—they had brown coats; yet we slew more of them than they did of us. The strong hearts and strong bodies are forthcoming; so is the proud *red* uniform of England; so is the British musket and bayonet; but some of our anonymous writers are trying to drive all these from the field, and turn our main battle into skirmishers, fighting the enemy at a vast distance. Perhaps they are right, but I do not think so. I think it will make men fearful of getting too near the enemy, and of closing with the bayonet. Some of these writers would almost make us believe that victory depended on *dress* and *rifle,* not on *discipline* and *stern soldiers.* If soldiers be constantly told that their arms are good for nothing, and their dress as bad as their arms (although in that dress and with those arms they carried England's glory to its greatest height), they will soon lose all confidence in their own superior physical powers.[61]

[60] Bruce, *Napier,* II, 449–50, 462–63, 471–81; *Times,* November 1, 1859. A detailed analysis of the volunteer movement is found in W. H. Chaloner and W. O. Henderson, *Engels as Military Critic* (Manchester, 1959), pp. 1–43.
[61] Quoted in "Sir Charles Napier on National Defense," *United Service Magazine,* 1852, No. 1, 420–21. For facts regarding the Minié rifle, see "Instructions in Musketry," *ibid.,* 1857, No. 2, 514–15; Fortescue, *History of the British Army,* XIII, 24–25; Cooper King, *Story of the British Army,* pp. 242–43.

Yet William insisted that his brother really was not opposed to the new rifle; he merely wanted it thoroughly tested before it was issued to all of the rank and file! His own attitude was scarcely less conservative:

The Minié rifle seems to be established by experiment as a real improvement on fire-arms, and is likely to supersede the old musket. I am sorry for it; not sorry that the better weapon should be adopted, but sorry that the improved weapon should have been invented. It will not serve England: take the following reasons.

A musket, which at 800 yards will enable its handler to knock down a man with tolerable certainty, must paralyse the action of cavalry against infantry, and of artillery within that range. No close reconnoitring can take place, as the generals would inevitably be killed, and hence battles will be more confusedly arranged, more bloody, and less decisive. Now also remark that an English army abroad can never be so numerous as French, or Russian, or Prussian, or American armies: and as our only real superiority lies in our resolute courage to close with the bayonet . . . the new weapon will be all in favour of the superior numbers. . . . the Minié rifle will probably deprive us of that moral force.[62]

During the Crimean War William Napier remained skeptical of the military value of the Minié rifle. Good as it was for particular purposes, he still preferred the simple weapon against the complex one, and comparing the battles of Salamanca (1812) and the Alma (1854), he concluded erroneously that "the musket proved more destructive than the Minié."[63] Napier later modified his opinion about the relative merits of the rifle and musket. In 1856 the troops in the Crimea were issued new Enfield rifles, a further improvement over the Minié, and the invasion scare of 1859 must have forced the realization, however reluctant, that no matter how effective Wellington's tactics had been in the Peninsula, they now finally belonged to the province of history.

Over the years Napier frequently contributed to public discussion on various aspects of army reform. In 1833 a Royal

[62] Napier's defense of his brother is found in the *Times*, December 15, 1864. His own views on the Minié rifle were published under his pen name "Elian" in the *Naval and Military Gazette* in 1853 and are quoted in Bruce, *Napier*, II, 377–78.

[63] *Ibid.*, II, 380–83. According to Fortescue, most of the Russian casualties at Inkerman were attributed to the Minié bullet, which sometimes killed or wounded half-a-dozen men or more among the densely packed Russian columns (Fortescue, *History of the British Army*, XIII, 142).

Commission had been appointed to inquire into the subject of military punishment, which opened the gates to an advancing flood of articles and speeches on promotions, pensions, and ways of enforcing military discipline. Normally receptive to social reform, Napier defended in public the practice of flogging in the army. The key to Wellington's victories had been stern discipline, he argued. Discipline could only be preserved by punishments or rewards, and without discipline no army could be really formidable. When it was pointed out that the best continental armies had already abolished flogging, Napier retorted that "the British army has always overthrown every army it encountered" and was therefore the one "to give, not take lessons." In indignation he sent a memorandum to the Horse Guards, which merely articulated the aroused sentiments of Wellington and the senior officers on the subject. To the crusading Manchester school he replied:

> Abolish it in your households, your public schools, in your prisons, in your penal settlements and then we meet on fair ground; but come not with eyes inflamed with passion, and hands red with the blood drawn from helpless children and prison delinquents by the lash, to stigmatize the military system for doing that publicly and with caution and after trial, to keep armed men in subordination, which you do in civil life without trial and secretly.

Napier also defended the army against charges of corruption, mismanagement, and maltreatment of the soldier voiced by Gladstone and the Liverpool Financial Reform Association.[64]

Even during the Crimean War Napier's instinct was to vindicate the army. He refused to join the Army Reform Association in 1855 on the ground that "if the persons composing the Society are military, their proceeding is an act of grave insubordination; if they are civilians, they are incompetent persons, perniciously meddling with what they do not understand." Lord Lucan's evidence before the parliamentary committee to inquire into the war struck Napier as "the best that has been given," and he evaluated the man most responsible for the charge of the light brigade as "a good soldier and a good administrator." He upheld the practice of

[64] Bruce, *Napier*, II, 196–97, 241. Napier's letters "exposing the calumnies of the Liverpool Financial Reform Association" are reprinted in *ibid.*, pp. 553–56.

purchasing commissions with minor modifications, because to give every soldier a chance of a commission would be to republicanize the army, "and then we must republicanise the Government; for the army is the principal support of the aristocratic form of our Government." Similarly, he opposed the idea of military crosses or awards, a French invention which constituted "a revolutionary measure . . . and will if introduced into our army produce revolution; if you make your army democratic, you must make your government democratic," and this was "meddling with a dangerous tool." Napier probably shared the antipathy of the older officers toward the Victoria Cross when it was introduced in 1856: in the old days Englishmen had been content merely to do their duty "without hope of outward adornment." As for the war itself, Napier followed the military movements attentively, anticipating in October, 1854, that the armies before Sebastopol were in for "a long siege" accompanied by fevers.[65]

Napier died in 1860, weakened by disease and defeated finally by news of the hopeless condition of his wife's health. His life had embraced not one, but three distinct careers. As an officer in the Light Division he had earned fame and respect for his exploits against the French. As the historian of the Peninsular War he had erected a lasting monument to the accomplishments of the army under Wellington. And finally he had devoted his last years to a spirited and uncompromising defense of his brother's record in India.

Napier was not only without peer among his contemporaries as a historian; he was also a foremost champion of the army, a respected and influential writer on military subjects, and above all, a most eloquent spokesman for the spirit of the times. He was instrumental both in creating and perpetuating the Peninsular tradition. Half a century later, Lord Wolseley was still urging the British soldier to read Napier's *History* so that his blood might "tingle as he hears of the heroic deeds of our fathers and grandfathers in that long struggle. . . ."

Unfortunately, Napier's eloquent testimonial to British arms in the Peninsula may in fact have brought harm to the institution he cherished above all others. For a chief obstacle to progress in the British army before the Crimean War was

[65] *Ibid.*, II, 373, 385–89, 398–99; *Times*, May 11, 1855; Fortescue, *History of the British Army*, XIII, 231–32.

the constant reference to and satisfaction with the results attained under Moore and Wellington. It would be many years before Wolseley also could write:

We have at last awoke to the conviction that we must cease to train our men for a condition of warfare that we can never see again, for war will not conform its procedure to the picturesque notions we had formed of it from field-days and from the pages of Napier.[66]

[66] Wolseley, "The Study of War," *United Service Magazine,* II, N. S., (March, 1891), 490; "The Standing Army of Great Britain," in *The Armies of To-day: A Description of the Armies of the Leading Nations at the Present Time* (London, 1893), p. 96.

2

THE NEGLECTED REBEL

Major General John Mitchell

NAPIER had a rival: the irreverent, impish Captain Orlando Sabertash, who disagreed with Napier's views of the present and most of his interpretations of the past; a capable biographer and historian, an authority on fashion, manners, and the art of love-making, and—most important of all—a prophetic and imaginative writer on military tactics and organization.

The captain wrote with a light touch. "We maintain no theories," he assured his readers in *Fraser's Magazine;*

folly may assert that bayonets, though never stained with the blood of fighting men, are yet formidable weapons of war; gentlemen who have risen to rank by purchase . . . may declare . . . that money is your best possible proof of military excellence, without, for the present, eliciting remark or reply from us. We may have some notion that the efficiency of military weapons is best proved by the melancholy work of destruction effected in the battle-field, and may fancy, that since the sale of negroes has been declared felony, the sale of whole troops, squadrons, and battalions, of whites, may be liable to objection; but on all points we say nothing, replying only to the encomiums passed on our modern system of tactics and promotion, by the words of power and deep import so often addressed to the incomparable Editor of this Magazine, "Yorke, pass the bottle!" [1]

Other essays he published over the signature "Bombardinio." Detached, sophisticated, and occasionally frivolous, they, too,

[1] Captain Orlando Sabertash, "Military Tableaux; or, Scenes from the Wars of Napoleon, sketched in the manner of Callot," *Fraser's Magazine,* XXVIII (1843), 696.

successfully masked the serious purpose and crusading zeal of the author who, when he wished to lash out against complacency and the sterility of military ideas, discarded all masquerades and went by the name that appeared in the army register—Colonel John Mitchell.

We know very little about Mitchell's personal life and military career. Born in Stirlingshire in 1785, at the age of twelve he accompanied his father, a veteran diplomat "of unusual intellectual powers," to the court of Frederick William III at Berlin. In Germany he attended the exclusive Ritter Academie at Luneburg, where he showed a special aptitude for languages, geography, and history. In 1801 he returned to England and two years later was commissioned ensign in the 57th Infantry of the Line. In 1804 he obtained a lieutenancy in the 1st Royals, where he became the protégé of the Duke of Kent, father of the future Queen Victoria. Promoted to the rank of captain in 1807, he subsequently served in the West Indies, Walcheren, and Spain. He joined Wellington's army in time to participate in the battles of Busaco, Fuentes d'Onoro, and Sabugal, and in 1813 he accompanied the 4th battalion of the Royals to Stralsund, where British forces were being sent to relieve the Swedish garrison. Here, and again during the campaigns of 1814 in the Low Countries, Mitchell served on the quartermaster general's staff. During the military occupation of France he frequently was used by Wellington as translator in dealings with the German and Austrian allies.

In 1826 Mitchell, by this time a major, was placed on the unattached half-pay list. Like Napier, he soon found a welcome outlet for his talents in literature. In 1831 he contributed an article on tactics to the *United Service Journal*. Rather to his surprise, his views became the object of so much attention and controversy that he felt encouraged to write on other military subjects, until finally most of the military institutions of England had passed in review before his writing desk. In 1833 he began a memorable association with *Fraser's Magazine*, a waggish publication founded three years previously for the purpose of capturing from *Blackwood's* those faithful Tory readers with a sense of humor. *Fraser's* was "one of the most important organs of progressive thought and open revolt in the Victorian age," and Mitchell joined with other distinguished Fraserians like Thackeray and Carlyle in assaulting Whig exponents of laissez faire and the Utilitarians. With firm editorial support he led the fight to correct abuses in the British army. For the next decade, writing under the pseudonyms "Bombardinio" and "Captain Orlando Sabertash," he wrote on serious subjects with levity and occasionally advocated nonsense with conviction. Manners, fashions, and travel served as convenient vehicles to carry his Tory convictions to the public and even to ridicule aspects of military life. The shako, he mentioned casually in one of his more frivolous essays, "is as heavy to wear as to look at; and has, besides, the double advantage of leaving the head as completely exposed to sun, wind, and rain, as to the sabres of the enemy." Mitchell also wrote a series of vignettes from the Napoleonic Wars and sketches of eminent contemporaries whom he had either known personally or else had observed from a distance. The vignettes were eventually republished in book form, but his "Reminiscences of Men and Things, by One Who Has a Good Memory" was too explosive to be acknowledged openly, even by the indomitable "Bombardinio." [2]

In contrast to Napier, who lived a more or less secluded life once he had committed himself to history, Mitchell was a well-known man of the world. Until 1848, when illness forced him to spend all of his time with sisters in Edinburgh, he devoted a part of each year to travel on the Continent, visiting old friends, seeing new places, and collecting materials for his historical works. "A man of handsome exterior and pleasing manners," he was welcomed even in the most select political and literary circles. Heine, Hugo, Guizot, Thiers, Chateaubriand, and Metternich were among his acquaintances and scarcely a court or an archive in Europe was not open to him. In his three-volume work on the fall of Napoleon, he claimed to have conversed with "nearly all the leading men named" except for Murat and Napoleon,[3] and his writings reveal that

[2] Details of Mitchell's life are found in the sketch by R. H. Vetch, in the *Dictionary of National Biography*, XIII (New York, 1909), 517–18; and the memoir by Leonhard Schmitz in Mitchell, *Biographies of Eminent Soldiers of the Last Four Centuries* (Edinburgh, 1865), pp. viii–xiv. He is also discussed briefly in Miriam M. H. Thrall, *Rebellious Fraser's: Nol Yorke's Magazine in the Days of Maginn, Thackeray, and Carlyle* (New York, 1934), pp. 27–28, 30. The quotations on style come from "Captain Orlando Sabertash, on Manners, Fashions, and Things in General," *Fraser's Magazine*, XVII (1838), 309; XX (1839), 192.

[3] Mitchell, *The Fall of Napoleon: An Historical Memoir* (London, 1846), I, ix. For his "Reminiscences of Men and Things," which indi-

he possessed a sophisticated wit to accompany his strong prejudices against the Whigs and everything French.

The contrast between Napier and Mitchell extends far beyond differences in temperament and politics. Napier was outspokenly pro-French; he worshiped Napoleon as an enlightened ruler and a great captain, and his military opinions rested on the theories of Napoleon and Jomini. Mitchell, on the other hand, especially admired the Germans. In his eyes Napoleon was an unscrupulous tyrant and greatly overrated as a general. Mitchell was influenced by the German theorists Berenhorst and Clausewitz, and his work on Napoleon betrays a strong sympathy for the awakening of a German national spirit.

The two differed also in their approach to history. According to Napier it was an art, a romantic and moral drama, and he resembled other Whig historians in their tendency to reduce history to deceptively simple patterns and to ascribe proper motives to heroes whilst equating villains and Tories.[4] Mitchell was more pragmatic. Military history should furnish practical lessons, otherwise it was "useless and unprofitable." To focus attention on the drama of a battle or campaign at the expense of the complicated factors that had decided the outcome may be good historical art, he contended, but it might easily contribute to a superficial view of what had happened. And to misunderstand the lessons of history would give rise "to new and fashionable doctrines, that are followed and upheld till some melancholy and unexpected catastrophe lays bare the feeble foundations on which they had been raised." More to the point, military history could be exploited to document false doctrine.[5]

Napier had treated war as an art; Mitchell studied it as a science, "the most complicated of all sciences," the only one still "covered with darkness" after a century of enlightenment. He offered several explanations for the lack of significant

---

cates both the extent and the success of Mitchell's social activity, see *Fraser's Magazine*, XXVI (1842)–XXIX (1844), *passim*.

[4] See R. W. K. Hinton, "History Yesterday: Five Points about Whig History," *History Today*, IX (November, 1959), 720–28; H. Butterfield, *The Whig Interpretation of History* (London, 1951), *passim*.

[5] Mitchell, *Thoughts on Tactics and Military Organization: Together with an Enquiry into the Power and Position of Russia* (London, 1838), p. 12; *The Life of Wallenstein, Duke of Friedland* (London, 1837), p. 170; *Fall of Napoleon*, I, vii.

progress in military science. Clearly the superficial study of military history was a factor. So, too, was human nature: men were always reluctant to abandon long-cherished opinions, and the science of war—having only general principles and no rules—was at a particular disadvantage in trying to overcome antiquated beliefs. Moreover, because military science until recent times had been exclusively controlled by kings and nobles, no theorist had dared go beyond the mental horizons of his prince. Bülow, the well-known Prussian military writer, had committed this error and later had good cause to complain that "military writings which are found to contain truth, novelty, and originality, or to bear proofs of genius and talent, invariably exclude their author from all promotion and employment, whether civil or military." The profession of arms itself was a barrier to fresh thought:

> Officers enter the army at an age when they are more likely to take up existing opinions, than to form opinions of their own. They grow up carrying into effect orders and regulations founded on these received opinions: they become, in some measure, identified with existing views, till, in the course of years, the ideas thus gradually imbibed get too firmly rooted to be either shaken or eradicated by the force of argument or reflection. In no profession is the dread of innovation so great as in the army. No sooner is an officer looked upon as a theorist and innovator than he is set down as an unhappy person, who ought . . . to be consigned to the care of compassionate friends.[6]

This attitude, Mitchell believed, was especially prevalent in the British army, where promotion was slow and officers owed their position to purchase rather than merit or professional knowledge. They had fought the French for over twenty years without discovering any better means of insuring success or calculating results than before; twenty years after Waterloo there still was no "single work on military science" in the English language. "Must military improvement" Mitchell asked, "be constantly purchased by a boundless waste of human blood?" History seemed to indicate that this was usually the case. Why could progress not come instead "from the power of human thought and reflection"? War is a time for action, not contemplation. One applies in war what has been acquired in peacetime.

[6] Mitchell, *Thoughts on Tactics*, pp. 1–2, 12, 15, 73.

> . . . a bold onset is probably worth all the science yet known in the world; but how to come well prepared, within reach of the enemy; how to nerve the army, and sharpen the sword that is to strike the blow; how to select the time and place for striking;— these are points that can only be learned by reflection, founded on . . . knowledge.[7]

There is ample evidence to support Mitchell's contention that the British army was making no attempt to encourage professional study. At the heart of the matter was the attitude, typical of the army at large, of the Horse Guards. According to an anonymous critic in 1848, most officers at army head-quarters devoted their time to "cutting out jackets, shaping of wings, the manipulation of shakos . . . and the eighteen or nineteen movements of Dundas, Torrens, and Co." An edi-torial in the *United Service Magazine* blamed the system in which

> . . . so large a proportion of the military are conversant chiefly with the Racing Calendar, the Sporting Magazine, Tom Oakleigh's Shooting Code, and the last novels, that any allusions to tactics or strategy awaken neither curiosity nor interest.

And those who desired to increase their knowledge too often faced the same obstacles that caused Sir Charles Napier to complain, when trying to induce his officers to read more, and to study their profession more seriously.

> Our *"chefs de bataillon"* will do neither, and will not instruct their young officers; indeed I doubt its being possible for them to do either, the orderly-room work is now so great. Regimental commanders are overwhelmed; there is no end to their work, and it is work which ought to be done by adjutants: but much of it ought not to be done at all! Every orderly-room is now a *little war office.*

With the general officers apathetic, regimental commanders either indifferent or else overburdened with paperwork, and junior officers inclined to be more interested in society than military science, Mitchell was probably correct in his assertion that whoever studied war seriously would suffer at the hands of "ignorant and incapable men" who were always "more ready to check, than to forward, the advancement of inferior officers possessing higher attainments." [8]

[7] *Ibid.,* pp. 6, 9–10, 113.
[8] Dioclides, "On Presence of Mind," *United Service Magazine,* 1848,

This lack of a scientific attitude toward the study of war explains why, in Mitchell's opinion at least, there had been no significant improvement in tactics since the Napoleonic Wars. "We have," he admitted, ". . . polished up and improved some matters of detail; we have also devised fine French names for plain old practices; but we have made no new discoveries." In fact, Mitchell believed the Napoleonic Wars to represent a step backward in the science of infantry tactics. The French had abandoned the linear tactics of Frederick the Great for the column formation. By thus massing infantry, the generals of the French revolutionary armies had placed most of their men where they could make no use of their firearms and yet would remain "needlessly exposed to all the fierce and fiery missiles of modern war." Other armies, imitating Napoleon, had hastened to discard the three-rank line in favor of massed formations: only the British adhered to the line and escaped "this French mania." Yet not to slip backward—this was progress of a sort. British tactics, according to Mitchell, resulted in a greater economy of life than the French columns of twelve or twenty-four ranks, where soldiers in all but the first two ranks were nothing better than "mere walking targets for the benefit of artillery practice." [9]

Even British infantry tactics, however, were hopelessly out of date in Mitchell's estimation. In principle and with but few variations in detail, the infantry drill manual was "exactly what Prince Leopold of Dessau introduced into the Prussian army about a century ago"—a fact deplored by other progressive soldiers as well.[10] The drill evolutions were nicely calcu-

---

No. 3, 5; anon., "A Glance at Some Defects in Our Military System, *ibid.*, 1840, No. 1, 1, 6. The quotation from Napier's journal is found in W. F. P. Napier, *The Life and Opinions of Gen. Sir C. J. Napier* (London, 1857), IV, 339–40. Other expressions of dissatisfaction with the British officer's indifference toward professional studies are found in Major Basil Jackson, "The Waterloo Campaign and Its Historians," *United Service Magazine*, 1844, No. 2, 1; anon., "A Chapter or Reflections on the Military Art," *ibid.*, No. 1, 108–9, and "General de Jomini and the *Spectateur Militaire*," *ibid.*, 1856, No. 3, 204–5.

[9] Mitchell, *Thoughts on Tactics*, pp. 5, 71, 148, 157–59; *Wallenstein*, pp. 280–81; *Fall of Napoleon*, II, 173–74.

[10] Mitchell, *Thoughts on Tactics*, p. 30. Prussian drill was first introduced in the British army in 1792 by Sir David Dundas, whose regulations remained in use almost unchanged until after the Crimean War. See Lieutenant Colonel C. Cooper King, *The Story of the British Army* (London, 1897), pp. 239–40. According to another critic, the regulations of "Dundass," as he was known to some reformers, were translated literally from "the ill-digested and confused treatise" of Von Saldern, who

lated to bring the greatest number of men into action in the shortest possible time, but Mitchell objected that British infantry were never trained for battle nor taught how to fight. This antiquated system

arms the soldier with a clumsy, unhandy musket, which, posted as he is in the ranks, he can never use to great advantage, and which he is besides never taught to use with skill. . . . Accurate marksmanship is therefore totally out of the question. . . . last, [but] not least, modern tactics teach us to fix bayonets and to charge the enemy. Of all the manoeuvres performed, this is the most irresistible—at a review.

A volley fired, a quick advance, muskets at the long trail, the martial display ending with a grand charge, delight the heart of the martinet tactician, astonish the spectators, and make the very nursery-maids scream for joy.

But in the field, Mitchell wryly observed, "its success has not always been so decisive." [11]

The reason for this was that tactical conditions had changed since the days of Frederick. The two-rank line may have been superior to the column as a tactical formation, but against an enemy that could harass it with swarms of skirmishers and spray the entire front with grape and canister from artillery firing at a distance, even the line was too rigid and exposed. For Mitchell had observed that as firepower increased, battles tended to become less decisive. In ancient times, when combatants had fought hand-to-hand with sword and spear, the defeated army usually had been annihilated and one general action had sufficed to decide the outcome of the war. Now battles were fought over great distances and the losses, although heavy, were usually evenly distributed. An army forced from the field could generally withdraw, reorganize, and prepare to fight another day under more advantageous conditions. Battles and skirmishes thus succeeded each other "with fearful rapidity," but an empty victory was the sole reward of the side that held out the longest.

---

utterly misrepresented the tactics of Frederick the Great. See "W.," "Cavalry and Infantry Tactics," *United Service Magazine*, 1832, No. 3, 11–16. For similar criticisms of Dundas and his system, see Major Patterson, "On the Utility and Importance of Light Troops and Cavalry in the Field, Exemplified by Several Instances during the War in Spain," *ibid.*, 1844, No. 3, 274–83; and anon., "Observations upon Infantry Drill," *ibid.*, 1845, No. 3, 97–106.

[11] Mitchell, *Thoughts on Tactics*, pp. 144–45.

The problem, therefore, was to devise some way of bringing the enemy "to close, prompt, and decisive hand-to-hand
combat. No option must be left him, but to fight or fly." This in
turn demanded new training techniques to develop the
physical strength and fighting qualities of the individual
soldier. Men must be provided with good weapons and
instructed how to use them. It was time, Mitchell insisted, that
the army benefit from its experiences in America and increase
both the general level of marksmanship and the proportion of
rifles issued to infantry. It was time, too, to learn from the
Napoleonic Wars that the use of the bayonet at close quarters
was a myth, for Mitchell insisted that this weapon under
normal circumstances was about as deadly as the family
toasting fork. [12]

Mitchell's condemnation of the bayonet as an effective
infantry weapon sparked a lively controversy among the
veterans of the Peninsula and Waterloo. He challenged "the
most experienced officers" of the army to answer

whether any one of them ever beheld a bayonet contest? Did they
ever . . . behold men thrust, and counter-thrust at each other
with their bayonets? . . . [A] soldier may perhaps have been
killed or wounded with a bayonet . . . but to suppose that soldiers
ever rushed into close combat, armed only with bayonets, is an
absurdity; it never happened, and never can happen.[13]

When Napier wrote that at Busaco "eighteen hundred British
bayonets glitter over a ridge," he used the word, according to
Mitchell, merely as a figure of speech. Napier, however, did
not agree. Although admitting that "the modern soldier
seldom uses his bayonet," he claimed that this was because
"few persons venture to stand its deadly thrust." Ridiculous,
Mitchell retored: Napier and his supporters were attempting
to defend a weak position by "resorting to mere incidents
related on anonymous authority." Back and forth the battle
raged, each side receiving reinforcements in the published
testimony of other Peninsular veterans. At last the editor of
the *United Service Journal* refused to print any more letters
on the subject, but not before Mitchell struck a final blow.
Napier, he wrote,

cannot, in military affairs, see beyond the existing practices and
institutions of the day, and is totally unable to try their value by

[12] *Ibid.*, pp. 49–50, 66–67, 156, 162.
[13] *Ibid.*, p. 43.

just, applicable principles,—by the effect of arms, and the power, qualities, and dispositions of men. In lauding the result of the British system of training, Colonel Napier overlooks the glaring fact that this boasted system leaves the infantry soldier as ignorant of the use of arms when brought into action, as he was on the day when he forsook the plough or the loom to enlist in the ranks.

Although the two had once felt a mutual respect for each other, this unpleasant exchange prompted Mitchell to complain that Napier's *History* "does not, from first to last, contain a single new idea or original thought upon war, or the science of arms." For military history as it should be written he referred British officers to a book just published in Germany by a still unknown Prussian staff officer: Mitchell must have been the first in England to appreciate the significance of Clausewitz.[14]

Controversy over the usefulness of the bayonet did not end with the truce of 1840. Captain Orlando Sabertash, who could contain himself no longer, observed that "the upholders of this weapon have, by collecting evidence of every kind, anonymous and hearsay, made out that nearly *a hundred men* were killed and wounded by the bayonet during our last great war of twenty-five years duration!" This, Mitchell calculated, "gives about four heroes per annum." Despite abundant supporting evidence the myth of the bayonet persisted. A decade later another critic noted: "If there is one subject upon which . . . writers have perpetuated the crudest notions and . . . the most erroneous ideas are still widely entertained, it is that of the bayonet charges of Line of Infantry." [15]

[14] Napier's views on the bayonet are found in his *History of the War in the Peninsula and in the South of France from* A.D. *1807 to* A.D. *1814* (new ed.; New York, 1890), IV, 416; and in the *United Service Magazine*, 1839, No. 2, 543; 1839, No. 3, 247; Mitchell's letters appear in *ibid.*, 1835, No. 1, 457; 1839, No. 3, 103–6, 531–36; 1840, No. 1, 105–8, 264. Support for Napier is found in *ibid.*, 1839, No. 3, 156–67, 247–49, 398, and mild criticism of Mitchell's arguments comes from Captain Kincaid of the Rifle Brigade, who suggested that the difficulty lay not so much with the weapon itself as the way in which it was used (*ibid.*, pp. 249–52). Mitchell was supported by an anonymous civilian writer in *ibid.*, pp. 393–97.

[15] Sabertash, "Military Tableaux," p. 696 n. For confirmation of Mitchell's view, see "Extracts from the Despatches and General Orders of Field-Marshal the Duke of Wellington," *United Service Magazine*, 1844, No. 2, 601–8; R. G. P., "Two-or-Three Deep," *ibid.*, 1850, No. 1, 279. In 1833 "Vielle Moustasche" had noted that "every soldier has observed on a field of battle, that most of the wounded with bayonets have received previous gunshot wounds." Yet the idea of a bayonet charge "is one of

Influenced by the Prussian theorist Berenhorst and the French Marshal Saxe, Mitchell proposed the replacement of the bayonet by a lance for use at close quarters. Spearmen should comprise half of the army and attack in small divisions or columns separated by intervals, through which skirmishers armed with rifles could fall back after covering the advance. To those who objected on the ground that infantry thereby would forfeit half of its firepower, Mitchell retorted: "We should certainly forfeit . . . half the noise and smoke . . . but we should . . . manage very ill, if we could not, by instruction, training, and position, far more than double the effect of the present practice." Flexibility and mobility would more than offset any loss in volume of firepower; extended formations would diminish the exposure to enemy fire. [16]

Assuming that Mitchell was correct in the belief that hand-to-hand fighting was the only way to gain decisive victory, was his novel suggestion one that ought to have been taken seriously? Probably not, for if bayonet duels rarely occurred, what justification was there for anticipating greater opportunities with the lance. Yet his writings did expose serious defects in the existing system, "not only in the arming and discipline of the troops, but still more in the method by which they are usually led into action," and his emphasis upon mobility, marksmanship, and more flexible formations was in accord with the requirements of modern tactics. He wrote nothing about the subject during the last years of his life, so we have no way of knowing how he would have reacted to the increased firepower produced by the needle gun and the Minié rifle. Probably he would have relied more extensively on artillery, and it seems likely that improved firearms would have induced him to expand his earlier views on intrenchments. When the Brown Bess still ruled the battlefield,

those visionary theories engendered by the 'reveries' of a twenty-years peace, during which, the reality of war is so apt to be lost sight of, and fantastic theories haunt the brain of the zealous but speculative soldier, which a single campaign would be sufficient to dispel" ("Use of Bayonet," *ibid.*, 1833, No. 3, 406–7).

[16] Mitchell, *Thoughts on Tactics*, pp. 158–69. Berenhorst's theories are treated in Ernst Hagemann, *Die Deutsche Lehre von Kriege. I. Von Berenhorst zu Clausewitz* (Berlin, 1940), pp. 6–20. Saxe's *Reveries on the Art of War* is contained in Major Thomas R. Phillips (ed.), *Roots of Strategy: A Collection of Military Classics* (Harrisburg, Pa., 1941), pp. 189–300. For Saxe's views on the training and equipment of infantry, see *ibid.*, pp. 192–202, 216–20. Mitchell discusses Saxe's place in military history in *Eminent Soldiers*, pp. 274–87.

Mitchell had questioned whether infantry could carry well-constructed intrenchments by frontal assault. Unless the position were destroyed by an artillery bombardment, he decided, "there will be few chances of success left to the assailants." [17]

Mitchell's views on cavalry were also disputed and with good reason. He was one of the few in England who continued to believe that infantry armed only with musket and bayonet could not withstand a determined mounted attack. Most British soldiers remembered the relative impotence of cavalry in the Peninsula: even Napoleon's elite cavalry had failed to break the infantry squares at Waterloo. So formidable did the square appear to most soldiers, in fact, that the initial proposals for applying steam to fighting on land were motivated by the need to find some way to break the infantry square. In 1833 a letter was published in the *United Service Journal* suggesting the construction of a nineteenth-century chariot.

> Secure the boiler and the machinery from the stroke of a cannon-ball, and you might drive a steam chariot triumphantly through a regiment. Imagine three or four of these machines driven at galloping speed through a square of infantry; the director might be seated in perfect safety in the rear of the engine, and a body of cavalry, about fifty yards in rear, would enter the furrows plowed by these formidable chariots, and give the *coup-de-grace* to the unfortunate infantry. The chariots might be armed with scythes, both in front and flank; and, if the first shock were avoided by men opening their ranks, they might easily be made sufficiently manageable to wheel round and return on any part of the square which stood firm.[18]

Mitchell did not harbor such fear of the infantry square. If the French cavalry had not succeeded at Waterloo it did not necessarily mean that cavalry as such was inferior to infantry; Napoleon's cavalry may simply have been inferior cavalry, and Mitchell insisted that this indeed was the case. The proper course for cavalry to take once the firing com-

---

[17] *Ibid.*, pp. 352–53; *Thoughts on Tactics*, p. 50. A favorable critique of Mitchell's views on infantry tactics, published originally in the *Caledonian Mercury* in 1832, is reprinted in *ibid.*, pp. 115–19, 149–50.

[18] *United Service Magazine*, 1833, No. 1, 118. Another soldier proposed the construction of "Chariots of Iron" for the same purpose and envisaged a "platoon of locomotives" advancing upon a line of solid infantry (*ibid.*, 1833, No. 2, 118).

mences was to hurl itself en masse on the infantry formations, relying upon speed and shock to win the day, but at
Waterloo the French had allowed themselves to be defeated
before a shot had been fired. They broke ranks and rode, "with
brandished sabres, in wild confusion round the square,
instead of rushing down upon it."

Once for all: in attacking accessible infantry, the cavalry must
throw doubts and hesitation aside, the moment that spurs are
dashed in chargers' flanks. . . . And, coming on thus, where are
the means of resistance that can enable modern infantry to withstand the fury of the shock? Their fire and bayonets?—earth is not
deep enough to hide from disgrace the soldier who should shrink
from a single volley of miserable musketry, or recoil from feeble
and useless bayonets—the bloodless toys of childish tacticians!

A square with spears bristling from every side would be
another matter, but at Waterloo "not a single one of the
enemy's horsemen perished on the bayonets of the kneeling
ranks." Mitchell contended that cavalry, properly used, could
not fail to produce a breach in any infantry square. That it did
not do so at Waterloo and in countless other actions during
the Napoleonic Wars meant only that cavalry had deteriorated
since the days of Gustavus Adolphus and Frederick. [19]

Here again Mitchell's views contrasted sharply with those
of Napier. By "actually making the events themselves give a
false evidence," Napier was guilty, he asserted, of perpetuating false doctrine. Take his description of the action of El
Bodon in 1811.

Then the fifth and seventy-seventh, two weak battalions
formed in one square, were quite exposed, and in an instant the
whole of the French cavalry came thundering down upon them.
. . . The multitudinous squadrons, rending the skies with
their shouts, and *closing* upon the glowing squares, like the
falling edges of a burning crater, were as instantly rejected,
scorched and scattered abroad; and the rolling peal of musketry
had scarcely ceased to echo in the hills, when bayonets glittered
at the edge of the smoke, and with firm and even step, the
British regiments came forth like the holy men from the Assyrian's
furnace.[20]

To Napier El Bodon demonstrated the inherent strength of
modern infantry, whereas Mitchell saw in the battle addi-

[19] Mitchell, *Thoughts on Tactics*, pp. 104–6, 109.
[20] Napier, *History*, III, 260. Italics mine.

tional proof "of the ignorance and misconduct of the French cavalry."

> . . . for there was no closing, nor anything like it in the whole affair. Not a single Frenchman came within arm's length of the square, and no collected body of horsemen came within twenty yards of the bayonets, though the trifling effect produced by the fire of the musketry, astonished all the officers present.

Analyzing the actions of the units participating in the action and eliminating casualties caused by elements of the Third Division and the British artillery, Mitchell concluded that no more than one hundred men were actually put *hors de combat* by the fire of the infantry.

> That is, it required eight hours exertion on the part of seven men to bring down one adversary. The horsemen who fled from enemies rendered so feeble, by their arming and training, should be held up to scorn and contempt. The action is a proof of their ignorance of duty, and nothing more.[21]

The more recent accounts by Oman and Fortescue seem to support Mitchell's basic contention,[22] which he bolstered further by taking other examples from the Napoleonic Wars. Mitchell analyzed the experiences of British cavalry during this period and discovered that of eight regular charges recorded against well-formed French infantry, five succeeded "completely," two failed owing to unusual circumstances, and "one alone remains to console the upholders of the delectable system of modern tactics." He cited numerous combats in which cavalry had overcome infantry by shock tactics,[23] although here it should be noted that his views rested on detached examples and that just as much evidence, if not more, could be mustered to document the case for infantry. Mitchell contended, however, that it was not necessary to demonstrate that cavalry had *always* defeated infantry drawn

[21] Mitchell, *Thoughts on Tactics*, pp. 126–27; "Promotion and Tactics," *United Service Magazine*, 1835, No. 1, 455, 458.

[22] Charles Oman, *A History of the Peninsular War* (Oxford, 1902–30), IV, 565–70; The Hon. J. W. Fortescue, *A History of the British Army* (London, 1899–1930), VIII, 261–63.

[23] Mitchell, *Thoughts on Tactics*, pp. 73–109 *passim*, 128–29; *Fall of Napoleon*, I, 310–13; II, 46, 153, 202, 293. In his description of the combat of Garcia Hernandez (1812), Sir Evelyn Wood specifically refutes Napier and reaches the same general conclusion as Mitchell, although the writings of the latter evidently were unknown to him. See Wood, *Achievements of Cavalry* (London, 1897), pp. 55–76.

up in a square; it was sufficient merely to show that *on occasion* it had done so, and under modern conditions of combat. The military scientist had only to prove that it was still possible for cavalry to succeed if properly trained, equipped, and led, and for this "one instance would have been sufficient." A similar argument was employed by Captain Nolen, the authority on modern cavalry whose indestructible faith in shock tactics played a role in the celebrated "charge of the Light Brigade" in the Crimean War.[24]

Two points about Mitchell's thoughts on cavalry deserve comment. First, he assumed that cavalry would be facing infantry armed with the smoothbore musket and bayonet and not the needle gun and Minié rifle, both of which appeared after he wrote his treatise. His target was the training manuals based upon the weapons of Waterloo, and some of his objections were valid. Why, he demanded to know, "must" cavalry charging "at full speed against a square of infantry, being exposed to only a single volley of miserable musketry. . . . quail before that one discharge of ill-aimed fire-arms" when at the same time infantry, marching with sloped arms in neatly arrayed lines at one hundred and eight paces a minute "are expected to press on against all the volleys that can be fired at them?" It should also be emphasized that Mitchell did not regard cavalry as inherently the stronger arm. Replace the bayonet with the spear, instruct the soldier to fire accurately with a rifle in place of the musket, and infantry "must at all times be able to resist cavalry." If he was misguided in his zeal for the *arme blanche* it was not because he was oblivious to the value of firepower: he merely felt contempt for the infantry tactics of his own day.[25]

Before it was possible to increase the tactical efficiency of the army and to teach soldiers to use their individual weapons with skill, it first would be necessary, according to Mitchell, to improve the soldier's condition and elevate his social status. The hero of Waterloo was an outcast in London: his very

[24] Mitchell, *Thoughts on Tactics*, p. 122. Criticism of Mitchell's theories together with his rebuttal, is found in *ibid.*, pp. 116–23. "The British Cavalry," *United Service Magazine*, 1831, No. 3, 473–76, also attacks Mitchell's claims for cavalry. For a summary of the views of Nolan, who often cites the works of Berenhorst, see Nolan, *Cavalry; Its History and Tactics* (3d ed.; London, 1860), pp. 319–20. Nolan does not mention Mitchell.

[25] Mitchell, *Thoughts on Tactics*, pp. 6, 55–56, 123, 192.

uniform prohibited him from entering Kensington Gardens, his living quarters were abominable, his pay inadequate, and his leisure time of necessity was spent in ways not calculated to build character. He was denied a decent family life, he had little cause to develop self-respect, and there was no agency within either the army or the government officially concerned with looking after his welfare.

Mitchell was among the first to fight for a more humane treatment of the rank and file. He deplored the ingratitude of the country toward the survivors of Waterloo, and he attacked the system which made it unlikely, perhaps impossible, for the army ever to have a constant supply of "good and well-behaved men." The ranks were filled with undesirables who had enlisted "for want of any more promising occupation." Military efficiency demanded that these men be well disciplined, and the only alternative to corporal punishment— which Napier defended against the attacks by a vocal and influential group of social reformers in the 1830's—was to elevate the lot of the soldier by improving his pay and comforts. Mitchell first expressed these views in 1835, at a time when Parliament was particularly hostile to any increased military expenditures. But the cry was taken up by others, and with the report of the Commission on Military Punishments in 1837 began "a new era in the career of the British soldier." Agitation for reform of the soldier's living conditions increased during the following decades and was expanded to include matters of recruitment, education, and even religion. A solitary voice on the subject of tactics, Mitchell found many to support him in his life-long attempt to promote the happiness and comfort of the British soldier.[26]

To increase further the efficiency as well as the comfort of the soldier, Mitchell recommended the introduction of more practical military uniforms. "Strapped into tight and narrow clothing . . . calculated to impede the action of the limbs rather than to aid it," and dressed in a sharptailed coat, the British soldier most nearly resembled "a peeled carrot." Soldiers, he felt, should be "rationally and comfortably dressed"; their clothes should permit free use of their limbs, provide maximum protection against the weather, and combine, with these advantages, "as much splendour and ele-

[26] *Ibid.*, pp. 242, 256–57: Fortescue, *History of the British Army*, XIII, 431–60.

gance" as possible to "improve the manly figure of the soldier
[and] make him proud of his appearance." Mitchell offered
no specific recommendations beyond the introduction of hel-
mets in place of hats, but he knew which articles deserved
to be discarded:

> We have no power to grant either rewards or decorations, but
> we can promise the best thanks of the soldiers to the first
> authority that shall rid the service of bearskin caps, infantry and
> light cavalry shakos, the ill-shaped helmet of the dragoons, and the
> jack-boots, cuirasses, and leather breeches of the life-guards, the
> stiff leather stocks of the whole army, that, nine times out of ten,
> prevent the men from coming correctly to the present when taking
> aim; [and] the worsted French epaulets . . . ; as well as to any
> one who shall contrive to divide equally between the two shoulders
> the weight of the sixty rounds of ammunition now supported
> exclusively by the left shoulder. What is called the Highland dress
> should also be abolished. The kilt is unfit for service . . . and
> the soldiers themselves dislike it after the novelty is over. The
> plumed bonnet is . . . fit only for fine parade wear and weather.

Officers at stations abroad likewise criticized the impractical
dress of the army on occasion, but it took the Crimean War to
demonstrate how "utterly unfitted" the soldier's uniform was
to fight in.[27]

Mitchell's harshest criticisms were directed against the
purchase and sale of commissions, an anachronistic practice
that had been abolished in the Continental armies. Defended
by those who hoped to gain by the system as well as men who
wished to see aristocratic control of the army continued,
promotion by purchase was assailed by Mitchell because it
made gold "the criterion of military merit." Of what good
were experience and competency to an officer of limited
means, when any wealthy dunce need only open his purse for
promotion? Worse still was the hopeless inefficiency of the
system. "On what principle," Mitchell wanted to know, "can
reasoning men defend the system of selling . . . the
. . . awful power of leading . . . soldiers into battle."
Money could make "a very ordinary man" lieutenant-colonel
and time alone was needed to see him a major general, while

[27] Mitchell, *Thoughts on Tactics*, pp. 230–35. The evolution of the
British uniform during this period is sketched in James Laver, *British
Military Uniforms* (London, 1948), pp. 18–20. Detailed changes are
described in Major R. M. Barnes, *A History of the Regiments and Uniforms of the British Army* (2d ed.; London, 1951), pp. 137–44.

"those who perceive that professional knowledge and acquirement are useless without money, and needless with money, readily grow indifferent to attainments more likely to become injurious than beneficial." There would be no significant progress in military science, Mitchell insisted, until the British army based promotions on merit alone.[28]

Once again Mitchell had anticipated, perhaps even precipitated public clamor for reform, for in 1840—five years after he first attacked promotion by purchase in the *United Service Journal*—a Royal Commission headed by Wellington investigated the subject. The Duke's opinions were well known: family connections, fortune, and influence were legitimate influences in determining promotion, and he used his powerful position to impede any changes in the system. "There is no one to beard him at the Horse Guards with proposals for amendment," a reformer later complained, and the professional men who sit in Parliament "are too much overawed to give their real opinions." The report of the Commission was inconclusive,[29] but it initiated a controversy that was to last until purchase was finally abolished in 1871. In a series of letters to the *Times* published in 1841–42, Mitchell continued to argue against the purchase system. He was joined in the attack by one Colonel Maurice Firebrace, who likewise attributed the ignorance of the typical British officer to the purchase and sale of commissions; and numerous other officers who were unwilling to see purchase abolished began to recognize the need to supplement money and seniority with some sort of proficiency test. Wellington continued to insist that purchase was "a saving of expense to the public and highly beneficial to the service," but the agitation of soldiers like Mitchell and Firebrace, intensified by the nagging of professional reformers such as Hume and Cobden, finally resulted in a modification of the system. Parliament was still unwilling in 1850 to make funds available to purchase commissions and establish pensions, but the Horse Guards

[28] Mitchell, "On Military Promotion by Purchase," *United Service Magazine*, 1835, No. 3, 296–304; 1836, No. 1, 297–307; *Thoughts on Tactics*, pp. 262, 265–66, 279, 290.

[29] Sir Herbert Maxwell, *The Life of Wellington: The Restoration of the Martial Power of Great Britain* (2d ed.; London, 1900), II, 122–23; Colonel Firebrace, "The Grand Job—Purchase in the Army," *United Service Magazine*, 1846, No. 3, 414; "Promotion in the Army," *ibid.*, 1854, No. 2, 493–98.

under pressure did issue an order that junior officers should be examined before receiving promotion. Now, in addition to "the Eighteen or Nineteen manoeuvres of Messrs. Dundas, Torrens, and Company," the British officer was expected to be proficient in mathematics, geography, and history, although in practice "both the teaching and the examination were for some time very much of a farce." [30]

Mitchell's final commentary upon the British army was written in 1850. Observing that "the tardy nature" of military operations had always given England sufficient time to recover from the usual initial defeats and to organize for victory, he now contended that "the progress of science has greatly altered this comfortable state of things." It was possible for a nation to concentrate its military strength and strike almost without warning. No longer could the British army afford to waste the years of peace. It must absorb the lessons of recent conflicts and accumulate professional knowledge because British soldiers could expect to be sent against any enemy, "in any quarter of the globe," at any time. And yet, Mitchell claimed,

there is not a single work on military science in the English language. There is no standard of what the different arms can effect; no instruction as to the best mode of combining the action of cavalry, artillery, and infantry; no principle is anywhere pointed out, according to which troops should be posted and employed under the thousand different aspects of war and battle. . . . No attempt is made to extract professional truths from the mass of well-defined results—the only possible mode of arriving at professional principles.

[30] Mitchell, *Eminent Soldiers*, p. xv, Firebrace, "On the Errors and Faults in Our Military System," *United Service Magazine*, 1843, No. 2, 196–207, 362–72, 537–47; 1844, No. 1, 202–13; "On Military Instruction," *ibid.*, 1846, No. 2, 62–72; "Instructions of Officer-Military Messes," *ibid.*, 1847, No. 2, 481–90; "Hint for the Military Student," *ibid.*, 1847, No. 3, 74–86, 219–33. For other criticisms of the purchase system, see "Promotion by Purchase," *ibid.*, 1842, No. 1, 31–47, 394–96; Colonel Hughes, "A Plan for a System of Promotion in the Army," *ibid.*, 1842, No. 2, 32–45; "Notes on the Army," *ibid.*, 1842, No. 2, 441–48; 1842, No. 3, 14–24, 233–37, 333–38, 481–92; 1843, No. 2, 21–26; "Military Education," *ibid.*, 1846, No. 2, 600–609; "A Glance at the British Army and Its Officers," *ibid.*, 1848, No. 3, 447–70. The officer examinations of 1830 are mentioned in Fortescue, *History of the British Army*, XIII, 20–21; the abolition of purchase is discussed in Captain Owen Wheeler, *The War Office Past and Present* (London, 1914), pp. 199–211. Wellington is quoted in the *United Service Magazine*, 1846, No. 3, 144.

In 1841 British forces in India had suffered an unprecedented disaster when a force of nearly 20,000 British and native troops was annihilated at Kabul, a conspicuous example, according to Mitchell, of poor planning and inadequate preparation. And yet the country had done nothing "to avert the possible recurrence of such disasters." Promotion by purchase continued, the army was still not large enough to perform adequately its task of policing the empire, and the rank and file, although unsurpassed in discipline, remained bound by rules that tended "to crush rather than improve the best of their moral qualities" and fettered to an outmoded system of tactics. Thanks largely to the campaign waged by the *Times* the lot of the soldier was improving, but in 1850 Mitchell considered the system still basically faulty. Too often, he lamented, it had been glossed over by victories won by brave men.[31]

Most of Mitchell's later writings belong on shelves devoted to history and *belles-lettres* rather than military science. As Bombardinio and Captain Sabertash he continued to amuse readers of *Fraser's Magazine* with his witty and revealing commentaries on public men and private morals and his frank appeal to their prejudices, while his military interests found expression in studies of Wallenstein, Napoleon, and eminent generals of the past four centuries. His biography of Wallenstein, published in 1837 and again in a second edition in 1853, was not superseded in English for a hundred years. Based upon thorough research among German records and a personal knowledge of the battlefields, Mitchell's *Wallenstein* impressed contemporary reviewers as "a masterpiece of historical composition," a book "of stirling merit." He did not possess Napier's gift of narrative and mastery of detail, but his piquant style, enlivened by a sense of humor, was scarcely less readable, and he was a perceptive student of human nature. Like the historian of the Peninsular War, Mitchell also hoped to re-establish a tarnished reputation, for the name Wallenstein in England was generally held to be synonomous with greed, deceit, and barbarity. Specifically, he refuted the hostile version of Schiller, who had condemned Wallenstein for treason "by poetry, before history had fairly tried the case." Mitchell naturally rendered a more favorable verdict,

31 Mitchell, *Eminent Soldiers*, pp. 345–55.

using Wallenstein's enigmatic career in the process as a vehicle for his own ideas on tactics and military reform.[32]

Mitchell's next effort was an attempt to destroy a reputation. He had never liked Napoleon, a man of "very ordinary talents"; and increasingly he resented "the false halo that events and partisan zeal" had placed over the figure of this spoiled child of fortune. In France the reaction against the Napoleonic legend occurred in the 1860's and marched in step with the opposition to the Second Empire, but Mitchell's hostility was due to other causes. Partly it was a lingering feeling of Tory opposition; to a considerable degree it represented moral indignation at the faithlessness and insatiable ambition of the man; there also was present an element of professional scorn for an unimaginative tactician and an emotional identification with rising German nationalism. Mitchell's prejudices against Napoleon were sufficiently strong to rob the *Fall of Napoleon* of some of its historical value, but it created such a sensation that a second edition was published the following year. For some unknown reason the work has been ignored ever since by historians and biographers of Napoleon. Mitchell devoted most of one volume to the Waterloo campaign, yet Colonel Charles C. Chesney, writing twenty years later, makes no mention of the work in his celebrated *Waterloo Lectures* although he emphasized the Prussian share in the victory. Even the debunkers of the Napoleonic myth have failed somehow to utilize Mitchell. The book deserves a better fate. Those who accused him at the time of being "crotchitty" and "wildly unjust" to Napoleon still respected Mitchell's views as a military critic and his abilities as an historian. He was well known; he understood Napoleonic warfare as well as any of his contemporaries, and his unrivaled knowledge of the German sources should have made the *Fall of Napoleon* a useful mine of information whatever the author's bias. Yet this book, like Mitchell himself and everything else he had ever written, passed quietly out of sight and was soon forgotten.[33]

[32] *Wallenstein* is discussed in Schmitz, "Memoir," pp. xii-xv, and "Life and Letters of Wallenstein, by Forster and Mitchell," *Quarterly Review*, LXI (1838), 164–203. Mitchell's comments on Schiller are found in *Wallenstein*, pp. xii–xiii, 145.

[33] Mitchell, *Fall of Napoleon*, I, vii–x; II, 35; III, 305–36 *passim*. Comments of reviewers are found in "Marmont, Siborne and Alison," *Quarterly Review*, LXXVI (1845), 245–47, and "Colonel Mitchell's

Mitchell died in 1859, preceding Napier by only a few months. Both must have died frustrated in their hopes for the British army. Although it was another decade before the military system would be turned entirely upside down, the organizational defects exposed by the Crimean War together with the development of improved firearms clearly foreshadowed the exit of the Peninsular army that Napier had loved and defended so vigorously. But Mitchell, who had struggled a quarter of a century to modernize the army, lived long enough only to have his worst fears confirmed. Had he lived a few years longer he would have seen many of his desires realized in the growth of the Staff College during the 1860's and the Cardwell Reforms—particularly the abolition of purchase and the institution of short service—in the following decade. Doubtless, too, he would have been pleased when British officers, impressed by the Prussian victories over Austria in 1866 and France in 1870–71, began to turn to the German army for guidance.

Denied this satisfaction, it seems all the more a pity that Mitchell is not remembered for his efforts to reform the army. He urged better living conditions for the soldier and promotions by merit ten years before there was any organized pressure for these reforms, and he was even further ahead of his time in his suggestions for a more practical military dress.

Except for an evaluation of the strategical questions involved in the event of a war with Russia in India or on the Continent, Mitchell had little to say about strategy. Partially this was a problem of definition, for strategy to him included what a later generation would have termed "grand tactics," that is, "the art of combining cavalry, artillery, and infantry together, so as to make their united efforts produce the greatest possible result." On what Mitchell regarded as "the broken crutches of modern tactics," no very rapid progress in strategy was possible. It also should be emphasized that strategy was universally neglected by British military writers during this period. Probably there did not seem to be much value in discussing the subject, for its principles were well

Historical Account of the Rise and Fall of Napoleon," *United Service Magazine*, 1847, No. 1, 174–88. See also Pieter Geyl, *Napoleon for and against* (New Haven, 1949), pp. 71–72, and the bibliography in Colonel Charles C. Chesney, *Waterloo Lectures: A Study of the Campaign of 1815* (4th ed.; London, 1907).

established, the ideas of most Continental theorists were available in translation, and the railroad, steamship, and telegraph had yet to revolutionize travel and communications. On one occasion Mitchell did deplore the fact that modern strategy had "been founded on the power of conscriptions rather than on intelligible professional principles," but he never worked out any new strategical principles of his own.[34]

Mitchell's thoughts on tactics were more constructive, although improved firearms soon made some of his proposals impractical. Nevertheless the underlying principles remained valid. In the nineteenth century clearly the trend was in the direction of looser and more extended formations for infantry. The American Civil War demonstrated the defensive value of field fortifications; the wars for German unification showed the increased power of modern artillery, the need for a strong skirmish line, and the decisive results of fire action at close quarters. (The French in 1870 had preferred to fight battles at a distance which, according to Mitchell, cannot be very decisive.) These wars, however, also illustrate the decline of cavalry as an offensive arm in battle, which would have come as something of a surprise to Mitchell.

Mitchell's proposals to increase the tactical efficiency of the army were well known, but entirely without effect. In the 1830's there was practically no interest in the army in tactics: the military journals rarely published more than a few casual remarks on the subject, and as late as 1860 the catalogue of the Prince Consort's Library at Aldershot listed but one book under the headings "Tactics" and "Minor and Secondary Operations of War"—and that a translation of a French work published many years before! The reason perhaps is indicated in the following quotation from an essay on the British army written in 1842:

Of formal books on tactics, indeed, whether by such are meant didactic essays or fanciful theories, our service has fortunately produced few, and not one worth the mention; nor can we say that we entertain any profound veneration for either the pedantries of rule or the speculations of self-constituted tacticians. On the contrary, we believe that more sound knowledge of the principles of our profession is to be gained by the attentive

[34] Mitchell, *Thoughts on Tactics*, pp. 148–49, 305–92 *passim; Wallenstein*, p. 186.

perusal of a few pages of such works as those of Jones or Pasley, Napier or Douglas, than from the study of whole volumes of professed tactical essays or declamatory lectures. . . . But the whole subject of the "Grande Tactique" will never be taught or learnt from mere books.[35]

If this was the conventional attitude in the British army at the time—and there is no reason to assume otherwise—we need look no further for the reasons why Mitchell's thoughts on tactics might just as well have been kept to himself. But this instinctive distrust of theorists was not the only cause for his neglect. The British army had, after all, won the Napoleonic Wars, and history indicates that it is the defeated army that is usually the most receptive to new ideas. By the time of the Crimean War, Mitchell's book on tactics was nearly twenty years old, and the campaign in Italy in 1859, the American Civil War, and the German wars for unification soon offered more practical evidence for consideration. Then too, before 1870 the foreign influence upon the British army was almost exclusively French; Mitchell represented the German theorists, but who in England would have rejected Jomini and the French disciples of Napoleon for Clausewitz and other obscure writers in Prussia before Königgratz and Sedan?

If for no other reason, Mitchell is significant because he was the first British officer after 1815 publicly to preach a doctrine of war developed in Germany rather than France. His pro-German sentiments jeopardized his interpretation of history, but his fresh approach to tactical problems owed much to the theories of Berenhorst, Bismark, and Clausewitz. From Berenhorst he learned to regard war as a science, to seek decisive victory in close combat, to develop more flexible formations, to place a higher value on the soldier's life and the way he lived, and to stress shock tactics for cavalry. Bismark strengthened his confidence in the power of cavalry against

---

[35] "The British Army, Past, Present, and Future," *United Service Magazine*, 1842, No. 1, 22. Mr. D. W. King's informed survey of British military thought before 1860 shows how little was written by British officers of a theoretical nature, while Friedrich Engels, a military critic as well as an economic and political philosopher, observed in 1860 that "the English subaltern is far less theoretically educated than the North German . . ." (King, "Military Thought, 1860," in *The Prince Consort's Library. Aldershot. 1860–1960* [n.p., 1960], and W. H. Chaloner and W. D. Henderson [eds.], *Engels as Military Critic: Articles by Friedrich Engels Reprinted from the Volunteer Journal and the Manchester Guardian of the 1860's* [Manchester, 1959], p. 4).

infantry, and Clausewitz taught him that it was a mistake to treat something as dynamic as war like a mechanical art, governed by laws similar to those which govern dead matter. He also owed much to the earlier writings of Marshal Saxe.[36]

Mitchell's tactical theories bear a striking resemblance to those of Colonel Ardant du Picq, a young French theorist who was killed in 1870 but whose ideas later were to have a shaping influence upon French military thought. Appalled by the incompetent military leadership during the Crimean War and convinced from his experiences in Africa that "the theory of the big battalions is a despicable theory," Du Picq also approached war as a military scientist. He, too, studied classical battles to learn more about the individual in combat, and he discovered that only close combat ("sword to sword combat was the most deadly") produced a sharp discrepancy between the losses of the victor and the vanquished. Du Picq observed on the eve of the Franco-Prussian conflict that improved firearms had "diminished losses in battle," that "the less mobile the troops, the deadlier are battles," and that "modern arms require open order." "The good quality of troops will more than ever secure victory." He had a higher estimation of Napoleon's military qualities than Mitchell, but he was no less critical of the tactics used at Wagram, Eylau, and Waterloo, where enormous masses of infantry were employed to little material effect and at the expense of

a frightful loss of men and a disorder that, after they had once been unleashed, did not permit of the rallying and re-employment that day of the troops engaged. This was a barbaric method, according to the Romans amateurish, if we may say such a thing of such a man; a method which could not be used against experienced and well trained troops. . . . Napoleon looked only at the result to be attained. When his impatience, or perhaps the lack of experience and knowledge in his officers and soldiers, forbade his continued use of real attack tactics, he completely sacrificed the material effect of masses. . . . In ancient battle victory cost much less than with modern armies.[37]

[36] Hagemann, *Die Deutsche Lehre von Kriege. I. Von Berenhorst zu Clausewitz*, pp. 10–17, mentions aspects of Berenhorst's thought that can also be seen in Mitchell. See also Mitchell, *Thoughts on Tactics*, p. 8.

[37] Colonel Ardant du Picq, *Battle Studies: Ancient and Modern Battle*, trans. Colonel John N. Greely and Major Robert C. Cotton (Harrisburg, Pa., 1957), p. 132. See also *ibid.*, pp. 89–116 *passim*.

The two men differed mainly in their views on hand-to-hand combat and cavalry. Du Picq maintained that "in modern combat, there never is hand-to-hand conflict if one stands fast," and that bayonet attacks therefore were to be "replaced by fire action." "Shock" was merely a term. He contended that "the mass impulse of cavalry has long been discredited." Even before the introduction of new weapons, cavalry was effective "only against infantry which has been broken." At the same time Du Picq insisted that increased firepower had not in fact altered the role of cavalry. Firearms might be useful in exceptional circumstances, but "look out," he cautioned, "that this exception does not become the rule." And he agreed with Mitchell that "if the cavalryman fires he will not charge." [38]

Du Picq was killed near Metz by a Prussian shell in 1870. His writings, some of which had already been published but had attracted little notice, "seemed to open an entirely new perspective" to an army disillusioned by repeated defeats, and his theory that success in war was largely a matter of morale inspired the school of the offensive that dominated French military thought toward the end of the century.[39]

The British army was ripe for reform in 1855, when the experience in the Crimea was still foremost in everybody's thoughts. Had Mitchell fallen in the assault on the Redan, leaving his views on tactics and organization where they could be found and in good enough shape to be prepared for publication, perhaps he would have had an inspirational influence on his own army. At the very least he would have been too important to dismiss as an interesting, prophetic, but nonetheless a neglected rebel.

[38] Ibid., pp. 116, 146–47, 149, 168, 179, 195–99; Stefan T. Possony and Etienne Mantoux, "Du Picq and Foch: The French School" in Edward Mead Earle (ed.), Makers of Modern Strategy: Military Thought from Machiavelli to Hitler (Princeton, N.J., 1943), pp. 206–17.

[39] Ibid., p. 218; Major General J. F. C. Fuller, The Conduct of War, 1789–1961: A Study of the Impact of the French, Industrial, and Russian Revolutions on War and Conduct (London, 1961), pp. 121–22.

3

BRIDGING THE GAP

Field Marshal Sir John Fox Burgoyne

BEFORE 1854, those who fought reform could always fall back on an intrenched position that seemed unassailable: "Why," they would ask, "do you require Army Reform, when we had so perfect an army in the Peninsula?"[1] The answer became self-evident during the Crimean War, and for the next two decades Britain's military institutions were the subject of searching discussion and controversy.

One of the most prominent officers involved in this general reappraisal was Sir John Fox Burgoyne, a distinguished veteran of the Peninsular War who is perhaps best remembered for his role in the siege of Sebastopol. Greatly respected as a military thinker, Burgoyne appeared to contemporaries "quite as old a soldier with the pen as with the sword."[2] He was by no means a prolific writer but he had something to say about nearly every phase of military activity. His career is all the more instructive because it spanned the distance in time—and the difference in outlook —between the Peninsular army and the new army created in the early '70's by the Cardwell Reforms.

Burgoyne came from distinguished stock. His father was General John Burgoyne, whose decisive defeat at Saratoga in

[1] C. C. Chesney, "The Study of Military Science in Time of Peace," *Journal of the Royal United Service Institution*, XV (1872), 255 (cited hereafter as *R.U.S.I. Journal*).
[2] *United Service Magazine*, 1858, No. 1, 99–100.

1777 marked the turning point in the war of the American Revolution. His mother was a professional singer by whom "Gentleman John" had four children, all of them without benefit of wedlock. The General, whose wife had died years before, publicly acknowledged his brood and tried to provide for them in his will, but he left barely enough behind when he died in 1792 to balance his debts. To young John Fox Burgoyne, however, he bequeathed his name and family connections, a far more useful legacy to an aspiring soldier in eighteenth-century England than the £1,000 he had intended to bestow.

John Fox Burgoyne, the eldest of the children, was born in 1782. Of his first ten years we know nothing and quite likely there would have been little unusual about the rest of his life had it not been for his father's companion and brother-in-law Edward, twelfth Earl of Derby.[3] This distinguished patron of the turf generously assumed the burden of maintaining and educating Burgoyne's young children. He sent the future field marshal first to Cambridge for a year's private tutoring and then to Eton, and in 1796 Burgoyne entered the Royal Military Academy at Woolwich. Upon graduation two years later he was commissioned second lieutenant in the Royal Engineers and ordered to Dover to work on fortifications.

Burgoyne's first active service came in 1800 in Egypt. Here again his father's connections were of assistance, for before the campaign was over he had been named aide-de-camp to Lieutenant-General the Honorable Henry Fox, commander of the army of the Mediterranean and brother of his godfather, Charles James Fox, the famous statesman. In 1807 General Fox selected Burgoyne as commanding engineer in the second expedition to Egypt and, upon recovering from illness contracted during this campaign, Burgoyne was named commanding engineer of the forces to be withdrawn from the Mediterranean for service in Portugal under the command of Sir John Moore. Moore's force was sent instead to Sweden in a clumsy attempt to oppose an expected invasion of French and Dutch troops from Zeeland. No sooner had Moore's troops returned to England in July, 1808, than they were ordered to reinforce the British army which in the meantime had invaded Portugal.

[3] Lady Charlotte Burgoyne, youngest daughter of Edward, the eleventh Earl of Derby, had died without issue in 1776.

Burgoyne's experiences in the Peninsula were extensive. He participated in the Corunna campaign but missed the worst part of the retreat, he was with the army when it landed again at Lisbon in 1809, and he witnessed the celebrated passage of the Duoro. After the Battle of Talavera he remained at headquarters, much of the time as senior officer of engineers, until May, 1810, when he was sent to Almeida to supervise the reconstruction of Fort Concepcion, a task which was nearly finished when the French advance made it necessary to blow up the fort. As the British and Portuguese forces retreated to Lisbon, Burgoyne was preparing for the destruction of numerous bridges. He was also present at Busaco and served as regulating officer in one of the six districts comprising the lines of Torres Vedras.

Burgoyne next saw action at the second siege of Badajoz, where he directed the attack on the left of the Guadiana against the castle. After the siege was raised he was attached to General Thomas Picton's division for the purpose of training 200 infantrymen in engineering operations. Promoted to major for his services in the siege of Ciudad Rodrigo in 1812, and lieutenant colonel soon afterward for his conspicuous part in the final capture of Badajoz, Burgoyne was commanding Royal Engineer in the reduction of the forts of Salamanca. His reputation was tarnished somewhat by the failure to take Burgos, but he won distinction at the Battle of Vitoria and during the siege of San Sebastian, where the commanding officer of Royal Engineers, Colonel Sir Richard Fletcher, was killed. Wellington's first choice to succeed Fletcher was Burgoyne, the most widely experienced officer in the corps, but Burgoyne was not entitled to the position by seniority and therefore he remained in a subordinate capacity throughout the campaign in southern France. When the war ended he was named commanding engineer to the expedition being organized under Major General Sir Edward Pakenham for service in America. He participated in the Battle of New Orleans and hence missed the final triumph at Waterloo.[4]

[4] The basic source for the career of Sir John Fox Burgoyne is the two-volume biography by his son-in-law, Lieutenant Colonel The Hon. George Wrottesley, *Life and Correspondence of Field Marshal Sir John Burgoyne, Bart.* (London, 1873). Sketches of Burgoyne's career are also found in Major General Whitworth Porter, *History of the Corps of Royal Engineers* (London, 1889), II, 406–33; H. Morse Stephens, "Burgoyne," *D.N.B.*, III, 342–44; and Sir Francis Head, *A Sketch of the Life and Death of the late Field Marshal Sir J. Burgoyne* (London, 1872).

Burgoyne evidently did not share Mitchell's belief that war is a time "for application far more than the acquisition of knowledge." In the midst of campaigns he often recorded his observations of some particular problem or event, seeking especially to benefit from the mistakes of others. He also demonstrated a growing interest in military intelligence. When a friend was ordered in 1810 to examine and report upon the Bayonne Islands in the mouth of Vigo Bay, it struck Burgoyne as "extraordinary that, as soon as we had the opportunity, the whole coast of the Peninsula was not examined; this would always be interesting intelligence, whichever way . . . affairs end." [5]

To young and enthusiastic engineer officers like Burgoyne, the situation in 1810 must have seemed discouraging indeed. The Royal Engineers were short of trained officers; often the means at their disposal were "lamentably insufficient," and there were practically no trained artificers, sappers, and miners available for trench work. Captain (later General Sir Charles William) Pasley, who was placed in charge of the first school for the instruction of a corps of sappers and miners in 1812, recalled later that "the very inefficient state of the Engineer Department, strange to say, appeared to be unknown, not only to the rest of the Army . . . but even to the senior officers of the Engineers themselves, though several of them had served in the American War." [6]

The impetus for reform came mainly from the younger officers. Those employed in the construction of the lines of Torres Vedras met whenever possible to discuss schemes for improvement, and they continued to exchange information in their correspondence. [7] Some indication of Burgoyne's concern is seen in a letter to his friend Pasley in April, 1810. Incapacitated by wounds, Pasley was free to devote all of his energies to writing and working for reform.

[5] Wrottesley, *Burgoyne*, I, 44–45, 74.

[6] The Hon. J. W. Fortesque, *A History of the British Army* (London, 1899–1930), VIII, 148, 221, 379; C. W. C. Oman, *Wellington's Army 1809–1814* (London, 1912), pp. 281–82; Lieutenant Colonel P. H. Kealy, *Sir Charles Pasley, 1780 to 1861* (n.p., n.d.) p. 7. Sir John Burgoyne to Lord Lynedoch, July 20, 1830 (Royal Engineers Museum, Chatham, Burgoyne Papers).

[7] "I enclose for your perusal an interesting letter . . . on the destruction and temporary repairs of the Alva and Ceira bridges. Send it me back when you have done with it" (Burgoyne to Captain John Squire, October 4, 1811 [Burgoyne Papers]).

I am entirely on your side [Burgoyne wrote] respecting the Corps, and everything else, and feel assured we want a great deal more than I will explain to you by letter. I had been brooding over these ideas for some time myself, but, meeting nobody to encourage me, or to whom I dare broach my opinions, I could scarce believe I was myself sincere in them. Yours and [Captain John] Squire's letters have given me confidence in these ideas and made me fit for anything. I have written to sound [Captain Edmund R.] Mulcaster and wait with impatience for his answer. I long to gain him, knowing him to be a clever fellow.[8]

Although it sounds like they were hatching a revolution, all Burgoyne and Pasley had in mind was the formation of an organization to encourage military study and aid in the procuring of information "theoretical, practical and local in our complicated profession." By the end of the year the "Society for producing useful Military Information" was actively working toward these goals, with six charter members (including Burgoyne) who were captains and field officers in the Royal Engineers then serving in the Peninsula and "inclined to be of the same way of thinking." In January, 1811, the membership was expanded with the hope someday of establishing "a grand Depot de la Guerre. . . . that shall . . . contribute to the advancement of the Art Militaire." Unfortunately the society never really flourished, despite the enthusiasm and energy of the reformers. Many members were casualties in the next few years and the others were prevented from doing much useful work by the demands of active service. But from the accomplishments of those who did survive, notably Burgoyne, Pasley, and Major General Sir John T. Jones, we may surmise that had the society still been functioning after 1815 it would have promoted many useful reforms in that uninspired era between Waterloo and Balaclava.[9]

Throughout the war Burgoyne remained an alert student of

[8] Quoted in Kealy, *Pasley,* p. 8. In November, 1810, Pasley published his *Essay on the Military Policy and Institutions of the British Empire,* a book written "to advocate greater energy and perseverance in prosecuting the war against France" (Porter, *History of the Corps of Royal Engineers,* II, 433). In 1812 he became the director of the first course of instruction for non-commissioned officers in military engineering at Chatham and he remained at the head of the Chatham Establishment until 1841. He also wrote several treatises on military engineering.

[9] Kealy, *Pasley,* pp. 8–10; Burgoyne to Squire, January 4, 1811; Captain S. Dickinson to Burgoyne, January 9, 1811 (Burgoyne Papers).

his profession. He prepared copious notes of his experiences in demolishing masonry bridges, revetting siege batteries, making fascines, and reconnaissance; he reflected upon the performance of British troops working in the trenches, the dangers of officers throwing responsibility upon others, and the relative merits of the line and the column. Probably Burgoyne intended his notes to serve as the basis for a history of the campaigns in the Peninsula, but the way in which his services were slighted after the war seems to have killed his interest in the project and he turned over his material to Sir John Jones for use in his well-known *Journals of Sieges Carried on by the Army under the Duke of Wellington in Spain.* Many of the notes later were published in a collection of Burgoyne's military writings and also in the massive *Aide-Memoire to the Military Sciences* compiled by a committee of Royal Engineers in 1845. For the most part these articles are too technical for the layman and too closely pinned to the Peninsular War to have survived the impact of the industrial age, but they do testify to Burgoyne's dedicated spirit and early attempts to improve the profession.[10]

Burgoyne also studied the latest books on theory. His remarks on Carnot's *De la défense des places fortes,* published in Paris in 1810, and Jomini's *Traité des grandes opérations militaires* which appeared the following year, show him to have been a discerning critic. Carnot he dismissed as a false oracle who wrote "in the true spirit of a controversialist, turning and twisting the subject in every way to his own side of the argument, in a manner unjustifiable in treating on any science." The bloody sieges in the Peninsula only appeared to

---

[10] Wrottesley, *Burgoyne,* I, 336; Wrottesley (ed.), *The Military Opinions of General Sir John Fox Burgoyne. Part I. National Defences. II. The War in the Baltic and Crimea. III. Military Maxims, etc.* (London, 1859), pp. 255–75 *passim,* 286–88, 295–97, 463–67 (cited hereafter as Burgoyne, *Military Opinions*); *Aide-Memoire to the Military Sciences. Framed from the Contributions of Officers of the Different Services, and Edited by a Committee of the Corps of Royal Engineers in Dublin* (London, 1846–52), I, 193–95, 520–21. Wrottesley did a careless job in editing *The Military Opinions of General Burgoyne* by occasionally combining papers written years apart without so indicating, incorrectly citing—and sometimes failing to do so altogether—the source of selections, and even altering isolated passages without acknowledgment. Compare, for example, Burgoyne's "Coast Defences, Chiefly as Applicable to the Coast of Great Britain," *Papers on Subjects Connected with the Duties of the Corps of Royal Engineers,* N.S., I (1851), 9, with the same passage as it appears in Burgoyne, *Military Opinions,* p. 372.

corroborate Carnot's principles of active defense, for according to Burgoyne,

these assaults have been nearly all perfectly *hors de regle,* and necessarily premature, from want of time or means which could not be given to the occasion, as well as from the faultiness of some of our military establishments most necessary to the reduction of fortified posts.

Despite Carnot's attractive proposals for a more vigorous and prolonged defense, Burgoyne maintained that the superiority of the attack over the defense "is precisely where it was before this celebrated work was published." Indeed, "no operation in war," he concluded, "can be so certain of success as a siege." [11] Nor was Burgoyne willing to accept Jomini's maxims at face value. He preferred the line to the column as a combat formation and he disagreed with some of Jomini's conclusions. Jomini, for example, had stated that a march on the rear of the enemy could lead to grand results only if it occurred immediately behind the enemy's line and that attacks far to the rear produced only "ephemeral successes." But according to Burgoyne, this was

a general maxim for what can only apply to particular occasions; on many the maxim should surely be decidedly the reverse. Suppose an army acting on the defensive, draws an enemy well into the country, takes up strong positions that can only be attacked to a very great disadvantage and at last checks him entirely without coming to a decisive action, what can be better than to employ all the troops beyond what are necessary to check the invader in front, upon his communications in the rear?—as was done by the Russians in 1813, and might as some think, have been done by Lord Wellington against Messena in 1811, when he was before the lines of Lisbon.[12]

[11] Burgoyne's "Remarks on Carnot" was among the papers given to Sir John Jones after the war and is reprinted in Burgoyne, *Military Opinions,* pp. 468–79. No date is given by Wrottesley, but it must have been written near the close of the Napoleonic Wars. According to a more recent authority, Carnot's calculations and figures were often "eminently fallacious," but he was ahead of his time "in insisting on a strong development of vertical fire as a powerful adjunct to the defence" (Major G. Sydenham Clarke, *Fortification: Its Past Achievements, Recent Development, and Future Progress* [London, 1890], pp. 22–23).

[12] Burgoyne, "Notes on Genl. Jomini's Book *Grandes Operations Militaires,*" pp. 31–32 (Burgoyne Papers). This thirty-nine-page foolscap manuscript is not dated, but from its contents, age, and appearance it too was written near the end of the Napoleonic Wars.

Although he emerged from the Napoleonic Wars the most distinguished of Wellington's engineers, Burgoyne was denied that public recognition extended to others of comparable rank and experience. By an oversight compounded by a technicality he did not receive the K.C.B. to which he was entitled, and he refused the subsequent offer of a civil knighthood on the ground that it represented a slight to the corps. He served as commanding officer of engineers in France (1815–18) and in the Medway district (1821–26); he accompanied Lieutenant General Sir W. Clinton's expeditionary force to Portugal in 1827 in a similar capacity; and in 1828 he assumed command of the engineer department of Portsmouth, a post which he resigned three years later for the less lucrative but more challenging position of chairman of the Board of Public Works—Ireland.

Burgoyne left the army in 1831 because he felt his services had been neglected and two junior officers had superseded him in rank, which virtually eliminated his prospects of becoming inspector general of fortifications, the only post in the service given to an officer of engineers with the rank of general. But his letters also reveal that he had lost much of his enthusiasm for military studies. If a vigorous and dedicated officer could grow stale so quickly, is it any wonder that the British army was barren of any original or constructive thought during the postwar years?

Burgoyne's duties in Ireland concerned civil engineering, and his only pronouncement upon military matters at this time was in response to a questionnaire sent him by the Royal Commissioners for Inquiring into the Practicability of Consolidating the Civil Branches of the Army. Burgoyne, who had been chairman of the Board of Public Works for three years, spoke out strongly against any similar organization in the War Office. "I conceive them," he testified, "to be more expensive, dilatory and inefficient than any departments under other systems, without a proper degree of responsibility, and producing a probability of a want of steady and uniform principles of proceeding." Actually he exceeded the limits of the questionnaire in urging a much greater consolidation than was anticipated when he proposed in 1834

uniting in one person the offices of Secretary of War, Commander-in-Chief, and Master-General of the Ordnance, under . . .

[what] would be more appropriately styled on the Continent, *Minister of War.* . . . This officer must necessarily be an influential member of one of the Houses of Parliament, and if possible, should be selected from those who had served with reputation in the army. . . . Such a charge given to one individual would in the first instance shock many prejudices, but I am myself satisfied that they are but prejudices.[13]

In recommending the concentration of powers in the hands of one civilian minister responsible to Parliament for the administration of the army, Burgoyne was twenty years ahead of his time. Not until 1855 were the initial steps taken, when the Board of Ordnance was abolished and the office of secretary at war merged with that of secretary of state for war. The Hartington Commission recommended in 1890 that the responsibilities of the secretary of state for war be increased and these proposals were reiterated dogmatically by the Esher Committee in 1904, when many of the recommendations finally were followed.[14]

In 1844 Burgoyne again had occasion to submit his thoughts on a military subject, this time the security of Ireland. According to his biographer, the memorandum he submitted to Sir George Murray, the master general of the ordnance, "affords a good specimen of a very rare quality of his mind, viz., the power of grasping the strategical features of an extensive country. . . ." Apparently this document impressed Sir George as well, for the following year he wrote Burgoyne offering him the post of inspector general of fortifications. Although Burgoyne had reached sixty-three years of age, the next twenty-three years proved to be the most useful of his military career. He served as the principal adviser to the government on national defense, he was for a time second in command to Lord Raglan in the Crimea, and throughout the entire period his pen was active in promoting measures to strengthen Britain's inadequate defenses.[15]

Within a year from the time Burgoyne assumed his new duties, he wrote to emphasize the defenseless state of the

[13] Wrottesley, *Burgoyne*, I, 397–400.

[14] Colonel J. S. Omond, *Parliament and the Army 1642–1904* (Cambridge, 1933), pp. 93–99, 135–37, 151–54; Captain Owen Wheeler, *The War Office Past and Present* (London, 1914), pp. 169–76, 244–45, 286 ff.

[15] Wrottesley, *Burgoyne*, I, 423–35. In 1838 Burgoyne had been promoted major general as a matter of course and nominated for the K.C.B. that he should have received twenty-four years earlier.

country. The French recently had committed themselves to
the construction of a steam navy strong enough to offset the
commanding lead in sail warships that Englishmen had come
to regard almost as a natural right. Actually the French naval
law of 1846 represented no immediate threat to British naval
supremacy, but to many it appeared to increase the danger of
an invasion or at least of raids against the English coast.[16]
English soldiers in particular, mindful of what had occurred
in 1805, feared that once again the French might succeed in
luring the fleet away from the Channel long enough to permit
an invasion, especially now that armies could be concentrated
quickly by rail and transported in swift vessels regardless of
unfavorable winds.

Burgoyne's reactions to this invasion scare can be measured
in a lengthy paper he submitted to the master general of
ordnance in 1846. Considering the possibility (although not
the probability) that the French might obtain naval superiority in the Channel long enough to stage an invasion "in
great force," Burgoyne looked at Britain's defenses and
concluded that such an attempt would probably succeed.
What existing forces, he asked, could repel an invasion? It
was a complete fallacy to think that the swarms of enthusiastic volunteers that might spring to arms overnight
could be of any use in the field against an army as well
organized and disciplined as the French. The militia too
would be unequal to French infantry unless bolstered by
regulars in the proportion of two to one, and Burgoyne
estimated that at most 10,000 regular soldiers could be
assembled on short notice for service in the field. Moreover,
the organization of the army had deteriorated since Waterloo,
available stores of equipment and provisions were "unsatis-
factory" at best and in some instances totally deficient, and
the country possessed practically no modern fortresses. In
brief,

a comparison of the land service and forces shows that France
could in a *very few* weeks from her first preparation, by partial
movements scarcely to be observed, collect from 100,000 to
150,000 troops on the shores of the Channel, within a few hours'
sail of the British coast, and where every coaster or large fishery

16 An excellent discussion of the technical questions involved is Bernard Brodie, *Sea Power in the Machine Age* (Princeton, N.J., 1941), pp.
17–45.

vessel, aided by steamers, would be an efficient transport; while England would have neither fortifications nor troops, nor means of equipment for a force equal to cope with even one fourth of that number.

Burgoyne recommended a large increase in the regular army, the immediate preparation and constant maintenance of ample military stores, an adequate peacetime organization of the militia, and the construction of fortifications "at every port in proportion to its importance." He estimated that a regular army of 30,000 free to take the field at any time and capable of being expanded in an emergency to 60,000 would suffice to discourage the French or any other nation from the temptation to plunder the wealth that industrialization had brought to Britain.[17]

This was the first authoritative warning that the defenses of Britain were inadequate in the day of iron and steam, and from the standpoint of the excitement it created it is probably the most important document Burgoyne ever wrote. Almost immediately it was ordered to be printed and circulated in confidence among the members of the cabinet. Lord Palmerston, the foreign secretary, was sufficiently alarmed to report to the cabinet that an immediate and effective remedy must be found before the next meeting of Parliament, and Wellington, when he read the memorandum, sent a lengthy letter to Burgoyne expressing approval of his observations and also the fervent hope that he himself would not live to see the tragic consequences of the government's inadequate defense policies.[18]

Burgoyne's efforts to bolster England's defenses were interrupted throughout most of 1847 while he served as president of the Irish Relief Commission. But as soon as he returned from Dublin in the fall, he renewed his effort to jar the government into action by emphasizing, in a second memorandum, the possibilities of a French descent upon the coast.

---

[17] Burgoyne's memorandum, entitled "Observations on the Possible Results of a War with France, under our Present System of Military Preparation," was later published in Burgoyne, *Military Opinions*, pp. 1–23.

[18] "Report on the Defence of the Country, Submitted to the Cabinet by Lord Palmerston. 17th December, 1846," is published in Wrottesley, *Burgoyne*, I, 436–44. Palmerston's private letters also reveal how impressed he was with Burgoyne's arguments (Major General T. B. Collinson, "On the Present Facilities for the Invasion of England, and for the Defence Thereof," *R.U.S.I. Journal*, XXI [1878], 1).

This time he supported his views by circulating Wellington's letter privately among persons of influence. By what Fortescue has called a "fortunate indiscretion" (in contrast to the present practice of deliberate leakage of information by responsible officials), the Duke's letter found its way to the *Morning Chronicle* and was published. The resulting furor, a mixture of alarm and surprise, infuriated Wellington, who despite his concern was still unwilling to be an instrument in mobilizing public opinion against the government, and it drew a cry of anguish from Burgoyne, who had no wish to compromise the good relations he enjoyed with his old chief. Although neither Wellington nor Burgoyne had communicated the letter to the press (actually it appears to have been a man named Pigou, "a meddling zealot who does nothing but read blue books and write letters to the Times and Chronicle" [19]), they cannot have been altogether unhappy at the opportunity thus provided to open the eyes of the people to the inadequate state of the country's defenses. But unfavorable economic conditions and the political upheavals of 1848 did not produce a climate conducive to any increase in defense appropriations, especially when any significant increase would necessarily involve a substantial addition to the recently introduced income tax. Indeed, by 1849 the actions of the new French government and the confidence of the British admiralty were such that the immediate fear of an invasion had diminished. The army estimates for that year were reduced accordingly, and for the time being, at least, Britain's new steam navy seemed to meet the requirements for national security.[20]

Burgoyne, however, continued to show anxiety over the state of Britain's land defenses. In May, 1850, he wrote still another memorandum, claiming that the facts in Wellington's celebrated letter "remain unchanged" and that the military posture of the country "is now absolutely awful." Continue the present policies, Burgoyne warned, and the nation's weakness would invite attack. Indeed, he main-

[19] Charles Greville, as quoted in Sir Herbert Maxwell, *The Life of Wellington: The Restoration of the Martial Power of Great Britain* (2d ed.; London, 1900), II, 361 n.

[20] Wellington's letter is reprinted in Wrottesley, *Burgoyne*, I, 444–51. Pertinent correspondence is found in *ibid.*, pp. 469–81, and Maxwell, *Wellington*, II, 364–66. Fortescue is in error in implying that Wellington's letter was responsible for the increase in army estimates in 1847; the letter was not published until January 4, 1848. See Fortescue, *History of the British Army*, XIII, 10–11.

tained that the army in 1850 was so inadequate that in the event of serious differences with the French, war would have to be avoided *"at any* sacrifice." Fortifications would help contribute to the defensive capabilities of the country, but the crying need was for more trained soldiers, arms, ammunition, and equipment. Moreover, he contended, the nation was losing sight of the real purpose of the army. British soldiers were more than a force to help preserve domestic tranquillity and police the empire; they also must be fully prepared to meet foreign aggression if and when it should occur.

Burgoyne based his appeal on the argument best calculated to impress the influential members of Parliament— it was good business to see that the empire was adequately defended. "In ordinary life," he argued, "we are not neglectful of providing a security for our own property and interests. We spend enormous sums in insuring our ships, our houses, and even our hay-stacks. . . ." To Burgoyne, the desired increases in the standing army represented cheap insurance against a national military disaster. His friend, Sir Francis Head, who was no less alarmed at the defenseless state of Great Britain in 1850, described the laissez faire attitude of the typical Victorian somewhat more dramatically.

I will, during every day of my life, enjoy cheap cotton, cheap silk, cheap linen, and cheap woollen clothes. I will warm myself in the evening at a cheap fire; I will sleep at night between cheap sheets and cheap blankets; I will travel 40 miles an hour at a cheap rate; I will read a cheap newspaper; say my prayers out of a cheap Bible—all cheapened by steam: but if I am called upon to contribute to repair the only little injury which this blessed beneficent power has created—an injury to the defences of my country which at any hour may deprive me and my family of our property, our lives, and our honour, I deliberately reply, "I know nothing about your *new inventions.* I have inherited a good *old* English hatred to a standing army; the thing, I tell ye, is *unconstitutional;* and besides this, I can't and *won't* afford it" [21]

Once again Burgoyne's timing was unfortunate, for the prevailing mood was for a further reduction in military expenditures. The International Exhibition in 1851 produced

[21] Burgoyne, *Military Opinions,* pp. 24–61 *passim;* Sir Frances Head, *The Defenceless State of Great Britain* (London, 1850), p. 278. Burgoyne and Head were in basic agreement on the necessary measures of defense.

much talk "of the brotherhood of man and of universal and perpetual peace." Newspapers claimed to see something symbolic in the public introduction of Richard Cobden, long regarded by soldiers as "our great adversary" because of his insistence on humanitarian reforms and reduced army estimates, to the aged Duke of Wellington in Hyde Park. Even the secretary at war contributed to this feeling of complacency when he announced that "the army never was in a more perfect state than at present." Of course he means "for its numbers," Burgoyne wrote to the Viscount Hardinge. There was fresh evidence that the invasion threat must be taken seriously.

> While we are thus progressively falling into imbecility and decay, the French are most energetic in their preparations against *us*, however they may economise in other matters. They have within the last three months passed a resolution for an expenditure of £275,000 for *sea* defences for Cherbourg— avowedly for the chance of collision with England; and two or three voices that ventured to oppose were at once silenced by a popular outcry that they were traitors. There is no mistaking this general feeling of preparing for war with England, which is constantly in action in France.[22]

Burgoyne's voice was heard only when Louis Napoleon seized power in December, 1851, and established a virtual military despotism. Palmerston did not wait for the formal restoration of the empire the following year to revive his old argument about the French capacity for throwing an army of 50,000 across the Channel. Soon rumors of imminent invasion were current and the press echoed the cry of alarm and defiance. Curiously enough, French naval expenditures had actually decreased steadily the past three years and in 1852 had reached the lowest point in over a decade, while the French army had recently been reduced by 50,000 men and the national guard had been practically dissolved. But the invasion panic in England was a demonstrated fact: the army establishment was increased by 5,000 in February, 1852, and a new militia bill providing for 80,000 men to be raised and trained was passed later in the year. Wellington's last major

---

[22] Wrottesley, *Burgoyne*, I, 488–90; "Cherbourg" is published in Burgoyne, *Military Opinions*, pp. 61–64. See also Fortescue, *History of the British Army*, XIII, 20–22; *United Service Magazine*, 1852, No. 1, 460– 61.

speech in Parliament forecast the importance of this measure.[23]

Burgoyne supported these defense measures. Although responsible for Britain's fortifications, he had the independence of mind to look to the army rather than brick and mortar as the first line of defense behind the navy. In May, 1852, he recommended that the government encourage the growth of local volunteer organizations—the first time, his biographer claims, since the Napoleonic Wars that a high-ranking official had advocated the re-creation of a volunteer force. The following year he published his proposals in greater detail. Asserting that "it takes at least a twelvemonth to make tolerable infantry soldiers," and that three years were required to produce "thoroughly good" soldiers, Burgoyne voiced little faith in "the spontaneous rising of an armed population": to rely upon the levy en masse in case of enemy invasion "would be futile." But militia and the best class of volunteers could serve usefully in the field if mixed with regular troops, and volunteers trained and organized for local defense against small enemy landing parties might be able to compensate for their inferiority by superior numbers. Burgoyne was quicker than Napier to see that the new Minié rifle would render volunteers more valuable because they would no longer have to fight "at very close quarters." "On the whole," he concluded,

> militia and volunteers, under duly considered arrangements . . . will afford powerful means in aid of our self defence; but it must not be forgotten, that the fate of the country will rest on a very insecure basis, in the event of having to fight the battle in our own land, unless the *regulars* shall be in sufficient force to sustain the main brunt of the operations.[24]

In 1854 Burgoyne, at the patriarchal age of 72, again saw active service, this time in the Crimea. In January, two months before Great Britain and France slipped into the war between Russia and Turkey, Burgoyne had smelled a war coming and in his usual fashion had submitted his "Reflections" to the government, recommending steps to be taken in

[23] Brodie, *Sea Power in the Machine Age*, pp. 59–69; Fortescue, *History of the British Army*, XIII, 22–24.
[24] Wrottesley, *Burgoyne*, I, 500 n.; "Militia and Volunteers" was first published in the *United Service Magazine*, 1853, No. 1; and is reprinted in Burgoyne, *Military Opinions*, pp. 91–112.

the Dardanelles and pointing to the dangers involved if wooden ships were to be used to bombard the stone forts at Sebastopol. By the end of the month he was in Paris endeavoring to persuade the French to undertake joint military operations in the Dardanelles, a mission which, so the English ambassador later informed him, had "produced a visible change in the Emperor's views." He reached Constantinople early in February and spent the final weeks of peace reconnoitering possible defensive positions covering the Bosphorus and conferring with Omar Pasha, head of the Turkish army. Despite "all the pressure of warlike reports and discussions," Burgoyne obviously enjoyed the assignment: he felt, he confessed, "like the old troop-horse at the sound of the trumpet." [25]

Burgoyne next turned his thoughts to the strategy of the coming campaign. His first concern was to establish in the Dardanelles "a firm base of operations." Once the Russians had committed themselves to a definite line of advance, he hoped that the allies might find openings to carry the war to Russian soil. Initially he had reservations about the proposal to land British and French forces in the Crimea: Sebastopol, he maintained, "can have little strength as a fortress, and its fate will depend upon the power of obtaining firm possession of the Crimea." The problem would be to land an army in the immediate neighborhood of powerful Russian forces. Watching the embarkation of the army at Varna Burgoyne, who had recently been appointed chief engineer of the British expeditionary force, confided to his family:

> It is not to be expected that I, coming out so late, and under the repute rather of a professional Engineer than otherwise, should have any opportunity of expressing any opinion upon the great project. . . . I must confess that I do not understand on what sound principle it is undertaken. This is not the time for discouraging anybody, and consequently I do not hold to a soul, opinions that I may give you at a distance, confidentially. It appears to me to be the most desperate enterprise ever attempted.[26]

An account of Burgoyne's activities during the Crimean War alone would fill a volume. He was the engineer in charge of British siege operations during much of the terrible winter

[25] Wrottesley, *Burgoyne*, II, 1, 12, 15.
[26] *Ibid.*, II, 37–40, 73–74.

before Sebastopol, but he also exercised considerable influence upon the conduct of the campaign as Lord Raglan's principal adviser on strategy and, after October, as second in command of British forces in the Crimea. Today an engineer' is often regarded as a technician who is either uninterested or inadequately informed in matters outside his specialty. But in 1854 the officers of the Royal Engineers and the artillery were the best educated in the service; the former especially "still looked upon themselves as the strategical, and even tactical, experts of the Army." Burgoyne had long been a student of Jomini, and as inspector general of fortifications he had also been forced to consider the strategical problems of the defense of Britain, so it was only natural that Lord Raglan should turn to him for advice even before the siege had commenced. His son-in-law and biographer is stretching a point when he claims that Burgoyne "held, in many respects, the same position during the Crimean campaign, which Count Moltke occupied with the Prussian head-quarters" in 1870,[27] but despite this reckless exaggeration the fact remains that Burgoyne was at Lord Raglan's elbow until recalled early in 1855, and even then the British commander retained him at headquarters for another month.

Burgoyne's field service falls beyond the scope of this work, but because his dismissal became a wartime issue and in view of the fact that his experiences in the Crimea helped to shape his subsequent military opinions, we cannot ignore altogether his role in the campaign. He was wrong, obviously, in estimating the Russian capability to resist a landing: the two armies went ashore in Eupatoria Bay well beyond reach of the main Russian field army, which was not encountered until the Battle of the Alma fully a week later. And it is still debatable whether Burgoyne's plan to slip around Sebastopol and attack the naval stronghold from the south was the best one under the circumstances. This had been in his mind even before Alma, and once the opportunity to exploit the victory by a swift advance against the northern forts had faded, Lord Raglan used Burgoyne to help persuade the French commander to agree to the flank march. Burgoyne's plan has been defended on the ground that the forts north of the city were too formidable to be attacked by infantry and that even had

[27] Lieutenant General Sir George MacMunn, *The Crimea in Perspective* (London, 1935), p. 182; Wrottesley, *Burgoyne*, II, 348–49.

the Russians been driven from them, "we should have found ourselves in a position of greatly augmented difficulty." [28] On the other hand, Lord Raglan's most recent biographer asserts that the northern attack was practicable, that the failure to assault the city immediately upon arrival south of Sebastopol was a still more grievous error, and that Burgoyne had erred when he had insisted that there be no unsupported assault before siege guns had arrived and were in position.[29] The question here turns on the state of the defenses south of the city at the time the French and British were first in position to make a determined attack. Perhaps, as one of the divisional commanders had observed, there was nothing for the siege guns to knock down during the first attempt to take the city; certainly the defenses became increasingly formidable. But it is doubtful whether any attack would have succeeded without sufficient artillery preparation. The Russian garrison was adequate in size and greatly strengthened with the addition of sailors from the fleet, and if the south side was still defended only by weak breastworks, 72 heavy guns were in position there—and for all Burgoyne and the others knew, so was half of the Russian field army. Burgoyne's judgment on this occasion seems to have been fundamentally correct: "The fortifications are poor concerns," he wrote privately, "but the situation is favourable for the enemy. They have an immense force of artillery mounted, and a large garrison, and it is not easy to get up all our means. . . ." [30] The real tragedy for the British was that later it became impossible "to get up" any of the necessary supplies from the base at Balaclava. Hopelessly lacking manpower to improve the British trenches and short of ammunition (during the whole month of December, 1854, the total amount of ammunition that reached the batteries from Balaclava was "little more than the expenditure for two days' and a half firing from one piece" [31]), the situation offered Burgoyne little scope for the conduct of the siege.

[28] *Ibid.*, II, 87, 91, 164–65; Major General Sir Edward Hamley, *The War in the Crimea* (London, 1891), pp. 69–70. MacMunn also believed that an allied attack on the northern defenses must have failed (*Crimea in Perspective*, p. 82).

[29] Christopher Hibbert, *The Destruction of Lord Raglan: A Tragedy of the Crimean War 1854–55* (London, 1961), pp. 95–97, 104–5.

[30] A penetrating analysis of the situation confronting the allied commanders is found in Emil Daniels' continuation of Hans Delbrück, *Geschichte der Kriegskunst im Rahmen der politischen Geschichte*, VII, *Neuzeit* (Berlin, 1928), 36–42; Wrottesley, *Burgoyne*, II, 94.

[31] The British even resorted to hitching the Turks to trench carts with man harnesses, but the men were too weak to pull the carts very far:

Burgoyne continually pressed for a combination of *"offensive* measures with those of defence," but the dwindling size and declining state of the army coupled with the problems of a joint command made it impossible to be as aggressive as he would have liked. Although he recognized the Malakoff Tower as the key to the defense of Sebastopol, the resources at hand were too limited to permit the British to seize it while Burgoyne remained in the Crimea. One of his final services to Lord Raglan was to impress upon the French the importance of this position, and when the city finally fell in September his successor, Major General Sir Harry Jones, wrote to Burgoyne that "Sebastopol was taken by the point you always indicated—the Malakoff." [32]

Burgoyne was not on hand to witness the final triumph. The English public had clamored for a change, impatient with the military stalemate and incensed by vivid accounts of suffering and mismanagement in the army sent home by the father of modern war correspondents, William Howard Russell. In February the new government led by Lord Palmerston, the prime minister, and Lord Panmure, the secretary of state for war, "yielded to the Storm." "Done nothing!" one member exclaimed indignantly before the House of Commons where he had been defending his colleagues: "We have recalled Sir John Burgoyne!" Originally, Burgoyne was to have been the scapegoat, but Lord Raglan's reluctance to let him go and rising indignation throughout the army forced the ministry to declare that he had simply been recalled "because his valuable services were required at home." As a matter of fact, his experience and judgment were not wasted in England, for a reorganization of the field army was both necessary and inevitable. A chief-of-staff—another Peninsular veteran—was sent out to bring the army under closer supervision; the land-transport service was reorganized, and Sir Harry Jones assumed the responsibility of directing the siege and co-ordinating the work of the various arms. If the public tended

---

several died in the attempt, which was not repeated (W. Edmund Reilly, *An Account of the Artillery Operations Conducted by the Royal Artillery and Royal Naval Brigade before Sebastopol in 1854 and 1855* [London, 1859], pp. 41–42).

[32] Wrottesley, *Burgoyne*, II, 121–23, 126, 137, 156, 304. The memoranda from Burgoyne dealing with the siege at all levels are found in Captain H. C. Elphinstone, *Journal of the Operations Conducted by the Corps of Royal Engineers. Part I. From the Invasion of the Crimea to the Close of the Winter Campaign 1854–55* (London, 1859), pp. 97–151 *passim.*

for a time to associate Burgoyne with the failure to take Sebastopol, his stock remained high in the army where his efforts had been appreciated and his difficulties understood. In the eyes of the *United Service Magazine* he had displayed an "eminent aptitude . . . for all the functions of a General" even though no longer in the hey-day of life; in the judgment of at least one historian his conduct of the siege was "admirable"; and according to the *Royal Engineers Journal,* it was "unfortunate" that Burgoyne was recalled "at the time when his judgment in engineering matters was beginning to be recognized, and his plans had come to be adopted," leaving others "to gather the laurels which he had planted and to some extent reared." [33]

Yet ultimately Burgoyne's military prestige did suffer in some army circles. Scarcely had Sebastopol fallen when the secretary of state for war ordered the compilation of an official record of the siege and Burgoyne, who persistently had refused to write of his own experiences for fear he would offend "private feelings, and perhaps public interests," now found himself accused of selecting as editor an officer who "would naturally be interested in giving the best colour" to his own services. "A large sum of public money has been expended," it was contended, "not alone on a failure, but on a production as unjust to our noble Crimean Army and its illustrious commander as it is discreditable to its authors." It was even intimated that many of Burgoyne's official papers printed in the Appendix "bore all the appearance of having been written when the siege was over," but there is no evidence to corroborate this suspicion and it is out of keeping with Burgoyne's character as revealed in his *Life and Correspondence.* Burgoyne defended his selection of Captain Elphinstone to prepare the first volume of the journal and assumed responsibility for the contents of each chapter, but he declined to answer publicly those criticisms which served "manifestly as a vehicle for decrying individuals or distinct bodies" like the Corps of Royal Engineers.[34]

[33] Head, *Burgoyne,* p. 45; *United Service Magazine,* 1855, No. 1, 108; 1855, No. 2, 119–20; MacMunn, *Crimea in Perspective,* p. 182; *Royal Engineers Journal* (November, 1871).

[34] Wrottesley, *Burgoyne,* II, 353; *United Service Magazine,* 1860, No. 1, 118–20; 1860, No. 2, 106; Burgoyne, "Remarks on the Journal of the Siege of Sebastopol," *Papers on Subjects Connected with the Duties of the Corps of Royal Engineers,* IX (1860), 139–40 (cited hereafter as *R.E. Professional Papers*).

Burgoyne continued to serve as inspector general of fortifications until he retired from the army in 1868 at the ripe age of 86. We are not concerned here with his policies or official acts—this would involve a detailed study of Britain's national defenses extending beyond the scope of the present work. But Burgoyne, despite his manifold duties and advanced years, was if anything more active than ever with his pen, and his military opinions during this period reveal a progressive outlook and increasing concern over the impact of technology upon war. To the end of his life, Burgoyne continued to study military developments: he learned from his own experiences in the Crimean War, he sent others to learn from the experiences of the Americans in their Civil War, and he lived long enough to pass judgment on some of the military lessons of the German wars for unification.

Burgoyne's writings during this period fall into several categories. Naturally he remained actively interested in the Crimean War. Upon his return to London he continued to submit memoranda on the strategy that should be followed and his friends with the army sent him regular reports on the progress of the siege. He provided Kinglake with material for his classic *Invasion of the Crimea,* and the appearance of Baron de Bazancourt's hostile *L'Expédition de Crimée* prompted him to contribute a vigorous defense of the British army to *Blackwood's Magazine.* He also criticized many of the claims found in the book by the great Russian engineer and the hero of the defense of Sebastopol, General Todleben.[35]

From the nature of his duties it was inevitable, too, that Burgoyne should retain a special interest in the development of new weapons and improved equipment. In contrast to the Napiers, he enthusiastically supported the introduction of the Minié rifle despite its imperfections. "It is impossible to stand still," he wrote two years before the Crimean War; "and therefore the least imperfect must be used until further assured improvement shall be devised. The expense of these changes will be very heavy, but *must* be borne. . . ." In a day

---

[35] Burgoyne's correspondence with A. W. Kinglake is found in Wrottesley, *Burgoyne,* II, 316–22, and among the Burgoyne Papers. The critique of Bazancourt's work is reprinted in Burgoyne, *Military Opinions,* pp. 220–232, and his objections to Todleben's account is found in Wrottesley, *Burgoyne,* II, 322–26. The Burgoyne papers also contain his "Notes on an Article 'Quelques considerations sur la campagne active d'Orient: Avril—Septembre 1854,'" that appeared in the March, 1866, issue of *Le Spectateur Militaire.*

when entire weapons systems grow obsolescent overnight we take this situation for granted, but when this youthful septuagenarian issued his "Memorandum on Rifled Small Arms" in 1852, the British army was in a "placid, stationary condition" and there were few indeed who could anticipate any need for change. Burgoyne was also one of the first to work for the introduction of wrought-iron guns, but in general his views on the type and caliber of rifled artillery best suited to the requirements of the army were not shared by the artillery authorities.[36] Nor were his interests in technology limited to new weapons: he instructed the official military observer sent to the Union Army in 1864 to learn what he could about any development in engineering, transport, or field equipment in a war that served as a unique testing ground.[37]

Burgoyne also became involved in the prolonged reappraisal of the British army after its experience in the Crimea. Recruitment, training, and the education of officers formed the principal subjects for debate and investigation, fresh interest was shown in the study of tactics, and numerous commissions and committees met to devise ways of overcoming weaknesses in the organization and administration of the army revealed by the Crimean War and the Indian Mutiny in 1857. Between 1815 and 1854 twelve such committees had been appointed to deal with army matters: between 1854 and Burgoyne's retirement in 1868, well over a hundred committees went to work on military problems.[38] At first the authorities "made the great mistake of repairing and patching, and propping up and adding to the worn-out, tumbledown fabric, instead of setting to work to demolish, and . . . to build up a sound edifice upon a new and solid foundation," but ultimately the agitation swept away many of the worst abuses and placed the British army on a relatively modern footing. If the army was to be found deficient in some respects during the initial stages of a future campaign and if officers continued as a class to show more enthusiasm for

[36] Wrottesley, *Burgoyne*, II, 383–86, 477–82; *United Service Magazine*, 1855, No. 1, 275.

[37] See Jay Luvaas, *The Military Legacy of the Civil War: The European Inheritance* (Chicago, 1959), pp. 36–38.

[38] These are listed in the *Abstract of the Recommendations of the Principal Commissions and Committees Which Have Reported on Army Matters 1806–1900* (London, 1901). See also Fortescue, *History of the British Army*, XIII, 555.

sports than for military studies, certainly it can be said that never again did the British enter a war quite so inadequately prepared: never again was the military profession in England looked upon, as it had been before 1854, "as the only one which required neither education nor instruction." [39]

The noisy clamor for reform tended to make Burgoyne something of a conservative in questions of military organization. Instinctively, he defended the army against all charges. "Nothing can be finer," he wrote from the Crimea, "than the primary organization of our infantry; the men are magnificent, well clothed and taken care of in quarters, of superb appearance, and in their training and movements as near perfection as any troops in the world." The officers, too, he considered excellent, although admittedly both officers and men "are particularly deficient in everything appertaining to the . . . practice of war—outpost duty, patrols, attack and defense of ground and posts. . . ." The cavalry was adequate although deficient in light horse; and the field artillery was "admirable" in every respect. The engineers, of course, were "well instructed" but the corps suffered for lack of adequate transport. Here was the one real weakness of the army in the Crimea, and Burgoyne urged the establishment of a regular transport service and of a commissariat which no longer depended upon local resources to keep the army fed and supplied. [40] He even defended the staff against what he thought were irresponsible charges and never seemed to appreciate the need for a well-trained, permanent staff. In 1855 he testified before the Sandhurst Committee that there was no need for a distinct staff corps as in the French and other Continental armies; again in 1868 he told a similar commission: "I deny that individuals competent for the Staff are not always available from the regimental officers of the Army. Among the mass of the Army there will always be found officers qualified for the Staff." [41]

[39] E. B. Fonblauque, "Reforms in Army Administration," *R.U.S.I. Journal*, XIII (1870), 92–93; "Remarks on Defects in Our Military System with a View to the Future," *United Service Magazine*, 1856, No. 3, 56–57.

[40] "Defects of Organization in the British Army," as reprinted in Burgoyne, *Military Opinions*, pp. 413–33.

[41] "On the State of the British Army," *Blackwood's*, LXXIX (1856), 115–24; "Our Military Colleges and the Staff," *United Service Magazine*, 1856, No. 2, 2; Brevet Major A. R. Godwin-Austen, *The Staff and the Staff College* (London, 1927), pp. 87, 89, 157.

In 1857 Burgoyne published a pamphlet entitled *Army Reform* in which he resisted the prevalent notion that educational tests for officers were highly desirable. As a member of the Royal Commission on Army Promotion before the invasion of the Crimea, he had opposed the method of promotion by seniority alone in the Ordnance Corps, advocating instead the superior claims of merit, but the Crimean War changed his outlook. Promotion by merit, as he saw it operating in the French army, struck Burgoyne as promotion by caprice, and his reactions to some of the younger staff officers, Trochu in particular, seem to have soured him on the idea of proficiency examinations to qualify for promotion.[42] By 1857, when the *Times* had joined in the campaign to improve military education in the British army, Burgoyne threw the weight of his authority on the side of old order.[43]

The burden of Burgoyne's argument was that the officer's duties were "essentially practical" and that there was "little to be acquired in books." Experience, observation, and intelligence were sufficient to produce a good officer: "Of what useful application to a regimental officer will be any minute knowledge of history. . . ." The army needed soldiers, not philosophers, hence Burgoyne would prefer the cricketeer to the scholar. He even defended some aspects of promotion by purchase because it maintained desirable social distinctions and also because he remained unconvinced that "those who have purchased are in the least degree inferior in military character and performances to the others." Purchase may be indefensible in principle, but Burgoyne insisted that promotion by merit was unworkable in practice and that relative qualifications in officers "cannot be absolutely tested." In his judgment, the "great popular movement for an educational test for a commission is uncalled for, delusive and mischievous. . . ." [44]

The army hierarchy was delighted, and the *United Service Magazine* rejoiced to think that "when the great engineer opens fire on a popular cry referring to the army, he usually

---

[42] *United Service Magazine*, 1855, No. 1, 275; Wrottesley, *Burgoyne*, II, 235, 331–32 n.

[43] See "Military Education the Panacea for All Our Shortcomings and Deficiencies," *United Service Magazine*, 1857, No. 2, 1–11; "Our Military Departments and the National Defences," *ibid.*, 1860, No. 1, 161–73.

[44] Burgoyne, *Army Reform* (London, 1857), pp. 10–16, 30. See also Burgoyne, *Military Opinions*, pp. 449–62.

bears down all opposition." The pamphlet would serve as "a serious discouragement to hasty changes," and the opinion of a practical soldier of Burgoyne's prominence was considered "of infinitely greater value in a question affecting military efficiency than that of all the members of all the learned societies put together." [45] Just why Burgoyne, himself a student as well as practitioner, should have reacted so strongly against a proposal to improve the preparation of the British officer is not altogether clear, but probably as a career soldier his first instinct was to close ranks when the pressure for reform was applied by individuals and organizations outside of the army. The example of the French and his own involvement in the Crimean campaign had exposed a nerve which became increasingly tender when the army became the subject of captious criticism in Parliament and in the press. One might almost suspect that Burgoyne's outlook had hardened before his arteries were it not for the fact that in other military matters his view remained flexible and even progressive. Like Mitchell he urged that the soldiers' uniform be designed to meet the needs of utility, comfort, and economy rather than appearance, and that the great shaggy grenadier caps, the kilts and caps of the Highland regiment, and the stiff stock and the shakos be replaced by "something more appropriate in campaigning." [46]

Burgoyne's views on fortifications changed in the decade following the Crimean War. Military opinion in England was divided over the relative merits of earthen parapets and works of masonry. To Sir Harry Jones, the superiority of earthworks "was fully and clearly shown at Sebastopol," but the author of the official history of the artillery operations asserted "that earthworks, however laboriously and skilfully constructed, cannot successfully withstand a heavy and continuous artillery fire." [47] Initially Burgoyne maintained that the capability of earthworks had been overrated, that had Sebastopol been protected with "masonry escarps and counterscarps on the

[45] *United Service Magazine*, 1858. No. 1, 99–100; J. W. F., "Our Schemes of Military Education and Reform," *ibid.*, 340–43.

[46] Wrottesley, *Burgoyne*, II, 275; Burgoyne, "On the Dress of Soldiers," *R.E. Professional Papers*, XII (1863), 121–25.

[47] Sir Harry Jones, *Journal of the Operations Conducted by the Corps of Royal Engineers. Part II. From Feb. 1855 to the Fall of Sebastopol, September 1855* (London, 1859), 577–78; Reilly, *Artillery Operations before Sebastopol*, p. 201.

bastion system, with a few outworks and with such a garrison, it would be as nearly impregnable as any place could well be." Even after the fall of the Russian stronghold he insisted that the notion that earthworks were superior to fortifications of masonry was erroneous. The Russians, he wrote, had utilized earthworks because they had had no choice: for permanent coastal defenses they continued to use "exposed masonry in fortification more than the engineers of any other country." Sebastopol had proven difficult to take because of the great strength of its natural position, the size of its garrison, and the fact that troops and supplies could move freely in and out of the city, and not because of any inherent superiority of earthworks over conventional fortifications.[48]

But the advent of rifled artillery altered the situation, and in February, 1859, Burgoyne issued his "Memorandum on the Probable Effect of the Rifled Cannon on the Attack and Defence of Fortifications." In this document, which guided the thinking of the committee especially appointed to consider the probable influence of the new rifled artillery upon existing fortifications, Burgoyne predicted that the range, penetration, and accuracy of the new siege artillery "will give much more advantage to the attack of fortresses . . . than to their defence." Escarp walls exposed to view

will be readily ruined from greater distance. Although the new shot and shells are not adapted to afford the regular effects of a ricochet fire, works will be subject to all the other evil consequences of enfilade, and that from much greater distances; parapets will be penetrated and ruined with greater facility; the interior of works will be plunged into from heights, at greater ranges than have hietherto been practicable; and where magazines, barracks, or other important military establishments are exposed to such heights, and have hitherto been safe from them, they will now be liable to direct cannonade or bombardment.

The solution?

Guns and ramparts . . . will require, more than ever, to be under bomb-proof cover; parapets must be thickened; openings of embrasures reduced to a minimum . . . and strengthened . . . escarp walls . . . and masonry in general, must be more covered than ever. . . . Bomb-proofs and screens of earth must be freely applied for covering.

[48] Wrottesley, *Burgoyne,* II, 125; Burgoyne, *Military Opinions,* pp. 190–207.

It was too soon, Burgoyne contended, to foresee specific solutions to the problems posed by rifled artillery or to arrive at
any fixed rules, but manifestly the new siege guns would force
a re-examination of the fortification question and the type of
works best adapted to coastal defense.[49]

The problem was brought into sharper focus by the American Civil War, where the increased range and accuracy of the
new rifled siege artillery heralded the end of brick and mortar
fortifications. Almost overnight the coastal defense system
that had been constructed in the 1830's to protect the eastern
seaboard had become obsolete. At Fort Pulaski in April, 1862,
solid brick walls seven feet thick and supported by massive
piers of masonry withstood the Union bombardment for two
days only, and the Union commander reported gleefully to the
War Department: "The result of this bombardment must
cause a change in the construction of fortifications as radical
as that foreshadowed in naval architecture by the conflict
between the Monitor and Merrimac. No works of stone or
brick can resist the impact of rifled artillery of heavy calibre."
On the other hand, earthen works like Fort Fisher and Battery
Wagner had provided adequate shelter from what were
probably up to that time the heaviest bombardments on
record.[50]

Burgoyne paid close attention to what was happening in
America. He was anxious to discover what changes in the
construction of field or siege works had been found necessary
and whether the inherent advantages of forts over ships had
been upset by the introduction of steam and rifled artillery.
Were the experiments being conducted at Shoeburyness
confirmed by the experiences of the Civil War armies? Often
the answers were inconclusive because the facts were not
known, as in the case of the bombardment and ultimate fall
of Fort Fisher, but enough information was received to reinforce Burgoyne in his conviction that the capabilities of steam
men-of-war against shore batteries had been grossly exaggerated, even when the ships were iron-plated. In 1860 he had
disagreed with the findings of the Royal Commission to
consider the defenses of the United Kingdom over this point,

[49] *Ibid.*, pp. 395, 396, 402; Burgoyne, "Memorandum on the Increased
Power of Breaching To Be Obtained by the Use of Rifled Ordnance,"
R.E. Professional Papers, N.S. (1861), 1–7.

[50] An adequate sketch of the most important sieges of the Civil War
is found in Clarke, *Fortification*, pp. 40–51.

and the *Report* of the British military observers in America seemed to demonstrate beyond any reasonable doubt that "ships cannot contend with forts when the conditions are anything like equal." After the Civil War he could still maintain that the fire of ironclads on shore batteries

may have a powerful effect upon one of exposed masonry, insulated and compact, when opposed for a considerable time to dispersed vessels with powerful guns; but where the shore batteries can be more or less separated in distance and height, with no exposure but of earthen parapets . . . the scattered shot directed on them in action will be thoroughly ineffective.[51]

One other aspect of Burgoyne's view of fortifications should be noted. While the Civil War did not convince him that permanent fortifications of masonry were necessarily a thing of the past, as some of the American military and naval leaders had boasted (the evidence reported by the military mission to the Union Army in 1864 indicated that thicker walls and new iron embrasures would make the partially built defenses of New York Harbor "very formidable" when completed[52]), it clearly pointed to the growing importance of earthworks. In 1860 Burgoyne's proposed scheme for the defense of London had rested on the establishment of a ring of twelve forts, half of which were to be earthen; two years later he had stated with regard to the defenses of Canada that while permanent works were desirable, they were too expensive and that intrenched positions could be "made very formidable"; finally, in 1870 he went so far as to claim that earthworks would provide the best fortifications, all other structures being too costly and requiring too much time to build. By this time he had become convinced that the increased power of rifled arms would lead to greater dispersion and use of cover in infantry tactics than before, and that intrenching tools should become standard issue.[53]

[51] Burgoyne, "Capture of Fort Fisher," Mss dated February 8, 1865, from the Palmerston Papers, Broadlands, Romsey, Hampshire. The writer is indebted to Professor Kenneth Bourne for calling attention to, and providing a copy of, this document. Burgoyne's criticisms of the *Report of the Royal Commission to Consider the Defences of the United Kingdom* (1860) is found in his memorandum to Mr. Sidney Herbert, January 27, 1860 (War Office Library, Whitehall). Burgoyne's later views are found in Wrottesley, *Burgoyne*, II, 421–22, and should be compared with those expressed earlier in *Military Opinions*, pp. 356–69, and in the *R.E. Professional Papers*, I (1851), 1–11; VI (1857), 115–18.

[52] Burgoyne, "On the Siege and Capture of Borgoforte, on the Po, June, 1886," *ibid.*, XVI (1868), 1–4; Luvaas, *Military Legacy*, pp. 40–41.

[53] "London the Stronghold of England," *Cornhill Magazine*, I (1860),

But fortifications to Burgoyne formed but one element—and not the most important at that—in the defensive posture of England. The first line of defense obviously was the fleet. Coastal fortifications were necessary to protect the vital harbors and dockyards. London, as the logical objective of any invading army, must be made impregnable. Significantly, Burgoyne continued to look upon fortifications as "the very complement of our volunteer movement," by housing untried troops and freeing the regular army to maneuver in the field.[54] Writing after the startling Prussian victory over Austria in 1866, Burgoyne relied still less upon fortifications to defend Britain. While still opposed to the levy en masse, he favored some adaptation of the Prussian system whereby the men would serve for a shorter period of service in the regular army and then pass into the organized reserves. Volunteers, he felt, could not possibly cope with the regular troops of Prussia or France, but they might be useful as garrisons and in the protection of ports. The main reserve would have to be the militia, which must be improved as rapidly as possible and organized on a county basis. Burgoyne died before the details of the Cardwell Reforms had been worked out, but already his thoughts were moving in the same direction. The basic difficulty as he saw it was reconciling short service in Britain with service in the colonies, a formidable obstacle to Cardwell and his band of reformers.[55]

Burgoyne retired from the army with the rank of field marshal. Three years later, broken in health and bereaved by the tragic death of his only son, he died at the age of ninety. For as long as he retained his mental and physical powers he continued to manifest interest in military matters. He attended reviews, wrote letters to the press, and followed the campaigns of the Franco-Prussian War as eagerly as any young officer. He anxiously awaited reports from the English observers and tried to discover the secrets of the success of the Prussian army, "the strongest and best organized" in the

---

641–51; "Memorandum . . . on the Defence of Canada," *Report of the Commissioners to Consider the Defences of Canada* (War Office, 1862), Appendix No. 2; "On Hasty Intrenchments in the Field," *R.E. Professional Papers*, XVIII (1870), 93–96.

[54] Burgoyne, "London the Stronghold of England," 641–43; "Memorandum on the Proposition for Covering Efficiently Our Principal Naval Arsenals, etc., by Defensive Works," March 5, 1860 (War Office Library).

[55] Burgoyne, *Our Defensive Forces* (2d ed.; London, 1869) *passim*.

world. Despite his admiration for the Prussians, however, Burgoyne felt that it would be a mistake to imitate them in every detail. He also continued to believe that it would be a mistake to abolish purchase in favor of seniority or selection, and probably the last piece he wrote was a letter to the *Times* opposing the proposed Army bill.[56] Thus Burgoyne lived just long enough to behold the dawn of a new era in warfare and the final hours of the British army as he knew it. He understood most of the technical and tactical changes that had occurred, but he was too much a part of the old army—and too closely associated with the Crimean War— to accept many of the organizational changes on the horizon.

In a sense Burgoyne's military opinions were never more than a series of oracular responses to specific situations. His written observations from the Peninsular War reflect some pressing problem or recent experience, but in each case they represent a practical answer to the questions of the day. When the revolutions of 1848 in Europe threatened to infect England, Burgoyne produced his thoughts on the "Defence of Large Towns against Popular Insurrections";[57] the invasion panic in 1859 induced him to write on the best way to defend London, and the Prussian victory over Austria provoked his reassessment of the defensive forces of England. As a pragmatist he was wedded to no special theory, which explains why his ideas changed as drastically as the pace in transportation and industry. In 1855 he had decried the notion that earthworks were largely responsible for the prolonged defense of Sebastopol; five years later he regarded the ability of the Russians to improvise defenses as one of the most useful lessons of the war.[58] But if Burgoyne's attitude changed, so had the basic conditions of warfare—a fact not always recognized by his critics—and as a rule the old soldier managed to keep pace with events.

Burgoyne occasionally was accused of enjoying "a higher reputation at Pall Mall than at Chatham."[59] In part this was a reaction to claims made about his services in the official account of the siege of Sebastopol, but it also testifies to the breadth of his vision. Although officially concerned primarily

[56] Wrottesley, *Burgoyne*, II, 441–44, 450–54.

[57] Burgoyne, "On the Attack and Defence of Open Towns, and Street Fighting," *Aide Memoire to the Military Sciences*, III, 584–91.

[58] Burgoyne, "London the Stronghold of England," p. 645.

[59] Editorial, *United Service Magazine*, 1860, No. 3, 102.

with fortifications, his interests included tactics, strategy, military organization and administration, and new weapons and equipment. Except for his views on promotion and military education Burgoyne's outlook was undeniably progressive, and it is perhaps significant to note that of those officers who contributed articles to the service journals in the 1860's, the most enlightened by far appear also to have been from the Corps of Royal Engineers: Captain H. W. Tyler, Captain T. Fraser, Colonel Charles Cornwallis Chesney, Captain H. Schaw, and Colonel Gerald Graham all understood the drift of modern warfare and especially the advantages increased firepower had given to the defense.[60]

Burgoyne's pen was nearly as mighty as his sword and adds appreciably to his military stature. No soldier in Europe could boast of such versatile experience as a military engineer; few understood better the fundamental changes forced upon armies by iron and steam. In intellectual history it is always difficult to document the path of ideas, and in the case of Burgoyne it is almost impossible: one can never be sure with Burgoyne whether it is the signature of the inspector general of fortifications, the prestige of an old and experienced warrior, or the wisdom of the ideas expressed that commands assent. Of this much we can be sure: whatever the extent of his influence as a writer, because he wrote memoranda rather than lengthy treatises and because his main concern always was with some imminent rather than an abstract problem, his influence was immediate rather than lasting and was limited to specific issues. But his influence at times was powerful. Often his memoranda served as the starting point for the deliberations of especially appointed committees;[61] usually

---

[60] See especially Tyler, "Railways Strategically Considered," *R.U.S.I. Journal*, VIII (1864), 321–43; Chesney, "Sherman's Campaign in Georgia," *ibid.*, IX (1866), 204–20; Schaw, "The Amount of Advantage Which the New Arms of Precision Give to the Defence over the Attack," *ibid.*, XIV (1871), 377–95; and Graham, "Shelter Trenches, or Temporary Cover for Troops in Position," *ibid.*, 448–78.

[61] Burgoyne's "Memorandum on the Defences for the Eastern Entrance of Spithead," February, 1861, is a case in point. It served as the starting point for the investigations of the Committee on Floating Obstructions and Submarine Explosive Machines (*Report on Active Obstructions for the Defence of Harbors and Channels, etc., and on the Employment of Torpedoes for Purposes of Attack* . . . [War Office, 1868], Confidential Papers 0357, p. 16). Burgoyne's influence on Palmerston in 1846, and his impact upon the committee concerned with the impact of rifled artillery have already been noted. See above, pp. 74, 90.

his short treatises on subjects connected with coast batteries
and the attack of fortresses were regarded as authoritative by
other military engineers, and occasionally his more general
papers on defense considerations were referred to by the
Admiralty, the Colonial Office, the India Board, and the
Foreign Office. Regardless of the nature of his inquiry,
Burgoyne remained throughout his remarkable career un-
impeded by prevailing opinions and traditions.

No system of fortification is associated with his name, and
his military opinions were not of enduring value, but this
should not detract from the imprint Burgoyne made on the
British army during the last thirty years of his life. If he
attacked local problems he did so from a broad base of
experience and study, and he lived long enough to comprehend the military significance of the Civil War and the
Prussian victories in 1866 and 1870. Neither a historian nor a
theorist—and certainly in no sense a prophet—Burgoyne
nonetheless deserves to be remembered for his commentary
upon contemporary military developments. In a day of rapid,
uncertain, and far-reaching changes, his military opinions
were of incalculable assistance to those who similarly were
anxious to bridge the gap between the old army and the new, a
gap that for a time threatened to grow wider with each invention at home and campaign abroad.

II THE ARMY IN TRANSITION 1856–73

THE Crimean War (1854–56) shattered complacency and jolted the public and army alike into a mood for
reform. Although spared the humiliation of military defeat,
the nation had to live with many uncomfortable facts: the
intense suffering in the trenches before Sebastopol, defective
hospital arrangements, lack of supplies, inefficient organization and mismanagement in the War Department. The new
Victoria Cross identified many of the heroes of the late war,
but to the wags, a C.B. now denoted "Crimean Blunderer."

Right on the heels of this rude shock came the Indian
Mutiny (1857), which added still another problem by demonstrating the inefficiency of the administration of India and the
dangers of relying too heavily on native mercenaries. The
renewed threat of a French invasion in 1859 led to a rapid
expansion of the volunteers and a significant increase in
expenditures to improve coast defenses.

Events abroad likewise excited public interest in military
affairs and kept alive the issues ignited in the Crimea and
India. The French campaign in Italy (1859) "afforded no new
lessons of importance," but the American Civil War (1861–
65) provided a unique testing ground for new weapons and
materiel and offered a preview of war in the industrial age.
This war gave birth to the "long era of costly trials of guns
versus armour plates." [1] The German wars for unification had

[1] Lieutenant General W. H. Goodenough and Lieutenant Colonel J. C.
Dalton, *The Army Book for the British Empire* . . . (London, 1893),
pp. 43–44.

a still more startling effect. The campaign in Denmark (1864) found England protesting, but too weak to intervene. The Seven Weeks' War with Austria (1866) established the superiority of the breech-loader and the importance of mobilization; the victory over France (1870–71) demonstrated the superiority of the Prussian military system in organization, training, tactics, and command. Henceforth German military literature set the pace, German uniforms the style, and the German system of short service the example to be imitated by every major power on the Continent.

Other developments, less spectacular, added to this ferment of discussion. England was experiencing a second round of political and social reforms in the 1860's, and the "general demand for a greater efficiency in the public services" affected the army as well as Parliament and the civil service. The relationship between Britain and the colonies also was changing. The West Indies, following the end of slavery, lost much of their importance; colonies began to assume more responsibility for their own defense; and the completion of the Suez Canal in 1869, coupled with the advent of the steamship, greatly reduced the dimensions of imperial defense.

Consequently, the years following the Crimean War were "unusually full of anxious changes." The volunteer movement in 1859, the Militia Act of 1860, and the Reserve Force Act of 1867 strengthened home defense and helped to establish an army of reserve. The Enfield rifle replaced the Minié in 1856; the Snider, a breech-loader, was adopted in 1866, and the Martini-Henry—"of smaller Bore, far greater range, lower trajectory and superior accuracy" [2]—was introduced on a limited scale in 1869. Rifled artillery, first used by the British in the Arrow War with China (1860), grew increasingly important. These new weapons led to the establishment of schools of musketry at Hythe and Fleetwood and the school of gunnery at Shoeburyness. Camps of instruction were organized at Aldershot, Shorncliffe, Colchester, and the Curragh, and training methods were further improved in 1871 with the institution of annual army maneuvers. The Staff College, founded in 1858, and the *Journal of the Royal United Service Institution*, which had been established the previous year, both stimulated interest in the study of war.

[2] The Hon. J. W. Fortescue, *A History of the British Army* (London, 1930), XIII, 549.

Most important of all were the reforms bearing the name of Edward Cardwell, Gladstone's secretary of war from 1868 to 1874. This gifted and courageous administrator reorganized the War Office in 1870, thus ending the system of dual control by bringing the administration of the army clearly under the thumb of the secretary of state. In 1870 Cardwell also introduced the short-service system—six years with the colors and six with the reserve—to create an effective reserve that had been lacking in the Crimean War and the Indian Mutiny. The next year he abolished the purchase system, and in 1872 he linked together the regular regiments in pairs, which he then assigned, along with battalions of militia and volunteers, to individual brigade districts. The district provided the recruiting area, and the brigade depot became a training center for both the reserve forces and the home regiment, which in turn served as a funnel through which recruits were fed to the linked regiment overseas. This went far to provide a better balance between service at home and abroad; it also greatly facilitated mobilization.

With greater awareness of the need to reshape military thought as well as organization during this period of transition from the old British army to the new, a number of soldiers became prominent for their writings. The subject of the next chapter, MacDougall, was one of these: his views on tactics and organization illuminate the issues even though his influence upon the Staff College and the Cardwell Reforms remains hidden. The subject of chapter v, Hamley, needs no introduction; he does need, however, to be viewed in perspective. Although the careers of both men stretched nearly to the end of the century, their varying contributions belong for the most part to the years when the British army was being refashioned into an instrument designed to meet the new requirements of war and empire.

4

THE NEW SCHOOL

Major General Sir Patrick MacDougal

IN 1844 Captain Patrick Leonard MacDougall arrived in Toronto to join his new regiment, the Royal Canadian Rifles. Quite likely he felt an attachment to the colony where his father, Sir Duncan MacDougall, had at one time commanded the 79th Cameron Highlanders, but the promising young Scots officer could not have anticipated the extent of his future involvement in Canadian affairs, nor could he possibly have foreseen how twenty years' cumulative service in North America would shape his military thinking.

MacDougall belonged to the first form in what Lord Wolseley described as "a new army school." Growing out of the misfortunes of the Crimean War, the new school embraced officers of various opinions and backgrounds who were united only in the recognition that "the study of their profession, both as a science and an art, was . . . all important." [1] They never formulated a common doctrine of war and often they disagreed among themselves over questions of tactics and organization, but together they were responsible for an intellectual awakening in the British army that occurred in the 1860's and after. They wrote about current military events and ancient campaigns; they lectured before the Royal United Service Institution and the several military colleges; they carried their arguments to the reading public in the great literary and professional journals of the day. Many of them were associated with Wolseley during his long and versatile career;

[1] Wolseley, *The Story of a Soldier's Life* (Westminster, 1903), II, 230–31.

others, like MacDougall, were administrators rather than men
of action and evidently preferred to work silently in the shadows. Much of what they wrote has not survived the subsequent transformation of war, but at least their writings enabled others to comprehend the significance of the changes
that were taking place at the time. Contemporaries recognized
MacDougall as one of the most influential of the new school
but history, unfortunately, has somehow allowed him to slip
quietly out of sight.

We know very little about MacDougall's personal life. He
was born August 10, 1819, at Boulogne-sur-Mer, France, and
received much of his education at the Military Academy, Edinburgh, and at the Royal Military College at Sandhurst. Entering the army in 1836, he served as a subaltern with the Ceylon
Rifle Regiment, the 79th Cameron Highlanders, and the 36th
Infantry of the line prior to being sent to Canada. He remained with his regiment in Canada for ten years before returning to England in 1854 as superintendent of studies at
Sandhurst. The following year he accompanied the army to
the Crimea, where he participated in the expedition to Kertsh
and later attended Lord Raglan in the trenches during the unsuccessful British assault on the Redan. After the war he resumed his duties at Sandhurst, and for the rest of his active
career his sword was used only for ceremonial occasions.[2]

MacDougall's concern for the future of Canada had already
prompted him in 1848 to write on the railroad as a stimulus
to colonization.[3] After the Crimean War he turned his attention to the deficiencies in the army, particularly the need to
sharpen the education of the British officer. MacDougall was
not yet a theorist, but he hoped to stimulate interest in the
subject by presenting in one book the basic theories expounded in the more unwieldy volumes of Frederick, Napoleon, Jomini, the Archduke Charles, "and from the only classical military history" in the English language, Napier's *Peninsular War.*[4] *The Theory of War*, which appeared in 1856,

[2] Robert Hamilton Vetch, "MacDougall," *D.N.B.: Supplement* (Oxford, 1921–22), pp. 993–94; *Canadian Illustrated News*, October 26,
1878.
[3] MacDougall, *Emigration: Its advantages to Great Britain and Her
colonies together with a Detailed Plan for the Formation of the Proposed Railway between Halifax and Quebec, by means of Colonization*
(n.p., 1848). Unfortunately no copy of this pamphlet could be located.
[4] MacDougall, *The Theory of War Illustrated by Numerous Examples
from Military History* (3d ed.; London, 1862), pp. viii–ix.

was an immediate success: within two years a second edition was necessary, a third was published in 1862, and the book later was translated into French and German. This was not the only military text in the English language, but the others had been neglected ("not from wanting merit," according to a contemporary, "but because our officers won't read") and none previously had treated the subjects of tactics and strategy as a whole.[5] If MacDougall advanced no original theories of his own in his first important book, at least he managed to digest the maxims of the foremost writers on war and serve these in a form digestible to others.

Like Napier, MacDougall relied absolutely on the accepted principles of strategy which, applied by Frederick and Napoleon and expounded by Jomini, he defined as follows:

1) To place masses of your army in contact with fractions of your enemy.

2) To operate as much as possible on the communications of your enemy without exposing your own.

3) To operate always on interior lines.

In MacDougall's opinion these principles, which he illustrated by describing Frederick's campaign of 1756 and Napoleon's campaign against Wurmser forty years later, supplied "an infallible test by which to judge of every military plan; for no combination can be well conceived, no maxim founded in truth, which is at variance with them." [6] Throughout the book he cited numerous other campaigns to show the successful application of maxims governing lines of communications and supply, marches, the choice of tactical positions, and the conduct of battles; in none of these major areas did he disagree with the established authorities.

Nor, in fact, did MacDougall disagree with the lessons Burgoyne had drawn from the Crimean War. Both recognized that the French staff organization had provided much greater unity throughout the army; both appreciated the fact that the Minié rifle had changed tactics; both initially would not concede that the earthworks protecting Sebastopol had been more formidable than conventional fortifications of masonry; and both remained skeptical of the practical value of educational tests for officers. MacDougall felt perhaps more strongly than Burgoyne that the responsibility for the blunders in the

[5] *United Service Magazine,* 1857, No. 1, 160; *R.U.S.I. Journal,* XVII (1873), 774.
[6] MacDougall, *Theory of War,* pp. 51–52.

Crimea lay "with our multiplication of independent departments," whereas Burgoyne was inclined to place the greater share of the blame on a deficient means of transport.[7]

In 1856 MacDougall was also more concerned than Burgoyne over the future of infantry tactics. He could not yet anticipate the evolutionary developments that would come within the next decade, but he felt sure that the fire of infantry armed with the improved rifle will "form the most important element in the decision of a battle." One hundred good marksmen, he contended, could now silence a battery at 800 yards distance, which means that

artillery will lose its preponderance, and infantry will become the arm whose superiority will be the most decisive on the issue of an engagement. For artillery to maintain its efficiency against such adversaries, the gunners must be covered by a mantelet, and this would afford a larger aim to the enemy's guns.

MacDougall's views on cavalry more nearly resemble those of Mitchell than Burgoyne, for he believed that "no formation of infantry can resist the shock of horses ridden . . . in earnest." Despite the introduction of the Minié rifle, MacDougall at this time still was an advocate of traditional cavalry in contrast to Burgoyne, who argued that more light cavalry was needed to perform the increasingly important role of reconnaissance and convoy duties, even at the expense of the mounted charge.[8]

Their views on fortifications were strikingly similar. Both dismissed as absurd the claim that the siege of Sebastopol had established the superiority of a new system of fortification devised by a Mr. Fergusson. Burgoyne wrote that it was the dispersion of the Russian guns that had given them their power, not the concentration provided by Fergusson's system. MacDougall pointed out that Fergusson's system had been misunderstood and that the only similarity between it and the fortifications of Sebastopol was the presence of earthworks. He personally inspected the Russian defenses after the siege and concluded:

[7] *Ibid.*, p. 37; Lieutenant Colonel the Hon. George Wrottesley, *Life and Correspondence of Field Marshal Sir John Burgoyne, Bart.* (London, 1873), II, 193.

[8] MacDougall, *Theory of War*, pp. 41–43, 238, 239; Wrottesley (ed.), *The Military Opinions of General Sir John Fox Burgoyne* (London, 1859), pp. 434–37.

The Russian earthworks were so knocked about by our fire that our soldiers could mount them without the aid of scaling ladders in every direction; if those works had been provided with deep ditches and masonry *revêtements,* although we now know that our vertical fire must have reduced the place, it never would have been taken by assault.[9]

On the question of military education, MacDougall emphasized formal instruction more than Burgoyne, although he too insisted that "it is of little importance to the state that the man who leads his regiment bravely should be a good classical scholar or general historian." What was essential, in his view, was that the officer "should be versed in military history, that he should be able to direct his men in strengthening a post by field-works, that he should have a good eye for ground, and that he should be able to speak other languages than his own." He recommended that all officers be required to attend a central military school for at least six or eight months before appointment to a regiment, and if specialized education were necessary for certain positions then he urged the establishment of a separate branch of the staff composed of scientific men, as in the French army. Even the United States had undertaken to give all officers a scientific education; only in England did the professional education of officers remain entirely voluntary.[10]

MacDougall pursued his ideas on military education in a pamphlet which he wrote in 1857 entitled *The Senior Department of the Royal Military College,* which probably led to his selection as first commandant of the Staff College when it was founded later that same year. He remained four years at the Staff College, where his most important achievement seems to have been the successful establishment of a course of instruction along the lines laid down by the newly created Council of Military Education.[11] Here he also found time to lecture on the campaigns of the great captains and even to write a book on the campaigns of Hannibal. Seeking always to illustrate the principles of war through an attractive presentation of some war or campaign from military history, MacDougall evaluated the generalship of Hannibal and his contemporaries in the

[9] Wrottesley, *Burgoyne,* II, 152; MacDougall, *Theory of War,* p. 114.
[10] *Ibid.,* pp. 29–33.
[11] Vetch, "MacDougall," p. 993; Major A. R. Godwin-Austen, *The Staff and the Staff College* (London, 1927), pp. 91–110, 127.

light of their adherence to the basic maxims considered in his *Theory of War*. Thus the march of a Roman general provided a "perfect example of the advantage of interior lines of operation" so popular with Jomini and Napier. MacDougall followed Napier's practice of offering detailed observations on the tactics and strategy of each campaign and, like the historian of the Peninsular War, he maintained that only a man of genius could safely depart from the prescribed rules of war. A respectable work of history, *The Campaigns of Hannibal* also shows MacDougall's flexibility on the subject of tactics: only two years previously he had expressed unbounded confidence in the traditional cavalry charge; now he recognized that "the relative strength of infantry has increased in constant proportion to the improvements of firearms"; before long he would maintain that the day of shock tactics for cavalry had passed altogether.[12]

MacDougall relinquished his post at the Staff College in September, 1861. Two months later he found himself suddenly involved once again in Canadian affairs when the crisis precipitated by the forcible seizure of Confederate representatives from the British ship "Trent" by a Union naval captain threatened war between Great Britain and the United States. Confronted with the urgent need to improvise a strategic plan in the event diplomacy failed, the War Office turned for advice to MacDougall and one or two others who were personally familiar with the type of forces available for the defense of Canada.

MacDougall submitted his thoughts "On the Prospect of War with the United States" early in December, 1861. The key to the successful defense of Canada belonged, he wrote, to whichever nation controlled the Great Lakes. Five years earlier he had called the attention of the secretary of state for war "to the paramount importance of England being supreme on the lakes," and now he asserted that if Britain were to gain

---

[12] MacDougall, "On Napoleon's Campaign in Italy in 1796," *R.U.S.I. Journal*, III (1859), 195–207; "The Military Character of the Great Duke of Marlborough," *ibid.*, III, 257–70; *The Campaigns of Hannibal Arranged and Critically Considered Expressly for the Use of Students of Military History* (London, 1858), pp. 99, 177, 195. G. P. Baker, a recent biographer of Hannibal, calls MacDougall's commentary upon Zama "shrewd and suggestive," adding that it convinced him "that in the usual accounts of the battle some important factors had been left out" (G. P. Baker to Captain B. H. Liddell Hart, March 14, 1930 [Liddell Hart Papers, States House, Medmenham, Marlow, Bucks]).

control of the Great Lakes "two thirds of the troops . . . required for the defence of Western Canada could be spared to reinforce the line of the St. Lawrence." Estimating the number of troops available in the event of war at 75,000 volunteers and 8,000 regulars, MacDougall evidently believed that Canada could be defended with the aid of intrenched positions at strategic locations and utilizing the railroad and telegraph to concentrate at threatened points. He assumed naturally that the Royal Navy would provide indirect aid by destroying the Union fleet and menacing the major cities along the eastern coast. He was even hopeful that the British would be able to invade Maine, which would enable them to reinforce Canada more rapidly and might even divert a significant portion of any army the Americans could assemble for the invasion of Canada. If the Americans were to advance on Montreal through Vermont, he argued, then a British army in Maine would pose a serious threat to their right flank. Once again, MacDougall's proposals do not differ appreciably from those suggested a few days later by Sir John Fox Burgoyne, who likewise advocated an invasion of Maine if possible. Both professed to believe that given "sufficient troops, a system of fortifications and command of the lakes," the British could defend Canada successfully.[13]

As a soldier MacDougall did not feel competent to suggest just how command of the Great Lakes might be secured: he knew only that this was fundamental to the successful defense of Canada. But his earlier experience in Canada did inspire a definite and far-sighted proposal for increasing the efficiency of the volunteer militia. Instead of keeping British regulars intact and treating the militia as a separate force—a mistake that the expanding Union army already had committed—MacDougall suggested that a regiment of volunteer militia should be attached to every regiment of regulars. If this were done, he predicted, "in a very few weeks" the volunteers "would not be much inferior to regulars in ma-

[13] MacDougall, "On the Prospect of War with the United States," in *Sir George Cornewall Lewis Papers* (Hampton Court Papers) 2943, National Library of Wales, Aberystwyth. The present writer is indebted to Professor Kenneth Bourne for calling attention to the schemes for the defense of Canada by MacDougall and Sir John Fox Burgoyne, and for his generosity in providing transcripts from the Lewis Papers. For a penetrating analysis of the military problems involved, see Bourne, "British Preparations for War with the North, 1861–1862," *English Historical Review,* LXXVI (1961), 600–32.

noeuvring." Burgoyne, it will be recalled, had made a similar proposal for amalgamation of reserves and regulars in his earlier memoranda on the defense of England.[14]

MacDougall's activities during the next three years are elusive. We know that he visited Canada in 1862, but in what capacity the sketch in the *Dictionary of National Biography* does not make clear. During the leisure hours on board ship while crossing the Atlantic he expanded his views on the defense of Canada in a pamphlet entitled *Forts versus Ships: Also Defence of the Canadian Lakes and Its Influence on the General Defence of Canada.* Because he was in Boston when he sent the manuscript to the printers, we may surmise that he learned something at first-hand about the Civil War: at any rate he had seen enough to be convinced that the Union army, "when time shall have conferred on it consistence and discipline, will be one of the most formidable forces the world has ever seen." [15]

The mystery deepens when we read that during this period MacDougall wrote the two-volume biography of his father-in-law, Napier, and that the work was actually published over the signature of H. A. Bruce, who had married another of Napier's daughters. Bruce explained that his editorial services were required because the author had written the book while abroad, "far from libraries and books of reference," but he declined to explain the "private reasons" that had induced MacDougall to remain in the background. Rereading the volumes in the twilight of his own career, Lord Wolseley suggests one possible reason why MacDougall had preferred to remain anonymous: MacDougall's name, he confided to Lady Wolseley, "was not a good one when the book was written.[16] Whether this means that MacDougall was momentarily under a cloud, which is unlikely in view of the fact that he stood high in the estimation of the Duke of Cambridge, the commander in chief, or that his name was not well-enough known, which is also improbable because of his prior publications, we have no way of knowing. Possibly the greater wealth

[14] MacDougall, "On the Prospect of War with the United States," Lewis Papers 2943.

[15] By an Officer (MacDougall), *Forts versus Ships: Also Defence of the Canadian Lakes and Its Influence on the General Defence of Canada* (London, 1862), p. 25.

[16] Wolseley to Lady Wolseley, April 17, 1894 (Field Marshal Sir Garnet Wolseley Papers, Royal United Service Institution, Whitehall).

and the political reputation of his brother-in-law, later Lord Aberdare, provides an answer.[17]

While in Canada MacDougall had also availed himself of the opportunity to study the Civil War campaigns which, according to Wolseley, were followed by British soldiers there with "breathless interest and excitement." [18] Today the conflict emerges as the first of the modern wars; the first great conflict waged by modern democratic states with the products of the industrial revolution; the first in which steam and iron were used on a large scale by both sides to transport and supply huge armies over vast areas. It also represents a prophetic departure in tactics, for the traditional formations used in Europe were not adaptable to requirements in America, where relatively untrained troops, many of them armed with rifles of unprecedented range and accuracy, grappled with each other over rough and often thickly wooded terrain. European soldiers at first did not know what to make of this strange conflict, and it was not until 1863 and later that the professional soldier could appreciate the clumsy efforts of the improvised armies and comprehend the real meaning of the transformation in tactics.

When MacDougall completed *Modern Warfare as Influenced by Modern Artillery* in 1863, he became the first European soldier to incorporate lessons from the Civil War into a military text. Although continuing to lean heavily on Napier's classic *History,* he tried also to analyze the experience of the American armies even though "the conclusions of one day" were "often overthrown by the events of the next." This book marks a significant turning point in MacDougall's literary career. No longer was he content merely to compile maxims from other military writers and to provide useful illustrations from history.

From the confusing and often contradictory accounts of Civil War battles, one hard fact could be deduced: modern firepower had forced a momentous change in tactics. The

---

[17] This is suggested by D. W. King, Librarian, War Office.

[18] Wolseley, "An English View of the Civil War," *North American Review,* CLXIX (1889), 725. For the reactions of English observers and military students of the Civil War, see also R. A. Preston, "Military Lessons of the American Civil War: The Influence of Observers from the British Army in Canada on Training the British Army," *Army Quarterly,* LXV (1953), 229–37; and Luvaas, *The Military Legacy of the Civil War: The European Inheritance* (Chicago, 1959), pp. 14–51, 110–19.

breech-loader, quick and simple to load, had doubled the firepower of infantry, and MacDougall ridiculed the arguments of those (including the Confederate General Robert E. Lee) who objected to this new weapon on the ground that it would cause soldiers to consume ammunition "in a reckless and aimless manner under the excitement of battle." Discipline could prevent this, he argued: the only legitimate question was whether firing should be "more in volleys by word of command and less by independent files." [19]

MacDougall predicted that improved firearms and the new rifled artillery would give an enormous advantage to the defense. Infantry in the future must advance in extended order and move swiftly through the fire zone in order to offer the smallest target possible; cavalry would find its traditional role in battle diminishing, "for its only power lies in the offensive" and there would be little opportunity for cavalry to charge infantry armed with modern weapons. MacDougall did not share the enthusiasm of his friend Colonel G. T. Denison, a Canadian militia officer, for mounted infantry, but at the same time he realized that increased firepower would no longer permit the massed assaults of Seydlitz and Murat in which dense formations of horsemen charged knee to knee into evaporating infantry formations.[20] Pointing to the great battles of the Civil War, MacDougall observed "that no open positions have yet been successfully attacked; the assailants have always been repulsed, though in several cases very superior in numbers."

So great, in fact, was the advantage given to the defense by modern artillery that MacDougall predicted even offensive

[19] MacDougall, *Modern Warfare as Influenced by Modern Artillery* (London, 1864), pp. 428–30. Lee's aversion to the breech-loader is mentioned in Lieutenant Colonel G. F. R. Henderson, *The Campaign of Fredericksburg, Nov.–Dec., 1862: A Tactical Study for Officers* (3d ed., Aldershot, n.d.), p. 131. Henderson notes that Lee was "speaking of troops whose standard of discipline was not a high one. . . ." In 1861 Sir George Cornewall Lewis, the secretary for war, had informed the House of Commons that "the military authorities appeared to be adverse to the adoption of a breech-loading rifle as there was an impression that it led to too hasty and lavish an expenditure of ammunition" (quoted in Brian Bond, "The Late-Victorian Army," *History Today*, XI [1961], 623).
[20] MacDougall, *Modern Warfare*, pp. 135–36, 414; Colonel G. T. Denison, *Modern Cavalry: Its Organization, Armament, and Employment in War* (London, 1868), pp. 30–31, 73–75.

warfare "must in future consist in taking up such positions as shall oblige the enemy to attack, on account of the deadly fire to which troops advancing to the attack of a position over open ground are now exposed." The battle of the future would be decided "principally by artillery"; there would be increasingly less combat at close range. (Mitchell would not have been surprised to learn "that the present fire-arms have no effect in deciding the issue of an engagement more quickly than of old.") And if this were so, MacDougall reasoned, then the difference between regulars and volunteers would diminish accordingly. When the outcome of battles had depended upon discipline and the speed with which soldiers could reload and move from one formation to another, volunteers obviously were inferior to trained infantry of the line. But in a strong defensive position, especially when armed with breech-loaders and supported by modern artillery, they must be nearly as effective as regular troops. Burgoyne had proposed using the volunteers in this way in the event England were invaded, but the Civil War convinced MacDougall that in the future all troops must learn to utilize field intrenchments. Napier had anticipated using the volunteers to good advantage as light infantry after the Minié rifle had proved itself in the Crimean War; now here is MacDougall asserting that "all infantry must be in future what has hitherto been distinguished by the name of light infantry" and he proposed the appointment of a committee to consider the best way to accomplish this.[21]

The impact of the new rifled artillery upon siege warfare represented a more striking departure still from familiar practices. MacDougall conceded

that at an enormous cost a fortress may be so protected that to break it will be impossible. On the other hand, any town may with certainty be destroyed by shells from a great distance, and this fact destroys the utility of many of the strongest European fortresses. No town will ever again be surrounded by a fortified enceinte; and the important places will be protected by a series of detached forts, mounting the heaviest ordnance, and of area so contracted as to present a small mark for shells . . . in short, entrenched camps will take the place of regular fortresses. It

[21] MacDougall, *Modern Warfare*, pp. 11, 13–17, 414–31 *passim*. See above, pp. 33–34, 79.

seems not improbable that in future warfare the blockade will supersede the regular siege, and that history will be spared the recital of the appalling slaughter of a Badajos or San Sebastian.

Union artillery had bombarded Charleston from a distance of 8,500 yards and Vicksburg had been forced to capitulate from want of provisions: to MacDougall these developments indicated the trend of the future.[22]

No European soldier in 1863 perceived more clearly than MacDougall the changing nature of warfare, and none was more obviously influenced by the American Civil War. As late as 1856 he had asserted that "the modern improvement in small arms renders it probable that the fire of the infantry will in future form the most important element in the decision of a battle"; in 1863 he prophesied that artillery would be the determining factor. In *The Theory of War* he had stated that the cavalry charge was still practicable; in *Modern Warfare as Influenced by Modern Artillery* he insisted that firepower had nearly destroyed cavalry as an offensive arm in battle. A year after the fall of Sebastopol he had commented on the inability of the Russian earthworks to withstand British and French artillery fire; within weeks of the fall of Vicksburg he had placed his faith in intrenched camps rather than regular fortifications. Anyone familiar with the battles and sieges of the Franco-Prussian War and, still more, the siege of Plevna in 1877 can appreciate the essential accuracy of his predictions, even though he was wrong in some details and it was not recognized until the next century that the attack upon an enemy sheltered in trenches "must either partake of the nature of a siege . . . or it must be made by night." In sharp contrast to many later theorists both in England and on the Continent, MacDougall distinguished between the natural advantages of the defensive and the dangers of a purely defensive attitude. The one led to victory in battle, but the other, carried to extremes, might render the destruction of the enemy impossible by preventing a vigorous pursuit and rob the individual soldier of his *élan*.[23]

At this point we will pass over MacDougall's career for the next ten years in order to follow his tactical doctrine, for such it had become when the time arrived to analyze the lessons of

[22] *Ibid.*, pp. 17, 23.
[23] *Ibid.*, pp. 13, 149, 169.

the Franco-Prussian War. In 1873 MacDougall, in protest against the rising tendency "to accept Prussian teaching without due investigation," wrote a short volume entitled *Modern Infantry Tactics*. In contrast to many contemporaries, he could see nothing in the recent war to upset his predictions based upon his knowledge of military history and his tactical deductions of the Civil War. The war of 1870–71 did not impress him as "altogether a safe guide in the future," since the conditions under which the French had been defeated were so "exceptional" that to judge by results alone "might be very misleading." Specifically he refuted those German theorists who asserted dogmatically that the attack had gained more from the breech-loader than the defense.

Actually the reverse was still true, MacDougall insisted. Frontal attacks were not impossible—to believe this "would destroy all enterprise and neutralize all genius." The enemy's defensive line might be stretched to a dangerous point by maneuvering and threatened attacks; a weak position could still be exploited, and assaulting troops "by the formation of a lodgment at no great distance from the enemy's position," could disrupt the defense. But to insist that modern firepower favored the offensive was sheer madness: if it enabled attacking infantry to throw a greater volume of fire against a specific target, as many German writers maintained, it also had obviously enabled the defense to place a greater proportion of the forces at hand in a mobile reserve without any corresponding loss in firepower.[24]

MacDougall criticized Prussian tactics: in his opinion the tendency to leave the basic tactical decisions in the hands of the company commanders seemed to "ensure the *maximum* of disorder," and although he could see merit in the company column as an attack formation,[25] he continued to advocate the line and to defend the British drill system. In his view the basic tactical problem was how to advance in open formation under fire and still concentrate to press home the attack. To move from line into columns would expose the flanks of the latter and leave dangerous gaps between them, yet it was

[24] MacDougall, *Modern Infantry Tactics* (London, 1873), pp. iii, 1, 15–20, 26, 27.
[25] The Prussian company comprised 250 men and the company column of six ranks was the basic tactical formation. In contrast the English company comprised 100 men and the basic tactical unit was the eight-company battalion.

essential at least to match the numbers of the enemy at the point of collision. The best mode of attack, then, was to throw a strong line of skirmishers in front to attract the attention and fire of the enemy (the value of skirmishers "has been materially increased" by the breech-loader), followed by a main line of battle in which each battalion carefully preserved its proper front. The attack should be by successive rushes of the different lines to the front, with only one line in an upright position at any given time. Even so MacDougall was not optimistic over the prospects of success. Although the line could be expected to work its way to within 300 yards of the enemy, "it is just those last 300 yards that will constitute the crucial test." A charge over that distance "must be impossible against good troops . . . unless the assailants have developed a very superior force, and are determined, as in the assault of a breach, to break in by sheer weight of numbers at any cost." On another occasion he even went so far as to state that the battles of 1870–71 were proof "that a front held by good troops undemoralized is practically unassailable under the present conditions of fire," and that future campaigns therefore "will in all probability be decided by strategic rather than by tactical manoeuvring." [26]

The ideal solution, obviously, was a combination of defensive-offensive tactics by which a general should try to occupy "such a position that his enemy may be forced to attack," and remain on the defensive until the enemy had wasted his strength in fruitless assaults. Then, utilizing his mobile reserve, the general should counterattack with sufficient force to win the battle and exploit the victory by a vigorous pursuit. This after all had been the pattern of most of Wellington's victories up to the Battle of Vitoria (it also was consistent with the teachings of Clausewitz), and it was peculiarly suited to the character of the English soldier who traditionally was stubborn on defense and endured hardship and fatigue with patience. MacDougall concluded that the British army in particular had benefited from the general adoption of breech-loading arms, for volunteers could now be trusted to hold their place in the line with a minimum of two months' continuous training.[27]

[26] MacDougall, *Modern Infantry Tactics*, pp. 30–50 *passim; R.U.S.I. Journal* (1873), 639.

[27] MacDougall, *Modern Infantry Tactics*, pp. 25, 53–59. Cf. Karl von Clausewitz, *On War* (Washington, D.C., 1950), pp. 354–55.

MacDougall's own experience with volunteers and militia contributed to this doctrine. Early in 1865 he had returned to Canada as adjutant general of militia, in which capacity he was responsible for forging that organization into an efficient military machine. The task was a formidable one. In the wake of the "Trent" crisis some emergency measures had been taken to improve the quality of the militia,[28] but as late as 1864 there were complaints that "not one single company has been organized, or received even the miserable six days' drill which is the maximum *permitted*." Despite four years' warning there was still not a single battalion of organized militia in all Canada ready to take the field: it would take six weeks at least, one critic estimated, to assemble an adequate defensive force, and this at a time when the United States had just become a military power.[29]

Fortunately, MacDougall was admirably equipped to carry through the necessary reforms. According to Wolseley, he

was gifted with the most charming, the most fascinating manner towards all men—by no means a poor recommendation for any one who has to get on well with politicians. . . . No man knew better . . . the difference between the educated officer and the ordinary amateur in uniform, and the best of the Canadian Militia soon came to recognize their new commandant's military worth, and the value of the new system he introduced.[30]

The heart of MacDougall's new system was the formation of independent companies of militia into battalions. Defects in the existing structure had become apparent in March, 1866, when it was found necessary to call out 10,000 of the volunteer force to guard the frontier against a threatened invasion by the Fenians. Within twenty-four hours 14,000 volunteer militia had responded, and an even larger force was mobilized again in June when the Fenians actually raided the

[28] In 1863 two militia acts were passed, one to facilitate the mobilization of the sedentary militia (comprising all able-bodied males between the ages of 18 and 60), and another to increase the size of the volunteer active militia, which had been established in 1855 to provide a force equipped and trained to deal with a sudden emergency. See George F. G. Stanley, *Canada's Soldiers 1604–1954: The Military History of an Unmilitary People* (Toronto, 1954), pp. 209–16.

[29] Sir Richard John Cartwright, *Remarks on the Militia of Canada* (Kingston, 1864), p. 607. The historical development of the Canadian militia is treated in C. F. Hamilton, "Defence, 1812–1912," in Adam Shortt and Arthur Doughty (eds.), *Canada and Its Provinces* (Toronto, 1914), VII, 379–460.

[30] Wolseley, *Story of a Soldier's Life* (Westminster, 1903), II, 230–31.

frontier. MacDougall was pleased with both the number and
the quality of the volunteers who had been mustered into
service on these occasions: what was lacking, he discovered,
was an effective organization. Most volunteers belonged to
isolated companies drawn from the rural areas, and it had
been necessary to form these into provisional battalions and
to improvise a staff for each "in a hurry, and at an obvious
disadvantage." [31]

MacDougall tried to eliminate this confusion in any future
mobilization by organizing all companies into permanent
battalions and, wherever possible, assigning to each a county
designation and permanent headquarters. His localization of
the militia was an immediate success. Battalion adjutants
reported that the new organization was "a source of strength,"
an aid "to unity of action and equipment," and was "of great
benefit, imparting a true *esprit de corps* . . . and far greater
efficiency into the force of each County." In Wolseley's
experience the battalions varied in efficiency "in direct proportion to the number of old army officers, and of those who had
graduated at the Military Schools" in each.[32]

But merely to assemble masses of volunteers on short notice
was not in itself adequate for the defense of Canada: it might
suffice to repel a raid by unruly Irish malcontents, but as
MacDougall reported in June, 1866: "The military system of
Canada . . . should be calculated with an eye to the future,
to resist the regular warfare which might be waged by a
powerful neighboring people, with immense resources in men
and material." To complete his system, he wanted to
organize the entire volunteer force into brigades. The suggestion actually had come from another British officer, and the
first brigade had already been organized on a temporary basis
as an anti-Fenian measure, but MacDougall deserves the
credit for seeing beyond the immediate crisis and for actually

[31] Only the volunteer companies from the principal cities had been
formed into battalions by March, 1866 (Canada. Department of Militia
and Defence, *Report on the State of the Militia of the Province of
Canada, for the Year 1867* [Ottawa, 1868], p. 1). This and earlier reports are cited hereafter as Canada, *Militia Report*.

[32] *Ibid.*, pp. 15, 18, 29, 34, 105; Canada, *Militia Report*, 1866 (Ottawa,
1866), pp. 16–21; Lieutenant Colonel Davis, *The Canadian Militia: Its
Organization and Present Condition* (Caledonia, Ont., 1873), p. 5;
Wolseley, *Story of a Soldier's Life*, II, 147–48. The military schools had
been established in 1864 for the purpose of training officers (C. P.
Stacey, *Canada and the British Army* [London, 1936], p. 151).

organizing the field force into brigades in the fall of 1866. Seven field brigades were created, each containing one battalion of regulars and three of militia, to serve (in MacDougall's scheme) as the advanced guard of the Canadian army. The remaining militia battalions were organized into brigades by districts and were intended, in times of emergency, to guard strategic points along the frontier and lines of communication and supply. MacDougall further recommended the establishment of depots in each district to accommodate the 100,000 men he believed could be raised in event of war, each depot to be protected by intrenched camps where the fighting population of Canada might rally.[33]

The amalgamation of militia battalions with the regulars had much the same effect in Canada in 1866 as a similar policy had had in France in 1793, when the newly raised battalions of volunteers and conscripts had been attached to old regiments of the line in the proportion of two to one. (Burgoyne, it will be remembered, had also urged a similar amalgamation for the defense of England.) Years later, a Canadian militia officer explained why his system had worked so well:

[T]he Volunteer Militia had models to guide them, and derived proportionate advantage from their superior knowledge. Moreover, the Regular officers in command, took all pains to create a healthy feeling of emulation whenever their Regiments and the Volunteers were brigaded together, and the prestige of victory was in the confidence felt by the men, as long as they knew they were to fight alongside the Regulars. Look at the moveable columns of Colonel MacDougall. Why, they were ready to go anywhere, and try to do anything, although there was only a wing of a Regular Regiment, and a couple of guns to each brigade. They knew that they would be properly led, that they were under the command of professional soldiers, and would have the advice and assistance of men whose trade was war.

When the decision was made to withdraw British troops from North America in 1871, one underlying cause for concern was

[33] Canada, *Militia Report, 1865–66*, pp. 24–25; C. P. Stacey, "The Fenian Troubles and Canadian Military Development, 1865–71," *Canadian Historical Association Annual Report, 1935*, p. 32; Canada, *Militia Report, 1867*, pp. 12–13. MacDougall's views on the defense of Canada after the Civil War had ended are found in his unsigned article, "Canada: The Fenian Raid and the Colonial Office," *Blackwood's Edinburgh Magazine*, CVIII (1870), 493–508.

the fear that the militia would deteriorate without the support of the regulars: where, it was asked, are the officers and men needed to give proper seasoning to the militia? [34]

MacDougall returned to England in 1869 and promptly became involved in the agitation that led ultimately to the Cardwell Reforms. Convinced by the Prussian victory over Austria in 1866 that Britain's military machine needed to be overhauled, MacDougall submitted his proposals in a booklet entitled *The Army and Its Reserves*. His views are worth noting.

In the first place, MacDougall was against any attempt to reproduce the Prussian military system in England merely because it had worked so well against Austria: the Prussian system, he pointed out, was based upon conscription for all forces and the introduction of this principle in England would "result in the extinction of the historical British soldier, and in the destruction of that *esprit de corps* which has always been the animating soul of the British army." Nor would the application of the "rigid localization" of the Prussian military system work in England without conscription to support it. The basic problem was how to augment the size of the army swiftly and efficiently in time of war, and MacDougall's solution embraced aspects of both the Prussian and Canadian systems. He suggested, for example, that soldiers should enlist for a period of fifteen years—seven with the regiment, three with the regimental reserve, and five with a regiment of local militia. This varies in detail but not in principle from the Prussian reforms of 1868 and it anticipates the essential features of Cardwell's reorganization of the British army on a short-service basis.[35] The key to MacDougall's scheme was the revitalization of the militia to constitute a ready reserve to reinforce the active field army, and for this he drew heavily upon his experiences in Canada. "It is very desirable," he wrote, "that as intimate a connection as possible, both physical and sentimental, should be formed and maintained between the regular Army and the Militia." The latter should be trained and brigaded with regular troops along the same lines

[34] *Ibid.*, pp. 497–99; Davis, *Canadian Militia*, p. 11. See also C. P. Stacey, "Britain's Withdrawal from North America 1864–71," *Canadian Historical Review*, XXXVI (1955), 185–98.

[35] MacDougall, *The Army and Its Reserves* (London, 1869), pp. 1, 5, 7–8. At the time MacDougall wrote this pamphlet the Prussian soldier served three years with the active army, four with the reserves, and five years in the *Landwehr*, or militia.

as the volunteer militia of Canada to facilitate training (in Canada "the corps which were thus brigaded learned more in a week than others . . . did in a month") and also to "create that feeling of connection between the regular army and the reserves, so much to be desired." While insisting that the regular army should be strictly a volunteer force, he maintained that conscription was "the surest and most natural foundation of any sound militia system." Possibly he was convinced of this from what he knew of the Prussian system, but it seems more likely that here again he was influenced more by what he had seen in Canada, where most of the militia who had volunteered during the Fenian troubles felt strongly that service should be compulsorily equalized by ballot. As adjutant general, MacDougall himself had prepared a militia bill recommending either the ballot, a bounty, or rotation of service.[36]

MacDougall continued also to write in the interest of Canadian defense. He knew as much about the subject as any man in England, and he threw himself vigorously into the fight then being waged by the Duke of Cambridge and other prominent soldiers to keep the Gladstone government from withdrawing all British troops from Canada to accommodate army reforms. He insisted in 1870, as he had during the "Trent" crisis and again in 1865,[37] that Canada could still be defended provided the militia were adequately armed and British regulars remained at hand to stiffen them and serve as

[36] MacDougall, *The Army and Its Reserves*, pp. 18–20, 22, 27; Hamilton, "Defence, 1812–1912," p. 421; Davis, *Canadian Militia*, p. 5. MacDougall's detailed proposals for the formation of a reserve in England in 1869 did not differ in any important detail from his reforms of the Canadian militia in 1866. A similar proposal is found in Major Arthur Leahy, "Army Organization: Our Infantry Forces and Infantry Reserves," *R.U.S.I. Journal*, XII (1869), 310–58.

[37] In February, 1865, during a debate in the House of Commons over proposed expenditures on the defense of Quebec, a Major Anson had maintained that it was utterly impossible for England to defend Canada. It took MacDougall just five days to write and rush into print an unsigned rejoinder entitled *Last Thursday's Debate in the House of Commons on Canadian Defence*, in which he denied that the defense of Canada was impossible. MacDougall is identified as the author of this pamphlet in the Duke of Cambridge's letter to Lord Granville, May 27, 1869 (Public Record Office 30/29/72), which also incloses a memorandum written in 1869 at the Duke of Cambridge's request in which MacDougall again insisted: "We *can* hold Canada without a doubt; and the chances of a war with America would *not* be against us, as too many Englishmen despondingly and increasingly assume." The writer is indebted to Professor Bourne for supplying transcripts of both of MacDougall's writings on Canadian defense.

a guaranty that England would not abandon her imperial interests. The "discipline and alacrity" of the Canadian volunteer militia "would have been a credit to the troops of any nation." [38]

The possible influence of the Canadian militia upon the Cardwell Reforms has never been explored. Although essentially English in origin and designed to correct evils peculiar to the British army, these reforms bear a superficial resemblance to practices in the German army, particularly some features of the newly adopted short service and enlistment on a territorial basis.[39] Yet a good case can be made that the localization of the British army came not from Prussia, as so often assumed, but instead had its roots in MacDougall's reforms of the Canadian militia in 1866; for in 1871 Mac-Dougall was appointed chairman of a committee to report on the organization of the various military land forces of the crown. Two of the five members of the MacDougall Committee—Wolseley, and of course MacDougall—were fresh from Canada, where they had seen convincing proof that localization had greatly facilitated mobilization and that brigading regulars with militia had quickly converted the latter into useful soldiers. Referring to training in 1868, MacDougall cited one militia battalion which maneuvered well both in close order and as skirmishers: "no troops of any army," he boasted, "could have executed the various movements performed, with greater steadiness, smartness and precision." [40]

[38] "Canada: The Fenian Raid and the Colonial Office," *Blackwood's*, CVIII (1870), 493–508; MacDougall to John Blackwood, August 10, 1870. National Library of Scotland, Edinburgh (Blackwood Papers 4265). MacDougall's articles usually were unsigned because to identify himself as author "would have been rather a breach of etiquette for a General on full pay" (MacDougall to Blackwood, March 3, 1885 [Blackwood Papers 4474]). For the reasons leading to Britain's decision to withdraw troops from North America, see Stacey, *Canada and the British Army*, pp. 256–57. The Duke of Cambridge's views are found in Colonel Willoughby Verner, *The Military Life of H.R.H. George, Duke of Cambridge* (London, 1905), I, 397–99.

[39] The German influence can also be seen in the institution of army maneuvers in 1871 and the establishment of an intelligence department two years later. The Prussian *Pickelhaube* even replaced the French *kepi* as standard headdress in most British regiments. See Sir George Arthur, *From Wellington to Wavell* (London, 1942), p. 72; Sir Robert Biddulph, *Lord Cardwell at the War Office* (London, 1904), pp. 189, 212–13; and James Laver, *British Military Uniforms* (London, 1948), p. 21.

[40] MacDougall, *The Army and Its Reserves*, p. 27. Wolseley was no less generous in his praise of the Canadian militia (*Story of a Soldier's Life*, II, 159, 174).

There is additional evidence to suggest that MacDougall and Wolseley (and who can imagine a committee of five not strongly influenced by the latter?) were more impressed by what they had seen in Canada than what they had read about the Prussian army. Neither had been blinded—as had so many in the British army—by the dazzling Prussian victory over France in 1870. True, this victory had opened the eyes of the British to their own military weaknesses, but Wolseley later felt compelled to advise British officers to "copy the Germans as regards work and leave their clothes and their methods alone," while MacDougall repeatedly protested that Prussian tactics were being overrated and that it would be unwise to import the German military system. "The successes of the Prussians," he announced, "have been purely strategical and have not in the least as yet touched the question as to whether a 3 years soldier or a 6 or 7 years soldier is the best to rely upon when the supreme moment of a decisive battle has been reached." Thus it would appear that both Wolseley and MacDougall resisted the impulse in 1871 to imitate the Germans, and it is significant that the final report of the MacDougall Committee emphasized that "localization must be understood in a sense different from localization in Prussia"; the scheme proposed by the MacDougall Committee and adopted by the British army in 1872 more nearly resembled the organization of the Canadian militia after MacDougall's reforms half a dozen years earlier.[41]

MacDougall was rewarded for his contribution to the localization scheme by being appointed first director of the Intelligence Department when it was established in 1873.[42] We know little of his activities during the five years he spent in this capacity, but his articles and printed memoranda indicate an active interest in mobilization schemes, German military organization, the route to India and the political and economic situation in Egypt, and of course the Russo-Turkish War.[43] And in his writings and testimony before various com-

---

[41] Major General Sir F. Maurice and Sir George Arthur, *The Life of Lord Wolseley* (New York, 1924), p. 222; MacDougall to John Blackwood, August 8, 1870 (Blackwood Papers 4265); *Final Report of Committee on the Organization of the Various Military Land Forces of the Country* (War Office, February 21, 1873), p. 13.

[42] Biddulph, *Lord Cardwell at the War Office*, p. 214.

[43] See MacDougall, "The Mobilization of the Army and National Defence," *Blackwood's*, CXX (1876), 509–20; "The Egyptian Campaign in Abyssinia. From the notes of a Staff Officer," (sent to MacDougall by Mr. De Leon, the American consul general in Cairo), *ibid.*, CXXII

mittees, he continued to hammer away at two major points: the need for gradual amalgamation of the forces and the folly of imitating the German military system in detail. Whether it was on the question of tactics, army organization, mobilization, or the most efficient size of a company, his reaction was always the same: "It is by no means desirable to cut an English coat out of Prussian cloth, until at least we have some better evidence than is now forthcoming, of the goodness of the material. . . ." [44]

In 1878 MacDougall returned to Canada as commander in chief of the forces in British North America. His five-year tenure in this position was uneventful except for one incident that provides still another example of his prophetic vision. Already in 1870 he had expressed confidence that the Canadians would respond to any appeal "to contribute their quota on just and equitable conditions towards the armies of the empire." During the tense relations between Great Britain and Russia in 1878–79, MacDougall officially offered "to organize a military reserve force of 10,000 men for general service in any part of the world." This offer was not accepted because the men were not actually needed at the time, but it would appear that MacDougall was one of the first in Canada to view the empire as a partnership of nations with respect to defense. [45]

MacDougall returned to England in 1883 and retired two years later. While in Canada he wrote sparingly on army

(1877), 26–39; and "The Khedive's Egypt and Our Route to India," *ibid.*, pp. 477–90. MacDougall also prepared weekly summaries of the Russian campaign in Turkey in 1877 for the Queen (MacDougall to Blackwood, December 15, 1877 [Blackwood Papers 4358]).

[44] MacDougall, *On the Proposal To Change the Organization of Our Field Battalions from 8 to 4 Companies* (War Office Confidential Papers 0768, March 8, 1877), p. 1; "Mobilization of the Army and National Defence," p. 520. MacDougall's arguments for the gradual amalgamation of the forces and the need to eliminate distinctions between the uniforms of the militia and regulars are found in his testimony before the Stanley Committee. See *Report of the Committee Appointed by the Secretary of State for War To Enquire into Certain Questions That Have Arisen with respect to the Militia and the Present Brigade Depot System* (London, 1877), pp. 217–30.

[45] MacDougall, "Canada: The Fenian Raid and the Colonial Office," p. 506; Alice R. Stewart, "Sir John A. Macdonald and the Imperial Defense Commission of 1879," *Canadian Historical Review*, XXXV (1954), 133–34; *Canadian Illustrated News*, October 26, 1878. See also C. P. Stacey, "Canada and the Nile Expedition of 1884–85," *Canadian Historical Review*, XXXIII (1952), 319–40.

matters, but once relieved of administrative duties he became considerably more active with his pen. Most of his writings during this last phase of his career were devoted to a spirited defense of Cardwell's reorganization of the army and particularly the localization scheme worked out by the MacDougall Committee. The Cardwell Reforms were the subject of much hostile criticism in the 1870's and 1880's, when many soldiers contended that the new system had failed to meet the test in the Ashanti War of 1873 and the campaign six years later against the Zulus. If the Cardwell Reforms had failed, MacDougall retorted, it was because they had never been fairly tested: the shortcomings were political rather than military in that Gladstone's government had reduced the army establishment to the point where its own scheme was no longer workable. The alleged breakdown of the Cardwell system was due primarily to the fact that England in 1878 had "carried on two difficult wars at the same time, with all the establishments on a peace footing," and Disraeli's government had compounded the error by refusing to ask Parliament for funds to meet the requirements of war in South Africa.[46] When the Airey Committee was convened in 1880 "with the idea of striking a blow at the roots of Mr. Cardwell's system," MacDougall, although a member of the committee, dissented from the published report because none of the machinery provided by the Cardwell Reforms had been utilized, and this remained his argument throughout the subsequent debates.[47] Wolseley, who on several occasions had commanded regiments of the new model army in the field, offered the same defense.

One aspect of the Cardwell Reforms, however, still did not please MacDougall: thirteen years after the abolition of purchase, he observed that the army had yet to produce a body of "professional officers." They were, he wrote in 1884, "so little in love with the army, that they are voluntarily leaving it in crowds." According to MacDougall the average number of years that the British officer spent in service from choice actually was less than it had been under the purchase system, and he criticized promotion by selection because the basis for

[46] "Army Reform," *Blackwood's,* XCI (1880), 553–62.
[47] Captain Owen Wheeler, *The War Office Past and Present* (London, 1914), p. 230; *Report of a Committee of General and Other Officers of the Army on Army Reorganisation* (London, 1881), pp. 24–66, 272–75.

judgment seemed "artificial and untrustworthy." Before 1870 French officers had been promoted by selection, he pointed out, "yet the annihilation of the French regular army was largely due to the incapacity of the officers." The German system of "pure seniority" modified by a rigid veto of promotion of men obviously incompetent was still "the only fair and reasonable" practice.[48]

MacDougall also questioned the tactical instruction of the British army. Ever since 1870 the tacticians had been experimenting with different formations for attack, but in MacDougall's day no system had yet been devised to avoid the mixing up of different commands in battle. Moreover, the annual maneuvers seemed to indicate that the advantages of the offensive were being exaggerated: at the Salisbury maneuvers in 1884, for example, MacDougall witnessed a battalion of 400 men in extended order attack on a front of 600 yards a line of "enemy" troops in close order, 1,200 strong! Convinced that the defense had gained more from improved weapons, MacDougall found the implications of such maneuvers frightening. In one respect only did he modify his earlier opinion. Whereas in 1864 he had written that the principal effect of increased firepower was to give new importance to extended order, he now maintained that

the formation of attacking troops in extended order is unnecessary, and . . . would not yield satisfactory results in actual conflict. The object of our various attempted formations is to bring up a battalion line two deep to the charging point with the least possible loss; and I am convinced that a closed line, each man occupying a yard of front, covered and protected by a thick screen of skirmishers, gaining ground by the rushes of alternate files or alternate companies, and lying down when not in motion, would not suffer more loss in advancing under fire than if the men were disposed in several open lines not covered by skirmishers.[49]

The army, too, had lost faith in extended order, but for different reasons. After 1870 the drill books conveyed the

[48] See MacDougall, *Short-Service Enlistment and the Organization of Our Infantry as Illustrated by Recent Events* (Edinburgh, 1883), pp. 5–7; "Have We an Army," *Nineteenth Century*, XIV (1883), 508; "Army Vivisection," *Blackwood's*, CXXXV (1884), 285–88; "The Inefficiency of the Army: A Reply," *ibid.*, CLII (1892), 267–72. Maurice and Arthur, *Wolseley*, p. 262.

[49] MacDougall, "Our System of Infantry Tactics: What Is It?" *Nineteenth Century*, XVII (1885), 833, 836; *Modern Warfare as Influenced by Modern Artillery*, p. 414.

impression that a battalion in four lines, unprotected by skirmishers, could carry almost any position. Then came the disaster of Isandlhwana in 1879, when a British column was destroyed by the Zulus, and this "overweening confidence gave way to an excess of caution." The British returned to close-line formations in their native campaigns; the square, once a human citadel against cavalry attacks, was reintroduced as an attack formation. MacDougall protested that such tactics would destroy the confidence of the troops and cramp them together where they could neither move nor fight properly: the latest tactical doctrine had no "semblance to reality or probability." [50] MacDougall failed, however, to see another danger arising from the colonial campaigns. In Africa the square worked well enough against natives armed with primitive weapons, but it had no place in a battle waged between armies equal in armament, training, and discipline. Yet in England, volunteers and militia were being forced to spend valuable time mastering these formations which were of little or no value in modern war.[51] As one who had long been concerned with the training of the reserve forces, it is curious that MacDougall should have overlooked this point.

MacDougall died in 1894 following a prolonged and painful illness. Except to defend a "violent attack" on the MacDougall Committee that appeared in print shortly before his death, he wrote nothing during the last years of his life. He was an administrator rather than a man of action, a thoughtful student of war who evidently preferred to work quietly in the shadows. He rendered lasting services to both the British army and the Canadian militia, yet he is virtually unknown in either country today.[52]

This is all the more curious because MacDougall apparently succeeded in every task he approached. His first book, *The*

[50] MacDougall, "Our System of Infantry Tactics: What Is It?" pp. 837, 842–45; "The Late Battles in the Soudan and Modern Tactics," *Blackwood's*, CXXXV (1884), 605–10; "The Fall of Khartoum, and Its Consequences," *ibid.*, CXXXVII (1885), 558–68.

[51] See J. F. Maurice, "The Advantages of a Simple Drill Nomenclature Consistent for All Arms, Apropos to an Incident of the Battle of Tel-el-Kebir," *R.U.S.I. Journal*, XXXII (1888), 95. See also Maurice's remarks in *ibid.*, XLIV (1901), 659.

[52] Wolseley to Lady Wolseley, December 9, 1894 (Wolseley Papers); MacDougall to John Blackwood, June 21, 1892 (Blackwood Papers 4590). The article in question is Field Marshal Sir Lintorn Simmons, "The Inefficiency of the Army," *Nineteenth Century*, XXXI (1892), 885–98.

Theory of War, earned him a foremost place among English military writers: it was known on the Continent and remained the basic text in the British army until Hamley's monumental *Operations of War* was published in 1866. His pamphlet on military education probably won for him the appointment as first commandant of the Staff College, in which capacity he obviously did well enough to retain favor with that influential patron of the institution, the Duke of Cambridge. His study of Hannibal's campaigns is still regarded as authentic history.

MacDougall's voice was heard when plans for the defense of Canada were being formulated during the "Trent" crisis. After the Civil War he continued to speak out with authority on matters pertaining to Canadian defense, and it is quite likely that his pamphlet in 1865 expressing confidence that an invasion by the United States could be repelled contributed to his selection as adjutant general of Canadian militia. To that "thankless office" MacDougall brought what Wolseley has described as "a clear brain and a bright imagination untrammelled by obsolete notions upon military subjects"; he left behind what the governor general regarded as "the foundation of a military system inexpensive, unoppressive, and efficient," a system which remained in force long after he had departed.[53]

In England he soon made his mark as a military reformer as head of the reserve forces from 1871 to 1873 and chairman of the influential Committee on Localization. "He was well aware of how thoroughly our antiquated military system required sweeping reforms to bring it up to a level with modern requirements, and he had also the courage of his opinions to say so. . . ."[54] Not blinded by the Prussian victories over Austria and France, he continued to work for improvements in British tactics and organization rather than join in the rush to reject both in favor of the Prussian system. We know nothing of the details of his tenure as first director of military intelligence, but presumably he was successful

[53] Wolseley, *Story of a Soldier's Life,* II, 231; Vetch, "MacDougall," p. 993; Lieutenant Colonel T. B. Strange, "The Military Aspect of Canada," *R.U.S.I. Journal,* XXIII (1879), 737. See also the dispatch from Lord Monck, the governor general, to the Right Hon. E. Cardwell, as quoted in Captain John A. Macdonald, *Troublous Times in Canada: A History of the Fenian Raids of 1866 and 1870* (Toronto, 1910), pp. 134–37.

[54] Wolseley, *Story of a Soldier's Life,* II, 231.

enough to warrant being sent to Canada as commander in chief of the forces in British North America; and in this post he had an early vision of an imperial rather than a purely British army representing common interests wherever they might be threatened. To the end of his life he also worked to uphold the reforms that he and other progressive soldiers had proposed during the Cardwell era.

Not the least remarkable of his accomplishments was his evident ability to get along with both Wolseley and the Duke of Cambridge. The former was progressive and impatient to introduce the much needed reforms; the latter, despite his contributions to military education, was growing increasingly suspicious of politicians and the "new school" which Wolseley and MacDougall represented, and his growing resistance to change was reinforced by the lurking fear that the royal prerogative was being endangered. But MacDougall somehow managed to remain in the good graces of both in what was one of the most crucial periods in the history of the army.

As a military writer MacDougall represents a sort of composite of the salient features of Napier, Mitchell, and Burgoyne. A friend of Napier's for many years, he learned from his father-in-law how history can serve a practical purpose in the education of officers. He followed Napier's format in his study of Hannibal, showing how even a campaign from classical times may illustrate the fixed principles of war, and he extracted from the *History of the War in the Peninsula* many military lessons applicable in his own day. Indeed, MacDougall understood much more clearly than Napier how history and theory march side by side. Napier wrote his *History* to vindicate individuals and relate the accomplishments of British arms: because he was a professional soldier he naturally drew upon military theory to help explain campaigns and evaluate generalship. MacDougall, on the other hand, looked to the past primarily for guidance into the future. It is from the acted past, he wrote in his most original work,

and not from the imagined future, that the theorist in War must take his rules and examples. It is impossible to anticipate the cases that may arise in practice; but the mind of a general will be better prepared to deal with any possible combination of events, in proportion as it is stored with examples afforded by former military operations. War must always remain a science of uncertainty and, to a great extent, of chance; and a careful analysis of past combinations and events is the only way even to approximate to exactitude in it.[55]

As a theorist MacDougall differed from Mitchell in several respects. He was more interested in strategy and more elastic in his study of tactics. Mitchell had utilized military history not so much to illustrate general principles as to document specific theories of his own; if he was more scientific than Napier in his approach he was every bit as dogmatic in his conclusions. But MacDougall over a period of years evolved a tactical doctrine that he was willing to modify in the light of recent developments, preferring, as had Mitchell, some modification of the English system of tactics to a slavish imitation of the prevailing foreign methods. And both recognized the desperate need for reform.

MacDougall may also be compared with Burgoyne in a number of respects. To a remarkable degree the lessons he deduced from the Crimean War corresponded to the views of that wise and experienced old warrior, and both changed their view of the capability of earthworks to withstand bombardment after the introduction of rifled artillery. Both recognized as well that volunteers and militia would have to play an increasingly important role in the defense of Britain and that modern firepower had increased the capabilities of the reserve forces. If MacDougall was more of a theorist than Burgoyne, he was equally vocal on defense issues and scarcely less influential in committee.

MacDougall's contributions as a military reformer are a matter of record; his significance as a theorist and military writer is equally profound. As a representative of the "new school" growing out of the Crimean War, he has been overshadowed by Wolseley and some of the men around him; as a theorist and military historian he is not as well known as Hamley and Colonel Charles Cornwallis Chesney, although both owe more to MacDougall than has ever been acknowledged. MacDougall was one of the first to advocate (in 1864) "the necessity of adopting an open formation for an attacking line in the face of breech-loading fire," and to recognize that the breech-loader and rifled artillery had greatly strengthened the defense. Although most military writers assumed the

[55] MacDougall, *Modern Warfare*, pp. vi, 92–93.

opposite and continued to stress offensive action, none other than Moltke agreed with MacDougall's basic conclusions, which received further confirmation in the defense of Plevna (1878), the trench warfare in Manchuria (1904–5), and especially the military operations in France and Belgium (1914–18).[56]

MacDougall once observed that "the successes of the German armies . . . were not so much owing to the manifestation of any great military genius . . . as to the vast capacity for taking trouble which was displayed in the bureaus of the military offices . . . in anticipation of war." [57] This is perhaps the most fitting commentary one can make on his own career. In his writings as well as his various administrative duties MacDougall showed that he too possessed a "vast capacity for taking trouble." It was his misfortune to have lived in an age that still idolized the dashing and successful field commander and had not yet learned to appreciate either the need for or significance of those members of the new army school who labored quietly and efficiently to prepare themselves and the army for the tests that lay ahead.

[56] MacDougall, *On the Proposal To Change the Organization of Our Field Battalions, passim.* Moltke did not mention MacDougall, but their views were strikingly similar (F. von Schmerfeld [ed.], *Generalfeldmarshall Graff von Moltke Ausgewählte Werke. I. Feldherr und Kriegslehrmeister* [Berlin, 1925], pp. 335–37). For German military thought during this period, see Colonel Eugène Carrias, *La pensée militaire allemande* (Paris, 1948), pp. 260–78. Useful excerpts from the various French, German, and English military writers on the question of offense versus defense are contained in Colonel Robert Home, *A Précis of Modern Tactics* (revised and rewritten by Lieutenant Colonel Sisson C. Pratt; London, 1892), pp. 53–58.

[57] *R.U.S.I. Journal,* XIX (1867), 398.

5

THE STRATEGIC PEDAGOGUE

General Sir Edward Bruce Hamley

IN 1860, in an unsigned review of the most recent biography of Wellington, it was aggressively asserted that

the first grand requisite for the biographer of a great soldier is, that he shall be sufficiently acquainted with military science to appreciate rightly the achievements of his hero. It is a common thing for writers of great eminence and ability to enter on the discussion of military questions with no more idea of military science than is supplied by a set of general impressions on the subject, which are common to educated and intelligent men of all professions. . . . On the other hand, a large practical acquaintance with war is generally incompatible with the cultivation of literary talent, to the extent requisite for the narration of important events, or the exhibition of remarkable characters. It is only when the union of experienced military judgment with literary power takes place that the achievements of great soldiers are faithfully and enduringly placed on record.[1]

Napier had possessed this rare combination; so, too, did the anonymous contributor to *Blackwood's* who, had he been identified, would have been widely known for his exploits in battle or his achievements in the more attractive field of belles lettres. Solidly established in both camps, Major E. B. Hamley was eminently suited to explain and illustrate the operations of war so that the soldier might read military history with intelligence and the reading public approach military problems with understanding and both, he held, were necessary if

---

1 "Wellington's Career," *Blackwood's*, LXXXVII (1860), 398.

the mistakes in the Crimea were to be avoided in a future war.

The Staff College provided Hamley with an opportunity to work with some of the most promising young officers in the army; *The Operations of War* in its many editions enabled him to place his views before a much wider military audience; *Blackwood's* furnished an admirable platform from which he could speak to a public curious but generally uninformed about military matters. For the next thirty years he stood high in the estimation of the public, while throughout the army he was looked upon as Britain's foremost teacher of strategy.

Edward Bruce Hamley was born in Cornwall in 1824, the youngest of four sons of a prominent English naval officer. Like the Napiers of the preceding generation, the Hamleys also were a distinguished military family: the father died a vice-admiral; William George, the eldest of the brothers, achieved the rank of major general of engineers; and Charles became a colonel in the Royal Marines and doubtless would have advanced further had he lived as long as the others. The three brothers contributed frequently to *Blackwood's*.

According to Hamley's biographer, who was too anxious to get on with his story to cast more than a hasty glance at his subject's youth,[2] "his precocious tastes even in childhood had set strongly towards literature," but he also manifested a feeling for art.

We know surprisingly little of Hamley's early development as a soldier. After grammar school he spent eighteen months at the Royal Military Academy at Woolwich. In 1843 he was gazetted to the artillery and sent to Ireland, where he spent a year before accompanying his battery to Quebec. Four Canadian winters gave Hamley abundant leisure for reading, if they did not whet his appetite for soldiering: he was bored by the trivia of regimental duty and preferred literature to military treatises. When he returned to England he turned to literature to supplement his pay, and in 1849 *Fraser's Magazine* carried his first publication, "The Peace Campaigns of Ensign Faunce."

[2] The basic source for Hamley is Alexander Innis Shand, *The Life of General Sir Edward Bruce Hamley* (Edinburgh, 1895), but E. M. Lloyd's sketch in the *D.N.B. Supplement* (New York, 1909), XXII, 807–10, is essential for a balanced appraisal of Hamley's writings.

In 1851 Hamley was promoted to the rank of captain and ordered to Gibraltar, where countless hours spent in the garrison library reading Shakespeare, Milton, Dryden, Pope, Richardson, and Fielding increased his commitment to litera-ture. It was here that he really began his literary career: a letter to the proprietor of *Blackwood's* about an article his brother William had published led to a contribution of his own—a poem entitled "Michael Angelo and the Friar." John Blackwood also encouraged Hamley to write about garrison life on the Rock, which emerged as a satirical series entitled the "Legend of Gibraltar" that "delighted the editor, and made a great hit with the public." [3] Other successful stories fol-lowed. Writing evidently came easy to Hamley.

The Crimean War recaptured his talents for the army. When his commander at Gibraltar, Lieutenant Colonel (later Sir Richard) Dacres, was placed in charge of the batteries of the first division, Hamley accompanied him as adjutant and later served as aide-de-camp. Present at every battle in the Crimea, Hamley was mentioned in dispatches and won the praise of the historian Kinglake.[4] But it was his pen that brought Hamley to the notice of most Englishmen. His picturesque and detailed letters in *Blackwood's* proved so popular that they were pirated by an American publishing firm. As a serving officer Hamley manifestly could not afford to publish facts or opinions that might prejudice British military operations, but the pictures he presented of camp life and battlefield—which he later illustrated with paintings and sketches of his own—do not suffer by comparison with the scenes depicted by the "Special Correspondent" of the *Times*. Both were vigorous and convincing writers; both excelled in describing scenes in a manner to kindle the imagination; both wrote of things that they saw or were acquainted with at first-hand. Here the comparison ceases, however, for Russell and Hamley wrote for essentially different purposes.

Russell represented a paper whose job it was to get the facts of the war before the public. He had a keen eye for a good story and was interested more in general conditions and the broad issues at stake than in the military operations and problems of strategy and command. But he enjoyed neither

[3] *Ibid.*, I, 51.
[4] A. W. Kinglake, *The Invasion of the Crimea*, adapted for military students by Lieutenant Colonel Sir George Sydenham Clarke (Edin-burgh, 1899), p. 356.

the respect nor the confidence of the generals because of his harsh judgments of the high command and also because his disclosures frequently were thought to have benefited the enemy. Russell's moving passages depicting the heroism of the troops against a background of bungling and inefficient leadership inflamed public opinion, and from his day to the present few generals have enjoyed immunity from the watchful and critical eye of the press.[5]

Hamley, on the other hand, wrote to educate the general reader. He resented the hostile tone in the press. If the new war correspondents gave a valuable picture of life in the field they also represented a dangerous influence upon public opinion, and Hamley wrote to counter "the false and self-depreciatory outcries of our own ill-informed and ill-judging countrymen." Why is it, he asked, that everybody considers himself an expert in military matters, when in fact the pretensions of the amateur in strategy and tactics were no more respectable than those of "barber-surgeons in pharmacy, inspired cobblers in religion, or gypsies in divination." Yet it was the amateur who through exaggeration and use of intensified colors was giving the public a distorted picture of events, thus helping to shape public opinion, which in turn was beginning to exercise powerful pressures on Parliament, the government, and ultimately on armies in the field. Fed on inaccuracies, public curiosity was a monster which must "be gratified at all hazards." [6]

Hamley defended the army. If the public needed a scapegoat, he argued, let it turn on those responsible for the defense of the country before the war, when the army was a mere skeleton with weak cavalry, half-equipped artillery, an insufficient medical staff, and a defunct commissariat. To those who looked upon the French army as superior to the British in training and organization, Hamley pointed out that the British had carried the brunt of the earlier battles and that the French too had suffered severe repulses before Sebastopol. "What would have been the feeling in England," he wondered, ". . . if it had been our batteries, instead of those of the

[5] See John Black Atkins, *The Life of Sir William Howard Russell: The First Special Correspondent* (London, 1911), I, 124–259; Rupert Furneaux, *The First War Correspondent: William Howard Russell of the Times* (London, 1944), pp. 20–94.

[6] "Lessons from the War," *Blackwood's*, LXXIX (1856), 234–35, 239; Hamley, *The Story of the Campaign of Sebastopol Written in Camp* (Edinburgh, 1855), p. vii.

French, which were silenced after a few hours' fire" during the initial bombardment of the city: British artillery had done its job well, the Russian defenses on the British front had been completely paralyzed, but the assault never was made because the French withdrew from the battle after a Russian shell had exploded one of their magazines.

Nor would Hamley concede that the British soldier was in any way inferior. "That the army was few and ill-provided," he argued, "only augments the glories of Alma and Inkermann [sic]." The present regimental system was "the most perfect" in the world; no troops were "more subordinate, better disciplined, or better led" than the British regular. The trouble with the British army was not so much in its component parts but rather in its inability to improvise divisions and a smoothly functioning field army complete with staff, commissariat, and transport. Staff and higher officers cannot master their new duties except in an army assembled, and, as Hamley pointed out, except for India no British officer had had an opportunity to acquire the necessary experience.[7]

Hamley emphatically refuted the charges of incompetent leadership in the Crimea. The British regimental officers, he maintained, compared favorably with the French; if British generalship had not displayed "any great genius," the public must recognize the fact that a siege does not offer much scope for development. Perhaps a speedy assault on the Russian defenses or "deliberate provision for wintering on the heights" would have spared much useless suffering, but once the army found itself before Sebastopol, "no arrangement or foresight within the scope of human minds could have averted, to any extent, the disasters which followed." Indeed, the campaign could be justified in the eyes of Hamley because, on balance, the allies had won this war of attrition.

Our own losses, though great, were nothing in comparison with those inflicted on the enemy, by forcing him to carry on the war at a distance from his resources, and with such a country as the Crimea intervening. Thus, and thus only, could be attained the result we behold; Russia, at the end of one campaign compelled to accept the terms dictated by the Allies.[8]

It was a defense that would crop up again in his later writings and find numerous adherents during the trench war

[7] *Ibid.*, pp. 136–39, 159, 162, 169; "The Crimean Report and Chelsea Inquiry," *Blackwood's*, LXXX (1856), 6–7.
[8] *Ibid.*, p. 24.

of 1914–18. Hamley's prediction that with peace the army "will shrivel to a skeleton—its members will be again the object of jealousy and taunts—until, in a new war, we shall again learn our deficiences from our misfortunes" also would bear repeating.[9]

He felt strongly about this because of his conviction that to learn "wisdom or precaution" from anything short of disaster and then to retain the knowledge thus purchased was "contrary to English national custom." The public was "indiscriminate and unreasonable"; and Hamley warned of new dangers in a day when public opinion was formed to a large extent by men ignorant of military affairs. "Reputations, beginning nobody knows how, have taken shape and substance," and the "mischief of this," according to Hamley, was "that these will be the men selected for trust in a future emergency."

Hamley did not join in the cry to broaden the education of the British officer: indeed, nothing struck him as more ridiculous than the first attempts to improve military education. Candidates for commissions were examined in science and literature by masters who evidently believed that the following questions asked in 1855 had something to do with professional skill. "Write a short life of Milton, with dates." "Perform the endiometric analysis of atmospheric air." "Tell what smoky quarz is." "Give a summary of Cousin's argument against the philosophy of Locke." "Draw a map of Britain in the time of the Roman occupation." The Reverend G. Butler's question: "What is the origin of Roman satire" impressed Hamley as a good point of departure for some satire of his own:

> Fancy the bewilderment of poor old Jomini, prince of strategists, at being required to tell the Rev. G. Butler what he knew "of the military organization of the Samnites,"—or the perplexity of . . . Wellington, when requested by the Rev. Mr. Brown to "illustrate from Homer the respect paid to the rites of hospitality."

The British officer may emerge more erudite than before, but Hamley was one with Burgoyne and MacDougall in not anticipating "the happy results which seem to be generally looked for." [10]

A more practical solution was the creation in 1857 of the

[9] Hamley, *The Campaign of Sebastopol*, pp. 139, 140; *The War in the Crimea* (London, 1891), pp. 302–7.
[10] Hamley, "Lessons from the War," pp. 236–39.

Council of Military Education and the subsequent establishment of the Staff College. Military history, which had been ignored at Sandhurst, became a part of the curriculum at Camberley, and Hamley was the man selected to teach the subject. He had served with distinction in the Duke of Cambridge's division in the Crimea, already he was marked as an officer "of great promise," and if he had not as yet turned his thoughts to a systematic study of military history, his *Story of the Campaign of Sebastopol,* published by Blackwood two years previously, was an auspicious beginning. His reputation as a military critic had even crossed the Channel when his refutation of De Bazancourt's account of the campaign attracted the attention of the Prussian authorities.[11]

As professor of military history, Hamley was expected "to point out to the students the objects of the various campaigns . . . as well as the manner in which these operations were conducted, showing when and why they were successful and where and why they failed." Evidently he "fully justified the hopes that had been entertained of his capacity"; his lectures have been described as "the most interesting delivered" at the new institution. Every teacher can sympathize with his complaint that "for every lecture I write I have to read twenty résumés or parodies of it,"[12] but this apparently is what he encouraged. For Hamley, as his own writings suggest and his students frequently testified, was a pedant. By comparison with his mediocre colleagues, he was a good performer in the lecture hall, but he "expected his pupils to accept his deductions as well as his facts, and did not encourage original research." Sir Evelyn Wood relates that the advice he gave to a fellow student who was preparing very superficially for an examination was met with the glib assurance: "No, I shall serve up Hamley, Hamley, nothing but Hamley; that always gets me full marks."[13]

[11] Brevet Major A. R. Godwin-Austen, *The Staff and the Staff College* (London, 1927), pp. 13, 63, 78, 112–13. In 1858 the course for the Staff College was set at two years and the subjects for examination were mathematics, military history, French, chemistry, German, geology, fortification, and military drawing (Colonel Willoughby Verner, *The Military Life of H.R.H. George Duke of Cambridge* [London, 1905], I, 144). For Hamley's criticism of this work see "De Bazancourt's "Narrative of the Campaign," *Blackwood's,* LXXIX (1856), 486–500.

[12] Shand, *Hamley,* I, 118–19; Godwin-Austen, *Staff and the Staff College,* pp. 11, 13–14.

[13] Evelyn Wood, *From Midshipman to Field Marshal* (5th ed.; London, 1907), pp. 214–15.

Hamley lectured on the major campaigns of Marlborough, Wellington, and Napoleon; he wrote an elaborate review of Carlyle's *Frederick the Great,* and his articles on the Belgian General Brialmont's *Life of the Duke of Wellington* were so comprehensive and well organized that they subsequently were published as a separate volume. His criticism of Thiers' account of Waterloo proved the Frenchman guilty of intense partisanship and of "manipulation of positive facts," and later was incorporated—without acknowledgement—in Chesney's well-known *Waterloo Lectures.*[14] His critique of the French official history of the war in Italy in 1859 shows a similar grasp of the most recent campaigns.

It also reveals a growing preoccupation with strategy. Hamley measured the movements of Napoleon III against accepted military principles and decided that the French emperor, as a general, was too much of a gambler. The march to Magenta in his judgment was "fatal" to Napoleon's character for generalship: "it was showy, unexpected, and therefore praised as brilliant; but it was extremely perilous, and all the danger was run without the prospect of a corresponding success." Hamley was quick to perceive that the nephew of the great Bonaparte would rather evade than fight a battle, and he predicted:

> Should he . . . take the field in another war . . . his combinations would be well calculated, his movements methodical and accurate; but we should doubt the resolution, not of the man, but of the general, and we should expect that, opposed to a skillful and resolute adversary, prompt and ready to fight, he might play for a high stake and lose it.[15]

If Hamley did not anticipate Sedan, clearly he understood the character of one of the men responsible for the debacle in 1870.

His knowledge of the American Civil War, on the other hand, was artificial. At first he shared the contempt felt by European professionals for the clumsy efforts of the American

---

[14] Hamley complained to Blackwood that Chesney "is particularly praised for . . . showing up Thiers. . . . and he has adopted all my views—but the only writing of mine he quotes as authority is *Wellington's Career*" (Hamley to John Blackwood, December 18, 1868 [Blackwood Papers 4234]). Hamley likewise refuted Victor Hugo's description of the battle. See "Victor Hugo on the 'Great French Puzzle,' *Blackwood's* XCII (1862), 647–57; and "Thiers on Waterloo," *ibid.,* pp. 607–33.

[15] "Louis Napoleon as a General," *ibid.,* XCV (1864), 339, 350.

armies. The first Battle of Bull Run, as reported by Russell,[16] had discredited the war in the eyes of many. To Hamley this battle was "certainly the greatest joke in the world" and the northern army was deservedly "filling all Europe with inextinguishable laughter." Frequently he expressed the hope that events in America, "a country where the impulses of the many swamp the logic of the few," would meet the derision they deserved. Hamley also made the common error of underestimating the war potential of the North. By 1862, however, when the first European observers reached the scene, he began to see the war in a different light and he watched the later campaigns with greater interest. According to his biographer, "Long before the termination of the war, he had come to the conclusion that the Northern American, like the Gascon, could plan and fight as well as swagger."

Nevertheless Hamley always remained a partial stranger to the campaigns in America. He knew enough about them to see the fundamental principles of strategy reaffirmed in the movements of the various armies and to cite examples as needed, but he had no personal knowledge of the terrain and he never showed any interest in Civil War tactics. His articles, which are for the most part political rather than military, do indicate, however, that Hamley regarded military history as a useful tool in interpreting current military operations. He was convinced that only the military student "accustomed to consider problems of strategy as exemplified in the practice of great Commanders, and able to apply his deductions to new combinations of circumstances" had the ability to perceive the important threads in modern wars and, by following these, to evolve "order and design out of hopeless confusion." [17]

[16] See Russell, *My Diary North and South* (London, 1863), II, 202–50.
[17] "Books on the American War," *Blackwood's*, XCIV (1863), 754. Other articles in *Blackwood's* that have been identified as coming from the pen of Hamley are: "Disruption of Union," XC (1861), 125–34; "Democracy Teaching by Example," XC, 395–406; "The Convulsions of America," XCI (1862), 118–23; "Spence's American Union," XCI, 514–36; "Trollope's North America," XCII (1862), 372–90; "American State Papers," XCIII (1863), 628–44; "Our Rancorous Cousins," XCIV (1863), 636–52; "Our Neutrality," XCV (1864), 447–61; and "General McClellan," XCVI (1864), 619–44. Despite his admiration for his "humane and honourable" spirit, Hamley had a low opinion of McClellan's fighting ability. He regarded him as "eminently a prudent and safe general," with radical defects of character which would always hinder him from ever achieving success (*ibid.*, pp. 637, 642). See also Shand, *Hamley*, I, 135–37; Mrs. Gerald Porter, *John Blackwood* (Vol. III of *William Blackwood and His Sons: Their Magazine and Friends* [London, 1898]), p. 268.

What was needed, therefore, was a knowledge of the essential principles of strategy, something to provide an effective technical background for further reading and investigation. Unlike the other sciences, the basic terms in military science had never really been defined or adequately explained: too often, Hamley contended, the military student was at loss to understand the comments and scientific expositions even of writers like Napier and Jomini; too often the theorist treated his subject in such an abstract form that he became "obscure in attempting to be scientific." The reverse side of this coin was the conventional military treatise, which often so resembled a textbook in geometry that even a corporal's guard, it was said, dare not cross a ditch without the aid of a logarithmic table. To illustrate complicated operations with Euclidean diagrams was to distort and oversimplify.

The student who is presented with a page of simple figures, squares, angles, or semi-circles with a few radii, and told that these are explanations of the art of war, is apt to ask if military problems can really be dealt with in this compendious fashion. He is told perhaps that when two strokes representing armies are placed in a certain way within two lines forming an angle, the one army has a great advantage over the other. But when he comes to apply this proposition to an actual campaign, which he follows on a map embracing extensive territories, covered with a network of roads, and diversified with innumerable accidents of ground, he finds . . . that he is at least as much bewildered as aided by his diagram. . . . [and] If . . . he is one of these facile disciples who accept implicitly whatever they find laid down by authority, it is evident that, in imagining he understands the art of war because he perceives the relations between sets of mathematical lines, he is in a fair way of becoming a pedant.[18]

Thus to read Napier without grasping the underlying theories, or to study some abstract treatise on theory while lacking the basic historical facts of the campaigns analyzed was in either case pointless and frustrating. The day had passed when an officer could be considered well informed by reading Napier in the same way that he had enjoyed Plutarch as a boy, free to "choose a side, drift with the course of the narrative, and accept the opinions of the historian." Now he must reduce the confusion of a campaign and the complexities of a map to manageable limits from which he could

---

[18] Hamley, *The Operations of War Explained and Illustrated* (Edinburgh, 1866), pp. 3–4.

deduce order and design. Unfortunately the average officer had not the time, if indeed he possessed the desire, to make a thorough study of the military literature even of a single period. The Napoleonic Wars, for example, would involve reading not only Napier and Jomini, but also the formidable works of writers such as Alison, Thiers, Gourgaud, Mathieu, Dumas, and Pelet, to mention only a few. *Wellington's Despatches* would have to be consulted; so would the biographies of generals like Messena, Ney, and Soult, and the accounts of others such as Foy and Marmont.[19]

Manifestly the only alternative for an officer who desired to be sufficiently grounded in military history to form theories of his own was to have someone else do it for him, and this was the intended function of Hamley's magnum opus, *The Operations of War*, which he completed early in 1866. He assumed that from the mass of historical records he could select campaigns and battles which would be "*representative* operations, each involving and illustrating a principle or fact, which, when elicited and fully recognized, will serve for future guidance." This would greatly simplify the problem that faced the new school of army officers after the Crimean War. Hamley would select and summarize, explain and illustrate in such a way that "a theory shall be formed on facts and experience which the student may confidently use for general application." With six years' experience in teaching military history at the Staff College and an unusual ability to handle technical problems clearly and succinctly, Hamley hoped that his book would clear new ground and enable the military student to study military history and current campaigns "with the confidence of one who does not grope and guess, but surveys and judges." [20]

The Operations of War is as original as most textbooks. Even the idea was not new, for ten years earlier MacDougall had written a similar text for students at Sandhurst in order "to render the study of the rules, which have been framed on the campaigns of the great masters of the art of war, easy and interesting." [21] Hamley's text was somewhat more comprehensive in scope and less dependent upon the work of Napier, but both were written with the same purpose in mind and both

19 *Ibid.*, p. 5.
20 *Ibid.*, p. vii.
21 MacDougall, *The Theory of War Illustrated by Numerous Examples from Military History* (3d ed.; London, 1862), Preface.

relied upon the case method to teach the principles of war. But in contrast to MacDougall, who had written a critique of Hannibal's campaigns, Hamley thought that it was "absurd to carry the reader back to times when the face of the earth was different, when armies were equipped and organized after another fashion, and when operations were conducted on methods long ago obsolete." Both writers, however, acted on the premise that the rules of war remain more or less constant, and in their works on theory they sought to explain and illustrate accepted rules rather than to arrive at any new precepts in strategy or tactics. In their later writings the differences between Hamley and MacDougall became more pronounced.

Hamley commenced his treatise with a discussion of the modern conditions of war in which, after a brief historical sketch of the main developments since the Middle Ages, he stressed the influence of communications on military operations. He then analyzed the conditions that usually preceded the opening of a campaign—the relative advantages and differences between the offensive and defensive, the selection of an object, and the considerations governing the choice of a theater and line of operations. In the third and fourth sections he concentrated upon the rules of strategy, explaining each carefully and summarizing pertinent campaigns to illustrate the various difficulties and alternatives involved. He concluded with a section on tactics and the minor operations of war.

Because Hamley has been credited with doing "more than any other Englishman to make known to English officers the value of a methodical treatment of the study of campaigns," [22] an examination of his method is in order. It becomes at once apparent that Hamley's approach was better calculated to reaffirm established truths than to discover new ones. *The Operations of War* was effective as a pedagogical technique to teach students the meaning of accepted principles; it was bound to be less successful, however, in preparing them to adjust to the changing conditions of war.

A second point is that Hamley's method of investigation was dangerously deceptive. For instance, in discussing "the

[22] Colonel F. Maurice, *War: Reproduced with Amendments from the Article in the Last Edition of the "Encyclopaedia Britannica" to which Is Added an Essay on Military Literature and a List of Books with Brief Comments* (London, 1891), p. 9.

effect of operating on a front parallel to the line of communication with the base," Hamley stated the general problem, spent half-a-dozen pages summarizing the campaign of Novara in 1849, and deduced:

1st, That when one of two opposing armies is operating on a front parallel to the line communicating with its base, and the other on a front perpendicular to the line communicating with its base, the latter has acquired a great advantage over its adversary.

2d, The advantage is of the same kind whether the armies are concentrated or operating on extended fronts.

3d, The distance of the front of the army from its parallel line of communication, when the front is extended, and when the space between is devoid of defensible positions, does not prevent, but only postpones, the catastrophe.

4th, That it must be a great error to place an army in such a position, without reasonable prospect of a counterbalancing advantage.[23]

Hamley's deductions in this case happen to coincide with the teachings of the conventional authorities, but this fact should not obscure the possibility that they may also be the result of bad argument from analogy or authority. What scientist would accept Hamley's maxim that "when a powerful cavalry is supporting offensive movements, its commander should be allowed considerable discretionary power; but that the cavalry of an army which awaits its adversary, especially if inferior in force, should be constantly under the direction of the Commander-in-Chief," when the only evidence to support such a contention is a random quote from Napoleon, that exponent of the offensive, and a contrary opinion expressed by Wellington, who preferred the defensive? [24]

Because many of Hamley's tactical deductions rested on such a sandy foundation, he was unable at first to understand the evolution of tactics in the 1860's. If the principles of strategy remain constant, then a knowledge of proven maxims may be a useful guide to an understanding of warfare in the mid-nineteenth century, despite the introduction of the railroad and telegraph. But the change in tactics was more abrupt and far-reaching; and to understand the significance of these changes inductive reasoning was a far more reliable tool than deduction from principle or example.

[23] Hamley, *Operations of War*, p. 72.
[24] *Ibid.*, pp. 331–32.

This is one reason why Hamley had nothing new to say about tactics: insufficient knowledge of what had happened in America was another. As late as 1866 Hamley still thought in terms of the classical battles of Frederick and Napoleon. He was strongly influenced by Jomini—more so on the subject of tactics than strategy—and from his excellent summaries of Austerlitz, Waterloo, and Solferino (1859), he deduced that "in ordinary circumstances the formation in two continuous lines prevails," that "columns are the only formation for the advance and the attack except for a defensive line counter-attacking," and that the battalion columns advocated by Jomini "have been most resorted to and most successful." [25] The three battles he selected are admirable examples of these particular deductions, but unfortunately Hamley's conclusions had already been proven false by the Civil War armies and within months would have to be revised again as a result of the Prussian victory over Austria. Yet Hamley could write in 1866 that "it is easy to imagine the effect upon a defensive line, already thinned and shaken by the enemy's fire, when through the smoke it perceives compact columns swiftly advancing upon its shattered array," and assert that cavalry "has no power of exercising a decisive influence on an action by its fire. . . . Its power resides in the impetus of the charge." Indeed, his views on cavalry closely resemble those of Mitchell, for both claimed that during the Napoleonic Wars

in place of the resolute home charge, cavalry began to manoeuvre defensively, to resort to file-firing, and to halt to receive the enemy. . . . The combination of impetuosity with determination in the attack was no longer . . . the characteristic of the arm. In the last great wars originated the notion which now prevails, that the cavalry cannot break steady infantry; though it is clear that in no formation can infantry really withstand a cavalry charge pushed home, and that when horse fail to break foot, it is from moral, not physical causes.

Like many contemporaries though by no means all, Hamley held that Civil War cavalry "was confessedly unfit to take its place in the line of battle."

Let us grant that cavalry will, in certain cases, suffer more than formerly, but, as Napoleon used to say, omelettes cannot be made without the breaking of eggs. The losses must be compen-

[25] *Ibid.*, pp. 367–68.

sated by increased efficiency, exhibited in power of manoeuvring and determination in attack. Let us grant also that *bad* cavalry, when the lines are about to close, had better get out of the way; that merely *respectable* cavalry will, while supporting the other arms, effect nothing that can be considered decisive of a battle. But let it also be granted that cavalry, properly trained and led, may play as great a part as ever on the stage of war. Combined with new and larger proportions of artillery, its actions may be decisive of the fate of battles; and, launched in pursuit of a broken foe, it may finish a campaign which would else wade through fresh carnage to its woeful end.

He scarcely mentioned rifled artillery at all in the first edition of *The Operations of War* and, like Napier, he believed that "much of the influence of artillery is due to the moral effect produced by the rush of the projectiles overhead." [26]

Hamley's idea of modern battle resembled his description of the Napoleonic battles with but slight modifications. He anticipated that a line of skirmishers would cover the front, supported by massed batteries of artillery wherever the terrain permitted. Then would come a line of battalions deployed, followed by a line of battalions in double column of companies 250 yards to the rear, with the cavalry massed on the wings ready to provide the final blow, and a grand reserve of infantry and artillery 800 yards behind the second line.

The war of 1866 caused Hamley to modify some of his opinions. He now recognized the fact that the breech-loader "has established an uncontested superiority" even though its effects at Königgratz were evident only in a single episode of the battle. He also appreciated the fact that "infantry can now direct a far more formidable fire than heretofore on approaching cavalry, and may thus attain a relative superiority greatly beyond that formerly conferred by arms of precision," although he still claimed that there were moments when cavalry "might have been launched forth with decisive effect." But the real lesson of the war, Hamley contended, was to be found in the organization and direction of the Prussian army itself: "Give breechloaders to the Austrians, and let them fight the campaign again, still who would doubt the issue? [27]

The Seven Weeks War was taken into account in revising

[26] *Ibid.*, pp. 328, 335, 396, 398.
[27] "A Review of the Continental War," *Blackwood's*, C (1866), 257–58. Hamley, *Operations of War* (3d ed., Edinburgh, 1872), pp. 31, 48–50, 211–14.

the second edition of *The Operations of War,* but the Franco-Prussian conflict made what Hamley called "a thorough revision" necessary. In the sections on strategy Hamley did not so much revise as add new passages on the influence of the railroad on military operations. This too he could have learned from the Civil War—the Germans did—but it took the example of the Prussians to incite his interest. Because of the time required to load trains and the vulnerability of railroads to raids, Hamley concluded that the defense would probably benefit most from this new method of transport. But in no instance did the advent of the railroad alter his original views on strategy. He did state, however, that the electric telegraph (which also had been used in America) would influence future military operations, particularly by diminishing the disadvantages of operating with divided forces against a concentrated army, as the Prussians had done in 1866 and 1870.[28]

Charleston had taught MacDougall the realities of bombardments at unprecedented distances by rifled siege artillery and Vicksburg had shown him the value of earthworks and intrenched camps. It took the Franco-Prussian War, however, to convince Hamley that many places "formerly deemed strong . . . are now easily commanded, and consequently untenable" and that "for the same reason fortified towns, which were formerly safe from bombardment while their outworks were held, are now liable to destruction while the defences are still unbreached." After 1872 he too maintained that

unless fortified towns are surrounded, at a considerable distance, by a girdle of forts on commanding ground, they are worse than useless; and that the only kinds of permanent fortresses which are admissible are intrenched camps, such as Metz should have been, and hill-forts closing important places.[29]

With the exception of these changes, Hamley's view of

[28] The Prussians had begun to study the military possibilities of railroads even before the Civil War, and in 1864, directly influenced by the Civil War, they added a railway section to the great general staff. In May, 1866, on the eve of the war with Austria, the Prussian war minister created a field railway section modeled directly after the construction corps of the Union army and designed to perform similar functions. The best treatment of the subject by an English officer during the war was Captain H. W. Tyler, "Railways Strategically Considered," *R.U.S.I. Journal,* VIII (1864), 321–43.

[29] Hamley, *Operations of War* (3d. ed.), p. 309.

strategy remained substantially the same: all that he felt was needed to bring *The Operations of War* up to date was to include an account of the campaigns of Metz and Sedan. On the subject of tactics, however, it was not sufficient merely to replace Solferino with Wörth: it was necessary to rewrite completely the chapter on "Changes in Contemporary Tactics." Hamley discarded the maps previously used to illustrate his ideal preferred battle formations for he now perceived that "columns, while under rifle-fire, dissolved into swarms of skirmishers.

While moving across the space swept by rifle-fire, the pace was of necessity rapid, in order to baffle the enemy's aim, and to shorten the time of exposure to it; frequent halts to recover breath and order were indispensable, and these were made lying down. . . . These evolutions would have been impossible for a line, even could a line have existed under the enemy's fire. So it came to pass that whatever the original formation of the troops—Prussian company columns or French battalion columns—this was the order they were constrained to assume, under penalty of repulse or destruction. And the second line likewise . . . found its dissolution into skirmishers, or small groups where there was partial cover, imperative, as did the reserves which followed.[30]

As for the defense, Hamley predicted in 1872 that hasty fieldworks, which he had not even mentioned in his earlier edition, would be "of greatly-increased importance, and will certainly be extensively used in the next war." Now—but not until now—he cited the American battles where intrenchments had been successfully improvised.[31] As the defense turned to shelter and extended order, with supports and reserves protected from rifle fire, a frontal assault became "a desperate enterprise." Flank attacks combined with pressure along the entire front to prevent an enemy concentration at the point of contact offered the best means of success.

Hamley also shared MacDougall's belief that Prussian tactics had not been the best possible under the circumstances.

The history of the victories of the summer of 1870 is, that the German corps march straight for the enemy, that the leading troops at once attack, that the rest hurry up to their support, extending and deepening the skirmishing line, and that, after a

[30] *Ibid.*, pp. 422–23.
[31] *Ibid.*, pp. 458–59.

severe engagement, an extension beyond a flank renders the position untenable. There is none of the higher manoeuvring which aims at an advantage by deceiving and perplexing the enemy—no feint to retain him on one point while the decisive attack is prepared elsewhere. All is sheer straightforward fighting, successful because of the discipline and training and spirit of the units, and, in the end, because of the weight of numbers.

The Prussians had won, Hamley contended, not because their system was perfect, but because it was superior to that of the French, who had been uninspired and passive on defense and "desultory and devoid of an important general purpose" in their offensive efforts. But the recent battles had nothing to teach of "higher tactics which . . . effect great results with small loss, or make skill compensate for inferiority of force"; and such tactics, Hamley maintained, were no less desirable under present than under former conditions.[32]

Hamley also shared MacDougall's reservations about the German tactical organization, feeling that the independence of the companies might render higher maneuvering difficult. He did not, however, believe that rifled artillery would dominate future battles: if its firepower had been greatly augmented, that of the infantry had increased comparatively still more, and the smaller and more flexible attack formations and use of trenches on defense would diminish the effectiveness of artillery despite the significant improvements in range and accuracy. "The effect, therefore, of artillery on infantry—its only decisive effect, and the very reason of its existence—is less than it used to be." And this from an officer of the Royal Artillery! [33]

As for cavalry tactics, Hamley now admitted that cavalry no longer could hope to attack the front of prepared infantry in any formation. He thought that opportunities still remained for pursuing retiring infantry "dispirited and despairing beneath the stress of combat," but unfortunately there were no examples he could point to in the campaign of 1870. He also contended that cavalry could still attack massed artillery, but this too was a hope rather than a judgment based on recent experience. Hamley supported this argument by citing the well-known example of the charge of the Scots Greys upon the French batteries at Waterloo.

[32] *Ibid.*, pp. 425–26.
[33] *Ibid.*, p. 430.

In one respect, however, Hamley's thoughts on cavalry were undeniably progressive: he urged the formation of a force which would combine the mobility of cavalry with the firepower of infantry. Most of the early exponents of mounted infantry took their examples from the Civil War, where cavalry had been used essentially as mobile firepower, depending upon the horse primarily as a means of loccmotion and fighting most of the time with rifles on foot.[34] Hamley never mentioned American cavalry, but the experience of the Prussians convinced him of the desirability of forming a separate corps of mounted infantry to guard advanced posts, maneuver on the flanks of the enemy, and execute distant raids against his communications. Such a force "has not been seen on any modern European battle-field," but Hamley was convinced that it would, "at small cost, produce great results." [35] Doubtless, he would have been pleased with the accomplishments of mounted infantry during the Boer War; but whether he ever would have been prepared to admit that shock tactics must yield to firepower for all cavalry is doubtful.

After 1870 Hamley envisaged a different type of battle altogether, with Germany the obvious key to the future.

It is very evident that the present training of the Prussians is, and their future tactics probably will be, largely influenced by their great and unbroken successes. They confide in cavalry, because cavalry did so much for them in France; their belief in the virtue of offensive tactics is confirmed, since their onsets on the French always ended in victory. This is a point for serious consideration by a commander who may oppose them in the next war. It is not to be expected that any army will be better fitted for fighting, by organisation, discipline, training, or spirit, than the armies of Germany. Success must be sought elsewhere than in a manifest superiority of this kind; and will be found mainly in anticipating and preparing to meet the peculiarities of Prussian warfare in its latest developments. An antagonist defending his own territory against them may calculate on finding all their movements at first characterised by audacity, and should seek therein his ad-

[34] See "The Last Campaign in America," *United Service Magazine*, CIX (1865), 370; Major Henry Havelock, *Three Main Military Questions of the Day* (London, 1867); and Lieutenant Colonel George T. Denison, *Modern Cavalry: Its Organization, Armament, and Employment in War* (London, 1868), *passim*. Even the Duke of Cambridge had recognized by 1866 that "Probably the day of heavy cavalry has somewhat passed by" (*R.U.S.I. Journal*, IX [1866], 220).

[35] Hamley, *Operations of War* (3d ed.), pp. 434–36.

vantage. He should meet their reconnoitring cavalry with a well-maintained cordon of mounted riflemen. Knowing that their advanced guards will be eager to engage, he should draw them into attacks on his own, bringing up a force of mounted riflemen to turn the scale against the infantry, and of cavalry to attack the great battery which will presently be seeking to overwhelm him. Except with manifest advantages on his side, he should not at first imitate their tactics by seeking to engage, but await them in position, combining his defence with the offensive action of a detached force . . . which would receive its impulses from the general-in-chief by means of the telegraph. Should the enemy seek to turn his position . . . he may throw himself across the heads of their columns, confident of finding that their eagerness to engage will have caused them to extend unduly, and that he will be met, in the successive stages of his attack, by numbers constantly inferior to his own. If the intercepting movement be already completed before he can meet it, he may strike boldly at their rear with the certainty of finding there a vulnerable point. When about to become the assailant, he should manoeuvre to base himself anew, and threaten their communications; for though this may have been foreseen by the enemy, yet the sudden change must derange their plans, complicate their movements, and deprive them, for the time, of the initiative.[36]

Would it be unfair to say that Hamley was expecting the next war to be conducted along the lines of 1870? Like MacDougall, he claimed that it was possible to learn from military history, but whereas the former looked to history for guidance into the future, Hamley, it would appear, valued history as essential to a better understanding of the present. The one could detect almost revolutionary changes in warfare, particularly in tactics and siege operations; the other could never quite divorce himself from the past that he had studied and mastered. After his first book MacDougall thought more in terms of tactics and organization than strategy; Hamley remained essentially a strategist, or rather a teacher of strategy since he developed no strategical theories of his own and remained content to explain and illustrate the accepted maxims of theorists like Jomini and the Archduke Charles and practitioners such as Napoleon and Wellington. This he did very well, thanks to his grasp of the principles involved and his gift for condensation and narrative writing. But whenever he wrote about tactics, one can almost accuse him

[36] *Ibid.*, pp. 438–39.

of backing into the second half of the century of iron and steam with his eyes still focused, however sharply, on the past.

The Operations of War enjoyed unprecedented success. The *Times* claimed that it had no rival in the English language "for enlightened, scientific, and sober teaching in the general art of war"; Moltke called it a "valuable and interesting" work; Lee wrote from America requesting a copy; and Sherman—after pointing out to Hamley that he had not made sufficient allowance for local conditions—praised the quality of the book. It soon became the official text in the various British military colleges and in 1870 the second edition was adopted as the textbook in the department of military history at West Point.[37]

In the 1890's a reaction set in against the book as a military text. It was discontinued in 1894 as the sole text for the Staff College entrance examinations, and according to the officer who was then professor of military history at the Staff College, applicants since that date "have had to rely on their knowledge and observation; and the papers set . . . have aimed rather at discovering the measure of their capacity for hard thinking, and of their ability to apply principles to concrete cases, than the mere strength and accuracy of their memory." Despite the author's intentions to the contrary, *The Operations of War* gave some officers the impression of viewing strategy as a geometric art. Spenser Wilkinson, who was probably the first writer on military literature to take Hamley severely to task, claimed that "if we read his book as a series of definitions with illustrations . . . I do not think any better book of the sort exists in any language. But if you read General Hamley's book and stop there you will get a very distorted idea of the different campaigns, because his purpose is merely to illustrate from different campaigns what is meant by such expressions as 'interior lines.' . . ." Lieutenant Colonel G. F. R. Henderson, shortly to become famous for his biography of Stonewall Jackson, went even further in his criticism:

The methods by which the great generals bound victory to their colours are scarcely mentioned in the tactical text-books; and in

[37] Shand, *Hamley*, I, 183–92. The *Times* is quoted in *Punch*, XCIII (September 24, 1887), 139.

Hamley's "Operations of War" the predominating influence of moral forces in alluded to only in a single paragraph. In short, the higher art of generalship, that section of military science to which formations, fire, and fortifications are subordinate . . . has neither manual nor textbook.[38]

Despite this reaction, however, most British soldiers would probably have agreed with the sentiments of an eminent soldier when he wrote in 1896:

Of the repellent pedantry which characterises much military writing there is no trace. The student is irresistibly led onwards by the charm of the author's style, and the path lies always in the sunlight. In breadth of treatment, in grasp, and in logical completeness, *The Operations of War* has no equal. Only the works of Jomini and the Archduke Charles can be placed in the same category. Behind these eminent writers, however, lay great traditions; while Hamley conferred unaccustomed *prestige* on an army whose achievements in original authorship had been relatively meagre.[39]

The book went through five editions in Hamley's lifetime and in 1907 it was revised at army headquarters so that it still could serve as a primer on strategy. Other than adding or interpolating a few paragraphs referring to the latest conditions, nothing was done to revise Hamley's sections on strategy. An entirely new section on the recent war between Russia and Japan replaced the old essay on tactics, but these were the only changes deemed necessary, and *The Operations of War* was reprinted periodically until 1923. Thus it is no exaggeration to say that Hamley continued to instruct the British officer in the rudiments of strategy until well into our own era.

Hamley was no longer at the Staff College when *The Operations of War* was completed, having been ordered in 1864 to rejoin his regiment upon promotion to lieutenant colonel of artillery. He spent eighteen months at Dover, where he found ample time to reflect upon his lectures at the Staff College and organize his material for the book. In December, 1865, the Duke of Cambridge nominated him to fill an

[38] *R.U.S.I. Journal*, XLI (1898), 707–9, 711, 718; Henderson, "Strategy and Its Teaching," *ibid.*, XLII (1898), 767.
[39] George Sydenham Clarke, Baron Sydenham of Combe, "The Life of General Sir Edward Bruce Hamley," *Quarterly Review*, XLXXXIV (1896), 9.

impending vacancy on the Council of Military Education, which had been established in 1857 to select examiners and prepare examinations for entry to the army and the Staff College and for promotion, and to recommend staff appointments for the several military colleges. Hamley served in this capacity until the council was abolished in 1870, when he became commandant of the Staff College.

Here he probably spent seven of the happiest years of his life. He was by this time a well-known figure; he was given practically a free hand in running the Staff College, and he much preferred this type of work to regimental duty of any kind. These were also perhaps his most fruitful years. In 1869 a Royal Commission "to enquire generally into the present state of Military Education, and to report especially upon the Course of Instruction in the Staff College" had noted in its *Report* that "expectations entertained of the Staff College had not quite been fulfilled," that the institution was "not popular with the Army, and sometimes failed to attract those most likely to prove good Staff Officers." Three months before Hamley returned to the Staff College, the regulations were revised to make possible some of the changes recommended by the commission, and it fell to Hamley to implement the necessary reforms. Within a year he "had infused a completely new spirit into the College." Supported by Cardwell, who made possible an increased training grant, he greatly extended the practical studies in reconnaissance and military sketching; he placed a greater emphasis upon sports and particularly horsemanship (of the four officers dismissed after six months as incompetent for Staff duties, one was failed for his inability to ride); he had students participate in the autumn maneuvers and he stimulated indoor work by introducing the German *Kriegspiel*. Stiff in manner and a born autocrat, Hamley was not universally popular at the Staff College, but whatever his defects it is nonetheless true that he "revived it when it was in danger of perishing from infantile debility." [40]

Hamley's experience with field exercises at the Staff College account for his next two military publications. *A Chapter on Outposts* grew out of the need for a more suitable guide for officers to follow in selecting the best ground for a line of

[40] Godwin-Austen, *Staff and the Staff College*, pp. 156–66, 171–82; Shand, *Hamley*, I, 202–8.

outposts and assigning the most efficient number of sentries, pickets, and supports. *Staff College Exercises* was what the title implies—a series of theoretical problems based upon topographical maps and existing military conditions. Future staff officers, for example, were asked to make "the dispositions consequent on the disembarkation of a force, with the design of an immediate advance on a specified line." Where would be the most suitable place to meet the invading army? What advantages could the defensive force exploit? What special problems in tactics, reconnaissance, and logistics had to be solved? Both volumes are too technical and detailed to warrant more than a passing mention, but Hamley's book on outposts led to an incident that may have had a bearing on his subsequent career. The officer commanding at Aldershot at the time wished to apply his theory on outposts in maneuvers, and a number of officers, among them the Duke of Cambridge, came to observe. Hamley later complained that his system, the essence of which was a flexible division of the outpost zone into sectors with sentries, pickets, and supports all from the same unit, never received a fair trial. He was not permitted to select his own ground, he had no previous opportunity to acquaint the troops and officers with his system, and although Hamley himself professed satisfaction with the experiment the opinions of the umpires were never solicited and the Duke of Cambridge made it obvious that he opposed the innovation. With more sense of humor, Hamley might well have smiled at an instance of tactics defined as "the opinion of the senior officer present." As it was, he bitterly complained that he had not received sufficient encouragement "to induce me to extend my enquiries . . . either practically or theoretically." [41] This was not the last time that peacetime drill would stifle evolutions better suited to wartime conditions.

We come now to the most controversial period in Hamley's career. In 1877 his tour of duty at the Staff College was over, and although he was generally acknowledged to have been a successful commandant, Hamley received no important military command for the next five years. For two years he

[41] *Ibid.*, pp. 238–43; Godwin-Austen, *Staff and the Staff College*, pp. 179–80; *R.U.S.I. Journal*, XXV (1882), 458. Hamley, *A Chapter on Outposts* (Edinburgh, 1875), went through two editions before it was incorporated into the 1876 edition of *The Operations of War. Staff College Essays* (Edinburgh, 1875) was better received by the Duke of Cambridge.

remained unemployed altogether. In 1879, as he was about to visit Italy, he was sent to the Balkans as the English commissioner for the delimitation of the Turkish and Bulgarian frontier following the redistribution of the territories Russia had recently conquered from Turkey by the Great Powers at the Congress of Berlin. Why he should have been thus sidelined is not clear: one admirer claims that it was because he "stood outside the dominant military clique" and was known moreover "to be somewhat bluntly outspoken." [42] But the so-called clique was that group of officers headed by Wolseley and known a few years later as the "Wolseley Ring," [43] and it was Wolseley himself who was responsible for obtaining the command of an army corps for Hamley in the autumn maneuvers in 1882.

The chief opposition to Hamley seems to have come from the Duke of Cambridge, who had come to tolerate rather than support the Staff College by the time Hamley was commandant: altogether too many products of the institution were associated with the new army school and worked for reforms that the Duke felt were unnecessary. MacDougall had been able to get along with the Duke and so even had Wolseley, for all his differences with His Royal Highness. Although Wolseley and the Duke each looked upon the other with a mixture of affection and mistrust, on most occasions the two somehow had managed to pull together in harness.[44] Hamley, however, lacked the charm of MacDougall and the tact and patience of Wolseley, and probably his reforms at the Staff College had alienated the commander in chief if his mannerisms had not done so already. We are told that the Duke "mercilessly lashed Hamley with vigorous destructive sarcasm" in front of the other officers who had witnessed the trial of Hamley's system of outposts at Aldershot,[45] which would indicate the presence of personal antipathy; and in all probability Hamley's enforced idleness after he left the Staff College was due in large measure to the hostility of the commander in chief. His feud with Wolseley and his satellites had its roots in the Egyptian campaign of 1882.

Hamley did not command a corps in the 1882 maneuvers

[42] Sydenham, "Life of General Sir Edward Bruce Hamley," p. 12
[43] See below, pp. 169, 173–74.
[44] Wolseley to Lady Wolseley, February 1, 1887; October 9, 1890; June 4, 1894; August 23, 1895 (Wolseley Papers).
[45] Godwin-Austen, *Staff and the Staff College,* p. 180.

after all; instead Wolseley chose him to command one of the two divisions destined for the expedition to Egypt. Hamley naturally was "extremely pleased" with the appointment—his first with the fighting army in over a quarter of a century— and he wrote to his friend Blackwood that Wolseley "has been most friendly in the matter, without solicitation." Presumably, Wolseley selected Hamley in the first instance because of his reputation as the foremost representative of English military thought, but he took Hamley to Egypt because of his desire to use the same troops and commanders designated for the maneuvers to have been held that fall.[46] Probably this explains why there were so many generals—eighteen—for the number of troops: with one general for every 900 men and two who felt responsible for determining the strategy of the campaign, there was bound to be friction.

It was not long in developing. Hamley had been on the scene scarcely a day when he offered gratuitous advice to Wolseley. According to Hamley's diary, Wolseley seemed politely interested up to a point but showed no desire to pursue the subject. For his own part, Hamley's attitude is best revealed in his statement: "If I call myself a strategist, I ought to behave as such." By nature a prima donna and by reputation an eminent strategist, he evidently believed that he was a sort of English Moltke sent to Egypt, not merely to command a division, but to act as adviser if not mentor to Wolseley. Wolseley's staff resented his presumption: "He has seen nothing, considered nothing, investigated nothing," one of the "Ring" later wrote,

but the moment he meets that commander he has a plan of campaign ready to loftily "suggest" to him. Those persons who had ever seen Sir Edward Hamley will not have any difficulty in forming a mental picture of the manner and method to which a "suggestion" would have been likely to emanate from him.[47]

If Wolseley was as annoyed on this occasion as some members of his Ring, he gave no sign; he did, however, relish

[46] Hamley to William Blackwood, July 29, 1882 (Blackwood Papers); Major General Sir John Adye, *Soldiers and Others I Have Known* (London, 1925), pp. 58, 60. The expeditionary force comprised two divisions of infantry, one of cavalry, and "the appropriate amount of artillery and engineers," a total of roughly 12,000.

[47] W. F. Butler, "Hamley and the Egyptian Campaign," *Contemporary Review*, LXVIII (1895), 217; Godwin-Austen, *Staff and the Staff College*, p. 200; Shand, *Hamley*, II, 86–87.

the thought that Hamley and his brigade commanders "are under the firm conviction that we mean to attack here [Aboukir Bay] on Sunday and that they are to take part in the attack. I am leaving sealed orders to be opened by Hamley at daybreak on Sunday . . . in which I tell him the whole thing is a humbug and that my real destination is the Canal." [48] Hamley's indignation at being thus deceived, along with the correspondents of the press, can be imagined. His pride was injured still further at the thought of being left behind.

On September 1 Hamley rejoined the main army at Ismailia. Wolseley, who meanwhile had written him a lengthy letter explaining the reasons for misleading him on the proposed landing in Aboukir Bay (he also had deceived his own superior, the Duke of Cambridge, as to his intentions), received Hamley cordially and invited him to breakfast, an invitation that Hamley refused on the ground that the two "could not have talked . . . on business at table." To meet Hamley's complaint that his division now comprised only a single brigade, the other having been left as a diversion at Alexandria, Wolseley assigned another brigade to the second division, but this failed to conciliate either Hamley or his biographer, who writes revealingly:

In his opinion he had been seriously crippled on the eve of an important engagement, on which his soldierly reputation and professional prospects were at stake. A long-desired opportunity had come to him at last, and failure, or even incomplete success, would have cast a cloud on the rest of his existence. [49]

As it turned out, this is precisely what happened. Tel-el-Kebir was fought and won in the early dawn, after a hazardous night march of five-and-one-half miles across the desert. The second division fought well, and in the first streaks of light, after the initial attack had faltered, Hamley's tall figure could be seen "on horseback in the press of foot-combatants, and his deep voice of command was heard above the confusion of the strife, as, seizing the broken bits of battle, he threw them again upon the enemy," reaching if not surpassing "the ideal of strength and efficiency he had so often, in his mental appraisement of self, previously attained." And that, our eyewitness assures us, "is saying much." [50] Unfortunately Hamley was not satisfied. His own

48 Wolseley to Lady Wolseley, August 18, 1882 (Wolseley Papers).
49 Shand, *Hamley*, II, 111.
50 Butler, "Hamley and the Egyptian Campaign," p. 223.

services had not been acknowledged, he claimed, and the contribution of his division was slighted in Wolseley's official report of the action; why, Wolseley had not even congratulated him for his role in the victory! Hamley submitted a lengthy report which Wolseley did not forward with his own dispatches, an act that Hamley interpreted as "a systematic attempt to rob troops and their leader of the credit due to them." He was humiliated further when he returned to England and discovered that many did not know what he had done in the battle. Had Wolseley been as generous in extending official recognition to his subordinates as his great rival Roberts in India, Hamley explained to Blackwood, he would not have felt himself in so embarrassing a position.[51]

So incensed was Hamley, in fact, that he violated professional etiquette and published his own official report of the battle, an act that even his admirers found difficult to defend. We need not concern ourselves with the charges and countercharges of the ensuing controversy; the battle flared up anew when Hamley's biographer attempted shortly after his death to readjust the reputations earned at Tel-el-Kebir. Colonel Frederick Maurice, the official historian of the campaign and editor of the rejuvenated *United Service Magazine*, rushed to see his old chief Wolseley and subsequently published two articles in his journal castigating Hamley and giving Wolseley's side of the affair.[52] Sir William Butler, another of Wolseley's lieutenants, similarly accused Hamley of attempting to substitute his own name for that of Wolseley as the victor of Tel-el-Kebir. Hamley's friends rushed to his defense in a battle that failed to enhance the reputations of any of the men involved. Most soldiers probably sided with Wolseley. The *Broad Arrow*, which at first tried to remain neutral, eventually tired of the controversy and indorsed "almost every word and expression" in Butler's article attacking Hamley, claiming that the latter was "professorial, dogmatic, . . . and difficult . . . to get along with," an "angry man with an exaggerated opinion of his own capacity as a commander." [53] Hamley's supporters were embarrassed to find their own position betrayed by Alexander Innis Shand, who had been

[51] Hamley to William Blackwood, October 10, 1882; November 9, 1883 (Blackwood Papers). Shand, *Hamley*, II, 122–23; Godwin-Austen, *Staff and the Staff College*, p. 202.

[52] See below, p. 214 n.

[53] *The Broad Arrow: The Naval and Military Gazette*, LV (July 6, 1895), 1–3; (August 3, 1895), 131; (August 17, 1895), 158.

asked to write the biography of Hamley and had rushed headlong into the battle without proper reconnaissance of the facts. Even Shand's dispositions were faulty, for before the volumes were published he admitted privately that he had suppressed those scenes "which show Hamley's violent temper and vindictiveness." In the course of the controversy, Shand discovered that he had been misled by the Hamley family, particularly the possessive niece who controlled the papers and, being an honest man, he retracted some of his statements publicly. The family was furious and published its own answer to Maurice; as for Shand, he was convinced that he had gained nothing and lost everything—"friends, reputation, the literary pursuits"—by relying solely upon Hamley's family and friends in trying to rehabilitate his memory.[54]

Hamley returned to London in the middle of October, 1882. Although he found supporters within the army—his good friend MacDougall, his old chief in the Crimea, Sir Richard Dacres, and Sir George Chesney—he was clearly out of favor with the Wolseleyites, and Wolseley, who as adjutant general was probably the most powerful man in the War Office next to the commander in chief, was in a position to end Hamley's military career for all practical purposes. He had found Hamley "to be quite useless and impossible as a Commander" and had come to despise him for his conduct after the war: "As soon as I find I have made a mistake," Wolseley wrote on another occasion, "I drop them remorselessly." So Hamley was dropped; at least he received no active employment for the next five years. He then was due to be retired from the service, but public indignation, reflected in the *Times* and a pungent

[54] A. I. Shand to John Blackwood, February 5, 1895; August 14, 1895; Maurice to Shand, August 5, 1895; Barbara Hamley to Blackwood, May 15, 1895; July 30, 1895; October 29, 1895; Edward Hamley to Blackwood, October 1, 1895 (Blackwood Papers). Letters by Maurice and Shand are printed in the *Times*, August 14, 1895. For the detractors of Hamley, see the Butler article, already cited, and Maurice, "Sir E. Hamley and Lord Wolseley," *United Service Magazine*, XI, N.S. (1895), 414–38, 439–63. Hamley's side is presented in the Sydenham article previously cited and also in A. C. Gleig, "Sir Edward Hamley," *Gentleman's Magazine*, CCLXXIX (1895), 515–25; and especially A. Allardyce, "Life of Sir E. B. Hamley," *Blackwood's*, CLVIII (1895), 583–608. The latter represents the family's point of view. Even before Shand's public withdrawal Wolseley received a letter informing him that "the feeling about the Hamley case is veering around very strongly in your favour, and even the Broad Arrow, which was the bitterest of all has come round" (——— to Wolseley, August 3, 1895 [Wolseley Papers]). A more recent confirmation is found in Godwin-Austen, *Staff and the Staff College*, p. 202.

cartoon in *Punch,* encouraged the officials to retain Hamley on the active list even though he was never again employed.[55]

Hamley turned therefore to politics. "Conservative to the core," [56] he was elected in 1885 and returned the following year as a member of Parliament for Birkenhead, which gave him a platform from which he could air his views on defense issues for the next seven years. He also continued to pursue his literary interests in *Blackwood's,* while at the Royal United Service Institution and in the pages of the *Nineteenth Century* he advocated policies pertaining to the defense of India and home defense, both of which were live issues in the 1880's.

Hamley deserves to be remembered during these years as the celebrated champion of the English volunteers. In the Commons he spoke repeatedly on their behalf, opposing any motion to place heavier demands on the volunteers, yet urging more practical training. He would have a greater proportion of time devoted to exercising in extended order; he wanted more firing practice at more realistic distances; he urged the government to provide more in the way of uniforms, ammunition, and supplies "and to construct and fill the necessary depots and magazines on all possible lines of invasion." Above all, he demanded that the training of the volunteer organizations be brought into line with the requirements for defense. In theory the volunteers were intended to free the regular army of garrison duty in the event of a national emergency; why not drill them, then, in garrison duties as well as in the evolutions prescribed by regulations. Let the rifles actually man the defenses and furnish the guards in a nearby fort; instruct volunteer artillery by giving them adequate practice with heavy ordnance; teach the engineer volunteers how to intrench positions; train the yeomanry as mounted infantry, which would "add immensely to their value as a national force." "Most readers," he concluded

will be astonished to find what a weapon we hold, and what we might achieve with it. . . . In endeavouring to complete its efficiency I have suggested nothing which would not make us a large return for a small outlay [Hamley estimated that one million pounds would suffice]. We might make a beginning at once, and

[55] *Ibid.,* pp. 202–3, 214; Wolseley to Lady Wolseley, June 15, 1895 (Wolseley Papers); *Punch* (September 24, 1887), p. 139; Shand, *Hamley,* II, 225–26.
[56] Sydenham, "Life of Hamley," p. 20.

so give the world a much-needed assurance that we are a practical people capable of opposing the evils which threaten us. It is the fashion to call our navy our first line of defence; but this refers only to material means. Our first line of defence should be the respect of Europe.[57]

When Hamley presented these views in a lecture before the Royal United Service Institution in April, 1885, he precipitated what surely must have been the longest and most animated discussion in the history of that institution. For three consecutive sessions officers from the volunteers stood up to pay tribute to "the most scientific soldier of the British Army." Hamley, they noted, had not always favored volunteers "and has only been recently converted to appreciate their advantages." His speech had "a true patriotic ring which is above party." One volunteer officer exclaimed that he "could hardly have believed that so perfectly accurate and complete a description of the organization of the Volunteer Forces could have been given by a writer who has not himself belonged to it." Another thanked him for articulating the desires of the volunteers. Throughout nearly fifty printed pages of discussion there was nothing but praise for the masterly way in which the eminent strategist had brought the condition of the volunteer forces before a public that seemed as indifferent as it was misinformed.[58]

Hamley also championed the volunteers in the House of Commons. In the debates on army estimates he continued to press for larger expenditures for the volunteers and for the construction of defensive works around London "in which the Volunteers might most effectively co-operate with the regular troops." He supported most of the plans of Edward Stanhope, secretary of state for war, dissenting only in detail in which he felt the volunteers were being discriminated against. In general he believed that Stanhope's proposals were excellent "as far as they go," and quite possibly Hamley's insistence on the establishment "by competent authority, and in open day" of a "standard of our military establishments for the defence of the Kingdom and the Empire" contributed to the famous

[57] Hamley, "The Volunteers in Time of Need," *Nineteenth Century*, XVII (1885), 405–23. Hamley's arguments before Parliament were condensed for this article. See Shand, *Hamley*, II, 266–70.

[58] "Discussion on the Paper by Lieut.-General Sir Edward Hamley, K.C.B., on 'The Volunteers in time of need' in the 'Nineteenth Century,' for March, 1885," *R.U.S.I. Journal*, XXIX (1886), 629–87.

Stanhope Memorandum of 1891 defining the role of the auxiliary forces in the defense of England: in any event Stanhope paid lip service to Hamley's proposals while working on a scheme of his own.[59]

On the broader question of national defense, Hamley was one of many in the 1880's honestly convinced that there was a real danger of war and even of invasion. In 1886 the first mobilization scheme was devised; in 1887 Stanhope's Committee on Fortifications and Armaments of Military and Mercantile Ports, of which Hamley was a member, submitted its *Report;* in 1888 General Sir Henry Brackenbury produced his "Memorandum upon French Invasion"; and in 1889 Stanhope announced construction of a series of fortifications to protect London, while the Naval Defence Act that same year provided for a significant increase in the strength of the fleet.[60] Hamley spoke out vigorously for greater funds for defense. The government alone was not to blame for military inadequacies; public opinion must also be educated if Britain was to respond to the perils that threatened her. He carried his case to the public in three articles that appeared originally in the *Nineteenth Century* and later were published in book form.[61] Except in matters of detail, Hamley's proposals did not differ greatly from those argued by Burgoyne half a century before: he was against placing absolute reliance on the fleet as the first line of defense and he would defend London with a ring of intrenched positions held by volunteers especially designated and trained for the task, thus leaving the regulars free to take the field against the invader.[62]

Hamley also considered the question of imperial security.

[59] See *Session 1887. Debates, Questions, etc. on Army Affairs in Both Houses of Parliament during the Session of 1887* (reprinted from Hansard's *Parliamentary Debates*, Vols. CCX–CCCXXI, 1887), pp. 324–34; *Session 1888*, pp. 4–5, 143; *Session 1889*, pp. 154–59, 444; *Session 1890*, pp. 62–64, 86, 529–31 (cited hereafter as *Military Debates*). For details on the *Stanhope Memorandum* and the ferment that produced it, see Colonel John K. Dunlop, *The Development of the British Army 1899–1914: From the Eve of the South African War to the Eve of the Great War, with Special Reference to the Territorial Force* (London, 1938), pp. 12–14, 307; Verner, *Duke of Cambridge* II, 342–49. For Hamley's views in detail, see his letter to Stanhope, May 10, 1888, in Shand, *Hamley*, II, 253–58.

[60] Dunlop, *Development of the British Army*, p. 12; Verner, *Duke of Cambridge*, II, 342.

[61] See Hamley, *National Defense* (London, 1899).

[62] Hamley, "The Defencelessness of London," *Nineteenth Century*, XXIII (1888), 633–40 *passim*.

As early as 1878 he had suggested a "firm alliance" with Austria to curb Russian ambitions in the Far East, even while maintaining that with appropriate precautionary measures the English "might view calmly any possible complications" along the Indian North West Frontier. But by 1884 he had grown more concerned: conditions for a Russian invasion now struck him as "formidable" and he favored a more positive or "forward policy" toward Afghanistan. Thus Hamley indorsed the views of Roberts, with whom he corresponded spasmodically, rather than Wolseley, in determining the best strategy for the defense of India. Four years later he criticized the appointment of the Hartington Commission "to enquire into the Civil and Professional Administration of the Naval and Military Departments," on the ground that the need to investigate and consider imperial defense requirements was infinitely more critical. It was essential, he insisted, that some group of qualified experts determine the minimum standards for the maintenance of regular forces at home and abroad, the creation of adequate reserves, the formation of an expeditionary force and the accumulation of supplies and ammunition sufficient to meet any crisis. Hamley made no pretense of knowing all of the correct answers, but he knew what questions ought to be raised and he did indicate the complexities of the problem.[63]

Hamley's last literary effort of any importance was *The War in the Crimea*, which he completed in July, 1890. It does not represent any significant change in the views he expressed in his letters from Sebastopol published in *Blackwood's* some thirty-five years before, but it remains today one of the best books ever written on the subject. The *Athenaeum* acknowledged it as a happy marriage of Hamley's "recognized mastery of the art of war" and his "very judicial frame of mind." His style, which had rendered technical aspects of the operations of war palatable and even interesting, revived the horrors, excitement, and frustrations of the Crimean War for a generation that had experienced only colonial campaigns and punitive expeditions. Most of the old soldiers probably agreed

---

[63] Hamley, "The Armies of Russia and Austria," *ibid.*, III (1878), 844–62; "The Strategical Conditions of Our Indian Northwest Frontier," *R.U.S.I. Journal*, XXII (1879), 1027–38; "Russia's Approaches to India," *ibid.*, XXVIII (1884), 395–418; "The Minimum Force Requisite for Security," *Nineteenth Century*, XXIV (1888), 789–98. Wolseley's views are summarized in Major General Sir Frederick Maurice and Sir George Arthur, *The Life of Lord Wolseley* (New York, 1924), p. 89.

with Sir Archibald Alison, commander of the Highland Brigade under Hamley at Tel-el-Kebir and his successor at the Staff College, when he described it as "really the most charming and the most able book that Hamley ever wrote. It has all his singular clearness and precision of style, and all the breadth and justice of his deep military thought." [64]

Hamley's last years were disappointing and bitter. He never fully recovered from the blow to his prestige at Tel-el-Kebir and he overlooked no opportunity to criticize Wolseley. On one occasion he utilized a review of a biography of Roberts written by a "Mr. Low, the same who wrote a biography of Wolseley of the most feebly fulsome kind," as a vehicle to attack Wolseley; when Sir Charles Wilson was criticized for his role in the abortive attempt to relieve Gordon in the Sudan, Hamley accused Wolseley of once again failing to acknowledge the services of a subordinate and recommended to his friend Wilson that he publish his own journal of the campaign.[65] In blaming Gladstone for the slaughters in the Sudan, he even claimed that the prime minister had taken credit from the Scots regiments in the Second Division at Tel-el-Kebir in order to increase proportionately the accomplishments of Irish regiments and thus flatter the Irish people.[66] (Another article in the same issue was entitled, appropriately, "A Vendetta"!)

Nor did Hamley ever fully recover from a severe attack of bronchitis which, beginning in 1888, recurred sporadically until his death in 1893. Gradually he withdrew from active political life and writing became increasingly difficult. His last article was a contribution to the *Pall Mall Gazette* on Irish Home Rule which he opposed on military grounds.

MacDougall's private life and much of his military career remain hidden from sight, but his accomplishments are easily appraised: with Hamley the reverse is true. His life and character are revealed—sometimes unwittingly—in a lengthy biography; he was well known to London society and often he was in the public eye; he was, in fact, much better known than MacDougall and on the surface a more conspicuous success.

[64] *Athenaeum*, November 29, 1890, p. 730; Shand, *Hamley*, II, 294–95.
[65] "Low's Life of Sir Frederick Roberts," *Blackwood's*, CXXIV (1883), 776–89; "Gordon, Wolseley, and Sir Charles Wilson," *ibid.* CXXXVII (1885), 872–79; Colonel Sir Charles M. Watson, *The Life of Major-General Sir Charles William Wilson* (London, 1909), pp. 354–55.
[66] "The Slaughters in the Soudan," *Blackwood's*, CXXXV (1884), 404.

Yet there is something enigmatic about Hamley; despite his obvious popularity and success he was in many respects—probably most in his own estimation—a partial failure. He never quite fulfilled the early promise he had shown at the time of the Crimean War and his first appointment to the Staff College. *The Operations of War* was by every standard a successful book, but in the final analysis it created a public image of the author as the peerless strategist which the Egyptian campaign failed to preserve, let alone enhance. His work as commandant of the Staff College bore tangible results, yet to Hamley it brought two subsequent years of unemployment and then the thankless task of helping to settle a boundary dispute far removed from his books and literary friends and of greater concern to the Foreign than to the War Office. His only opportunity for command in the field contributed more to Wolseley's fame than to his own and abruptly ended his active military career. He entered Parliament too late to achieve the position he had expected, and his literary ability, although genuine, never placed him among the literary elite. He failed even to convince his biographer of his greatness, for poor Shand's letters to his publishers are full of incidents and references to Hamley's shortcomings that had to be suppressed in deference to the family's wishes and to avoid, as Roberts had warned, stirring up "a hornet's nest" that would add new injuries to his reputation.[67]

But if Hamley was a partial failure by his own standards or expectations, there were many contemporaries who considered him an undoubted success. "Hamley will be best remembered," it was predicted, "as the most brilliant military writer that this country has yet produced, and as a teacher who set before the British Army a new standard of attainment."

Hamley set a new intellectual standard, awakened dormant thought, and showed the way to an independent judgment. It is just to say that the uprising of a national military literature was due to the stimulus he supplied, and that the increasing band of writers who now represent with credit the intelligence of the Army draw their inspiration largely from "The Operations of War."[68]

No English military writer in the nineteenth century equaled Hamley in prestige, and there were many who interpreted his

[67] Shand to Blackwood, August 1, 1895 (Blackwood Papers).
[68] Sydenham, "Life of Hamley," pp. 10, 23.

failure to find military employment during the five years before Tel-el-Kebir to his "dangerous reputation for ability" among conventional soldiers at the War Office,[69] and attributed his subsequent troubles to the jealous intrigues of the Wolseley clique, feeling that despite his contentious disposition Hamley could not have been his own worst enemy as long as Wolseley and the Duke of Cambridge were around.

Ignoring the personalities and discounting the claims of his friends and supporters, claims which sometimes prove only that those who preceded Hamley had been even more neglected and unappreciated, what should be the verdict of history upon Hamley's contributions to English military thought? *The Operations of War* is unquestionably one of the most significant books ever written by a British soldier, if only because it was so widely known and frequently quoted. Although it contained no original strategical views and was conservative and occasionally wide of reality in its tactical deductions, at the very least it did define terms and frame the important issues, and it did, as Maurice has stated, popularize "the value of a methodical treatment" in the study of war.

In many ways it is unfortunate that Hamley did not devote more of his talents to military history: his account of Marengo brightened the otherwise dull pages of the *Journal of the Royal United Service Institution* when it appeared in 1860,[70] while his history of the Crimean War written thirty years later deserves to stand beside the narratives of Napier and a later successor at the Staff College, Colonel G. F. R. Henderson. His mastery of the principles of war together with a pen that could describe a sunset as graphically as a turning movement would have enabled him to develop into one of the truly great military historians. His friend MacDougall, who appreciated Hamley's rare talent, urged him to channel his energies in this direction, but he preferred instead to dabble with poetry, literary criticism, and book reviews: in place of a biography of Napoleon or Moltke, he wrote about Voltaire and Carlyle, which at once frustrated his friends and alienated his fellow officers. "As a soldier at the Staff College, Hamley was a civilian; as a civilian in his literary club, he was a soldier," Sir

---

[69] See Hamley's obituary in the *Athenaeum*, August 19, 1893, p. 261.
[70] Hamley, "The Campaign of Marengo," *R.U.S.I. Journal*, IV (1860), 25–44.

William Butler has observed; "and equally in college or club he was an autocrat." [71]

Hamley deserves to be remembered for his accomplishments at the Staff College. Perhaps he was not a provocative teacher; he seems at least to have been a thorough one, respected if not adored by those who went through the Staff College in the sixties. Hamley's reforms as commandant saved the institution, even though a later generation—the same that criticized the pedantic tone of *The Operations of War*—found it necessary to rejuvenate the teaching, and pour, in the metaphor of the historian of the Staff College, new wine into old bottles.[72]

Hamley is significant for still another reason, one so obvious that it often is overlooked. He was the first military writer of any consequence in England to write specifically for the public. His letters from Sebastopol were inspired in part by a desire to instruct the public in the complexities of the problems encountered in the Crimea. His articles after the war were written in the conviction that he was one of the few, the very few, soldiers who could write and writers who understood soldiering, and *The Operations of War* was intended to educate soldier and civilian alike. Hamley never retreated behind obscure pseudo-scientific language in describing a military movement or analyzing a campaign. His reputation as a writer undoubtedly helped to prepare the way into the field, and he had the additional good fortune of writing at a time when the public, aroused by the disasters in the fifties and stimulated by the German successes in the following decade, had "displayed an unwonted interest in the army." Hamley was instrumental in recruiting what John Blackwood liked to think of as "the military staff" of his magazine: C. C. Chesney, Sir George Chesney, Sir Archibald Alison, Colonel Henry Knollys, Sir John Adye, MacDougall, and Maurice, all in one way or another owed their start in *Blackwood's* to Hamley.[73]

Consequently, throughout most of his military career Hamley had a large public following. The *Times* applied pressure to have him made commandant of the Staff College in 1870

[71] Butler, "Hamley and the Egyptian Campaign," p. 224.
[72] See Godwin-Austen, *Staff and the Staff College,* pp. 195–234.
[73] Hamley, *Operations of War* (3d ed.), p. viii; Porter, *John Blackwood,* p. 267.

and, together with *Punch,* fought to have him retained when
the attempt was made to superannuate him in 1887. His
vigorous support of the volunteers naturally won for him new
followers in the auxiliary forces, and he was a familiar figure
in the clubs of Pall Mall and St. James. Wolseley was known
in the late Victorian Age as Britain's "only general"; to many
officers not admitted to Wolseley's select circle, Roberts
became "our only other general," but the public looked upon
Hamley as "the great strategist" and could not understand
why he was less successful with his sword than with the
pen.

His personality was one reason: as his biographer discovered, "there is not one of Hamley's friends—not even his
aide-de-camp . . . who is attached and devoted to him—who
does not tell something of his harshness and hasty temper." [74]
His lack of rapport with the Duke of Cambridge and his feud
with the "Wolseley Ring" was another. Many soldiers doubtless would have agreed with Sir William Butler, who offered
still another explanation:

> On one hand he found himself in the position of an absolute
> despot, whose schoolmaster word no staff-student dared venture
> to call in question. On the other he was completely removed from
> the practical soldiering of his time, and from contact with scores
> of hard-headed soldiers who, if they had not a tenth part of
> Hamley's knowledge of theory, had had a hundred times his
> experience of actual campaigning." [75]

And besides, what would the typical fighting soldier be
expected to make of a man who, despite his reputation for
personal bravery, had preferred the company of women and
cats in garrison life and was seen more often in literary than
military circles in London, and who in addition wrote poetry!
Similar literary tastes, as General Sir Ian Hamilton and Field
Marshal Earl Wavell could testify, were an imposing handicap
in the British army even in our own century.

We hear often of the "military mind" (as though soldiers
could ever be of one mind) and how it is typically conventional, conservative, suspicious, and even intolerant of new
ideas. Hamley's friends and supporters sometimes maintained that he was a victim of this antiquated outlook, an

[74] Shand to Blackwood, August 1, 1895 (Blackwood Papers).
[75] Butler, "Hamley and the Egyptian Campaign," pp. 214–15.

English Clausewitz or Jomini who struggled vainly against the forces of darkness in the War Office. "Time will bring its gentle revenge, and the lack of Algerian prestige [a reference here to the new generals of the Second French Empire and Wolseley's own rise to fame in Africa], which possibly militated against Hamley's career, will seem a pitifully small thing in view of the rich legacy which he has bequeathed to the army." [76]

Unfortunately for those who would take this view, it was not Hamley's theories that were new or different and therefore unacceptable: the men of originality already were in the War Office, and Hamley's ideas were never so radical or unorthodox as to represent a threat to any of them. In Hamley's case it was not the strategist and military writer who was discriminated against—rather it was the man himself, and particularly the man Hamley conceived himself to be. Hamley was unacceptable, but not his ideas! This is perhaps the greatest irony in the career of Britain's most famous pedagogue of strategy.

[76] Sydenham, "Life of Hamley," p. 23.

PART III THE WOLSELEY ERA
1873–99

I<small>N</small> 1873, when Sir Garnet Wolseley was sent to command a small expedition against the Ashanti in west Africa, the British army entered a new era. To some the success of the campaign seemed to vindicate the recent reforms; for Wolseley, forty years of age and a major general, it brought recognition and promising opportunities; and the hand-picked group of officers who had accompanied him to the Gold Coast followed "our only general" to still greater fame and power. The Wolseley Ring, as they were called, became the dominant clique within the army, both in the field and at the War Office. Although the Duke of Cambridge remained the military head until 1895, the prime mover within the army was Wolseley, who succeeded the Duke of Cambridge as commander in chief only to find the office stripped of much of its former power. By the time old age, dissension, and Boer victories finally allowed others to crash this charmed circle, the army had taken on a new character.

The issues that divided soldiers also were different. Although there was by no means universal agreement on the subject of tactics, the appearance of texts such as Home's *Modern Tactics* (1873) and Clery's *Minor Tactics* (1875)[1] implied a consensus, and few changes were made in the drill or the tactics of the British army after 1880 except in the direction of simplification. Because there were no wars

[1] Colonel Robert Home, *A Précis of Modern Tactics* (London, 1873); Lieutenant Colonel Clery, *Minor Tactics* (London, 1875).

between the Continental powers during the Wolseley Era, the campaigns of 1870 continued to dominate military thinking, and, hence, no abrupt departure in tactics was possible without some reappraisal of Prussian methods. (Nor were the small wars in Africa and Asia likely to stimulate a revolution in tactics.) For this reason military history became a useful tool to enable progressive soldiers to understand present trends and even, in a vague sort of way, to peer into the future. Wolseley himself was a prolific historian.

The Cardwell Reforms did not remedy all organizational shortcomings overnight. Recruiting remained a problem despite improved living conditions for the rank and file; short service found many critics; and the joining of regiments together in pairs under a territorial designation in 1881 in an effort to convert "a collection of regiments into an army" offended regimental pride.[2] But most reformers were content to work for greater efficiency within the framework provided by Cardwell. What they sought was an effective scheme for mobilization, the preparation of an army corps for service abroad, the establishment of something akin to the Army Service Corps to facilitate supply, the formation of a general staff, and better co-ordination between the services. They worked also to improve the instruction of officers, the training of soldiers, and the quality of the militia and volunteers.

Most of all, thoughtful soldiers were concerned about the acute need for a national military policy. Committed to the defense of India, home defense, and the formation of an expeditionary force, in vain they pleaded with their political leaders for a definition of the army's role and responsibilities and an order of priorities within the broad context of national policy. They became interested in seapower; they grew increasingly aware of the military implications of European alliances. They had demonstrated their ability for improvisation in numerous campaigns against native levies; they now demanded systematic preparation to increase the chances for success in a modern war of major proportions.

The subject of the next chapter, Maurice, was one of the most articulate spokesmen for the Wolseley Ring. Aggressive and independent, he often reflected the views of his chief, and his writings embrace most of the problems that plagued the

[2] The Honorable Sir John W. Fortescue, *Following the Drum* (Edinburgh, 1931), p. 148

army between the Cardwell Reforms and the Boer War. Henderson, who is treated in chapter vii, was another of Wolseley's protégés, but he belonged to a younger generation and never became an active member of the "Ring." Beginning as a student of tactics, Henderson gradually expanded his interests to include strategy and policy at the highest level. He was a thoughtful student of war, a gifted teacher, and an outstanding historian; and along with Maurice he typifies the progressive type of officer who worked to blend the new with the best of the old and to educate the army for war as well as drill it for parade.[3]

[3] A penetrating glance at the British army during the Wolseley Era is Brian Bond, "The Late-Victorian Army," *History Today*, XI (1961), 616–24.

6

THE SECOND PEN OF SIR GARNET

Major General Sir John Frederick Maurice

HISTORY can offer no more striking example than Sir Garnet Wolseley of the truth of Don Quixote's observation that "the sword hath never blunted the pen; nor the pen, the sword." Hamley's success with the one had jeopardized his reputation for the other, but Wolseley surpassed most men in both. "All Sir Garnet" became a fashionable synonym for "all correct" as a result of Wolseley's victorious campaigns in western Canada, south and west Africa, and Egypt; and his accomplishments in military literature were scarcely less impressive. He wrote graphically of his experiences in the Arrow War with China (1860), his visit to the headquarters of Lee and Jackson (1862), and the successful expedition he organized and led to the Red River (1870); *The Soldier's Pocket Book,* which he finished in 1869, went through five editions and anticipated the functions of the official *Field Service Pocket-Book* by forty years; he produced frequent articles about the past accomplishments and present problems of the British army; and he published essays about recent military heroes to supplement his income and a book on Marlborough primarily for his own amusement.[1]

Wolseley naturally attracted other officers who, in addition

[1] That Wolseley was not motivated solely by a desire to widen the mental horizons of the British officer is clear from his letters to Lady Wolseley. Thus *The Soldier's Pocket Book* "gives me occupation and . . . amuses me also," the Marlborough manuscript provides "a real day of enjoyment," and an article on Moltke yielded £75, making a total of £275 so far for the year, "very nearly enough to pay for Taylor's Bill to move our belongings here. I must try to earn another couple of hundred before

to being good soldiers, also shared his progressive ideas and intellectual interests. These men were nearly all militantly loyal to the general, "our only general," who gave them opportunities to prove themselves in the field and encouraged them at all times to take their profession seriously. Maurice was one of these; in time he became Wolseley's closest and most faithful friend; and because he excelled even Wolseley as a military writer he may be considered the most articulate voice of the Ring. As a special correspondent, official historian, editor and proprietor of a service journal, and in a variety of books and articles, Maurice presented the campaigns of Wolseley and represented the views of his chief. A difficult man at times, and one who thrived on controversy, Maurice's views were not always accepted as "all Sir Garnet." Most would have agreed, however, that no matter what he wrote, he was all *for* Sir Garnet: that he was, in fact, what Hamley himself had suspected [2] and his biographer to his lasting sorrow had finally discovered, Sir Garnet's second and in many respects his most able pen.

John Frederick Maurice was born on May 24, 1841, the eldest son of Frederick Denison Maurice, a famous theologian and social reformer. His mother, who died when he was four, came from a military family of some renown, a fact which may have influenced young Maurice in his decision to enter the army, but it was his father who introduced him to books and taught him "the habit of expressing himself clearly and forcibly on paper." [3] The elder Maurice assumed responsibility for his son's education; he taught him to read widely and

the year is up to keep the pot boiling" (Wolseley to Lady Wolseley, June 13, 1885; August 1, 1889; June 29, 1891 [Wolseley Papers]). To William Blackwood he was equally candid: "Making money is one of life's pleasures that survives even ambition and adds to one's comforts and ease of mind, which ambition never does. Writing in my spare moments is my only means of money making, and on many accounts it is a pleasure that never seems to diminish in the enjoyment" (Wolseley to Blackwood, March 17, 1889 [Blackwood Papers]).

[2] Regarding Maurice's official history of the Egyptian campaign, Hamley wrote: ". . . it is difficult for me to avoid the conclusion that he has been gratifying a hostile animas . . . possibly he is gratifying the animas of somebody else" (Hamley to William Blackwood, January 1, 1888 [Blackwood Papers]).

[3] Lieutenant Colonel Frederick Maurice, *Sir Frederick Maurice: A Record of His Work and Opinions, with Eight Essays on Discipline and National Efficiency* (London, 1913), p. 6 (cited hereafter as Maurice, *Work and Opinions*).

independently, encouraged him to cultivate his own views, provided opportunities for him to meet and talk with distinguished friends from many walks of life, and by example he imparted principles that guided the future soldier throughout his life.

Maurice's education was intended as preparation for Cambridge, but the excitement of the Crimean War and the Indian Mutiny induced him to choose the army for a career, and he went to the Royal Military Academy at Woolwich instead. Commissioned in the Royal Artillery in 1862, he served at Woolwich, Shorncliffe, Leith (near Edinburgh), and in Ireland before entering the Staff College in 1870. Two years later he was appointed instructor in tactics at the Royal Military College, Sandhurst.

Quite likely the appointment to Sandhurst saved Maurice's career, for having decided relatively late in life to become a soldier and facing slow promotions (he remained a subaltern for more than thirteen years) in a profession in which there were fixed ages for retirement within the various ranks, his professional prospects must otherwise have seemed dim. By habit a voracious reader, liberally endowed with a retentive memory and fascinated by military history, Maurice capitalized upon this opportunity. While engaged in the study of the recent Prussian campaigns, he learned that the second Duke of Wellington had offered a prize of £100 for the best essay submitted on the subject of preparing a British army to fight a war under modern conditions. Although still a subaltern Maurice decided to enter the competition. For weeks he burned the midnight oil. Completing the essay only minutes before it was due, he then committed the unpardonable sin of arousing Hamley, who was to act as judge, from his slumbers in order to make the deadline. The commandant, whose job it was to stimulate interest in such matters, evidently did not like to do so after working hours: he swore at the messenger, threw the essay into a corner, and vowed that it would be the last to be read. For Maurice's sake it was perhaps just as well that all papers had to be submitted anonymously, especially since some of the other thirty-six contestants were officers of general rank.[4]

Maurice won both the contest and a reprieve from Hamley, who wrote:

[4] *Ibid.*, pp. 14–20.

[I]t may be doubted whether any essay, in any language, has handled the subject with a more comprehensive and vigorous grasp, or discussed it with a more logical precision. . . . It displays in an eminent degree . . . knowledge of the theory of modern war, extensive reading of contemporary military literature, and the power of drawing from theory and fact new and original deductions.

"Were this essay the only result of the offer of a prize," Hamley publicly assured the Duke of Wellington, "it could be one on which your Grace might be justly congratulated." [5] When one considers that five other entries ultimately were selected for publication including one by a general officer and another by Colonel Wolseley, who won second prize, Lieutenant Maurice's accomplishment is all the more impressive. Hamley used his influence with John Blackwood to have the essay published, General Crauford, one of the contestants, arranged for its translation into French, and it brought Maurice to the attention of the most promising officer in the British army—Wolseley.[6]

The most striking feature about Maurice's essay, *The System of Field Manoeuvres Best Adapted for Enabling Our Troops To Meet a Continental Army,* is his judicious, even skeptical use of evidence from the Prussian wars. Unlike most British officers, Maurice was not astonished "that an army whose organization had decayed should have been utterly beaten by one led by more able chiefs, numerically very superior, [and] perfectly prepared for war"; nor did he favor imitating the Prussians merely because they had succeeded. Each army, he noted, of necessity had changed its tactical formations during the course of the war, the French because ultimately they had to rely largely upon half-trained levies and the Prussians as the need "for further developing the system of manoeuvring in the presence of highly-trained troops passed away." Maurice, in fact, regarded the Prussian formations as the less trustworthy of the two, "for as the experience of the Germans increased, so their need of employing it with care diminished." "On the whole," Maurice concluded,

the following deductions appear to be legitimate. At the commencement of the campaign the German leaders had not been

[5] *Times,* May 6, 1872.
[6] Maurice, *Work and Opinions,* p. 15; Maurice to John Blackwood, April 20, 1872 (Blackwood Papers). It was Maurice's understanding that the second Duke of Wellington assumed the financial risk in publishing the Wellington Prize essay.

prepared to adopt those modifications in tactics which were proved to be necessary almost at once by their first experience of fighting against the breech-loader and the mitrailleuse. Such modifications as were subsequently introduced, so far as they proceeded from the orders of the generals commanding, were therefore only tentative. They had not been carefully tried and studied in the school of mimic war. Moreover, they were never perfected even under the more rapid tutorship of battle itself. The need for perfection passed away. The time came when the only thing that was dangerous was not to dare enough.

Maurice therefore contended that it was not possible to determine future tactical developments on the basis of what even the Prussians themselves had learned in 1870–71: "For in the first portion they had not learnt the necessities of the new conditions of things; in the latter, other circumstances had rendered even these new conditions of comparatively secondary importance." [7]

Insufficient or misleading evidence added another hazard in the evaluation of the tactical lessons of 1870–71. According to Maurice it was too early for the publication either of detailed personal accounts in any significant number or regimental histories, which were instructive if read between the lines. Most of the available evidence, therefore, had to come from "the little better than casual illustrations introduced by those who would defend a particular theory," a shortcoming that received partial compensation from the fact that the Germans more than any other people loved "to pay the most plodding devotion to fact." [8]

Working on ground "of an altogether different kind from the distinct positive study of such clearly-recorded battles as those of Austerlitz, Waterloo, or Solferino," Maurice's conclusions corresponded to MacDougall's deductions on the impact of the breech-loader upon tactics. Assaulting troops must adopt flexible formations and make better use of ground; "an attack in column is a thing no longer possible"; "if an army is to retain *the power of attack* at all, it must nowadays attack in skirmishing order, with a proper system of supports and reserves"; finally, flank attacks offered by far the best and in most cases the only real prospect of success.[9]

[7] Maurice, *The System of Field Manoeuvres Best Adapted for Enabling Our Troops To Meet a Continental Army* (Edinburgh, 1872), pp. 4, 14–15, 17.
[8] *Ibid.*, pp. 17–18.
[9] *Ibid.*, pp. 19, 26–31.

He was more specific than MacDougall in his solutions: there should be greater freedom of action on the battlefield. Command should be elevated from a habit "of exact prescription" to one "of clear instruction"; unity between tactical formations and harmony among the officers was more essential than ever, "but it must be arrived at by a thorough appreciation of the spirit rather than by a strict adherence to the letter." The British army was at a disadvantage here, in Maurice's estimation, because battalions were scattered the world over. How could a regiment from Tipperary, for example, be expected to co-operate as closely with one from Bombay as German units from neighboring districts who were already accustomed to working together in brigade maneuvers? Admittedly this was a weakness, but one which must be overcome or at least minimized if British troops were to achieve maximum efficiency.

One way to overcome this in Maurice's opinion was to develop aptitude rather than cultivate memory in the education of officers and noncommissioned officers. Another was to enlarge the size of the British companies to correspond more nearly to the German company of 250 men by reducing the number of companies in a single battalion. Maurice suggested an increase in both the number and responsibilities of noncommissioned officers, so that fewer men in each rank were placed under the immediate orders of the next above them. Finally he advocated organizing the army into corps and holding combined maneuvers to insure co-operation, minimize friction, and increase mutual confidence among the three arms. Maurice recognized the uneven quality of the auxiliary forces but offered no constructive suggestions as to how the militia and volunteers might be improved and incorporated with good troops: "for troops without discipline there is no place in modern open war." [10]

Maurice agreed wholeheartedly with MacDougall that the defense had benefited most from the breech-loader. Merely because the victorious army in 1870 had nearly always assumed the offensive, it did not necessarily follow that the offensive was the stronger method of waging war. In the first period of the war, the Prussians had nearly always greatly outnumbered the French, except at Spicheren and there, by the time the French position finally fell, the Prussians again

[10] *Ibid.*, pp. 34–71.

enjoyed a numerical superiority. Yet "in each of these cases the loss of the victors so enormously exceeded that of the vanquished, that it would have been impossible for any army to have long borne the exhaustion produced by such work." If, after fighting "for hours with marvelous success under the most unfavorable circumstances against overpowering numbers," the defenders of the key position at St. Privat finally were driven off because of a shortage of ammunition, is it to be inferred that men on the defensive "are specially apt to be left without ammunition?" Maurice concluded that

in those cases in which the German victories were obtained under conditions such as in any conceivable state of warfare would insure success, there they were due to bold attacks, in the course of which the victors suffered fearful losses, and till the moment of victory inflicted hardly any. In those cases in which the German victories were strange, unprecedented, overpowering, they were due to a brilliant application of offensive strategy, but of defensive tactics.[11]

Metz, Paris, and Sedan would fall into the latter category.

Here then was the solution—offensive strategy and defensive tactics. The commander should take up a position that would force the enemy, from strategic considerations, to assume the tactical offensive on a large scale. Modern weapons dictated this course; British tradition supported it; and "national characteristics" made it the strongest form of warfare for any British army. But if massed attacks no longer provided the road to victory, it was now easier for comparatively weak bodies to threaten front and flank simultaneously and thus to force an enemy to stretch its lines to the breaking point. Victory in this instance would likely go to the army which, "having prepared for attack, is awaiting the opportunity of striking at weakened points when the extension has reached its limit." The Prussians had not been the first to demonstrate that an army could continue this process until the entire opposing army had been actually outflanked or even surrounded—"this phenomenon of constant flank attacks was quite as marked a feature of the American war as of the late one. The Americans seem to have habitually intrenched themselves against one another in front, and then to have worked round to a flank." [12]

[11] *Ibid.*, pp. 74–79.
[12] *Ibid.*, pp. 84–98, 162, 173.

As for the role of the three arms in the attack, Maurice recommended a new tactical organization for infantry corresponding to the Prussian company column which would enable small units better to adapt themselves to the ground.[13] The present British infantry drill book would suffice "with as little alteration as possible": some expressions were outdated, but the principles themselves were as sound "as if all the experience of the war had been before the writers." The main change that had occurred was in the functions of the skirmisher: whereas previously skirmishers had existed to protect columns, columns now were designed to feed successive supports and reserves into the skirmish line. Maurice cited the need for shelter trenches even in the attack, and because of the enormous superiority of the Prussian artillery he was reluctant to accept the claim of German theorists that artillery on the offensive enjoys the advantage of mobility and a fixed target. Actually he believed that the reverse was probably true, although he conceded that the Prussian practice of placing artillery in advanced positions had much to be said in its favor, even at the risk of occasionally losing a few guns.[14]

Maurice was somewhat more conventional in his thoughts on cavalry. Recognizing that mounted infantry was ideally suited to assist in reconnaissance and as protection for artillery, he accepted the prevailing view that even if the role of cavalry in battle had been reduced by the breechloader, there would still be opportunities for a decisive charge against shaken infantry and exposed artillery, while in encounters between cavalry and mounted infantry the former would enjoy a natural advantage. Maurice did not think that it was possible to develop a hybrid to fight equally well on horse and dismounted, and he insisted that even with modern firearms cavalry would have opportunities to make local attacks and to exploit victory by vigorous pursuit.[15]

Thus in most respects Maurice shared MacDougall's interpretation of the war of 1870 and his view of war in the future. Both resisted the impulse to imitate the Prussians in detail;

[13] Maurice recommended a battalion of four companies, each company comprising 200–250 men, divided into four sections (*ibid.*, p. 61).

[14] *Ibid.*, pp. 88, 92, 142–43, 148–51, 162–63.

[15] *Ibid.*, pp. 104, 130–32, 144, 155–59.

both contended that the defense had gained more than the offense from modern weapons, that more flexible formations and better use of skirmishers were necessary to prevent excessive losses, that flank attacks offered virtually the only means of carrying a position, and that the best way to wage war was to combine offensive strategy with defensive tactics. They differed in matters of detail: Maurice placed greater faith in conventional cavalry and would allow company commanders greater tactical independence, while MacDougall emphasized linear formations, the counterattack, and the destructive power of modern artillery. Both were agreed, however, that British drill regulations need only be modified to meet the requirements of modern infantry tactics, although Maurice in addition would reorganize the company and battalion.

Maurice's essay had no immediate effect upon the British army. Word reached him from friends in Germany that "the Germans preferred the essay to any deductions which had been made by their own officers," but by the time it was published in England "the motive force of public opinion" which had enabled Cardwell to introduce his reforms was spent. Hamley obviously incorporated some of this studious subaltern's ideas into *The Operations of War* when it was revised six months or so later, but Wolseley soon afterward departed for the Gold Coast and the others involved in the Cardwell Reforms were quickly scattered. Maurice himself did not expect that the essay would make much of an impression upon the army. "The colonels of the regiments," he reported to Blackwood, "as a rule [are] fighting hard to stand to the old ways. . . . I am quite convinced the best chance of a sale is among the Volunteers and Militia who know they are out of the way of hearing what has been going on. . . ." [16]

The Wellington Prize essay did produce quick profits of another sort, however, for Wolseley, solely on the strength of Maurice's essay, took him to west Africa as a special service officer and his own private secretary when he was sent in September, 1873, to prepare for an expedition against the Ashanti. Only a select group of officers, thirty five in all, accompanied Wolseley, but among them were the men

[16] Maurice, *Work and Opinions*, pp. 15, 19; Maurice to John Black-wood, (April), 1872 (Blackwood Papers).

destined to provide the intellectual leadership of the British army and command most of the military expeditions sent out from England over the next thirty years—Lieutenant Colonel (later Field Marshal Sir) Evelyn Wood; Captain (afterward General the Right Honorable Sir) Redvers Buller, who as commander in South Africa in the first months of the Boer War failed to live up to the expectations encouraged by previous accomplishments; Major (later Colonel) Robert Home, whose *Précis of Modern Tactics*, first published in 1873, became the official textbook; Major (later Major General Sir) George Colley, "intellectually perhaps the most brilliant of them all" and a casualty at Majuba Hill; Captain (later General Sir) Henry Brackenbury, described by Wolseley as "*the* cleverest man in the British army," and Captain (later Lieutenant General Sir) William Butler, who wrecked his career by his reluctance to serve in the field against the Boers. No ordinary men, these, and it is little wonder that they incited envy and in time bitterness among those outside of the charmed circle. They accompanied Wolseley in most of his campaigns, following a respectful distance behind in prestige and promotions—a fact which outsiders often attributed to favoritism—and to many their ranks seemed closed "to those who loved the sword and despised the pen." Sir Ian Hamilton was one who encountered the corporate feeling of the Ring. Passing through the Canal in October, 1884, when the Gordon Relief Expedition was about ready to start for Khartoum, Hamilton promptly forgot about his leave and tried to wangle a position with Wolseley's army. "Nothing," he wrote,

could have been more inhospitable or forbidding than the response from that special preserve of the Wolseleyites. There was a ban on "medal hunting"; all and sundry were to be properly appointed from London; if we wanted to relieve Gordon we must do so *via* Pall Mall; anyone attempting to cut in from any benighted country like India would be summarily dealt with; arrested certainly; probably tried by court martial. . . . I *was* an intruder: I was alone in a hostile camp.

Hamilton even attributed Wolseley's creation of the Desert Column instead of following the river route to "the pressure of the Ring; the urge to do something for his pals." Correct or not in his judgment, there is no mistaking the hostility of his feeling: nor is there much doubt that his own motives were questioned by those as loyal to Wolseley as he himself was to Lord Roberts.[17]

A very junior member of the "Ashanti Ring," as Wolseley's circle originally was called, Maurice performed his duties well. As Wolseley's private secretary he handled all of the correspondence with the Colonial Office, but he also managed to participate in every engagement of the war and to represent the *Daily News* as special correspondent. When he returned to England the following year, he published in book form his letters to the paper. One is tempted to comment that this, together with the history of the campaign written by Wolseley's military secretary, Captain Brackenbury, also in no small way contributed to the success of the expedition.[18]

Back in England, Maurice was posted to the Royal Horse Artillery at Woolwich until promoted captain in 1875, after which he served for two years in Canada. Like MacDougall, he too grew interested in the Canadian local forces, an interest which in his case later ripened into the suggestion that an exchange of officers of imperial and local services between England and her colonies would greatly strengthen both the defense of the empire and the ties that bound it together. Eventually the imperial general staff did promote such a system of exchange between Great Britain and the Dominions, although how much of this was due to Maurice's insistence it is difficult to say.

In 1877 the paths of Maurice and MacDougall may have crossed briefly, for Maurice was assigned to work under Home in the Intelligence Department just as MacDougall left that office to assume his duties as commander in chief in British North America. In 1879 Maurice accompanied Wolseley as deputy assistant quartermaster general in the successful campaign against the Zulus in South Africa. Shot through the lung leading a charge in one of the final operations of the war,

[17] General Sir Ian Hamilton, *Listening for the Drums* (London, 1944), pp. 172–77; Maurice, *Work and Opinions*, pp. 183–84; Major General Sir John Adye, *Soldiers and Others I Have Known* (London, 1925), pp. 106–8; Major General Sir Frederick Maurice and Sir George Arthur, *The Life of Lord Wolseley* (New York, 1925), pp. 63–64, 224; Brevet Major A. R. Godwin-Austen, *The Staff and the Staff College* (London, 1927), p. 183. There was another aspect of the Ring worthy of remark: the majority were Staff College graduates. See Wolseley, *The Story of a Soldier's Life* (Westminster, 1903), II, 276.

[18] *The Ashantee War: A Popular Narrative.* By the "Daily News" Special Correspondent (London, 1874); Captain H. Brackenbury, *The Ashanti War: A Narrative* (Edinburgh, 1874)

Maurice was invalided home and awarded the rank of brevet major. During convalescence he began work in earnest on a biography of his father, which consumed most of his leisure time for the next three years. He was serving as brigade major at Cork when Wolseley once again summoned him, this time as deputy assistant adjutant and quartermaster general on the headquarters staff of the expeditionary force that was being assembled for service in Egypt.[19]

Maurice returned to the War Office after the campaign of 1882 and for the next two years worked day and night with his pen. He completed the biography of his father, a work regarded by some as "his chief literary attainment." He also investigated the occasions within the past century when nations had plunged into war without previous strain or a formal declaration of war. There was talk at the time of a tunnel to be built under the Channel, and many soldiers professed to fear that the French someday might utilize the tunnel for a surprise stroke against England. No doubt this fear was intensified upon publication of Maurice's *Hostilities without Declaration of War* in 1883, for Maurice's research had revealed that in the period 1700–1870 there had been "less than ten instances in which 'declaration of war' had been issued prior to hostilities . . . while in 107 cases, war had begun without any formal warning." Needless to say, Maurice opposed the tunnel scheme whenever it was revived.[20]

His work as official historian of the recent Egyptian campaign was more important. Official history had come a long way since the compilation of engineer and artillery records during the siege of Sebastopol. This and the official history of the 1867 expedition to Abyssinia had been the responsibility of the secretary of state for war; when the Intelligence Branch was founded in 1873, one of the duties it inherited was the preparation of the official history of the numerous small wars in which England was engaged from the Ashanti expedition in 1873 until after the turn of the century.

Among these campaign studies, Maurice's *Military History of the Campaign of 1882 in Egypt* stands alone. Hitherto most

[19] Maurice, *Work and Opinions*, pp. 23–41.
[20] *Ibid.*, pp. 43–45; Maurice, "The Revived Channel Tunnel Project," *Nineteenth Century*, LXI (1907), 176–81. Wolseley also opposed the project. Maurice and Arthur, *Wolseley*, pp. 168–69.

British official historians, like soldiers everywhere, had been content to follow the practice of the Germans. They imitated the German staff histories in approach as well as organization, quoting voluminously from official documents and narrating the campaigns in elaborate detail. The German official account of the Franco-Prussian War was generally held up as "an example for all time," presenting

a picture of war on a gigantic scale, slowly unrolled before the reader, with all its complex purpose and involved action calmly traced by a master hand. Effect is evolved from cause with the merciless logic of a mathematic problem. Hardly ever rising to the level of eloquence and never didactic, this great book carries with it a power which no eloquence and no professorial periods could command; while the entire impersonality and the cold inflexible treatment . . . complete the conviction of solid and substantial truth.[21]

Maurice could see no wisdom in imitating the Germans by producing a book crammed full of dull facts: he wrote with another purpose in mind.

Guided by the same impulse that drove Hamley to defend the record of the army in the Crimea, Maurice hoped to counter the effect of the "undisciplined haste for news" created by the penny illustrated papers and intensified by the telegraph. Wolseley had attempted to alleviate the problem by establishing rigid regulations for all special correspondents and by censoring every communication sent to the papers;[22] Maurice endeavored to solve it by being his own war correspondent in the Ashanti War and later, as official historian of the Egyptian campaign, by educating the public about the complexities of small wars. Recognizing that responsible

[21] "Military History of the Campaign of 1882 in Egypt," *Edinburgh Review*, XLIV (1888), 286; Godwin-Austen, *Staff and the Staff College*, p. 219. The Intelligence Branch produced histories of the Ashanti Expedition of 1873, the Zulu War of 1879, the Egyptian Campaign of 1882, the campaign in the Sudan in 1885, and the operations in Somaliland, 1901–4. The history of British military operations in China, Burma, and the North West Frontier, became the official responsibility of the Intelligence Branch, India.

[22] "As long as the British public's craze for sensational news remains as it is now, the English General must accept the position." See Wolseley's "Rules for Newspaper Correspondents at the Seat of War," in *The Soldier's Pocket-Book for Field Service* (5th ed.; London, 1886), pp. 178–80.

government must always be sensitive to the pressures of public opinion, Maurice considered English ministers to be less well informed about military affairs than many statesmen on the Continent, and he feared that the sensational press, in satisfying the craving of readers hungry for "morsels of exciting news," might force the government to make unreasonable demands upon generals struggling with slender means to overcome time, distance, and hostile native populations. Any expedition overseas involved preparations and problems hidden from public view:

> As certainly as these delays occur, newspaper correspondents on the spot will begin to croak that nothing is going on. Whilst this particular form of croaking is taking place will be almost certainly the time when the hardest work is going on, and when the successes of the future are being assured. But unless people at home are much less mere news-hunters than they are at present, the croakers will be believed and the nation will suffer.[23]

Perhaps the fate of the next expedition to leave England would depend upon the public understanding those factors which had been ignored after the initial landings in Egypt, when it had taken considerable time to accumulate supplies, repair railroads, and remove obstacles from the Canal. Even the Prussian victors at Sadowa would have been detained by similar conditions, Maurice contended, but the English people had overlooked the difficulties in the happy assumption that "the moment was immediately at hand when a final forward movement upon Cairo was to take place." Years before, Sir Arthur Wellesley had observed that the English public never formed "an accurate estimate of the difficulties attending *any* military enterprise which they undertake." Maurice believed that this was still the case, only now the risks of disaster had increased because governments were more responsive to public opinion and the larger and more complex armies required longer preparation before those at home could see the results.[24]

As a record of the campaign, Maurice's *History* has many

[23] Maurice, *Work and Opinions*, p. 225. Maurice's essay, "Undisciplined Haste for News Apropos of the Egyptian Campaign of 1882," is reprinted in *ibid.*, pp. 209–26.
[24] Maurice, *The Military History of the Campaign of 1882 in Egypt* (2d ed.; London, 1908), pp. 25–28, 54–55; Maurice, "Critics and Campaigns," *Fortnightly Review*, XLIV (1888), 128.

shortcomings. He was, in many respects, comparable to a court historian, and one might easily conclude from reading his pages that Wolseley never made a mistake. He neglected to mention the dispute between Wolseley and Hamley and to recount the whole story of Hamley's leadership at Tel-el-Kebir—as his public disclosures in the *United Service Magazine* and private correspondence to Hamley's biographer and publisher later attest.[25] His book is far less detailed than the *United States Naval Intelligence Report* on the campaign issued two years previously,[26] and one hostile reviewer pointed to occasional confusion of military titles and "vague passages alluding to time sequences." Maurice was also criticized for having taken longer to write his brief history than the historical section of the German General Staff required to produce the official history of the war of 1870–71 or the British Intelligence Branch to translate this work, but this accusation, although true, is unjust. Maurice was called away from his desk to participate in the expedition to relieve Gordon in 1884–85, and the work was further delayed for more than a year after his return by disagreements among the chief actors, principally Hamley, over points of fact. Maurice was able to satisfy everybody else with minor alterations, and after frequent interviews he and Hamley were able to agree on all but two sections which, because Hamley's version was at variance with the testimony of others, Maurice used, citing Hamley as his source. Hamley regarded these footnotes as "gratuitously unpleasant," and he never forgave Maurice for using as evidence the first report of one of his subordinates, Sir Archibald Alison, which he himself had suppressed.[27]

Of far greater significance was the eternal problem—or plight—of anyone in Maurice's position: Is the historian of a military campaign who writes under official auspices really an independent agent? Maurice insisted that he was, that no evidence had been withheld although secret documents had to

[25] Maurice, "Sir E. Hamley and Lord Wolseley," *United Service Magazine*, XI (1895), 414–38, 439–63; Maurice to William Blackwood, July 27, 1895; (Maurice) to Alexander Innis Shand, August 5, 1895 (Blackwood Papers).

[26] See Lieutenant Commander Caspar F. Goodrich, *Report of the British Naval and Military Operations in Egypt in 1882* ("Information from Abroad," War Series, No. III; Washington, 1885).

[27] "Campaign of 1882," pp. 294, 318; Maurice, *Work and Opinions*, p. 58; "Sir E. Hamley and Lord Wolseley," pp. 417–21; Hamley to William Blackwood, January 1, 1888 (Blackwood Papers).

be released by competent authority before they could be cited, and that "no one ever had, in the composition of any history, official or other, a freer hand or more ample resources." He reluctantly conceded, however, that "an official historian is not his own master," and his later comments on the German official history of 1870–71 perhaps reveal something of his own troubles. The German official historian, Maurice told a military audience in Dublin some fifteen years later, "does not frankly tell you the plain fact. He ought not to tell you, because *there are some things that an Official Historian must conceal.*" [28]

Maurice's next experience with official history was more frustrating still. In 1903 Colonel G. F. R. Henderson, the official historian of the Boer War, died while his work was in early stages of preparation and Maurice was asked to succeed him. "The offer," he wrote,

was couched in what were to me personally very flattering terms. Yet, when I first received the conditions on which I was to edit the history, I felt very much like Hamlet must have done at the time when he opened the letters of the King of Denmark to the King of England. They propose to consign me to penal servitude for life, and to the more modern punishment to add the ancient one, that I am to spend my time with a hornets nest about my ears, trampling a bottomless bog in pursuit of an unapproachable bauble. Naturally, I prefer to retain my freedom.

Maurice and Henderson had already discussed the plan and scope of the projected work and were agreed on the need to write something that would appeal to the general reader as well as the soldier and explain the political and military lessons of the war in terms that the layman could understand. Henderson had even made arrangements to have a commercial firm publish the volumes, so anxious was he to break away from the dreary format of His Majesty's Stationery Office.

Unfortunately, changes at the War Office compromised the work soon after Maurice had agreed, with considerable misgivings, to complete Henderson's first volume. The new army council replaced the office of commander in chief, which

[28] Maurice, "Critics and Campaigns," p. 126; "Sir E. Hamley and Lord Wolseley," p. 414; *The Artillery in 1870–71: From a General Army Point of View* (Military Society of Ireland Lecture, No. 14; Dublin, 1892), p. 26. Italics mine.

deprived Maurice of a powerful supporter in the person of Lord Roberts and brought him directly under civilian control. The new regime scrapped Henderson's chapters because his harsh judgments of former Boer leaders might prejudice current conciliatory negotiations and directed that the official history should follow the general lines of the German staff history of 1870–71.[29] Maurice publicly denied the rumor that his two volumes were subedited "in the interest of Departments concerned," but in private he denounced the official criticism to which his work was subjected. It was customary for several offices to read the proofs to safeguard against leakage of confidential documents, but frequently Maurice had to conform to the views and impressions of interested individuals as well.

In his first attempt at official history Maurice had to cope with the vanity of a divisional commander; now he had also to satisfy politicians, many of whom were concerned with the repercussions of earlier mistakes upon their parliamentary careers. Maurice was not the first to labor under this handicap: the author of the *History of the Sudan Campaign* evidently had produced a manuscript that "suited the soldiers affected by it very well" but which failed to satisfy the politicians "who had been responsible for the campaign," and the latter, with the tacit consent of both front benches, "decided . . . to mutilate it." [30] Working under similar restraint, Maurice feared that his history could have little educative effect, particularly since no compromise was possible between the kind of work he and Henderson had planned and that insisted upon by a general staff "with definite views of what it wanted to teach." [31] Probably the War Office was happier than Maurice with the results, for the *History of the War in South Africa* conformed tactfully to German standards as a literal, fully documented record of the campaigns with

[29] Maurice, *Work and Opinions*, pp. 119–21. When the office of commander in chief was abolished in February, 1904, and replaced by the newly created Army Council, Lord Roberts left the War Office to become a member of the new Defense Committee (Colonel John K. Dunlop, *The Development of the British Army 1889–1904* [London, 1938], pp. 208–9). For Henderson's part in the official history of the Boer War, see below, pp. 239–40.

[30] Charles Williams, "The Nile Campaign—a Reply to Mr. Forbes," *United Service Magazine*, IV (1892), 418–19.

[31] Maurice, *History of the War in South Africa 1899–1902* (London, 1907), I, Preface; *Work and Opinions*, pp. 123–25.

reputations adequately protected. When illness forced Maurice to give up the project, his staff prepared the final two volumes in the belief that official history "would be valueless to military students if it could not be referred to for information concerning the minutiae of the campaign." Thus in a narrative such as this, the only casualty, one is tempted to remark, was the civilian reader.[32]

Yet the lessons were there for all to see. British armies had suffered once again from inadequate peacetime preparation, inferior staff work, and lack of a general doctrine. The Boers had succeeded initially because of their greater numbers, mobility, mastery of the terrain, and the longer range of their guns, advantages which eventually were offset as the British built up their forces, adopted more realistic tactical formations, and learned how to utilize mounted infantry. The weakness of this official *History* is not the occasional misstatement of fact, for Maurice did a painstaking job of research: [33] the weakness lies in the fact that Maurice was never free to analyze motives and describe all of the circumstances behind the basic military decisions. In vain he protested that military history was "worthless except in so far as it places the man who reads it in the position of those whose actions he is studying, and therefore enables him to profit by their experience, and to learn both from their failures, their misfortunes, and their successes." [34] *The Official History of the Russo-Japanese War* was much better in this regard, for the authors were free to criticize and comment upon the actions of both armies—no British military reputations were at stake.

[32] Captain Maurice Herold Grant, *History of the War in South Africa 1899–1902* (London, 1910), IV, v–vi.

[33] Maurice, *War in South Africa*, I, 88–90, 205, 228; II, 103, 105, 111–13, 204–5, 522. Writing of Maurice's treatment of Elandslaagte, General Sir Ian Hamilton has revealed something of Maurice's methods—and sense of frustration—in compiling the official history. "I was out in Manchuria at the time the Official History was being written and never got the proofs which . . . Maurice had sent me 'for remark.' When the book came out I pointed out to him the mistakes and he was so angry that I left the matter alone and never explained that I had not received his first letter. His point was that I had waited till the whole thing was printed and then found fault. Actually . . . the various times of the movements are muddled up. . . . The Times *History* is on the right lines but, so far as I recollect, is somewhat inadequate as a military study" (Hamilton to Colonel C. À Court Repington, July 2, 1924 [Liddel Hart Papers, States House, Medmenham, Marlow, Buckinghamshire]).

[34] Maurice, *Work and Opinions*, p. 121.

The campaign in the Sudan was a watershed in Maurice's military career. Prior to 1885 he had alternated between service at the War Office and in the field; after that date his duties were confined to the classroom and the writing desk. He much preferred the field to the desk (Wolseley once described him as "the bravest man I have ever seen under fire"), but clearly his talents made him a more effective fighter with the pen. Wolseley used him on his staff because he could "do what I want well enough" and his "sincerity and honesty and loyalty in the eye of ingratitude endear him to me, more than any man I have ever known"; but he later confided to Lady Wolseley why Maurice had no future as a commander in active service. Maurice, he wrote while the two were on a trip together in 1897,

has become more violently argumentative than ever, and if you venture to say you think he is wrong or has formed his opinions on very insignificant and incomplete evidence, he flies at you like a tiger. He becomes worse as he grows older in this respect. I always feel guilty and regret having said anything to produce this excitement in him, for I fear at times for his brain. His eyes distend and for the moment he is not responsible for his actions much less his words. Then comes sleeplessness and then that worn, haggard look which invariably follows upon it. I am so fond of him that I am torn with remorse as I think that some words or chaff of mine has brought this state upon him. You know how suspicious he always was about men and women conspiring against him or me. Well, he is worse than ever in this respect. He evidently hankers after military command and thinks that would be his special role if he were given a chance. This shows more unbalance in his mind for if he but knew the truth there is not a man amongst all his military friends who would give him any command in war of any sort or kind knowing him to be absolutely unfitted for it. He has less method than ever, is less tidy than formerly, but much abler with his pen and is a better reasoner upon many subjects than ever. The pen is his weapon not the sword, and yet he thinks the exact opposite. I often wonder to myself whether I am as incapable of weighing my own capacity, weaknesses, folly. . . .[35]

[35] Wolseley to Lady Wolseley, September 12, 1897 (Wolseley Papers). For similar reasons the Duke of Cambridge apparently would not let Maurice join Wolseley's staff when the latter was commander in chief in Ireland. See Wolseley to Lady Wolseley, January 19, 1891 (Wolseley Papers). Wolseley's comments upon Maurice as a fighting soldier are found in Maurice, *Work and Opinions*, pp. 54–55.

In 1885 Wolseley, now adjutant general, appointed Maurice professor of military art and history at the Staff College. Characteristically Maurice resisted the appointment and objected that the title "professor" might jeopardize his chances for active service; but Wolseley knew his man and Maurice knew what had to be done to improve the instruction at the Staff College. His predecessor had been a "steady, persevering," but uninspiring instructor to whom the knowledge of facts was often confused with the understanding of the subject. Maurice, who had been taught by his father to question and ponder rather than to memorize and repeat, had a different concept of the instructional value of military history.

In all professional study it is essential for a soldier at all events to keep before him the fact that the object is not merely to "acquire information concerning operations, battles, skirmishes, and charges, or, indeed, any mere information at all," but to improve his judgment as to what ought to be done under the varied conditions of actual war. . . . And to this end, in the study of military history, it is necessary in each separate case first to ascertain accurately what the facts really are; secondly, to endeavour to ascertain what the causes were that led to the facts; and, thirdly, to endeavour to draw sound conclusions for the future from the sequence of facts upon the causes.

In his teaching, Maurice followed much the same principle advocated by Arnold in his well-known lectures on modern history. The student, Maurice contended, "is likely to acquire a much better knowledge of general history by the close and intimate study of one particular section of it, as a preliminary to all his reading, than he is likely to acquire by merely covering a very large amount of ground." Here then is the fundamental difference between Hamley and Maurice: the one digested military history for his students, while the other was concerned primarily in teaching the student how to digest it for himself. In Maurice's opinion this was the most that could be accomplished in the course at the Staff College, but to introduce the student to a method of studying campaigns that would guide him in his independent reading was infinitely more valuable than to impart factual information which in itself was "of very little interest" and "absolutely useless" to the average officer. Carried to excess, the latter approach had produced the type of soldier who reputedly a few years before had announced, after passing through the Staff College, that he was unfit for the specific duty assigned him because "he had not learnt to move bodies of less than 100,000 men." [36]

Maurice was ideally suited for the position. A thorough and imaginative student of war, he was able to bring to his classes the experience of active campaigning and the knowledge that springs from wide reading in the field. He was also an experienced and conscientious teacher, having spent two years as an instructor at Sandhurst after the Franco-Prussian War. His first year as a teacher, he later told the Committee on Military Educational Establishments, was "the hardest year of all my life." Not content merely to read his lectures out of a textbook, Maurice sometimes used as many as sixty books for a single preparation and this, together with the reading he had to do to keep up with his profession and the time spent with individual students, made the year so strenuous that Maurice could testify "I had very nearly at the end of that time got brain fever." [37] At the Staff College Maurice was known for his stimulating and at times profound lectures, although he soon acquired a reputation for a habit which, harmless and even endearing in a professor, posed serious handicaps to the staff officer or commander: Maurice was absent-minded. Often he said French when he meant German, confused the Archduke Charles with Prince Frederick Charles and the Peninsular War with Waterloo, and more than once while touring the battlefields of 1870 with his students he managed to catch a southbound train when the next object of study lay well to the north. That his bravery was not limited to active

[36] *Ibid.,* pp. 58–62; Godwin-Austen, *Staff and the Staff College,* pp. 208–9.

[37] *Report of the Committee on Military Educational Establishments: Royal Military Academy, Royal Military College, Royal Artillery College, Royal Military School of Music, with Minutes of Evidence and Appendices* (London, 1888), pp. 135–41. American readers may be interested to know that Maurice's teaching load was eight hours. In his estimation one lecture a day would keep a conscientious teacher busy, and he testified: "I doubt if it is possible to improve upon the perfect education they get at West Point, from anything I have seen of it." Even at the time of the Civil War, English soldiers had been favorably impressed with the caliber of instruction at West Point, and in fact many of the features of the Royal Military College of Canada were borrowed from West Point rather than Sandhurst and Woolwich. See Lieutenant Colonel Henry Charles Fletcher, *Report on the Military Academy at West Point, U. S.* (n.p., n.d.), pp. 20, 24; George F. G. Stanley, *Canada's Soldiers, 1604–1954: The Military History of an Unmilitary People* (Toronto, 1954), p. 244.

campaigning nor his confusion to the lecture hall is suggested by the stories that grew out of his semi-annual trips to the battlefields, when Maurice provided great amusement by his fearless attempts to negotiate in French and German. On one occasion a puzzled German officer was overheard to remark: *"Der Herr Oberst ist nicht leicht zu verstehen, aber er hat 'courage'!"* But his students respected him for his intelligence and integrity. "He was then a mine of information, and as he was one of Wolseley's men he had a good knowledge of what was going on." [38]

Maurice somehow managed to find time during seven busy years at the Staff College to continue writing. In 1887, the same year that his *Military History of the Campaign of 1882 in Egypt* was published, he created a stir in military and political circles on the Continent as well as in England with a series of provocative articles in *Blackwood's* on the subject "The Balance of Military Power in Europe." Wolseley, who was in a good position to pick up repercussions, reported that one of the articles in particular, dealing with possible English alliances, "has been extensively read abroad and by all the ambassadors here—It is a most powerful and able paper and I hope may be well digested by our own Cabinet." None other than Herbert Bismarck, the son of the German Chancellor, wrote suggesting that the articles be reprinted and expressing the hope that Maurice's views would find a receptive audience in England: Count Karolyi, the Austrian Ambassador, also "praised them in the highest terms and agreed with all the views they contain." When the articles were reprinted in book form under the same title the following year, the military attaché at Berlin wrote that it was one of the "very few" English military works to be found on the shelves of German officers.[39] Maurice also wrote his well-known essay on "War" while at Camberley. According to

[38] Godwin-Austen, *Staff and the Staff College*, pp. 209–10: Major General Lord Edward Gleichen, *A Guardsman's Memories: A Book of Recollections* (Edinburgh, 1932), pp. 111–12; Adye, *Soldiers and Others I Have Known*, p. 41; Major General Sir C. E. Callwell, *Stray Recollections* (London, 1923), I, 293; Lieutenant Colonel Charles À Court Repington, *Vestigia: Reminiscences of Peace and War* (Boston, 1919), p. 141. See also Maurice, "Round Foreign Battlefields," *United Service Magazine,* IX (1894), 77–85, 280–89, 413–18.

[39] Wolseley to A. C. Gleig, December 23, 1887 (Gleig Papers, National Library of Scotland, Edinburgh). Herbert Bismarck to Wolseley, November 11, 1887 (Wolseley Papers); Wolseley to Maurice, December 19, 1887

Wolseley, had Maurice never written another word on the subject, this article alone would "stamp him as the ablest English writer on military subjects." [40]

In addition to these works, Maurice frequently lectured before literary and political as well as military societies. Beginning in 1890 he also became the most prolific contributor to the *United Service Magazine*, which he owned and edited for the better part of a decade. Although unsuccessful as a business venture, this once-popular magazine was restored to good health by Maurice and it fulfilled a useful purpose during the years preceding the Boer War as an organ for reform. Accused in the press of being the mouthpiece of the Wolseley Ring, Maurice's magazine in fact served as a platform for anyone interested in military or naval reform. Naturally Wolseley and his followers frequently contributed articles; so, however, did Rudyard Kipling, the Duke of Argyll, Lord Charles Beresford, Sir Geoffrey Hornby, Sir Charles Dilke, and Spenser Wilkinson—all men who either belonged to the naval school or else were recognized opponents of Wolseley and his ideas. Even Hamley gave private support to the venture.

Maurice intended the *United Service Magazine* to assume some of the functions of the *Revue Militaire des armées étrangères* by diffusing knowledge of military and naval events elsewhere in the world and serving as a sort of unofficial press for both the War Office and the Admiralty. He contributed editorials, book reviews, articles on history and current events—everything, one suspects, needed as ballast to complete a forthcoming issue. Despite his protest that he was hard up, even Wolseley occasionally made a gift of his contributions and purchased ten copies a month as a subsidy, but Maurice's business sense was little better than his sense of direction in the German railroad station and ultimately he was forced to sell out at a heavy loss. [41]

(copy in the Blackwood Papers [No. 4505]); Maurice, *Work and Opinions*, p. 66. *The Balance of Military Power* appeared in Germany in the Tauchnitz edition.

[40] Wolseley, "War," *Fortnightly Review*, CCLXV (1889), 1.

[41] Maurice, *Work and Opinions*, pp. 73, 76; "The Wolseley Ring and the United Service Magazine," *United Service Magazine*, II (1891), 474–76; Wolseley to Lady Wolseley, October 28, 1894; March 14, 1896 (Wolseley Papers). There is no mistaking the economic motivation in Wolseley. He frequently urged his wife to contribute to the family pot by writing, and in 1898 he informed her: "I may run over to Ireland

Maurice by this time was no longer connected with the Staff College, having left when his appointment expired in 1892 for successive artillery commands at Aldershot, Colchester, and Woolwich. He continued to investigate and write about a wide variety of topics: army organization and administration, current military operations in Korea (1894–95) and Africa,[42] military history and biography.[43] Significantly, his monthly reviews of the Sino-Japanese War show Maurice to have been one of the first European soldiers fully to appreciate the military capabilities of Japan: as early as 1895 he predicted that Russia would be "decidedly inferior at sea and no stronger on land" in any future war with Japan.[44] In all of his writings Maurice seems to have been motivated by a desire to explain the facts, to "guide and calm" the judgment of the

for a day and see the Boyne once more for I could then write an article or a little book on it that would certainly give me £100 or perhaps £200, which would help to keep our pot boiling" (Wolseley to Lady Wolseley, July 28, 1898 [Wolseley Papers]).

[42] See Maurice's analysis of Japanese military operations in the *United Service Magazine*, IX (1894), 540–46; X (1894–95), 94–102, 200–210, 307–11, 422–26, 531–36, 630–37; XI (1895), 105–8, 201–7. Maurice's articles on the various colonial campaigns include "Tactics in Matabele Land. Luck or Skill," *ibid.*, VIII (1894), 618–23; "The Dongola Campaign," *ibid.*, XIII (1896), 113–23; and "Omdurman," *Nineteenth Century* XLIV (1898), 1043–54.

[43] Maurice's articles on Waterloo are found in the *United Service Magazine*, I (1890), N.S., 61–81, 137–52, 257–63, 344–55, 533–50; II (1890), 73–80, 330–39. His edition of *The Franco-German War 1870–71* (London, 1899; reprinted 1914) appears to be modeled after *Battles and Leaders of the Civil War*, which Maurice considered "of incalculable importance and highly instructive" (*R.U.S.I. Journal*, XXXIII [1890–91], 1076–87). Maurice did not complete his biography of Moore, but he did uncover Moore's journal, which had disappeared ninety years before. In 1904 Maurice published *The Diary of Sir John Moore* in two volumes. Other historical articles include "Assaye and Wellington," *Cornhill Magazine*, I (1896), 291–304, and lengthy reviews of Wolseley's *Marlborough* (*Quarterly Review*, CLXXIX [1894], 439–62), Maxwell's *Wellington* (*Edinburgh Review*, CXCII [1900,] 91–116), and Henderson's *Stonewall Jackson* (*ibid.*, CLXXXIX [1889], 48–75).

[44] Maurice, "Chinese Puzzle No Puzzle," *United Service Magazine*, XI (1895), 205, 207. Most English authorities recognized the superiority of the Japanese army in the Far East after the Sino-Japanese war but considered Japan a "military power of the second rank" when compared with the major European armies. See Lieutenant Colonel E. G. Barrow, "Military Japan after the War," *ibid.*, XII (1895), 13–20; H. W. Wilson, "England and the New Japan," *ibid.*, XI (1895), 109–22; Colonel Henry Knollys, "China's Reputation—Bubble," *Blackwood's*, CLVI (1894), 714–26. The writer is indebted to the researches of Mr. Ralph Kinney Bennett for confirmation of the reluctance of western observers to recognize the military power of Japan until 1905.

public, particularly whenever Britain's own interests were involved.[45]

His writings also reveal that his views on tactics had not changed materially since the day he submitted his Wellington Prize essay. With infantry the fundamental problem continued to be "how to maintain the old unity under the new conditions"; the solution was still to be found not so much in the adoption of specific tactical formations but in training officers and men to observe certain necessary conditions in battle. Infantry must learn "to place themselves instinctively and as quickly as possible under the orders of some officer who can get them into order," officers must learn to reform dispersed men at the first opportunity and to maneuver small units without sacrificing unity of action. Some system had to be devised to provide for the continual replenishment of ammunition close to the fighting line; fire discipline must be stressed, and after the experience of the Russians in their attacks on Plevna in 1877, when the unaimed fire of the Turks was deadly at great distances, Maurice recognized the possibilities of "an extensive employment of long-range fire." Maurice continued to recommend the use of intrenchments, but with reservations, sharing the popular view among professional soldiers that troops too accustomed to trenches somehow lost their spark. The Boer War confirmed his conviction that "the great power of modern weapons for purposes of defence in a position prepared by field intrenchments is probably the best basis for offensive tactics." Maurice criticized his old comrade in arms, General Sir Redvers Buller, for failing to imitate Sherman by using trenches and the local defensive to contain the Boers while preparing to attack one of the enemy's flanks.[46] (Maurice assumed, as did nearly all soldiers before 1914, that however well fortified, the enemy would always have flanks.)

He assumed also that there was still a need for cavalry: even though the infantry and artillery in position were now

[45] Maurice, *Work and Opinions*, p. 94; "Terms Used in Modern Gunnery," *Nineteenth Century*, XLVI (1899), 905–14.

[46] Maurice, *War*, p. 42–62; "How Far the Lessons of the Franco-German War Are Now out of Date," *United Service Magazine*, X (1894–95), 556; "Battles and Leaders of the Civil War," pp. 1084–86; "The War in South Africa," *Quarterly Review*, CXCI (1900), 555–56; *History of the War in South Africa*, I, 74, 243; II, 140, 319.

impervious to a mounted attack, "cavalry striking by sudden surprise on the flank of unprepared infantry or artillery, engaged with other enemies, may produce an effect, great to an extent of which as yet we have no adequate example in modern war." And by cavalry attack clearly he meant shock tactics, "the impetuous power and moral effect of the man and horse" armed "with their proper weapon, the . . . sword or lance." Maurice belittled the arguments of those who contended that mounted infantry had replaced cavalry in battle. "The Germans," he pointed out in 1887, "continually, at their maneouvres, practise their cavalry in surprise charges with the *arme blanche*," and no one on the Continent feared the Russian cavalry now that it had abandoned shock tactics for dismounted fighting.[47] He did not oppose mounted infantry as such; but he did insist, along with Wolseley, that the two should be separately organized and trained and that each should adhere to its own proper function. To dismount cavalry "tends directly to weaken and destroy the very spirit and quality on which the efficiency of true cavalry depends"; mounted infantry fighting on horseback "necessarily becomes a very inferior cavalry." Maurice recommended that mounted infantry should be under infantry, not cavalry, officers, and he proposed that the bicycle be utilized to supplement the horse, an idea that appealed to many officers particularly in regard to home defense. But Maurice never lost faith in cavalry proper: even after the Boer War he contended that it remained superior to mounted infantry and he cited the pursuit of Cronje as proof "that the conditions of modern fighting still permit cavalry and Horse artillery to play a role of supreme importance in war." In this conviction Maurice was heartily indorsed by most cavalrymen everywhere: *The Cavalry Journal* was conceived in 1904 and first appeared in print two years later in an effort to promulgate a similar doctrine.[48]

[47] Maurice, *War*, pp. 62–63; *The Balance of Military Power in Europe: An Examination of the War Resources of Great Britain and the Continental States* (Edinburgh, 1888), pp. 55–58. For a contrary opinion, see Colonel F. Chenevix Trench, *Cavalry in Modern War, Being the Sixth Volume of "Military Handbooks for Officers and Non-commissioned Officers"* (London, 1884), *passim*. Chenevix Trench was at one time British military attaché in St. Petersburg and was convinced by his study of the American Civil War that mounted infantry rather than cavalry proper was the arm of the future.

[48] Maurice, as quoted in the *R.U.S.I. Journal*, XLIV (1900), 661; *War*,

As for artillery, Maurice insisted that while technical changes since 1870 may have caused some modification in tactics, the concentration of artillery fire nonetheless remained an immutable principle, and he resisted any attempt to introduce the idea of distributed fire in the drill books. He also maintained that despite the enormous improvement in the destructive power of artillery in recent years, the most significant contribution of the arm continued to be—as it was in Napier's pages—"the great moral effect which is produced." Increased ranges meant merely that guns would open fire at greater ranges,

but as it is usually impossible for guns to see over the whole of the vast area of ground which is occupied by a modern battlefield, any distant fire, however destructive, tends rather to drive men out of the positions in which they are than to cause them to remain where they are to be slaughtered. Thus the victory-winning power of artillery is essentially connected with its moral rather than with its material effect.

The essential job of artillery, therefore, was to prepare for the attack, and to do this, Maurice argued, it was not necessary to destroy the enemy infantry but only to deprive defending troops of the will to resist by making the effect of the bombardment appear much worse than it really was.

Here it should be noted that Maurice had always emphasized the importance of destroying the enemy's will to resist. In 1872 he had commented that losses themselves were no adequate test of the results of battle: "Our object is to make

pp. 65–68; "Cycling as an Aid to Home Defence," *R.U.S.I. Journal*, XLVI (1902), 1–12; *History of the War in South Africa*, II, 103; *Work and Opinions*, pp. 97–103. Maurice first conceived the idea of using the bicycle for mobile infantry in 1890. In 1900 maneuvers demonstrated the military use of the bicycle when a volunteer battalion covered 100 miles in a single day, a distance that far surpassed anything that the horse could do, and on the eve of the First World War the territorial force had twelve cyclist battalions for the purpose of rushing infantry to meet an invader. For the views of Wolseley on mounted infantry, see "General Forrest," *United Service Magazine*, V (1892), 1–14, 113–24, *passim*.

According to the review of the first issue of the *Cavalry Journal*, "It is evident, from the number of articles devoted directly or indirectly to the subject, that the editors have deliberately elected to commence with an exposure of the ridiculous contentions of the mistaken school of thought by whom it is fatuously asserted that the days of Cavalry, quâ Cavalry, are over; and at the same time to illuminate, if possible, the dense intellects of others who have merely failed to comprehend the true functions of cavalry in modern war" (*United Service Magazine*, XXXII [1906], 604–6).

them run rather than to kill them—to break the effective force of the army opposed to us by destroying its moral power and cohesion, rather than by placing a certain number of men *hors de combat*." Twenty years later he still believed that "to produce a moral effect is the aim of all strategy and tactics and of each arm," a conviction upheld—at least as far as Maurice was concerned—by the experiences of the Boer War.[49]

If Maurice's tactical concepts represent substantially a crystalization of the solutions he formulated in 1872, this does not necessarily mean that he was inflexible or that he ignored the lessons of more recent wars. Actually the reverse is true. He never pretended to do more than indicate general conditions that would probably prevail in the next great war between European powers, and for this purpose the war of 1870 was unquestionably a better guide than subsequent campaigns in Africa and India, where the experience of one war often was reversed by the next. It was almost necessary, Maurice once told a military audience, for the British army to change tactics every year. The extended skirmishing order adopted after 1870 had proven useless against the Zulus at Isandlhwana, but the close-order formations that worked well in savage warfare no longer served any useful purpose in Europe. Moreover, in a day of rapid technical change, when British soldiers were apt to be employed anywhere in the world under conditions that varied widely and could not be anticipated because the tactics, equipment, and transport requirements differed with the circumstances of each campaign, the British army could not even preserve "one uniform pattern, such as is established everywhere by the nations of the Continent." About all that could be done to prepare the army to fight was to retain elasticity in outlook, simplicity in drill, and to adopt a common, simplified nomenclature in the various training manuals. When the next war came the British would have to feel their way amidst new conditions, but at least their feet would not be chained to a rigid system of tactics long since outmoded.[50]

[49] Maurice, *System of Field Manoeuvres*, p. 74; *War*, pp. 80–82; "War in South Africa," *Quarterly Review*, CXCI, 289; *History of the War in South Africa*, II, 418; III, 156. See also Maurice's comments following a lecture on modern artillery at the Royal United Service Institution (*R.U.S.I. Journal*, XXXIII [1889–90], 108).

[50] Maurice, "The Advantages of a Simple Drill Nomenclature Consistent for All Arms, apropos to an Incident of the Battle of Tel-el-Kebir,"

While still at the Staff College, Maurice also became concerned with the increasingly complex problems of grand strategy and national defense. In 1883 he had declined a request to do a volume on national defense because he considered it a more appropriate subject for a sailor to investigate and also because he did not feel that the time was ripe for such a book. He changed his mind a year or so later, however, after the Right Honourable W. H. Smith—the creator of the railway bookstall—had entered the War Office and Lieutenant General Sir Henry Brackenbury had become director of military intelligence. The one was a quiet, unassuming, businesslike secretary of state for war to whom Lord Salisbury soon turned for leadership in the House of Commons; the other has been described as "the most competent administrator in our Army"; and between them they began serious work of a kind that many British soldiers "had been praying for for years"—the creation of an expeditionary force equipped and trained to strike anywhere in the empire, and the strengthening of the defenses of coaling stations to the point where the fleet "could rely upon them, instead of having to defend them." [51]

Anxious to support these reforms and angered by "the very serious miscalculations" in Sir Charles Dilke's articles in *The Fortnightly Review* on the relative military power of the European nations, Maurice contributed a series of articles on the same subject to *Blackwood's*. For once he agreed with Hamley: it was imperative, he wrote, that a non-partisan commission be established "to determine the purposes for which we maintain our army and navy, to consider how far our present forces fulfil the necessary conditions, and to decide what forces we do or do not require to maintain." Until these fundamental decisions had been reached British soldiers must always grope in the dark, and Maurice accused Dilke of writing with a "beam" in his own eye while at the same time posing as one who was above party passions and pressures.[52]

Ibid., XXXII (1888–89), 91–102; *History of the Boer War*, I, 88; II, 113, 204–205. See also Maurice's comments in the *R.U.S.I. Journal*, XLIV (1900), 658–59, *Work and Opinions*, pp. 129–91, *passim*.

[51] Maurice, *Balance of Military Power*, pp. viii, 39, 206; Captain Owen Wheeler, *The War Office Past and Present* (London, 1914), pp. 237–39; Hamilton, *Listening for the Drums*, p. 179.

[52] Maurice, *Balance of Military Power*, pp. x, 9; Maurice to William Blackwood, April 23, 1887 (Blackwood Papers). Dilke's articles, which

There is no point in describing Maurice's view of the military posture of Europe and the colonies in 1887 except in the most general terms: the political climate has changed drastically since then, and much of what he wrote was intended specifically to refute facts or opinions in Dilke's analysis. The most striking fact in Maurice's work—one which separated him from many soldiers at the time—is his conviction that naval power alone could be translated into an effective force equivalent to hundreds of thousands of soldiers upon the Continent. One would expect such an argument from the American theorist, Captain A. T. Mahan and British naval writers like the brothers Colonel Sir John and Admiral Philip Colomb, but it is somewhat surprising to find such a strong supporter of sea power in one whose writings hitherto had been focused primarily on the land campaigns between France and Prussia.

Briefly stated, Maurice contended that Britain's power, by virtue of her command of the sea and an "unrivalled" merchant marine, was best exerted in those places where, in Kinglake's phrase, "land and sea much intertwine." With her unique ability to land a small army on an exposed coast anywhere in the world, Britain was in a unique position to exert an "enormously potent military influence" in Europe as well as the far corners of the empire. It was necessary therefore to make the requisite military force available by shaping the disjointed lots of regiments, batteries, and squadrons into a concrete amphibious force; to keep the navy overwhelmingly powerful and insure its mobility by strengthening the armament and garrisons of coaling stations and harbors.

Military writers during this period have been assigned somewhat arbitrarily to the "military" school of thought—men who would not rely absolutely on the navy for the defense of England—and the "blue water" school, which contended that the fleet alone was an absolute bar to invasion and adopted as a slogan the stirring words of Mahan: "those far distant, storm-beaten ships, upon which the Grand Army never looked, stood between it and the domination of the world." Military men themselves were further divided over the

were at once attributed to him although written anonymously, were published later in the year as *The Present Position of European Politics* (London, 1887).

goal of British military preparations: some opposed armed intervention on the Continent under any circumstances, others maintained that in view of the immense size of the conscript armies on the Continent, effective intervention was impossible, and many argued that the main efforts should be directed toward reinforcing the garrisons of overseas possessions, especially India.[53]

Maurice's position in this spectrum is not easily identified. Hamley, for example, fits neatly into the military school, in which he was an outspoken advocate of the "forward" policy in defending India. Maurice on the other hand looked to the navy rather than a special frontier force to defend the North West Frontier. In his view the only sound policy was to be prepared to retaliate against any Russian encroachment in the area by striking Russia where she was most vulnerable—her seaboard, fleet, and commerce, and perhaps the sensitive lines of communication through Persia. The Boer War, like the Egyptian campaign of 1882, clearly demonstrated Britain's unique power to dispatch and supply "a large army at an immense distance from home." [54]

Yet Maurice cannot be considered representative of the "blue water" school of thought if it meant subscribing to statements like Admiral Sir John Fisher's assertion that "The Navy is the 1st, 2nd, 3rd, 4th, 5th . . . ad infinitum Line of Defence! If the Navy is not supreme, no Army however large is of the slightest use." [55] The difference between Maurice and the extremists was essentially one of emphasis, but he could not agree with those who denied the possibility of an invasion of England under any conceivable circumstances or who claimed that the army was of value primarily as a missile to be launched by the fleet. As an observer of the naval maneuvers in 1888, he saw the squadrons com-

[53] Arthur J. Marder, *The Anatomy of British Sea Power: A History of British Naval Policy in the Pre-Dreadnought Era, 1880–1905* (New York, 1940), pp. 65–83; Maurice, *Work and Opinions,* p. 65.

[54] Maurice, *Balance of Military Power,* pp. 50, 53, 179; "The True Policy of National Defence," *Contemporary Review,* LIV (1888), 214–23, *passim;* "Frontier Policy and Lord Lytton's Indian Administration," *Edinburgh Review,* CXCI (1900), 226–46. For a clear sketch of the issues involved, see C. C. Davies, "The North-West Frontier, 1843–1918," in H. H. Dodwell (ed.), *The Indian Empire 1858–1918: With Chapters on the Development of Administration 1818–1858 (The Cambridge History of the British Empire,* Vol. V; New York, 1932), pp. 448–75.

[55] Quoted in Marder, *Anatomy of British Sea Power,* p. 65.

manded by Sir George Tryon successfully frustrate the efforts of a stronger blockading fleet and he concluded:

> The English fleet is completely unable, with its present strength, to save our shores and commerce from even one foreign fleet. The man who from this time forward in the House of Commons or on any platform endeavours to lull us into security by telling us that our navy is supreme because it has a superiority, ship for ship and gun for gun, over the French, is simply an unscrupulous scoundrel. There is no use in mincing the matter. It is the safety of our homes and the food of our population that is at stake. . . . Our navy is not strong enough. It must at all costs be made so.[56]

The maneuvers of 1889 seemed to justify Maurice's conviction that a naval blockade under modern conditions was impossible to maintain. Later he attacked the views of a small group of naval writers who exhibited "a kind of quarterdeck jealousy of every attempt to render our land forces efficient."[57] As a soldier Maurice was criticized for "pleading before all things for the navy," but he did so on military grounds and not at the expense of the army. Both a supreme navy and an adequate army were necessary if England were to realize commanding amphibious power, and there was always the possibility that Britain might lose command of the Channel long enough to permit an enemy landing on the coasts: the sea was an "unstable" line of defense because the navy could not always overcome delays caused by storms, fog, mechanical difficulties, or loss of communications. To insist, therefore, upon sufficient training and equipment for the reserve forces did not imply any lack of confidence in the navy; but to reduce the inhabitants of Eng-

---

[56] "The Naval Manoeuvres," *Fortnightly Review*, XLIV (1888), 402–4. Maurice later wrote that he invaded Sir Charles Dilke's base of operations at the request of the editor of *Fortnightly*, who was so impressed by Maurice's arguments for sea power that he invited him to contribute an anonymous article stressing "the need of looking to our navy for Imperial Defence" (Maurice, *National Defences* [London, 1897], p. 6).

[57] Maurice, "China and Japan," *United Service Magazine*, X (1894–95), 210; "Two Years of Naval Manoeuvres," *Contemporary Review*, LVI (1899), 534–35. The latter was approved in proof form by Admiral Sir George Tryon himself, while Maurice's views on the impracticability of the naval blockade were supported by Admiral Sir Geoffrey Hornby against the arguments of Admiral Philip H. Colomb, one of the best known and most influential members of the "blue-water" school with whom Maurice frequently crossed "friendly swords" (Maurice, *National Defences*, pp. 188–89; Colomb, "The Functions of Armies and Navies: A Demurrer to Colonel Maurice's Pleadings," *United Service Magazine*, X [1894–95], 220–25).

land "to a condition of helpless dependence" upon the navy and allow them to enjoy secure ease was not in the national interest, for such an attitude would neither build character nor create more public minded citizens. Maurice supported Wolseley's program for the formation of a permanent and well-equipped expeditionary force of two army corps and a cavalry division, roughly 70,000 men: less than half this number had been decisive in Egypt in 1882, and Maurice believed that such a force could have intervened with decisive effect against Austria and Prussia in Denmark in 1864, and against the Russians in Constantinople in 1878.[58]

But more than an expeditionary force was needed to defend the empire and preserve the military balance of power in Europe: England must have allies, and Maurice recommended an alliance with the Central Powers against Russia and France. From England's point of view such an alliance would insure the defense of the empire by threatening decisive action in Europe against her two foremost colonial rivals while the command of the sea, the possession of an effective expeditionary force, and vast financial power would make England a desirable ally for Italy, Austria, and Germany. By guaranteeing the defense of the Italian coast against the possibility of a French attack from the sea, British naval power alone would free 300,000 Italian soldiers for service on the land frontiers. England could offer additional strength to Germany and Austria out of all proportion to the number of soldiers actually comprising the expeditionary force. Thus Maurice was one of the first in England to realize that isolation was not "splendid" and to point out emphatically that if England were to wait to fight a war in her own interests it would be impossible to secure allies "who will fight for us when we have refused to fight for them."

[T]his much is certain . . . if we do not help ourselves no other power will help us. If we cannot and will not give help, we cannot get help. It is a question simply of securing for a moderate price the incalculable blessings of peace, or of being involved in certainly the most costly, and probably the most fatal, war in which we have ever engaged.[59]

[58] "The War Office and the Army," *Quarterly Review*, CLXXXIII (1896), 189–90; *National Defences*, pp. 7, 197–98, 209; *Balance of Military Power*, pp. xiii–xiv, 31, 33, 50, 200 n.
[59] *Ibid.*, pp. 197, 200, 240.

Maurice did not of course predict the First World War, but in view of the opening campaigns in 1914 some of his strategical conclusions are of interest. First, he assumed that the next great war would involve Germany and Austria on one side and France and Russia on the other, although he wrote in the same year that the Reinsurance Treaty was signed between Russia and Germany and seven years before a formal alliance between Russia and France. Second, he recognized the threat to the neutrality of Belgium but did not believe that Germany would use this route to avoid the French frontier defenses. In any case, Maurice assumed that neither Germany nor France would dare march through Belgium as long as there remained the probability that England would land an army, even a small one, on the direct line of communications of the invader: "If Belgium arms, and England forbids violation of her territory, the territory of Belgium will not be violated." Finally he forecast the strategy that enabled the Germans to defeat Russia at Tannenburg: a Russian attempt

to move in two separate columns, unless each column was in overwhelming force, which, from the nature of the country, would not be easy, must give opportunities to a German general for dealing blows right and left against either army while separated by the lake region of East Prussia. Thus an attack by Russia upon Germany appears to be one which offers every kind of advantage to the Germans, either for a prolonged resistance with inferior forces, or if in approximately equal numbers, for striking deadly blows against the invader.

Maurice did not hazard a guess as to whether Germany would assume the offensive in the east or the west—this would naturally depend upon circumstances—but he recognized that

there are possibilities involved in the possession . . . of a middle position covered with a most perfect and carefully devised railway system, and a telegraph network as complete, which stagger one as to the terrible grandeur of the drama which may be enacted by their means almost under our eyes. In a time far shorter than it took Napoleon to transfer his force from Boulogne to Ulm and Austerlitz . . . a German army might be nowadays transferred from the Rhine to the Vistula, or from Königsberg to Metz. Under given conditions, such a transfer of men from one side of Europe to the other might be made without any knowledge of the movement reaching either of the hostile armies until one that had been advancing triumphantly was crushed by the new and overwhelming power suddenly thrown into the field.[60]

Picking the wrong enemy for England disqualifies Maurice as a prophet but in no way diminishes his acumen as a military analyst. Subsequent military developments and revelations of the strategical thinking of the German General Staff show that his evaluation of the military situation in Europe in 1887 was fundamentally sound, even though later events suggest that he rated too highly the quality of the Austrian army and the importance of Italy to England. When he wrote again on the subject ten years later, the international situation had changed and Maurice, although still convinced that a combination of Britain and the Triple Alliance was best for the peace of Europe and the security of the empire, no longer believed such an alliance possible. By this time too he had begun to be suspicious of the growing naval power of Germany, although he mistakenly thought that Mahan's influence would lead to a greater appreciation in the minds of Continental statesmen "of the enormous importance to them of the alliance of the Great Sea Power." In 1897 the nation that Britain had most to fear, in Maurice's estimation, was still France.[61]

Maurice ended his active military career in 1902 when his term at Woolwich, having been extended to the end of the Boer War, at length expired. His pen, however, remained as active as ever. In 1903 he succeeded the ailing Henderson as official historian of the Boer War. The following year he published the two-volume *Diary of Sir John Moore*, which he had discovered and edited, and he wrote running commentaries on the Russo-Japanese War for the *Daily Telegraph*. Maurice continued to show an interest in contemporary problems, although the only new ideas he had to contribute at this time were in the field of social rather than military reform. True to his father's spirit, he devoted countless hours to the cause of improving the health of the under-

---

[60] *Ibid.*, pp. 110, 117, 147–48, 169–70. This of course was the fundamental goal of German strategy. Moltke and his successor Waldersee planned on a powerful offensive in the East and "a more or less offensive defence" in the West; Schlieffen shifted the emphasis from east to west in his memorandum of August, 1892, and planned ultimately on an envelopment of the French left wing by an advance through Belgium. See Gerhard Ritter, *The Schlieffen Plan: Critique of a Myth* (London, 1958), pp. 17–45.

[61] Maurice, *National Defences*, pp. 72, 140–55.

privileged. He was one of those responsible for the National League for Physical Education and Improvement, "and he was constantly occupied in working, writing, and speaking, on behalf of the League until his health broke down." He also was instrumental in the establishment of the St. Francis Hospital for Infants. But the old soldier had his own reasons for improving national health: he had discovered that of every five men who enlist in the army only two remained as effective soldiers by the end of two years' service. Obviously, the real problem therefore was not to obtain recruits in greater numbers, but rather to find men in better health in order to reduce the wastage. Maurice blamed inadequate diet, bad teeth, flat feet, and the lack of physical exercise as the real obstacles to be overcome, none of which was removable by conscription or some form of compulsory service. The shortage of recruits, therefore, was a problem for the nation rather than the War Office, and the answer was to be found in a more systematic development of the health of the country's youth.[62]

Maurice s own health broke down in 1908, and he was forced to give up work on the official history. He lingered on for four more years, but his day clearly was over. As a matter of fact, his most effective pleading had been before the Boer War, when he and Wolseley still retained their intellectual powers and progressive outlook. The young reformers of 1870 had grown old by the turn of the century, and although they lived until the eve of the First World War, in many respects neither had survived the Victorian Age. The army was in other hands; the war they had spent a quarter of a century preparing for had already been fought—and against the wrong enemy. Many of their friends were gone and few of the problems they had lived with remained: England at last had an expeditionary force backed by a territorial army for home defense, a navy far more powerful than those of her rivals, and, after 1907, England had allies that removed the threat to the North West Frontier and the hope expressed so often by Wolseley—usually on the eve of his birthday—that he might die at the head of an army that had just defeated the French![63]

[62] "Miles" (Maurice), "Where To Get Men," *Contemporary Review* (LXXXI, 1902), 78–86; "National Health: A Soldier's Study," reprinted in *Work and Opinions*, pp. 259–81.
[63] "I feel as convinced as I can be of anything that we shall have a war

It would not be fair to Maurice to judge his theories on tactics and strategy solely in the light of what happened during the First World War. Admittedly some of his tactical deductions did not weather the storm that burst over Europe in 1914: he underestimated the destructive power of modern artillery when discussing the moral effects of concentrated fire and he greatly overestimated the importance of cavalry after the Boer War. Yet Maurice was on the right track in predicting the importance of trenches and in stressing flexibility and realism in training infantry for the attack. According to Henderson, the views on drill and discipline expressed in the Wellington Prize essay were still valid at the time of the Boer War, and in essence many of Maurice's ideas on training could have been indorsed by army reformers after the First World War as well. It should be noted, however, that Maurice never attempted to find a formula for victory in all wars: as he stated in another connection, "There the absolute tactical deduction stops." [64] His ideas on strategy were conventionally sound and there was no way he could have anticipated the growth of the Triple Entente twenty years before the event. He appreciated both the dangers and advantages to Germany of waging war on two extended and widely separated fronts, and he was fully aware of the military value of sea power. There is a significant contrast between Maurice's enthusiasm for Mahan's theories and the statement of Sir Henry Wilson, director of military operations, in 1913 that whereas he did not consider the British navy "worth 500 bayonets" in a war with Germany, the French generals Castelnau and Joffre "did not value it at one bayonet! Except from the moral point." [65]

Significantly, the period of Maurice's greatest influence corresponds almost exactly with the period Wolseley was the

---

with France before ten years come and go—it might come now at any moment. We shall make no preparations for it, and consequently, we shall have a French army in Ireland and possibly one in England also, before the generation now in their youth are gathered to their fathers. I should like to die commanding an army that had just utterly destroyed a French army" (Wolseley to Lady Wolseley, June 3, 1885 [Wolseley Papers]). See also his letter to Lady Wolseley, June 3, 1895.

[64] Maurice, "The Army-Corps Scheme and Mr. Dawkins's Committee: An Historical Retrospect," *Nineteenth Century*, L (1901), 145; *System of Field Manoeuvres*, p. 54.

[65] Maurice, "Mahan's Testimony to England's Power," *United Service Magazine*, VII (1893), 792–98; "Mahan on Nelson and Pitt," *ibid.*, 972–81; *National Defences*, pp. 51–58; *Work and Opinions*, pp. 109–12. Major General Sir C. E. Callwell, *Field-Marshal Sir Henry Wilson: His Life and Diaries* (London, 1927), I, 122.

guiding spirit in the army. The Wellington Prize essay first brought the two together; *The Ashanti War* helped to popularize Wolseley as well as explain the facts of the campaign to an awaiting public; *Hostilities without Declarations of War* documented the opposition of Wolseley and the War Office to the projected Channel tunnel; *The Military History of the Campaign of 1882 in Egypt* was of sufficient historical value to warrant a new edition in 1909, a precedent not followed by any other official campaign history until the early volumes of *Military Operations, France and Belgium, 1914,* were revised to incorporate fresh material; *The Balance of Military Power* added volume to the voices clamoring for a stronger fleet and thus contributed to the agitation that produced the Naval Defence Act of 1889: it also supported Brackenbury's scheme in 1886 for the mobililization of two army corps for service outside the British Isles.

Maurice was influential in the Royal United Service Institution and instrumental in arresting the atrophy and perhaps even preventing the demise of the *United Service Magazine.* At the Staff College from 1885 to 1892 he was respected for his knowledge, beloved for his idiosyncrasies, and regarded as the most accomplished among the professors. Although cramped by the need to prepare students for examinations that varied little from year to year, Maurice nevertheless tried to treat military history as an academic discipline. In this he never quite succeeded to his own satisfaction, but he indicated the path to be followed and before he departed he made sure of a successor who would make his own way along a parallel route. "I am deeply conscious that at present the Staff College produces a monstrous deal of bread for very little sack," he wrote to Henderson soon after handing over the chair.

The able men who would make good Staff Officers benefit greatly; so do those who have strong character or practical experience of war to guide them; but from the ruck we have turned out, I fear me, some cranks and not a few pedants. I am sure that under the new regime you will succeed where I have often failed.[66]

The work of Maurice should not be measured by what he wrote in the last ten years of his active life. *National Defences,* published in 1897, was received by the critics with mixed

[66] Quoted in Godwin-Austen, *Staff and the Staff College,* p. 231.

feelings: it contained "very much more than a grain of truth," and yet much of it applied to conditions which no longer prevailed.[67] It was the only book Maurice ever wrote that did not "command a ready sale." *The Diary of Sir John Moore* was "highly controversial" because Maurice was as much captivated by Moore as Napier had been: Sir John Fortescue, *the* historian of the British army, condemned the "careless and inadequate treatment" of Moore's journal and called for a new and revised edition "by a competent editor." Nor was Maurice's *History of the War in South Africa* the book that it might have been: Maurice went out of his way (and somewhat out of character) to avoid controversy, and the *Times* was harsh but not altogether unfair in its comment that the work as a consequence was "a colourless statement of facts rather than one which might guide and form the opinions of a soldier." [68]

Perhaps the most significant aspect of Maurice's military thought is his unwillingness to cast aside English military institutions and organization when everybody else was rushing to the corner to watch the Prussians march by. He greatly admired the Prussian army, particularly the independence it allowed subordinate commanders and the discipline that can be defined as an aptitude for working together, but he felt that British tactics could be adapted to modern conditions, particularly if the British were to reorganize, as they did in 1913, the battalion to include larger but fewer companies.[69] Similarly, he believed that it was not necessary to turn to the German General Staff as a model in order to increase the

[67] Maurice, *Work and Opinions*, p. 80; *Spectator* (November 27, 1898), 773–74.

[68] C. W. C. Oman, *Wellington's Army 1809–1814* (London, 1912), p. 37; Sir John Fortescue, *History of the British Army* (London, 1899–1930), IV, 184, 199; *United Service Magazine*, XXIX (1904), 95–97; *Times* obituary, January 13, 1912.

[69] The British army adhered to the traditional battalion organization until the eve of the First World War. The question of the four-company battalion divided military opinion in England "in a way that no other military question" had done in modern times. The turning point seems to have come in 1911, when Brigadier General (later General Sir Ivor) Maxse, later to gain fame as the trainer of the armies in France, advocated the adoption of the four-company battalion at the Royal United Service Institution. The next year the four-company battalion was tried in training at Aldershot, and in a special army order dated September 16, 1913, it was adopted in battalions of the foot guards and all regular infantry battalions (*ibid.*, December 20, 1911; May 18, 1912; September 17, 1913).

efficiency of the War Office. He disagreed with the recommendations of the Hartington Commission in 1890 to abolish the office of commander in chief (Wolseley was next in line for the position) and to create a general staff—by which was meant staff officers in the usual sense of the term—under a chief of staff responsible to the secretary of state for war. All that was necessary, Maurice contended, was to free the commander in chief of needless details in order that he might be free to devote the bulk of his time to reflection and planning. Maurice even broke away from the German pattern of official history, feeling that "the duties of an official historian writing for a country under a constitutional and parliamentary government like that of England are not the same as those of a German historian." [70]

Maurice was unusual in another regard: unlike many professional soldiers of his day, he welcomed the "fresh thought and independent views" of the volunteer officers, even though he did feel that some of those who wrote about military problems might, "as a matter of military discipline," adopt "a less aggressive tone in referring to the decisions of military authority." He had the volunteers in mind when he decided to publish his Wellington Prize essay in 1872 (the regular British officer, he wrote to Blackwood, "hates literary work").[71] He greatly respected the views of volunteer officers like Spenser Wilkinson and J. H. A. Macdonald and from the latter, who ultimately became lord advocate of Scotland, he derived many of his views on fire discipline and tactical organization. Addressing an audience of volunteer officers in 1873, Maurice confessed that "you have done much more for us than we have been able to do for you," an opinion he still held after he had retired from the army.[72]

[70] "War Office and the Army," pp. 204–5; "Critics and Campaigns," p. 123.

[71] "I have been for some time intending to mention to you certain facts about the characteristics of that somewhat queer animal in the matter of books, the British officer. . . . I believe the great difficulty in getting a sale for books in the army is that partly from the habit of being a good deal away at out-stations, partly because never possessed of much literary connection, partly because largely sprung from classes very much dependent for their reading on local circulating libraries the British officer as a rule *does not know where to get books.* . . . He hates literary work even in the form of letter writing, has hardly the energy to undertake it" (Maurice to John Blackwood, n.d. 1872 [Blackwood Papers 4308]).

[72] Maurice quoted extensively from Macdonald's treatise, *Common Sense on Parade, or Drill without Stays* (Edinburgh, 1886). Maurice, *Work and Opinions,* p. 160.

Maurice's son, who later acquired a reputation to rival that of his father as a military writer, has recorded that

During his long illness Maurice was able to watch with pleasure and interest the effect of the recent introduction of many of the reforms which he had spent much of his life in advocating. He welcomed the good results which followed the decentralization of War Office business, the formation of a General Staff [but not at the expense of the office of commander in chief], the growth of co-operation between the army and navy, the grouping of the army in fighting formations, trained and staffed in peace by the men who would serve with them in war, the earnest attempts to provide us with second-line troops adequate for home defence; in all these he saw signs of steady and satisfactory progress, but perhaps nothing gave him greater pleasure than the frank recognition of our interest in maintaining the balance of power in Europe.[73]

The *Times* predicted that Maurice

will be best remembered . . . as a writer, a thinker, a student of war and of national problems, and this at a period when the average officer had but little encouragement, even if he had the inclination, to devote himself to this side of his profession. A clear and forcible writer, accurate in his facts and of sound judgment, his voluminous publications form a series which will have special value to the future student of military thought in the latter part of the nineteenth century.[74]

Both the recollections of the son and the forecast of the *Times* were essentially correct, yet neither goes quite to the heart of the matter. No complete evaluation of Maurice is possible without taking into consideration his special relationship to Wolseley. In a very real sense he was the second pen of his good friend and chief. This is not to imply that he was merely a hack: Wolseley had been attracted to him in the first instance for his original analysis of Prussian tactics, and Maurice did not hesitate to differ with his chief over questions of detail in organization (Wolseley, for example, favored the existing eight-company battalion) or to praise the accomplishments in South Africa of Britain's "only other general," Roberts, whom Wolseley neither liked nor trusted.[75] But the

[73] *Ibid.*, p. 125.
[74] *Times* obituary, January 13, 1912.
[75] "I have always regarded him as a scheming little Indian who had acquired a great reputation he would never have had but for the necessity of getting someone up to counteract my influence in the army" (Wolseley to Lady Wolseley, August 1, 1895 [Wolseley Papers]). See also Maurice's unsigned article, "War in South Africa," pp. 557–59.

minds of the two seemed always to operate on the same wave lengths. Both fought against the imitation of everything German, wrote of the importance of sea power, and worked to increase the power of the commander in chief.

There is no doubting the mutual respect and affection that existed between the two. Maurice greatly admired Wolseley, and in the eyes of Wolseley, Maurice was

full of honest enthusiasm and of courage that equals the enthusiasm; not always discerning nor always wise in public matters. Above all meanness and yet very suspicious of others and inclined to attribute men's actions to unworthy notions and to see conspiracy in their conduct. But his fine qualities put these small peculiarities so much in the shade that it is only those who know him well who know of their existence.

And in addition to these was the one quality that Wolseley prized most—loyalty.[76] So loyal was he, in fact, that often his pen was mistaken for that of his chief,[77] but this does justice to neither the motives nor the character of either man.

Perhaps the clue to Maurice's importance to Wolseley is contained in the observations by Archibald Forbes, who wrote (in language making it difficult to comprehend his popularity as a war correspondent) of the Wolseley Ring:

The keynote to the constitution of that group of devoted adherents . . . I take to be its completeness for the functions which it has to perform as a composite whole. In each of its constituent

[76] Wolseley to Lady Wolseley, July 31, 1895; August 15, 1897 (Wolseley Papers). Wolseley never forgave Brackenbury and Buller for trying to increase their authority at his expense, the former through the recommendations of the Hartington Commission to create a chief of the staff to advise the secretary of state upon strategic matters (Brackenbury, according to Wolseley, proposed this office "with a view to its being filled by Brack himself. . . . I am glad that Brackenbury is in India at this juncture for it is one disturbing element out of the way" [Wolseley to Lady Wolseley, August 6, 1895 (Wolseley Papers)]), the latter for intriguing to land the office of commander in chief for himself upon the retirement of the Duke of Cambridge (Wolseley to Lady Wolseley, August 6, 1895 [Wolseley Papers]).

[77] Broad Arrow, LV (July 6, 1895), p. 1: Maurice, Balance of Military Power, pp. xi, 236 n. Wolseley doubtless wanted to avoid criticism of this sort when he left the country at the time the Hamley controversy was renewed. Maurice visited him and together they discussed what Maurice would write, yet Wolseley confided to his daughter "I am glad I am abroad so none will be able to say that I have had any hand in whatever Maurice writes on the subject" (Wolseley to Lady Wolseley, June 15, 1895; Wolseley to Francis Wolseley, June 22, 1895 [Wolseley Papers]).

elements, [Wolseley] . . . has discerned some specific attribute, of which, when the occasion calls it into requisition, he shall take astute and purposeful avail. As a whole, then, it is . . . an engine effectively adapted to a wide range of potential uses. The individual units of that whole do not strike one as by any means . . . men of exceptional general military ability. Some of them, indeed, may be called dull men. But never a one of them but has his specialty. One has a genius for prompt organization; another a rare faculty for administration. A third has a winning manner and a good address, a fourth is the scout of scouts. . . . The "gang" as an aggregate is a weapon of extraordinary and diverse force; break it up and its parts are but the withes of a faggot, with here and there a stick of exceptional stoutness.[78]

If this description is correct, then there is no mistaking Maurice's function: he possessed the pen, not to be used at Wolseley's bidding and most assuredly not to sway the decisions of Britain's foremost general, but rather to articulate the thoughts that passed between them.

He was also "a stick of exceptional stoutness," and it is singularly appropriate that the second pen of Sir Garnet should have been the first in England to receive the coveted Chesney Gold Medal in 1907. Instituted in 1899 in memory of Sir George Chesney, an imaginative military writer and a successful administrator, this was to be awarded from time to time "to the author of an original literary work treating of Naval or Military Science and Literature, and which has a bearing on the welfare of the British Empire." [79] The only previous recipient had been the American, Mahan, whose writings were regarded the world over as the gospel of sea power. Long aspiring for a command in the field, Maurice died with the satisfaction of knowing that at the very least he had been recognized for his command of another field.

[78] Archibald Forbes, *Souvenirs of Some Continents* (London, 1885), pp. 175–77.

[79] *R.U.S.I. Journal,* XLIV (1900), 1097–98. Only seven medals were awarded between 1899 and 1914: in addition to Mahan and Maurice, the other recipients were Sir John Fortescue, Sir J. D. Laughton, Sir Charles Oman, Sir Lonsdale Hale, and Sir Julian Corbett. Of the total number, three can be classified as naval writers, two as military historians, and two as military writers on a variety of subjects. The most recent recipients are Major General J. F. C. Fuller and Captain B. H. Liddell Hart (see chapters X and XI), who were awarded—belatedly, to be sure—The Chesney Gold Medal on October 31, 1963.

7

THE UNFINISHED SYNTHESIS

Colonel G. F. R. Henderson

In 1886 there appeared in England a small, rather insignificant-looking volume entitled *The Campaign of Fredericksburg,* written by an anonymous "Line Officer." To the average soldier this book was probably just another campaign history, better written than most tactical studies but otherwise no different from many similar volumes in the regimental library. But to those concerned with the education of the British officer this book had a unique appeal. Written with an intelligence and insight unusual in such literature and filled with thoughtful observations on the military significance of the campaign, it represented a skilful blending of personal knowledge of the terrain, careful study of the available sources, and a lively, readable style. Maurice, who was in his second year as professor of military art and history at the Staff College, reviewed the book with enthusiasm and then, recalling that Wolseley had visited the Confederate army a few weeks before the battle and perhaps mindful of the benefits that had proceeded from his own first effort as a writer, he forwarded his copy to Wolseley. Wolseley read it, liked it, and made inquiries about the identity of the author. As adjutant general he was charged with the military education of British officers and could use an able instructor.[1]

"Line Officer" proved to be Captain George Francis Robert

[1] Lieutenant Colonel Frederick Maurice, *Sir Frederick Maurice: A Record of His Work and Opinions* (London, 1913), p. 64; Major General Sir Frederick Maurice and Sir George Arthur, *The Life of Lord Wolseley* (New York, 1924), p. 236. The standard sources for Henderson's career

Henderson of the York and Lancaster Regiment. Although he did not live long enough for all of his ideas to mature or perhaps even to perform his greatest services as a military writer, Henderson nevertheless wielded an enormous intellectual influence in the British army, and in many respects his writings represent a synthesis of the views of those who have preceded him in these pages. He wrote in a style as polished and lucid as the best passages of Napier and Hamley; as an observer of contemporary military developments he remained as flexible and capable of growth as Burgoyne and Mac-Dougall; although he lacked the cruasading zeal of Mitchell he was anxiously concerned about modernizing tactics, and he was more successful as a teacher than either Hamley or Maurice. Henderson's writings on the American Civil War and the Franco-Prussian War were carefully constructed on a firm foundation of fact and theory and were accepted as supremely authoritative in both respects. In a very real sense he even bridged the gap between Wolseley and Roberts: the former provided Henderson with his first opportunity and wrote an introduction to his most famous historical work, while the latter was responsible for his last employment and contributed a biographical appreciation to Henderson's most significant book on the science of war. Had Henderson lived long enough to complete his history of the Boer War and to analyze the lessons of the war in Manchuria, there can be little doubt that he would have been in a position, considering his influence and insight, to provide unique services for the army in preparing for the next great war: had he lived to retirement age, he might even have been able to include in his synthesis the military lessons of 1914–18.

Henderson was born in 1854, the eldest of fourteen children of the Reverend William George Henderson. Educated at Leeds Grammar School, where his father was headmaster, he was a good enough student to gain a history

are Lieutenant Colonel R. M. Holden, "Lieut.-Colonel G. F. R. Henderson, C.B.," *R.U.S.I. Journal,* XLVII (1903), 375–82; E. M. Lloyd, "Henderson," *D.N.B. Supplement,* II, pp. 240–41; and a biographical appreciation by Field Marshal Earl Roberts in Henderson, *The Science of War,* ed. Captain Neill Malcolm (London, 1906), pp. xiii–xxxviii (cited hereafter as Roberts, "Memoir"). The latter is also included in Lieutenant Colonel Ralph Henderson, *Records of My Family* (Carlisle, 1926). No new information is presented in Alexander Smirnoff, "A Tribute to the Memory of Colonel G. F. R. Henderson," *Army Quarterly,* XVII (1929), 335–41.

scholarship at St. John's College, Oxford, and Henderson left home to prepare for a career in the church. But in 1877 Henderson left the university for Sandhurst, where after a year he was gazetted as second lieutenant in the 65th Foot. He was sent first to India but remained there only a few months when he was promoted to lieutenant in the 84th Foot which then was stationed at Dover. Henderson was in Ireland when the expeditionary force to Egypt was organized in 1882. His battalion was assigned to Hamley's First Division and at Tel-el-Kebir he won distinction by leading his company into an enemy redoubt. After the Egyptian campaign Henderson was stationed in Bermuda and later Halifax, which enabled him to spend his leave tramping over many of the battlefields in Virginia and Maryland. Here he developed his life-long attachment to the men who had fought the Civil War, and when he returned to England Henderson applied for and received assignment to the Ordnance Department, where his duties would provide him with sufficient time and income to continue his study of the American campaigns.

Until 1886 Henderson apparently "lived the usual life of the subaltern of that day—he did his duty, played cricket, fished, and was ready for any harmless amusement at any time." One wonders what first prompted him to invest his own meager funds in the standard military works which were lacking in the "relics of Government libraries" where he had been stationed,[2] and if he anticipated at this time that his pen would soon become far mightier than his sword.

Henderson intended *The Campaign of Fredericksburg* to serve as a tactical text for officers of the volunteers. He had known many of these men while stationed at Fort George, in Inverness-shire, and probably he was aware of the great discrepancies between the volunteer regiments in training and quality. Aware too that the volunteers might have to face a Continental army superior both in manpower and in train-ing, Henderson wished to improve the practical and theoret-ical training of the officers. He maintained that a sound knowledge of military history was the best substitute for ac-tual combat experience, that if volunteer officers would only study past campaigns with intelligence they would find them-selves "instinctively doing the right thing." [3]

[2] Holden, "Henderson," p. 376.
[3] Henderson, *The Campaign of Fredericksburg* (3d ed.; London, n.d.),

The "lessons" this thoughtful soldier tried to communicate in his account of Fredericksburg all center in his conception of the role of the officer in modern battle. European military observers with the Civil War armies had noticed that battles often escaped the effective control of the field commander. Henderson also recognized this apparent trend, for he emphasized that at Fredericksburg Lee brought his troops to the selected positions, notified his lieutenants of his general plan, "and then gave frankly into their hands the conduct of the fight." Manifestly it was out of the question to demand of volunteer officers that sort of cohesion and disciplined independence Maurice so admired in the Prussian army, but perhaps much the same result could be obtained by studying how officers similar to themselves in background and training had reacted under fire.[4]

The use of intrenchments at Fredericksburg helped to convince Henderson that "good infantry, sufficiently covered . . . is, if unshaken by artillery and attacked in front alone, absolutely invincible." He recommended a well-directed fire by volleys as the best defense against enemy frontal attacks, and he considered a movement against the enemy flank or rear the most likely to succeed against fortified positions. These views harmonized with official doctrine in the years immediately preceding the war in South Africa, when volley firing was the "backbone of all musketry training"[5]; yet it is doubtful whether Henderson at this date fully respected the value of modern firepower. He thought Lee's comments on the use of the breech-loader "worth consideration." "What we want," he quoted Lee as saying, "is a firearm that cannot be loaded without a certain loss of time; so that a man learns to appreciate the importance of his fire."

According to Henderson, the object lessons of Fredericks-

p. 126. This volume, together with four essays on the Civil War contained in *The Science of War* and an appreciation of Stonewall Jackson written especially for Mary Anna Jackson's biography of her husband, is found in Jay Luvaas (ed.), *The Civil War: A Soldier's View* (Chicago, 1958).

[4] Henderson, *Campaign of Fredericksburg*, pp. 72–73, 125.

[5] *Ibid.*, pp. 85, 124; Major General J. F. C. Fuller, *The Army in My Time* (London, 1935), pp. 69–70; Colonel John K. Dunlop, *The Development of the British Army, 1899–1914* (London, 1938), p. 37. Wolseley advised: "From first to last use volleys as much as possible in preference to individual firing, over which latter it is so very difficult to exercise any effective control" (*The Soldier's Pocket-Book for Field Service* [5th ed.; London, 1886], p. 386).

burg could be summarized in two words—leadership and discipline. The conditions of modern battle made it necessary for junior officers to assume greater responsibility; flank marches and volley firing could be successfully executed only through strict discipline. Henderson admired "the splendid fighting qualities" of the American volunteer soldiers and he saw no reason why the English volunteers, *"if knit together by strict discipline and led by well-trained officers,"* could not "excel even Lee's battalions in mobility and efficiency." [6]

The Campaign of Fredericksburg was a complete success. It brought Henderson his first opportunity when Wolseley, solely on the strength of the book, appointed him an instructor at Sandhurst, and it was in sufficient demand that two subsequent editions were published. The book also created a new interest in the American Civil War at a time when Wolseley, Maurice, and a few other imaginative soldiers were beginning to react against the exaggerated study of everything German. A few years earlier Wolseley had written from the German maneuvers that "we can really learn very little here," but urged a close re-examination of the Civil War. Maurice too had begun to appreciate the lessons "to be derived by a careful student from the American war," and from far-off India came an anonymous appeal to look again at the Civil War. Thus there was already a receptive audience for Henderson's book, which in turn was instrumental in introducing the Civil War campaigns to most British officers. [7]

Henderson's appointment to Sandhurst was timely. For several years he had been disappointed in his professional prospects, even to the extent of contemplating leaving the army. At Sandhurst, however, he found himself. He greatly enjoyed teaching and his association with the cadets. One incident occurred which suggests his independence from tradition and authority. In 1891 Henderson founded, edited, and contributed many articles to the *Royal Military College Magazine,* which he hoped would be a means of fostering

[6] Henderson, *Campaign of Fredericksburg,* pp. 131, 147.

[7] Colonel Frederick Maurice, *War* (London, 1891), pp. 12, 107; Wolseley to Lady Wolseley, September 17, 1880 (Wolseley Papers). Wolseley, "An English View of the Civil War," *North American Review,* CXLVIII (1889), 556–57; CXLIX (1889), 567; see also "A True Reformer" (Captain F. N. Maude), *Letters on Tactics and Organization* (Calcutta, 1888), pp. 299, 312; T. Miller Maguire, "Our Art of War as 'Made in Germany,'" *United Service Magazine,* XIII (1896), 124–34; 280–91.

esprit de corps among the students. Instead the publication was ordered discontinued by the War Office, presumably because it was "too progressive." [8] By temperament Henderson was not a professional reformer, but throughout his career he approached every problem with the same vigor and freshness that characterized his tenure at the military college.

Henderson's next book, an elaborate tactical study of the battle of Spicheren, was published in 1891 and was written primarily for the student, although the book, "the first detailed study of a modern Continental battle in which British troops were not engaged," deserves to stand on its historical merits as well.[9]

We have here a new concept of the use of military history. Henderson did not study Spicheren to develop tactical ideas or to illustrate "the tabulated maxims and official regulations"; he was not even concerned particularly to discover the reasons for the Prussian success. Military history to Henderson offered "an efficient substitute for practical acquaintance with almost every phase of active service." Rather than to test memory, Henderson used military history to test the ability of his students.

> To gain from a relation of events the same abiding impressions as were stamped on the minds of those who played a part in them —and it is such impressions that create instinct—it is necessary to examine the situations developed during the operations so closely as to have a clear picture of the whole scene in our mind's eye; to assume, in imagination, the responsibilities of the leaders who were called upon to meet those situations; to come to a definite decision and to test the soundness of that decision by the actual event.

Thus military history helped to train the judgment of the student, and it taught him how all arms function in battle.

Finally,

> It is only from the experience of others . . . that we can obtain knowledge of the more startling and decisive aspects of the breech-loader battle. The effect of fire, the intense strain on the nerves produced by a protracted engagement, the dispersion of units, the tendency and the temptations to straggling and dis-order, the moral effect of flank attacks and turning movements,

[8] Holden, "Henderson," p. 377.

[9] Spenser Wilkinson, "Notices of Books," *United Service Magazine*, V (1892), 108–9.

the difficulty of transmitting orders, and, more than all, the importance and influence of ground, with these, not all the experience and exercises of peace can afford more than the most superficial acquaintance. If we would realize them, we must have recourse to history.[10]

Writing in a day when it was generally assumed that events could be recreated as they actually occurred, Henderson insisted that history be accurate and extremely detailed. The student should follow single companies and even sections through the battle with the same knowledge available at the time to the local commander. He must have enough information to enter the mind of the actor and develop and test alternate plans of his own. Henderson combed the mass of literature in Germany and France, the official and regimental histories, and even the observations of noncombatants; he selected a battle where the terrain was in many respects similar to the ground between London and the Channel—"the same steep hill-sides, covered . . . with woods, and with the same open plateaus and deep gullies behind the crest"—so that officers (particularly volunteer officers whose commands had been designated to occupy positions in Kent and Surrey in the event of invasion) might learn from the manner in which the Spicheren position was attacked and defended. Henderson also followed Napier's example "by showing how the received maxims and established principles of war, were violated or adhered to." The historian, particularly one whose knowledge of war is second hand, may feel reluctant to censure generals with such freedom, but manifestly "a work which professes to teach cannot avoid showing up errors, however excusable." [11]

What makes *Spicheren* unique here, however, is Henderson's method and purpose and not his description of the battle or judgment of individuals. His treatment embraced every subject he considered pertinent; the characteristics, mobilization, and concentration of the armies, the step-by-step development of the battle from the appearance of Prussian scouts to the ultimate retreat of the French. Occasionally he would punctuate his narrative by pointing an obvious moral: "A

[10] Henderson, *The Battle of Spicheren August 6th, 1870, and the Events That Preceded It: A Study in Practical Tactics and War Training* (2d ed.; London, 1909), pp. vi–vii.
[11] *Ibid.*, p. viii.

commander who commits his troops to action cannot withdraw without heavy loss in men and in *moral* from the deadly zone of fire which girds a modern battle-field." "If a subordinate leader . . . by a too precipitate attack, involve the mass of the army in a premature and unforeseen engagement, he may utterly destroy the combinations of his superior. . . . "Success in battle turns, as a rule, upon the skilful employment of reserves." [12] Henderson revealed his own views on tactics and organization, commenting frequently upon conditions that ought to determine the choice of a defensive position, the value and dangers of initiative in subordinate officers, and the type of discipline that should be cultivated.

But even without Henderson's own theories, his treatment of Spicheren admirably fulfilled its purpose. He devotes, for example, two pages to a minute description of the situation and disposition of the garrison of Saarbrucken, which consisted of three squadrons of Uhlans and a battalion of Fusiliers and then asks the reader: "How would you dispose the outposts of 1 battalion of 500 men and 3 squadrons on the Saarbrucken Ridge? What orders would you give as to patrolling?" Or again, after discussing the intelligence reports received by the commander of the first Prussian division to reach the field, he fired a series of questions: "As commander of the 14th Division, what would be your action on learning at Guichenbach that the Saarbrucken Ridge had been evacuated? . . . What would be your action on reaching the ridge? . . . What would be your action on learning that the enemy was retreating?" Readers who followed the Fusiliers "through the widely scattered trunks of the lofty beeches" in the Stiring Copse did not dare skim pages to see if the attack succeeded for fear they might have to answer "As commanding II/74, what would have been your action when III/39 began to fall back?" [13] In this way Henderson combined literary skill and meticulous research to recreate the atmosphere of battle and present military readers with an opportunity to display their own skill in a similar situation.

The Campaign of Fredericksburg brought Henderson to Sandhurst and *The Battle of Spicheren* led to his appointment in 1892 as Maurice's successor at the Staff College: rarely, one

[12] *Ibid.*, pp. 110, 111, 141.
[13] *Ibid.*, pp. 52–53, 106–14, 143–44, and Appendix III, pp. 10, 11.

is tempted to remark, has publication resulted in more rapid promotion even in an academic atmosphere. At the Staff College Henderson continued the good work of Maurice in attempting to elevate the reputation of the institution. In Maurice's day the courses there had often been dull and formal. Sir George Aston, who attended the Staff College in 1889, recalls that one of the best students in his class, a Royal Engineer "who had earned great fame by his surveys of large areas on the North West Frontier of India," had had one of his maps returned by the instructor with the comment, "You should practise gravel-pits." But with the arrival of the new regime such pedantry was discouraged. "We want officers to absorb, not to cram," insisted Colonel H. T. H. Hildyard, one of Wolseley's men who became commandant in 1893, and thereafter the accumulation of facts as preparation for examinations gave way to "the solving of problems of strategy, of tactics, and of organisation" and to "a continued series of practical tests, applied on the ground."

Henderson's teaching was in line with this policy. He broadened the course in military history to include the Civil War campaigns and gave each student personal attention such as he might receive in a university seminar. His students soon learned to respect him for his intelligence and "extraordinary capacity for work." Always questioning and interested above all in developing the process of reasoning, Henderson did not restrict his teaching to the classroom. Many were the days he spent in the field working with students on their tactical schemes, and one suspects that he most preferred to spend leisure hours conversing with some young officer over points of dispute in a recent lecture or discussing a new work on military literature. Indeed, according to Hildyard, "it would be difficult . . . to say where most was really learned by the officers anxious to acquire knowledge in the military art—in the lecture-hall or in the anteroom of the Staff College Mess." [14]

At the Staff College Henderson found his sphere of action greatly enlarged. He worked six or seven hours daily on his teaching, and in addition to preparing "most carefully

[14] Hildyard, as quoted in Roberts, "Memoir," p. xxx; Major General Sir George Aston, *Memories of a Marine* (London, 1925), pp. 100–101; Brevet Major A. R. Godwin-Austen, *The Staff and the Staff College* (London, 1927), pp. 231–33. Hildyard's philosophy of education is briefly described in Henderson, *Science of War*, pp. 402–3.

thought-out lectures," he appeared frequently before military societies throughout the United Kingdom and contributed regularly to the *Times,* the *Edinburgh Review,* and various service journals. He received more offers from publishers than he could possibly accept, the new *Military Magazine* offering up to a guinea a page, still the standard rate, for anything he cared to write. He also covered foreign military maneuvers for the *Times,* and whatever time was left over from his official duties and literary obligations he devoted to the preparation of his major work, *Stonewall Jackson and the American Civil War.*

Henderson continued to use the Franco-Prussian War as an aid to teaching. His published lectures on the battle of Wörth show that he continued to frame tactical questions with the material of history, resorting even to a sort of Platonic dialogue to enable the reader to converse with participants. Thus a student, "discussing" with a French officer the reasons for his decisions during the battle, asks: "In fact, after considering what happened at Wörth, you have come to the conclusion that when once the artillery of the defence is driven in it can only play a subordinate part, and should not occupy positions which interfere with the fire and formations of the infantry?" The Frenchman replies: "That is my opinion, for I find, on reflection, that the teaching of Wörth is in accordance with the teaching of all military history. The infantry is the arm which decides the battle, and, on the defensive, it should be kept intact and under cover until the enemy's infantry advances. To this all other considerations must give way." [15]

Although it is not generally so recognized, Henderson's biography of Stonewall Jackson was also written to instruct the British officer in the art of command. Convinced that Hamley's *The Operations of War* had grievous shortcomings as a military text because the author had "deliberately omitted all reference to the spirit of war, to moral influences, to the effect of rapidity, surprise and secrecy"—those vital intangibles so essential to good leadership and, incidentally, so characteristic of Jackson [16]—Henderson obviously in-

[15] Henderson, *Short Tactical Studies,* I. *The Battle of Wörth, August 6th 1870* (Yorktown, Surrey, 1899), p. 29.

[16] Henderson, *Science of War,* pp. 169–75; "Strategy and Its Teaching," *R.U.S.I. Journal,* XLII (1898), 767; Godwin-Austen, *Staff and the Staff College,* p. 114. Also see above, pp. 150–51.

tended his biography of the great Confederate general to fulfil on a higher level the same practical purpose as his monographs on Spicheren and Wörth. Henderson wrote from the eye level of Jackson, describing each situation as he thought Jackson himself would have viewed it and focusing his attention upon the commander's methods and psychological reactions. This technique enabled the future staff officer to accompany the men of Jackson's staff: it also enabled Henderson to inject his own philosophy of war so skilfully into the narrative that on occasions where the facts were not known —or did not appear to reflect the usual credit on the Confederate general—Jackson's actions are explained and justified by Henderson's own strategical concepts. While this practice occasionally led to minor distortions of fact, it did not necessarily detract from the value of the book as a military study and probably even enriched it as a military treatise.

Stonewall Jackson differs from Henderson's earlier works in several respects. He had become far more interested in strategy. His study of Fredericksburg had been written when, as a company officer, he had been primarily concerned with what he later termed "Minor Tactics," a phrase used to describe "the formation and disposition of the three arms for attack and defence." But after teaching seven years at the Staff College his outlook had naturally broadened to include more general problems of military policy, organization, and especially that "higher art" of generalship known as strategy or "Grand Tactics," which Henderson defined as "those strategems, manoeuvres, and devices by which victories are won, and concern only those officers who may find themselves in independent command." Strategy, Henderson discovered, was "a far more difficult art to master than tactics." [17]

It is also evident that the longer Henderson studied the Civil War campaigns, the more convinced he became that the tactical lessons of the Franco-Prussian War had been overrated. He continued to take students on extended tours of the battlefields of 1870, but he became increasingly absorbed in his study of the Civil War. In 1891, the same year that *Spicheren* was published, Henderson wrote:

[T]he tactics of the American troops, at a very early period, were superior to those of the Prussians in 1866. . . . The success

[17] Henderson, *Science of War*, pp. 168, 310; *R.U.S.I. Journal*, XLI (1898), 707–9.

with which from the very first that cavalry was employed on the outpost line puts to shame the inactivity of the Prussian horsemen in Bohemia; and, whilst the tactics of the Prussian artillery . . . were feeble in the extreme, the very contrary was the case in the Secession War. . . . Nor were the larger tactical manoeuvres even of 1870 an improvement on those of the American campaigns. . . . Flank attacks and wide turning movements were as frequent in one case as in the other; and not only were the victors of Sedan anticipated in the method of attack by successive rushes, but the terrible confusion which followed a protracted struggle, and for which Prussian tacticians still despair of discovering a remedy, was speedily rectified by American ingenuity. . . . [The American tactical] formations were far better adapted to preserve cohesion than those of the Prussians.

To those who still discounted the lessons of a war waged before the universal introduction of the breech-loader, Henderson pointed out that the Americans, compared with the Prussians in 1870, "made more careful preparations for the attack, were far more zealous to re-form the ranks after every phase of battle, and, whilst developing a broad front of fire, kept within proper bounds the initiative of their company commanders." [18]

Nor was Henderson's growing reluctance to depend upon the military lessons of 1870 limited to the subject of tactics. He considered both the Civil War and the Egyptian campaign of 1882 more valuable for the purpose of preparing the auxiliary forces for war than any of Moltke's campaigns.[19] Both had been influenced by sea power and hence were of "very special value" to British soldiers. They also were more instructive in another problem that confronted every British general—how to improvise organization and administrative services on the spot "with insufficient means, inexperienced officials, and auxiliary troops." [20]

No matter what the occasion, Henderson saw lessons in the Civil War of special significance to his own army. One of the main military questions of his day, for example, concerned the auxiliary forces—the volunteers and militia. There was general concern about the efficiency and capabilities of these

[18] Henderson, *Science of War,* pp. 129–30.

[19] In this connection, see Henderson's estimation of Wellington as a general in *ibid.,* pp. 87–107.

[20] These views are the essence of Henderson's comments following a lecture by Lonsdale Hale on "The Professional Study of Military History," *R.U.S.I. Journal,* XLI (1898), 708.

organizations, for while much attention had been given to their assignment in war, many still doubted that untried soldiers such as these could stand up against a large professional army from the Continent.

Henderson's writings and speeches reflect that concern. Unlike his patron Wolseley, who had been content merely to state that "the armies of raw levies" ought to be taken into consideration when one was evaluating the generalship of the Civil War, Henderson pleaded for a better understanding of the special problems of the American armies. The Civil War after all had been fought by elements comparable to the auxiliary forces. Admitting that the Civil War armies had suffered initially from lack of discipline, Henderson also noted that they had improved steadily as the war progressed, until by 1863 they were "in very many respects . . . superior and more advanced in military knowledge than even the Germans in 1870." He asserted that the volunteers could be trained to the point where they would be "fully equal" to the Continental armies and in fact he anticipated that the next great war would be fought largely by armies comprising just such soldiers. Henderson's remarks to a military audience in 1894 seem almost prophetic:

> If I see in the future an English general at the head of an army far larger than that which drained the life-blood of Napoleon's empire in the Peninsula, if I see our colours flying over even a wider area than in the year which preceded Waterloo, you may think that I am over-sanguine; but to my mind the possibility exists, and with it the probability that the forces which are employed . . . will be constituted, at least in part, as were the armies of the American Civil War. Our men will not all be regulars. They will come straight from civil life, and to civil life they will return. The habits and prejudices of civil life will have to be considered in their discipline and instruction, and officers will have to recognize that troops without the traditions, instincts, and training of regular soldiers, require a handling different from that which they have been accustomed to employ.[21]

The experiences of the Americans in raising, equipping, and training their volunteer armies in the 1860's was, to Henderson's way of thinking, "one of the most important lessons" the British soldier could learn from the Civil War.

Still another difference between Henderson's tactical stud-

[21] Henderson, *Science of War*, p. 310; Wolseley, "General Sherman," *United Service Magazine*, III (1891), 304.

ies and his biography of Jackson is that in the intervening years he had become a recognized theorist on the science of war. *The Campaign of Fredericksburg* may have enlightened volunteer officers about their probable role in battle but it contained few original ideas, and the same is true of *The Battle of Spicheren.* In the latter work Henderson employed his knowledge of theory to explain and evaluate what had occurred in the battle in much the same way as Napier, and if his analysis of tactics compares favorably with that of Maurice in his Wellington Prize essay, it is also apparent that Henderson had not yet formulated his own philosophy of war or found solutions for current tactical problems. But by the time he completed his two-volume study of Jackson, his own theories had begun to evolve, a fact acknowledged by one prominent reviewer who praised the work as really three important volumes in one—a military biography, an authentic campaign history, and a general treatise on the art of war.[22] Both as history and biography *Stonewall Jackson* can be considered a military classic: Henderson captured the spirit of Stonewall and his men as no foreign and few American writers have succeeded in doing. He succeeded so well, in fact, that the casual reader is apt to miss many of his cogent observations on various phases of military activity, from problems of a purely technical nature, such as tactical formations for infantry, to the more general questions of discipline and morale and even the sensitive relationship between soldier and statesman in a democracy at war.

Henderson probably learned more about war during his tenure at the Staff College than did any of his students, for his writings in the 1890's reveal a steady growth. His ideas on cavalry were the most subject to change. When he wrote *The Campaign of Fredericksburg,* Henderson evidently still believed that the American cavalry in fighting dismounted was not "exercising its proper functions," which elsewhere he defined as, first, "to drive the hostile horsemen from the field" and, second, "active participation in the struggle of the infantry and artillery for the key of the position." The opportunity of cavalry, he wrote in 1891,

will still come, as it did at St. Privat. . . . One great victory is less costly than a series of indecisive battles, and to win a great

[22] Sir Henry Brackenbury, "Stonewall Jackson," *Blackwood's,* CLXIV (1898), 722.

victory, to become master of every opportunity, our generals must have in their cavalry an auxiliary that can act as skilfully and as resolutely in the centre of the field against opposing infantry as on the flanks of the battle against the opposing cavalry.

Accompanied by "mobile infantry," cavalry had acquired a strategical independence: "Its offensive strength has expanded, and, at the same time, it has been supplied with the defensive capacity it has hitherto lacked." [23]

For several years Henderson continued to think that the dismounted tactics so much in evidence in the Civil War resulted primarily from unfavorable terrain, but further study, supplemented by the experiences of the Boer War, convinced him that the rise of mounted infantry was due instead to the increase in firepower which as early as 1861 "had already become the predominant factor in battle." Henderson nevertheless refused to side with those extremists who asserted that regular cavalry had no place in modern war. Rather he believed that the Civil War cavalry had succeeded because it had been able to strike the true balance between shock and dismounted tactics. The Boer War found Henderson moving still further away from the position taken by Maurice and Wolseley, neither of whom could place much faith in a "military Jack-of-all-arms." It took the experience in South Africa, however, fully to convince Henderson that "cavalry trained to fight as infantry, and carrying a magazine rifle, is the ideal arm." [24]

A similar change can be seen in his view of infantry tactics. In his account of Spicheren he emphasized that a bayonet charge, "made by troops whose tactical unity is still intact, and bringing about the insertion of an ordered body of rifles into the midst of the enemy's line, is essential to decisive success." Six years later he declared that the bayonet had become subordinate to the bullet and that the bayonet assault had lost its importance.[25]

More significant still are Henderson's observations on intrenchments, for here he was years ahead of his time.

[23] Henderson, *Campaign of Fredericksburg*, p. 132; *Science of War*, pp. 111, 116.

[24] *Ibid.*, pp. 70, 278; "National Defense," *Edinburgh Review*, CLXXXV (1897), 531.

[25] Henderson, *Battle of Spicheren*, p. 265; *Science of War*, p. 135. The later view is represented in *ibid.*, p. 100 (1897), and *Wörth*, Introduction (1899).

Although preferring offensive action, he was realist enough to see that trench warfare greatly strengthened the defensive. He had already made this point in his study of Fredericksburg and he recognized the limited role of earthworks at Spicheren, but not until he became acquainted with the facts of the Wilderness campaign did he fully appreciate "the importance of the spade." Even before the Boer War he warned repeatedly that intrenchments "as a tactical expedient and precaution, and especially as an essential adjunct to attack, do not receive, at field-days and manoeuvres, the attention they deserve," and the military events in South Africa confirmed his prediction in 1894 that Grant's operations in the Wilderness provided "a better clue to the fighting of the future than any other which history records." Henderson considered mobility the best antidote to trench warfare. Sudden seizure of key tactical points, outflanking maneuvers, and marches against the enemy's line of retreat had frequently enabled the Americans to overcome the natural advantages of the defensive. Thus Grant's ability to maneuver had forced Lee out of successive defensive positions in Virginia, while Sherman's campaign for Atlanta offered additional proof that "against troops which can manoeuvre earthworks are useless." [26]

From the first Henderson questioned the effectiveness of the Prussian company column, which in one form or another had been adopted by every major army of Europe except his own. This formation "was too hastily accepted," "its disadvantages were never pointed out," and no endeavor had been made "to secure to the new formation the sound principles of that which it superseded." The company column had worked well enough in 1866 against an enemy armed with a weapon inferior to the needle gun, but against French troops, firing the superior Chassepot, "its results were very far from being so decisive." Often it forced the enemy lines to yield ground, but never did it lead to "the end at which the attack should aim"—annihilation. In Henderson's judgment the companies were too inclined to independent action, the fire of the skirmishers was employed—mistakenly, he believed—to blaze a path into the enemy's position and not, as

[26] Henderson, *Campaign of Fredericksburg*, p. 123; *Battle of Spicheren*, pp. 135, 137–38, 164, 220; *Science of War*, pp. 68, 308, 340–41; *Stonewall Jackson and the American Civil War* (new impression; New York, 1906), II, 347.

in the late war in America and the most recent drill books in England, merely to cover the advance of assaulting lines; and the Prussian formations lacked sufficient depth. For these reasons the Prussians had been unable to throw sufficient weight into the attack for it to succeed under modern conditions. Thus the confusion of the Prussian battle was due, in Henderson's view, "to their neglect of the immutable principles of tactics," and therefore "are a bad model for us to follow."

> Had the battles of the Secession War been studied in Berlin instead of being dismissed with a contemptuous allusion to mobs of skirmishers . . . [these faults] would have been foreseen; and a knowledge of the modifications of the old formations necessary to achieve decisive results would have been gained without the lavish expenditure of life which the defective tactics of 1870 entailed. . . . In the first place, the unity of the battalion was scrupulously respected; and although the leaders of the units in the fighting line were allowed a free hand as soon as superior control became impossible, they were neither encouraged to ma-noeuvre nor permitted to deviate from the line of direction the commander had assigned. Secondly, the traditional formation in three lines was the basis of all dispositions for battle. Thirdly, the second and third lines of each division were, as a rule, supplied by its own brigades, and not by strange units; that is, the division went into battle on a narrow front and with great depth. Fourthly, the preliminary dispositions were carefully carried out: and lastly, as both common sense and experience taught the leaders that to carry a position, line after line, re-gardless of cohesion, must be piled one on top of the other, the process of rallying, not only when the enemy had been driven back, but at every pause in the attack, was a universal rule in battle, and constantly practised in the camp.[27]

Two points in Henderson's analysis of infantry tactics deserve comment. First, he was still convinced in the early 1890's of the efficacy of the frontal attack of successive lines of infantry and of the value of the bayonet in the climactic act of battle. Commenting on the French maneuvers in 1891, Henderson seemed favorably impressed by the offensive spirit that was evident everywhere, a spirit that permeated in

[27] Henderson, *The Science of War*, pp. 148–49. This was written in 1892: for other similar observations, see *Spicheren*, pp. 264–70, and "The Offensive Tactics of Infantry," *United Service Magazine*, VII (1893), 945–61 *passim*.

exaggerated form the French infantry regulations for 1895 where it was prescribed that

as soon as the battalion has arrived within 400 metres of the enemy, bayonets are fixed, and individual fire . . . of the greatest intensity delivered. The portions of the reserve that are available are advanced. . . . The battalion in second line in the meantime gradually advances closer. The advance is made by successive rushes followed by a quick fire of short duration. The fighting line reinforced by the reserves . . . gradually reaches to within 150 or 200 metres of the enemy. At this distance magazine fire is commenced, and all available reserves . . . close up for the assault. At a signal from the Colonel the drums beat, the bugles sound the advance and the entire line charges forward with cries of *"en avant, à la baionette."* [28]

In justice to Henderson, however, it should be noted that he praised the French army for not depending exclusively upon shock tactics and he complained gently of an "over-scrupulous regard for the niceties of the parade-ground" and neglect of the "importance of cover during an advance." His observations on the German maneuvers in 1895 show a growing respect for firepower but his faith in frontal attacks remained undiminished. "Whether these deep columns of assault are a formation adapted to modern conditions," he reported to the Intelligence Division,

is a question which does not concern me here; but I may point out that these columns would not be formed in actual war until the attack had gained a decisive superiority of fire, and the enemy was demoralized. It can hardly be doubted, I think, if the first line is able to advance to 250 yards from the position, and at that close range to pour in a magazine fire, that the assault, in whatever formation it may be made, is nearly bound to succeed. [29]

The second point to be observed in Henderson's treatment of infantry tactics is the conviction he shared with Mac-

[28] Quoted in Major General J. F. C. Fuller, *War and Western Civilization 1832–1932: A Study of War as a Political Instrument and the Expression of Mass Democracy* (London, 1932), pp. 152–53. Henderson's observations are recorded in a lecture he gave before the Royal United Service Institution ("The French Manoeuvres of 1891," *R.U.S.I. Journal*, XXXVI [1892], 859–79); *Spicheren*, p. 267.

[29] "French Manoeuvres of 1891," p. 874; *Science of War*, p. 162; War Office, Intelligence Division, *Extracts from the Reports of Various Officers on the Manoeuvres in Austria, Belgium, France, Germany, Italy, Roumania, Russia and Servia* (London, printed at the War Office, 1896), p. 55.

Dougall that British tactical formations were inherently superior to those of the Prussians. Both criticized the freedom exercised by Prussian company commanders in seeking cover at the expense of abandoning the line of direction in the attack. Cover thus "exercised a magnetic influence" which the integrity of the battalion, disregarded both in theory and in practice, could not overcome. "Well has it been said," Henderson commented, "that 'the company leader who, regardless of losses, carries out the task assigned to him, is a better servant than the company leader who manoeuvres." He further agreed with the final view of MacDougall that close order remained the backbone of the attack and that the extended order so popular after 1870 was nothing more "than an essential accessory"; and he rejoiced that the latest edition of *Field Exercise,* which until 1888 had followed the lead of the Prussians, had finally reached the "true mean": "Close order whenever . . . possible, extended order only when . . . unavoidable." [30]

Both Henderson and MacDougall insisted that British tactics prior to 1870 had been based on sound principles. Whereas the Prussians had used the skirmish line both to prepare for and execute the main attack and had regarded the second line as useless except as a means of feeding the firing line, the British traditionally had employed skirmishers merely to cover the advance of the main body which, "moving shoulder to shoulder, was to pass through the firing line and carry the position with the bayonet." If the two differed in their estimation of the chances for success of a modern frontal attack, they agreed that the failure of most Prussian assaults had been due to the neglect of the same principles advocated in the English drill book, where it was stressed that force must be marshaled in several distinct lines and "that at the moment of the final rush strong supports were at hand, in good order, and obedient to control." In Henderson's view, the traditional attack formation of the British infantry, reinforced by the lessons of the American Civil War, was still the most likely method of producing victory, and in the early nineties he was "firmly convinced" that "the attack of a large force upon a single point, whether as stroke or counter-stroke, is still the crowning act of battle." [31]

[30] Henderson, *Science of War,* pp. 134, 146–47, 153.
[31] *Ibid.,* pp. 132, 158, 162. According to Henderson, the traditional at-

In trying to assimilate lessons from the Civil War and the more recent campaigns in Europe and along the North West Frontier of India, Henderson adhered to still another English military tradition. For he concluded that there was no surer guide for training infantry in its "multifarious duties" than Sir John Moore's system. In contrast to Maurice, who looked to the Prussians for methods to develop cohesion, initiative, and intelligent co-operation in battle, Henderson found the answer in the type of leader Moore had produced—men capable of carrying out the plans and even anticipating the wishes of their superiors rather than docile subordinates who obeyed orders to the letter but were devoid of imagination or initiative. Whenever Moore's officers had been left alone, Henderson observed, "they almost invariably did the right thing. They had no hesitation in assuming responsibility. They could handle their regiments and companies . . . as independent units; and they consistently applied the great principle of mutual support." Because the problems Moore had faced at Shorncliffe—how to preserve order in disorder, make the best use of ground, improvise formations as needed and develop an effective fire—shed light on the requirements of modern infantry, Henderson contended that "in training our officers and men as light infantry after Sir John Moore's model, we shall be giving them the best training to fit them for battle, on whatever ground it may be fought." [32]

By a curious twist of history, if we can believe Henderson, Moore's spiritual successors fought under Moltke and not

---

tack formation of Wellington's infantry rested upon the following: "(1) As a preliminary disposition, the troops were divided into three lines before they were set in motion. (2) The objective of each division was clearly indicated, either by direct instructions, or by the division being placed opposite that point of the enemy's position which it was to assault, and being allotted a space in the line of battle that it could adequately cover, and no more. (3) During the attack itself, the skirmish line was given a free hand, and the leaders of units were allowed to act on their own initiative. . . . (4) The second and third lines in close order behind the skirmishers maintained their tactical unity throughout the advance. When the position was carried, no time was lost in resuming the original formation, and the troops were in a position . . . to follow up the enemy, or to check a counter-stroke. (5) The knowledge that strong supports were close at hand . . . not only added that element of moral strength to the attack which is above all things essential, but shook the *moral* of the staunchest enemy" (*ibid.*, p. 133). It should be noted that Henderson and Maurice held essentially the same view of the function of skirmishers.

[32] *Ibid.*, pp. 347, 352.

Wolseley, Roberts, or Kitchener. At the German maneuvers in 1895 Henderson observed that the soldiers "act like intelligent beings, who thoroughly understand their duty, and the fact speaks volumes for the way in which even the privates are taught to use their initiative, and for the excellence of the system of individual training." In contrast, "Foreign officers who have visited Aldershot have remarked . . . that our men did not seem to be able to act for themselves, but that they always required some one to tell them what to do; and it is evident that if officers have to look closely after their men, they will have little time to give to a consideration either of the ground or of the enemy." [33] It is significant that many of the details of Sir John Moore's system of training not known to Henderson were finally deduced by another great English military historian and theorist, Colonel (later Major General) J. F. C. Fuller, who occupied his ever active and creative mind during several months of idle employment in 1915 trying to discover the details of Moore's system and an answer to the tantalizing question: "What . . . must we do if the spirit of John Moore is to live in us?" [34]

Certainly the spirit of Moore was alive in Henderson. Both men were imaginative students of tactics and military training, both sought to foster originality and initiative alike among officers and men, and both were receptive to the idea of change and therefore were able to assimilate the lessons of contemporary war. Compare, for example, the difference in Henderson's own concepts of the training of infantry for attack in 1891 and 1899. Initially, he had preached the advantages of deep attack formations and decisive waves of infantry lines, and his formula for success was deceptively simple:

[33] Intelligence Division, *Reports of Various Officers on Manoeuvres*, p. 53; Henderson, *Science of War*, p. 355. Henderson observed that the French soldiers were not as smart as the English on the parade ground, but that constant smartness was not too important. "To see a French battalion forming fours or presenting arms would make the hair of an English sergeant-major stand on end. . . . It is when the attack begins that steadiness, regularity, and strict discipline are first apparent . . . all other branches of military training, except marching, are made subordinate to duties under fire . . ." ("French Manoeuvres of 1891," p. 875).

[34] Fuller, *Sir John Moore's System of Training* (London, 1924), p. 222. It is interesting to note that Fuller's book, although written originally in 1915, was published after the war when he, too, was an instructor at the Staff College (Fuller, *Memoirs of an Unconventional Soldier* [London, 1936], p. 48).

"careful arrangements, a precise objective, great depth, and
the local assault." But on the eve of the Boer War he no longer
relied upon bayonet and volley fire, he advocated greater use of
cover and exalted the characteristics of light infantry—all of
which were confirmed by the experiences of the British in
South Africa. The same evolution is evident in Henderson's views on cavalry, for year by year he became increasingly convinced of the futility of shock tactics and the
need to develop mounted infantry of the type that fought
under Forrest and Stuart in America.

Perhaps the difference in outlook was nothing more than
the difference between studying one campaign waged by Continental armies and anticipating thirty years later the conditions that the British army might have to face in the next
war. Or perhaps, as Henderson delved more into the Civil War
and scrutinized the campaigns between Russia and Turkey in
1877–78 and on the North West Frontier, he became less sure
of previous deductions. Most certainly the continued improvements in weapons caused him to modify earlier convictions. At all events Henderson, in contrast to Maurice, was
still searching for ways to improve tactics and training at the
time of the Boer War, instead of falling back upon old
methods which, however rational and adaptive at the time, no
longer were adequate to meet the demands of modern war.

The year after *Stonewall Jackson* was published war broke
out in South Africa. After British forces had suffered a series
of setbacks, Roberts was called to assume command. Convinced that Henderson "would be able to turn his knowledge
to practical account," Roberts in January, 1900, appointed
him to his newly formed staff as director of intelligence. On
the long sea voyage out, the two spent hours together
discussing strategy and its application to the coming campaign. During the days of preparation at Cape Town, Henderson's "fertile suggestions and sober criticisms . . . played
no small part in confirming the native intuition and strengthening the resolution of his chief." He performed useful service
in obtaining maps of the theater of operations, and, doubtless
guided by Jackson's dictum, "Always mystify and mislead" (a
phrase that has become idiomatic in English military
parlance), he even took pains to plant misleading newspaper
articles to camouflage the British plan of campaign. Roberts
himself has recorded that during the campaign Henderson's

former students would file into his tent at odd hours, "eager to discuss those actual problems which they had so often studied in theory, glad of the chance given them of referring their doubts and difficulties" to their esteemed teacher.[35]

Unfortunately, Henderson's health was not equal to the strain of active campaigning. Malaria and excessive fatigue forced him to leave Roberts at Paardeberg and return to England. Roberts continued to make good use of Henderson, however, first by ordering him to revise and bring the old *Infantry Drill Book* up to date and then by selecting him to write the official history of the war. Henderson died before completing either task, but he left enough behind to indicate the drift of his thought.

Henderson's tactical deductions from the Boer War clearly pointed the way to the future. Another revolution in tactics, he asserted, had occurred since the advent of breech-loading rifles in the 1860's: now the superiority of the small-bore repeater was such that infantry "attacking over open ground, must move in successive lines of skirmishers extended at wide intervals"; cavalry "armed, trained, and equipped as the cavalry of the Continent, is as obsolete as the crusaders"; and reconnaissance had increased in importance. The war in South Africa convinced Henderson of the fallacy of depending upon mere weight of numbers, and he decried the spirit of *L'audace, l'audace, toujours l'audace* then prevalent in French military doctrine. To pile battalion on battalion, brigade on brigade, to believe that stern discipline, high morale, and hard hitting would compensate for the increased advantages of the defense, was an expensive doctrine even according to the conditions of 1870 and 1877: against an enemy such as the Boers, sheltered in trenches and concealed through the use of smokeless powder, the cost of using the old formations had become prohibitive. Under modern conditions a frontal attack could succeed only through close co-operation between artillery and infantry, and even then the best opportunities were to be found in envelopment and the seizure of key tactical positions that would force the enemy to suffer enfilade fire, attack at a disadvantage, or else withdraw.

Henderson anticipated many of the conditions that dominated the battlefields of 1914–18—"the difficulty of recon-

<hr/>

[35] L. S. Amery, *My Political Life*, I. *England before the Storm*, 1896–1914 (London, 1953), p. 126; Roberts, "Memoir," pp. xxxvi–xxxviii.

naissance, the increased power of the defence against direct attack, the difficulty, owing to the wide front occupied by a defending force, of developing flank attacks, the general use of entrenchments"—and he predicted that these conditions

will make the fight for each locality long and exhausting; and it will consequently be necessary for a general to proceed with the utmost caution, and to make certain of securing one point of vantage before he attacks the next. The attack . . . of each point will consume far more troops, in proportion to the strength of the army, than heretofore. The whole army . . . may be employed in mastering one single point, part keeping the enemy employed elsewhere, the remainder combining for the decisive attack. The battle . . . will thus resolve itself into a distinct series of engagements, each ranging round a different locality and each protracted over many hours.

Manifestly, Henderson did not foresee the trench deadlock or a protracted struggle of attrition where maneuvering was confined largely to intrigues in the various army head-quarters, nor would he have derived much comfort from the thought that conscription would replace the principle of voluntary service in Britain. But the English generals of the First World War would have done well if, instead of giving lip service to Henderson's writings, they had observed some of his maxims written fifteen years before Passchendaele, particularly one which asserted: "It should always be the aim of a general, even when in command of a superior force, to destroy his enemy with as little loss as possible to himself." [36]

Henderson's bout with the official history of the war in South Africa has already been mentioned. Appointed in the autumn of 1900, he spent as much time as failing health would allow gathering material and writing almost to the day he died. Evidently he had already completed much of the initial volume when Maurice took over the work, but his chapters were suppressed both because his harsh judgments of former Boer leaders might prejudice current conciliatory negotiations and also because he was not afraid to criticize British leaders for their mistakes. The suppressed chapters portray the former Boer president, Paul Kruger, as a man to whom "pledges had never meant anything . . . but tem-porary expedients of policy and intrigue," while elsewhere

[36] Henderson, *Science of War*, pp. 80–81, 372, 376, 411–12, 416.

Henderson alluded to "the gross blunders perpetrated in South Africa by British Ministries" and complained that the British drifted into faulty strategical decisions at the outset of war because no machinery existed at the War Office for devising any scheme of operations.[37] Considering Henderson's supreme mastery of the language, powers of synthesis and organization, and relative freedom from professional prejudice, it may be asserted that had he lived to complete the official history it probably would have been the best thing of its kind and might even have had a beneficial effect on the compilers of the *Official History of the Great War*. Unfortunately, Henderson died in 1903 in Egypt, where he had been sent to avoid the rigors of another English winter; civilian control in the War Office was extended with the replacement of Roberts by the Army Council a year later, and Maurice was too old and tired to do much more than record the actions of British soldiers, and thus it was left to other hands to reveal the mistakes that had been committed.

"The influence of such a man must bear good fruit." Roberts expressed his hope that Henderson's writings would have as much influence on British military policy as the books of Mahan had had in naval matters. The obituary that appeared in the *Times* likened Henderson's influence in the British army to that of Moltke in Germany, and while this statement is doubtless an exaggeration, Henderson did in fact have a wide following and his views on military subjects were well received. Through his teaching, lectures, frequent publications, and numerous friendships he was able to reach a large and appreciative audience, and his death left a gap which, to quote one admirer, "contemporaries regard as impossible to be filled." [38]

For several reasons Henderson's evolutionary theories never grew to maturity. He died before his thoughts on war had crystallized: his *Science of War*, regarded by some as his most important military work, may have provided "the solid foundation of a complete education in the art of war," but it

[37] Proofs of Henderson's first three chapters, labeled "Confidential," are preserved in the War Office Library, Whitehall. For his views on British mistakes, see *Science of War*, p. 389, and Henderson's unsigned article, "The War in South Africa," *Edinburgh Review*, CXCI (1900), 277.

[38] Roberts, "Memoir," pp. xxxvi–xxxviii; *Times*, March 7, 1903; *United Service Magazine*, XXXI (1905), 452.

represents a collection of exploratory essays rather than a carefully thought out synthesis of Henderson's views, and if there is any unity at all to the volume it is the evident desire of the author to provide "a clear insight into the innumerable problems connected with the organization and the command of an armed force."

Even Henderson, moreover, was suspicious of "pure theory." War, to his way of thinking, was no exact science, because it lacked even a fixed code of rules: those who exalted theory at the expense of practical considerations soon degenerated into formalists of the type Napoleon had met and conquered in his early campaigns. There was no sealed pattern to be followed, nor was it possible even "to dictate a normal procedure for the combination of the three arms." Henderson conceded that certain principles demanded respect, but these were not new and the key to success in battle depended on knowing when to disregard the so-called rules of war, when to subordinate theory to the needs of the moment and invent new methods of attack and defense.[39] "No doubt," he once told a military audience

. . . it would be simpler by far to lay down a normal formation, and to practise nothing else. But when we turn to military history, and fail to discover a single battle in which the initial formations of the infantry have not had to be very greatly modified, we may be permitted to believe that a system which accustoms officers and men to constant modifications of formation, compels them to use their own judgment, and brings peace-training and battle-practice into line, is a thoroughly sound one.[40]

This was true also of strategy, where principles were to be obeyed "rather in the spirit than in the letter." According to Henderson, the successful strategist was a man like Stonewall Jackson who, knowing "exactly how far he can go in disregarding or in modifying" the so-called principles of war, was at the same time "ingenious enough to bring those into adjustment which are apparently irreconcilable." [41]

The essential theme, therefore, of Henderson's writing and teaching was "to train the judgment of officers, so that when left to themselves they may do the right thing." And the best

[39] *Ibid.*, p. 452; Henderson, *Science of War*, pp. 71–72, 367, 395.
[40] Henderson, "Offensive Tactics of Infantry," *United Service Magazine*, VII (1893), 961.
[41] Henderson, *Science of War*, p. 42.

way to accomplish this, he believed, was through the intelligent study of military history: for this purpose even the lessons of "Red Indian Warfare" were not without value.[42] Henderson maintained that the study of past campaigns offered a more comprehensive view of the processes of war than experience itself and enabled the diligent student to become so familiar with the few great principles "that to apply them, or at all events to respect them, becomes a matter of instinct." MacDougall and particularly Hamley had attempted to digest the lessons of history for soldiers who had neither the time nor inclination to do as much for themselves, but Henderson insisted that the student himself become involved. Those who heard Henderson's lectures at the Staff College or who read his *Spicheren* or *Stonewall Jackson* found themselves expected to replace the actors, to work out the operations step by step with map and compass, to investigate the reasons behind each decision, to ascertain the relative importance of moral and physical factors, and to deduce the principles on which the generals had acted. Doing this, the student probably would only discover what had been discovered already, but he would have discovered it for himself, and Henderson had taught long enough to realize that knowledge "gained by hard labour and independent effort is of higher worth, and much more likely to be permanently absorbed, than that which comes in by the ear." [43]

Henderson must have been an unusual teacher, and there is abundant evidence that he was an effective one. By "the charm of his personality and the inspiration of his teaching," he exercised an influence that was "almost unique" in the history of the Staff College. He was intrusted with some of the best minds in the army, men who later were to attain positions of high command in the First World War, and these men, wrote a future Chief of the Imperial General Staff, "would readily admit that such successes as attended their leadership were largely due to the sound instruction and inspiring counsel which they received from their old tutor some twenty years or so before." Perhaps the *Times* sounded the right note when it predicted, in 1903, that Henderson's influence would be felt "in the next great war, if that should take place when those who have passed through the Staff College in the

[42] "Red Indian Warfare," *R.U.S.I. Journal*, XXXV (1891), 181–202.
[43] Henderson, *Science of War*, pp. 48–49, 160, 182.

nineties are in positions of command," although one may be permitted to wonder what had happened to the spirit of Henderson's teaching.[44]

Certainly the spirit of Henderson's *Stonewall Jackson* was distorted, for Henderson, whose primary intent had been to develop a flexible and inquisitive attitude in the minds of his students, quickly became the agent of a dogmatic approach to the Civil War. Most of the books and articles written in England on the subject were stimulated by the need to assist hopeful young officers in mastering the intricacies of Jackson's campaigns in preparation for the promotion examinations, which, thanks to Henderson's popularity, usually contained some question on the Civil War; and the average campaign study written after Henderson's death was often little more than an abridged and mutilated version of *Stonewall Jackson*. By writing to drum facts into the heads of candidates for promotion, the authors of these cram books succeeded only in eclipsing the main lessons Henderson had contrived to teach. And as all armies were shortly to discover, "to be able to enumerate the blades of grass in the Shenandoah Valley and the yards marched by Stonewall Jackson's men is not an adequate foundation for leadership in a future war where conditions and armament have radically changed." [45]

---

[44] Sir William Robertson, *From Private to Field Marshal* (Boston, 1921), p. 83; Sir Frederick Maurice, *The Life of General Lord Rawlinson of Trent* (London, 1928), pp. 26, 84; *Times*, March 7, 1903. The following extract from a letter printed in the *Times* years after Henderson's death may be of interest: ". . . in May, 1897, Colonel Henderson said to a small gathering of whom I was one, 'There is a fellow in your batch who will be Commander-in-Chief one of these days'; and on being asked who it might be, said 'Douglas Haig.' The fulfilment of this forecast came at St. Omer at the end of 1915" (as quoted in Ralph Henderson, *Records of My Family*, pp. 111–12). In view of the fact that Haig failed his entrance examination to the Staff College and was appointed finally upon nomination of the Duke of Cambridge, who knew his elder sister, one naturally wonders whether Henderson's predication was based upon his assessment of Haig's intellectual powers or the latter's known friendship with the Prince of Wales. See Alan Clark, *The Donkeys* (London, 1961), p. 22.

[45] Captain B. H. Liddell Hart, *The Remaking of Modern Armies* (London, 1927), pp. 170–71. General Fuller writes: ". . . in 1913, I remember a Major recommending Henderson's *Stonewall Jackson* to a brother officer, and then, a few minutes later, when this book was being discussed, committing the error of supposing that [the battle of] 'Cross Keys' was a public house in Odiham and Jackson the name of the man who ran it" (*The Army in My Time*, pp. 53–54). See below, p. 369.

Henderson's writings reveal even more clearly than those of Maurice the plight of the military analyst in England. Until the role of the army could be more sharply defined, the theorist and military planner must always grope about in the dark. In Germany and France the military leaders could anticipate every detail of mobilization beforehand and shape their strategy accordingly, but in England, as Henderson was well aware, the problem was more complex:

> It is as useless to anticipate in what quarter of the globe our troops may be next employed as to guess at the tactics, the armament, and even the colour . . . of our next enemy. Each new expedition demands special equipment, special methods of supply and special tactical devices, and sometimes special armament. . . . Except for the defence of the United Kingdom and of India, much remains to be provided when the Cabinet declares that war is imminent.[46]

And Henderson, like Maurice, discovered that the British army still was not much interested in books. Soon after publication of *Stonewall Jackson*, a success by any standard, Henderson complained to one friendly reviewer:

> Besides yourself, only one other General, or even Colonel, on the active list has said a word about the book to me; and so far from its having attracted any notice, I find that very few of the senior officers even know that it is in existence. We are certainly not a literary army, and the unfortunate soldier with a turn for writing history does not get much encouragement from the service. The Volunteers, however, are noble creatures: they actually buy military books, and spend their money freely in educating themselves, so there is hard cash to be made out of writing, and that is a consolation.[47]

These two protégés of Wolseley in fact had much in common. They shared essentially the same view of national defense problems, War Office organization, the value of the volunteers, and the amphibious potential of Britain. If Henderson did not apply his theories to the situation confronting Britain on the Continent, he always reminded his readers of "the enormous strategic advantages which accrue to the army that has the sea behind it," and he firmly believed that

[46] Henderson, "War in South Africa," pp. 251–52.
[47] Sir Henry Brackenbury, *Some Memories of My Spare Time* (Edinburgh, 1909), p. 86.

amphibious power represented a "far more terrible weapon" in the age of steel and steam than had been the case in the days when it crushed Napoleon. Finally, both Henderson and Maurice, while critical of much of the literature obscuring the realities of the Franco-Prussian War, were influenced by the views of German theorists. Maurice seems to have been most impressed by the writings of Prince Kraft zu Hohenlohe-Ingelfingen and Von der Goltz, but Henderson, significantly, preferred the views of Von Verdy du Vernois, a writer of a more independent turn of mind. By the end of the century Henderson had begun to suspect that German military thought as well as practice had been dulled by the long peace since 1870: although he did not mention the German army in particular, there is no doubt whom he had in mind when he wrote in 1901 of a Continental army where "order, steadiness, and uniformity [had] become a fetish; officers and men are drilled, not trained; and all individuality, however it may be encouraged by regulations, is quietly repressed in practice." [48]

England has produced few military writers to compare with Henderson. Whatever he did, he did extremely well. His *Campaign of Fredericksburg* is still the best study of the battle, despite the countless water-soaked items floating by in the current flood of Civil War books. Even his analysis of such a routine subject as "The French Manoeuvres of 1891" drew the comment from a prominent officer present that it was "one of the best lectures" ever heard at the Royal United Service Institution,[49] and a review he wrote of several books on the subject of national defense attracted the attention of the *Spectator*, where it was described as "a very remarkable article" on an old subject "freshly and intelligently treated.[50] Henderson's unfinished revision of the *Infantry Drill Book*, particularly his section on tactics, was found to be so meaty in doctrine common to all the arms that the committee intrusted with the completion of the work issued it under a new title, *Combined Training*. Regarded as the forerunner of a new concept of military texts, this work represented a definite break with the past, and Roberts instructed that it was to be

[48] Henderson, *Science of War*, pp. 26–36, 93, 365, 375; "National Defense," *Edinburgh Review*, CLXXXV (1897), 507–39 *passim*. In 1894 Henderson translated Verdy du Vernois' *The Battle of Custozza: A Tactical Study*.
[49] Sir Archibald Alison in *R.U.S.I. Journal*, XXXVI, 879.
[50] "National Defence," *Spectator*, XXVIII (April 17, 1897), 536.

regarded as "authoritative on every subject with which it deals." [51]

Similarly, *Stonewall Jackson,* "an admirable exposition of the generalship of small semiprofessional armies," became a popular military text: Wolseley claimed that he knew of no book that would add more "to the soldier's knowledge of strategy and the art of war," and General Fuller has testified that its influence was "enormous." It introduced succeeding generations to military history. If we can believe the statement of one who became Chief of the Imperial General Staff between the wars, "the impression it left on me . . . chiefly of the very human tone of it, has never faded. Many decisions I helped to arrive at date from those easy readings and the impressions it left in me." [52] *The Science of War,* despite the lengthy treatment of tactical questions no longer at issue after 1914–18, was reprinted after the war for use as a military text.

Henderson's writings survived the war because the basic approach to military history changed after 1918. No longer was it fashionable to concentrate on a few battles and memorize all of the maneuvers in detail. After the First World War the emphasis was more upon strategy, morale, and the psychology of generalship—factors which had not been outmoded by the recent revolution in warfare.

Because Henderson excelled as historian and military critic, because he used history to stimulate independent thought rather than illustrate conventional views, because he wrote with care, imagination, and in a brilliant style, his books are read still today. He left the army "a priceless legacy of instructional works"; [53] and his influence over the years has been inspirational, which explains why many British officers in the 1930's still thought it profitable to visit Civil War battlefields, particularly the Shenandoah Valley and Chancellorsville, where, book in hand, they could share the experience

[51] Dunlop, *Development of the British Army,* pp. 225–26, 291. In 1905 *Combined Training* became Part I of *Field Service Regulations,* which was superseded in 1909 by a new manual (Sir James E. Edmonds [comp.], *Military Operations, France and Belgium, 1914* [London, 1922], I, 9).

[52] Wolseley, Introduction, *Stonewall Jackson,* I, xvi; Fuller, *Army in My Time,* p. 122; General (later Field Marshal), Montgomery Massingberd to Captain B. H. Liddell Hart (August 25, 1926 [Liddell Hart Papers]).

[53] *United Service Magazine,* XXXI, 453.

of Henderson's students and follow Jackson through his most exciting and successful maneuvers.

But the man "who stood head and shoulders above his contemporaries in his brilliant gifts of analysis and exposition of war" [54] died with his work unfinished. He did not live long enough to write the projected sequel to *Stonewall Jackson,* the life of Robert E. Lee. He did not live to see many of his views confirmed in the Russo-Japanese War or to assist in the effort to apply the lessons of the Boer War to military doctrine and organization. With his knowledge of history, command of theory, mastery of language, and with the prestige he had earned and the support he enjoyed from men like Lord Roberts, it is possible, indeed probable, that Henderson's most productive work was still before him. For in the ferment of discussion in the years preceding the war, Henderson would have spoken out with vigor and authority. And he would have been heard.

[54] The Military Correspondent of the *Times* (Lieutenant Colonel Charles À Court Repington), *Imperial Strategy* (London, 1906), p. 213.

IV THE YEARS OF PREPARA-TION 1899–1914

H ENDERSON died on the eve of the greatest changes in the British army since the Napoleonic Wars. The Cardwell Reforms had altered army organization, but the changes that occurred in the decade before 1914 touched everything from tactics to the newly established Committee of Imperial Defence. For the Boer War had jolted Englishmen into a sense of insecurity, and the lengthening shadows of approaching war in Europe added fresh anxieties.

Some of the changes represent attempts to correct flaws uncovered by the recent operations against the Boers. The elaborate report of the Elgin Commission in 1903, for example, pointed to inadequacies in military preparations, manpower, materiél, and transport and served as a basis for reforms in these areas. The appearance of Henderson's *Combined Training* (1902), *Cavalry Training* (1904), *Infantry Training* (1905), the *Manuel of Engineering* (1905), the *Field Service Regulations* (1905), and *Field Artillery Training* (1907) reflected some of the tactical lessons of the war and provided common doctrine governing the employment of the army and its component parts. In 1904 the office of commander in chief was abolished in favor of an army council comprising two civilian and four professional advisers to the secretary of state for war; in 1906 a general staff finally was created to assist "in promoting military efficiency, especially in regard to the education of officers and the training of the troops," and "to advise on the strategical distribution of the

Army . . . to collect and collate military intelligence, to direct the general policy in Army matters, and to secure continuity of action in the execution of that policy." [1] Planning and co-ordination on a still higher level was made possible by the emergence of the Committee of Imperial Defence on a permanent basis in 1904. An "organ of inquiry and persuasion," the C.I.D. provided "the basic machinery necessary to the comprehensive planning of imperial security" and "rendered outmoded the dangerous vacuum caused by the lack of planning so general during the nineteenth century." [2]

Other reforms were designed to create an army permitting Britain to fulfil new obligations should war break out on the Continent. The entente with France in 1904 and with Russia three years later signified a reversal in foreign policy and led to measures increasing the effectiveness of existing forces and enabling their rapid expansion in time of war. The Haldane reforms created a modern expeditionary force, transformed the volunteers into the territorial force to provide a stronger second line of defense, and instituted the national reserve to increase military strength in times of emergency.

These reforms were accompanied by organized efforts to mobilize public opinion and to increase the public's knowledge of military affairs. The National Service League under the vigorous leadership of Lord Roberts demanded compulsory military service as the only means of national survival; the Navy League, founded in 1895, clamored for the support of all classes in maintaining the fleet "at the requisite standard of strength"—meaning, of course, to keep well ahead of Germany in the naval race. One has but to scan the pages of any English periodical to appreciate the extent to which the public was kept informed on military matters. In 1905 the *Times* appointed its first regular military correspondent in the expectation that his columns "would stimulate thought concerning the art of war." Soon afterward Oxford established a chair in military history, bringing the study of war within the scope of higher education.

[1] Brevet Major A. R. Godwin-Austen, *The Staff and the Staff College* (London, 1927), pp. 243–44; Brigadier General J. E. Edmonds, *Military Operations France and Belgium, 1914* (London, 1922), I, 2–14; Colonel John K. Dunlop, *The Development of the British Army 1899–1914* (London, 1938).

[2] Franklyn Arthur Johnson, *Defence by Committee: The British Committee of Imperial Defence 1885–1959* (London, 1960), p. 81.

Within the army there also were signs of a great intellectual awakening. The Manchester Tactical Society was increasingly active and served as a sounding board for discussion of proposed reforms. Inexpensive editions like "The Wolseley Series," which originated in 1897, "The Pall Mall Series," which appeared in 1903, and "The Special Campaign Series," the first volumes of which were published in 1907, facilitated publication and encouraged soldiers to write. Works of foreign military writers—Clausewitz, Foch, Von der Goltz, and Bernhardi—were translated; new military journals such as *The Cavalry Journal* (1906) and *The Army Review* (1911) gave direction to British military thought. Altogether there was enough activity of this sort to give the pacifists after 1918 a field day.[3]

The two most prolific and influential military writers during this period moved in army circles but operated from a civilian base. Wilkinson was a volunteer and Repington was forced to leave the army, but personal contacts and a large public following gave both an influential voice in the shaping of military policy. Differing in character and temperament, they were alike in their crusading zeal and both were motivated by the realization that much work and little time remained to fit the army for its new role on the Continent and to educate the public about its responsibilities in a modern war between nations.

[3] George Arthur, "The Soldier as Student," *Fortnightly Review*, LXXXVIII (October, 1907), 620–29; Lieutenant Colonel Alsager Pollock, "A Military Education," *ibid.*, LXXXVII (February, 1907), 537–47; T. Miller Maguire, "The Military Education of Officers," *National Review*, XXXVI (December, 1900), 507–16. A pacifist's view of these proceedings is Caroline E. Playne, *The Pre-war Mind in Britain* (London, 1928), pp. 140–55.

8

THE VOLUNTEER ADVOCATE

Spenser Wilkinson

DEAR MR. WILKINSON:
The King has decided to appoint a Royal Commission on the Militia and Volunteers.

I am permitted to ask if you will accept the honour of serving upon it.

I hope you will see your way to do so, as I know from your writing how deep an interest you take in the efficiency of the Auxiliary Forces.[1]

To the drama critic of the Manchester *Guardian* this letter from the secretary of state for war, coinciding with the official arrival of spring, must have signified regeneration of another sort. After twenty years of special pleading, Wilkinson's case for the volunteers was about to be judged. By vocation a lawyer, he had dedicated his lifework to his avocation. When the Norfolk Commission finally was constituted in 1903, it almost had to include this most articulate and outspoken advocate of the volunteers.

Wilkinson's memoirs were written too late in life to recapture his thoughts on this occasion, but probably he approached the task with mixed emotions. Relieved that the bleak months for the moment were behind him, he must have felt uneasy about the clouds that were beginning to gather on

---

[1] Mr. St. John Brodrick to Spenser Wilkinson, March 21, 1902 (Wilkinson Papers, Ogilby Trust, the War Office). Most of the letters to Spenser Wilkinson are in the custody of the Ogilby Trust but a few of special interest to the family remain in the hands of a daughter. Miss Victoria Wilkinson, and will be so designated.

the horizon, for Spenser Wilkinson understood the extent of the preparations necessary if the British army were to weather the next storm.

Henry Spenser Wilkinson was born in 1853 in Manchester, where his father, Thomas Read Wilkinson, was a banker and a crusading liberal in the tradition of Cobden and Bright. As a young boy he had been exposed to the propaganda of the Union and Emancipation Society and involved in the efforts of his father to bring about compulsory education, so it was natural that he should grow up convinced "that the mark of any man worth the name was public spirit." At Owens College, where he spent six years, inspired teaching led to a mastery of German and a lifelong enthusiasm for history; and at Merton College, Oxford, which he attended in 1873 as a postgraduate scholar, he stumbled into a cause that was to give meaning to his life and consume his special skills and interests.[2]

Wilkinson spent his first vacation at Oxford touring Germany, where he happened to pick up an Austrian pamphlet on the comparative strength of the armies of Europe. Having shown no previous interest in military affairs—the liberal spirit that pervaded his father's household was against it—he was shocked to discover how insignificant was the British army compared with the great armies of the Continent. His curiosity aroused, he borrowed copies of Hamley's *Operations of War* and Maurice's Wellington Prize essay, and during the next term at Oxford he joined a university volunteer corps and organized the Oxford Kriegspiel Club. At this time his interest in war was "patriotic and political." He had no desire for a soldier's life and in any case he was too old to enter the Army, but while reading law he felt a compelling desire to discover his own answers to questions which lay well beyond the horizons of his early environment. He wanted to know, for example, if John Bright and the Quakers were right in refusing to have anything to do with war. Was it a citizen's duty to defend his country? Was it in fact possible ever to eliminate war? [3]

[2] Most of the information relating to Spenser Wilkinson's career comes from his unpublished papers and his autobiography, *Thirty-Five Years 1874–1909* (London, 1933). Some material has also been gleaned from the files of Captain B. H. Liddell Hart and the correspondence and writings of perhaps Wilkinson's most devoted pupil, the late Colonel J. Marius Scammell, U.S.A.

[3] Wilkinson, *Thirty-Five Years*, pp. 5–7.

In 1880 Wilkinson was called to the bar and started practice in Manchester. He had previously taken a commission in the 2d Manchester Volunteers, where the problems he encountered were of quite different character from those which first had prompted him to become a volunteer. Here he was struck by the sharp contrast between what he had read and what he was taught in the regiment; the officers were eager to learn but ignorant of theory, and the drill books specified evolutions that long since had ceased to serve any useful purpose in war. It was to remedy this state of affairs that the young barrister and six other enthusiasts formed in 1881 the Manchester Tactical Society; although Wilkinson probably did not realize it at the time, for all practical purposes his legal career was already behind him. He continued to practice law, but his happiest hours were those spent with friends discussing war games or tactical problems. They developed a camaraderie rarely seen among volunteer organizations, and by frank discussion of their blunders, a demanding program of reading and study, and rigorous self-examination they learned a great deal about the practical aspects of war.

Originally, Wilkinson had intended the law to serve as a gateway to a useful career in public life, but instead his opportunity came from the Manchester Tactical Society. The need for a set of realistic exercises in applied tactics induced Wilkinson to translate French and German military texts, and before long he had converted the Society into a publishing fund which for many years issued at nominal prices books and pamphlets on tactics and their application to the volunteers. In this way Wilkinson published *Suggestions for a New Field Exercise for the Volunteer Infantry* (1886), *Essays on the War Game* (1887), and translations (some in collaboration with colleagues) of Gizycki's *Exercises in Strategy and Tactics* (1887), *The Command of Artillery in the Army Corps and Infantry Divisions* (1889), and *The German Order of Field Service* (1893). Although the latter was adopted by the War Office and, according to Wilkinson, was "perhaps the most valuable book on the details of war that has ever been published," few soldiers bought these publications. They did go far, however, to establish Wilkinson's reputation as spokesman for the volunteers, and they served as a solid foundation for his own military education.

The immediate influence of the Society is seen in the growth of many kindred organizations and the institution by the War Office in 1881 of a voluntary, if elementary, examination on the theory of tactics. Unfortunately this proved a failure because, as Wilkinson pointed out, the authorities "had no idea how to examine and encouraged a bad text-book instead of a good one." During the Boer War the Manchester Tactical Society submitted a memorandum to the commander in chief suggesting various improvements in the organization and training of the volunteers, some of which were incorporated in regulations issued by the War Office during the next two years. All of these suggestions were recommended in the report of the Norfolk Commission on the Militia and Volunteers in 1904, and, with but two exceptions, were adopted by Lord Haldane in his famous reorganization of 1907.[4]

Wilkinson's activities with the volunteers led directly to a new vocation—journalism. In 1881 he wrote an account of the great volunteer review in Windsor Park for the Manchester *City News,* after which he was asked to represent the *Guardian* on similar occasions. From time to time the *Guardian* also printed the articles he wrote for the Tactical Society. Wilkinson first made his mark as a military critic by writing daily commentaries on the 1882 campaign in Egypt. Maurice, in defending Wolseley's conduct and his own history of the campaign, tempered his accusations against the press by making a deep bow to "the very able military critic" of the *Guardian* who had provided "the most valuable [public] support that was given to the general during all that trying time." The Egyptian campaign proved to Wilkinson "not only that I could write, and liked it, but that I understood something of war." He turned from the bar to journalism, and the newspaper in turn provided him with a new platform for his ideas on the reform of the volunteers and army reorganization.[5]

[4] *Ibid.,* pp. 18–29; Wilkinson, "An Experiment in Military Education," *Army Quarterly,* III (1921), 51–69; "The Practical Value of the War Game," *R.U.S.I. Journal,* XXXII (1888–89), 69–79; Wilkinson to Lord Charles Beresford, October 9, 1894 (Wilkinson Papers). The weekly activities of the Society are recorded in the Minutes which Wilkinson deposited in the War Office Library after the First World War.

[5] Maurice, "Critics and Campaigns," *Fortnightly Review,* XLIV (1888), 128; Wilkinson, *Thirty-Five Years,* pp. 30–36.

For the next twenty years Wilkinson remained the principal advocate for the volunteers, using his pen to help educate the officers, alert the public, and win War Office support for much needed reforms. In 1883 he made a number of proposals in a little volume entitled *Citizen Soldiers,* and if Wilkinson's views had no immediate effect at least he could claim, ten years later, that no modification in the volunteer system had been introduced by the War Office "which was not suggested in that book."

But still he was dissatisfied: many of the measures adopted —higher standards of marksmanship, formation of brigades, voluntary examinations in many subjects—impressed Wilkinson as mere caricatures of his original proposals,[6] and when his friend Lord Roberts suggested a fresh look at the auxiliary forces and their role in the defense of the empire in the 1890's, Wilkinson was far from pleased with the view. The mobilization scheme worked out a few years earlier had "hardly been taken seriously," the volunteers were not a homogeneous organization, the necessary stores were lacking, the official textbook was "far from lucid, and by no means embodies the best modern military thought," the artillery was too heavy and immobile to serve as field artillery under modern conditions, and drill, even with the adoption of some of his earlier suggestions, had yet to be reduced to essentials. Marksmanship, for example, must come before bayonet exercises; battalion squares and marching in open column, movements which had disappeared from the field of battle, should also be cut from the *Field Exercise;* and more attention should be paid to the construction of field works "in their simplest form." Wilkinson was one of the few in the 1890's to become convinced that in future battles "the spade will frequently be used" even in the attack.[7]

In Wilkinson's judgment more money was needed, training must be brought up to date, and the authorities must learn to recognize the inherent virtues as well as faults of Britain's citizen soldiers. But the most serious deficiency was in the number of qualified officers: the volunteers desperately needed more officers of the type Henderson was trying to

[6] Wilkinson to Roberts, August 24, 1892; Wilkinson to Beresford, October 9, 1894 (Wilkinson Papers).
[7] Wilkinson, *The Volunteers and the National Defence* (Westminster, 1896), pp. 17, 23–24, 33, 64, 90–91, 114–15.

groom at the Staff College, men interested in tactical theory and military history and dependent upon insight and judgment rather than "facts stored in the memory." One could master the details of *Field Exercise* without becoming a slave to them. As Sir Ernest Swinton shortly was to point out in his delightful indictment of the pre-war training of the British officer, *The Defence of Duffer's Drift*, what Wilkinson was looking for in the volunteers was hard enough to find among regular officers even after the painful lessons of the early campaigns in South Africa.[8]

In his fight to improve the volunteers Wilkinson received encouragement from Roberts and assurances of support by Wolseley,[9] but not until the authorities, stung by the revelations of the Boer War, appointed him to the Royal Commission on Militia and Volunteers did he have an opportunity to play an official role in determining policy. Reading the minutes of the Norfolk Commission one can see the volunteer advocate skilfully lead witnesses from the militia and volunteers to build his case. He fought tooth and nail for the volunteer system, and the draft report which ultimately was accepted came largely from his pen. The government did not act on the report, probably because it appeared to indorse some system of compulsory service, but Wilkinson had sufficient faith in the volunteers to believe that if the suggested reforms were adopted, compulsory service would not be necessary. He worked with Haldane during the next three years and saw many of his hopes realized in the Haldane reforms, although he was never satisfied with the financial adminstration and training of the new territorial force and he feared that by changing their name and becoming subject at all times to military law, former volunteers might also lose something of that unique spirit which had animated them ever since they were first organized to meet the invasion threat of 1859.[10]

[8] *Ibid.*, pp. 67–71, 94, 149.
[9] Wolseley to Wilkinson, February 17, 1896 (Victoria Wilkinson Papers). Roberts to Wilkinson, April 6, 1896; March 19, 1897 (Wilkinson Papers).
[10] Wilkinson, *Thirty-Five Years*, pp. 263–67, 306–8; Wilkinson to H. H. Asquith (later Earl of Oxford), September 18, 1914; Haldane to Wilkinson, October 27 and December 15, 1905, January 6 and October 12, 1906 (Wilkinson Papers). *Minutes of Evidence taken before the Royal Commission on the Militia and Volunteers,* I (London, 1904), *passim.*

Ten years' writing on behalf of the volunteers convinced Wilkinson "that the reform of the army could not be effected from below by teaching war" [11]—he had to begin at the top. His next attempts, therefore, were directed toward a reorganization of the War Office. In 1887 General Sir Henry Brackenbury, testifying before a select committee appointed to examine the army and navy estimates, struck a responsive note in Wilkinson when he referred to the lack of any "great central thinking department" in England comparable to the German General Staff. The next year the Hartington Commission—of which Brackenbury was a member—was appointed "to enquire into the Civil and Professional Administration of the Naval and Military Departments," and it seemed to Wilkinson that the time was ripe for an historical examination of the German General Staff to see how in fact it operated and "to perceive which of its peculiarities are local, temporary, and personal; and what are the unchangeable principles in virtue of which it has prospered." [12]

By coincidence *The Brain of an Army* was published on the same day in 1890 as the Hartington Commission *Report*. It was one of Wilkinson's most successful efforts. German military leaders, including the great Moltke, praised the book for its accuracy and confessed surprise that a foreigner—and a civilian at that—could describe so faithfully "the organisation, spirit, and working of our General Staff" when "this has not been yet done in German." [13] British generals, notably Roberts and Brackenbury, likewise were impressed. The former had reservations, maintaining that a chief of staff was necessary only "if the nation thinks it desirable to reserve the appointment of a Commander-in-Chief for a member of the Royal Family, irrespective of his qualifications." According to Roberts, the ideal solution would be to find a really capable commander in chief and then build upon the present system.[14] Brackenbury naturally supported the idea of a chief of staff and encouraged Wilkinson—*"very private and confidential"* —to

[11] Wilkinson to Beresford, October 9, 1894 (Wilkinson Papers).

[12] Wilkinson, *Thirty-Five Years*, p. 120; *The Brain of an Army: A Popular Account of the German General Staff* (London, 1890), pp. v–vi.

[13] Wilkinson, *Thirty-Five Years*, pp. 121–22. Moltke's letter to Wilkinson is printed in the Preface to the second edition.

[14] Roberts to Wilkinson, September 11, 1891; December 31, 1891 (Wilkinson Papers).

stick to your guns about a Chief of the Staff and fire away. But pray don't quote me on the subject. It is the very devil that the Duke [of Cambridge] has my professional life at this moment in his hands. He has always called me a dangerous man on this very question, and thinks that a Chief of the Staff would destroy the Crown's hold on the army and threaten its very existence. Still, I say—Hope! but don't pretend to sources of information. Only stick to the line you are upon.[15]

Brackenbury himself worked, quite possibly in his own interest, to abolish the office of commander in chief when he drafted the Hartington Commission *Report,* but Wilkinson regarded this as only one of several ways to achieve the desired goal, that being to create a special military adviser, an English counterpart to Moltke, to the civilian minister responsible for the army. For his part Wilkinson did not care whether such an official were to be called "chief of the staff" or "commander in chief," as long as he had the authority, "limited only by that of the Cabinet, to carry out, during peace, the training of the army for war," and as long as it was his responsibility to resign when his advice on basic issues was disregarded. Before remodeling the whole structure at the War Office along the lines suggested by the Hartington Commission, Wilkinson wanted first "to try the effect of a change of persons upon the present system." Once the Duke of Cambridge was retired and safely out of the way, he thought it possible for a Roberts or Wolseley to improve upon the present system by incorporating those features of the German General Staff essential to its success and at the same time compatible with the English Constitution.

In this as in other matters where he had strong convictions, Wilkinson the reformer did not tamper with Wilkinson the historian. *The Brain of an Army* was an honest "endeavour to describe the German General Staff and its relation to the military institutions from which it is inseparable" [16] and not,

[15] Brackenbury to Wilkinson, March 7, 1889; March 12, 1889; March 29, 1890; May 14, 1890; June 2, 1890 (Wilkinson Papers). According to the future Field Marshal Lord Nicholson, "it is perfectly notorious that the report of the [Hartington] Commission was drafted by Genl. Brackenbury to suit his own ends, and that most of the members . . . knew little and cared less about the subject." "Talking to me on the subject at Simla, Brackenbury certainly gave me to understand that he was really responsible for the report" (Nicholson to Wilkinson, June 24, 1894; July 28, 1894 [Wilkinson Papers]).

[16] Wilkinson, *Brain of an Army,* p. vi.

as one might suspect, a weighted argument, cloaked in the seductive garments of history, for Wilkinson's own point of view. This he expressed in numerous articles and in the joint letter that he and three distinguished members of Parliament, all men of different political philosophies who stood above party differences in their sincere efforts to reform the army, addressed in 1894 to the prime minister.

His collaborators on this occasion were Sir Charles Dilke, Maurice's brilliant antagonist in the debate over national policies and imperial defense, a man of exceptional ability who, were it not for his tragic involvement in a sensational divorce trial a few years previously, might reasonably have aspired to succeed Gladstone as leader of the Liberal party; Sir George Chesney, the imaginative writer who had attempted in his provocative and controversial *Battle of Dorking* (1871) to jar England into a state of military preparedness, and a tireless advocate of army reform; and H. O. Arnold-Forster, a relative newcomer to the ranks of the reformers and the only one who, as war minister after the turn of the century, would ever be in a position to act on his own proposals.

Although the joint letter on national defense was Dilke's idea, the driving force behind it was Wilkinson. The authors hoped to increase military efficiency by means of more systematic planning and preparation and through closer co-operation between the services. Whereas the Hartington Commission had proposed abolishing the office of commander in chief in favor of a chief of staff to co-ordinate administration and policy, Dilke and Wilkinson advocated appointing the same minister to the offices of both secretary of state for war and first lord of the admiralty or alternatively the amalgamation of these two offices. Thus in place of the decentralized War Office Council comprising the prime minister, the cabinet heads of both services, and the principal military and naval advisers as recommended by the Hartington Commission, the joint letter urged the cabinet to select, for each service, "an officer whose professional judgment commands its confidence, to be at once the responsible adviser of the Cabinet upon all questions regarding the conduct of war . . . and the principal executive officer" for the respective services.

The basic weakness in the Hartington Commission *Report,* in Wilkinson's judgment at least, was that while it recommended in vague terms the establishment of a "thinking department," it had ignored the nature and unique merits of the German General Staff system. The chief of staff envisaged in the *Report* would be given "no authority over the army," merely the "general power to meddle." Therefore it was essential, the authors of the joint letter concluded, that the military adviser be freed of all administrative burdens so that he could concentrate upon planning in peace and direction of the army in war. He should be responsible for the advice he gives, and he should remain in power "only so long as his judgment upon the professional matters . . . is acceptable to the Cabinet." This had been the secret of the Prussian victories, and it was the only way to cement the relationship between strategy and statesmanship.[17]

The joint letter succeeded only in stirring up controversy. Despite its publicity and Dilke's determined efforts in Parliament, the measures it proposed were never accepted. When the government changed hands in 1895, the new ministry followed the recommendations of the Hartington Commission by creating a Defense Committee of the Cabinet and stripping the new commander in chief, Wolseley, of much of his power, to the dismay of Dilke, Wilkinson, and most of all, Wolseley. Convinced by this action "that there was no one in the cabinet who had thoroughly thought out the relations between policy, war, and naval and military preparation," Wilkinson volunteered his services to the Defense Committee in the hope that through personal contacts and an occasional memorandum he might "be able unobtrusively to get the essential questions" before the proper authorities. His offer was refused, as it was again during the early months of the Boer War when he indicated a willingness to bury himself in some government

---

[17] For the story of the joint letter, see Stephen Gwynn and Gertrude M. Tuckwell, *The Life of the Rt. Hon. Sir Charles W. Dilke* (2d ed.; London, 1918), II, 413–26, 451–57; Wilkinson, *Thirty-Five Years,* pp. 182–83, and Wilkinson's letter to the Duke of Devonshire (Marquis of Hartington), December 26, 1899 (Wilkinson Papers). Wilkinson's views on the Report of the Hartington Commission and his own recommendations for a modification in the existing structure are found in his essays reprinted in *War and Policy* (New York, 1900), pp. 259–84; Wilkinson and Dilke, *Imperial Defence* (new and rev. ed.; Westminster, 1897), pp. 169–71; and Wilkinson, "The General Management of the Army," *Nineteenth Century,* XLVII (1900), 175–86. The problem in retrospect is treated briefly in Franklyn Arthur Johnson, *Defence by Committee: The British Committee of Imperial Defence 1855–1959* (London, 1960), pp. 23–34.

department as a subordinate despite the increased demands for his pen.[18]

Frustrated in his desire to see a general staff anticipating and preparing in advance for an emergency such as that confronting the British Army in South Africa in 1899, Wilkinson carried his case to the public in his regular commentaries in the *Morning Post*. The army itself was "never in better condition" to fight, he wrote: the officers were zealous, the men well trained and disciplined, and the field services appeared to be well organized. But the government had "deliberately handicapped" the army by conceding the strategical advantage: reinforcements to South Africa had been too late and too few. Wilkinson took the line that "the war is doing us good. It is giving us the beginnings of political education in a department that has been utterly neglected." Success in war, as in other business, "depends on putting knowledge in power." [19]

The disasters of Black Week (December 11–15, 1899), during which three British forces were defeated, sharpened his criticisms of command by committee. "You cannot expect a Cabinet of twelve or eighteen men ignorant of war to create a good war-fighting machine," he wrote on the day London learned of the failure at Magersfontein, where 13,000 of England's finest troops were defeated in the open field. The trouble lay with the cabinet and the War Office. If the country was not indignant enough to insist upon the formation of a ministry competent in the management of war, then at the very least the present ministers "should choose a war adviser who can convince them, even though . . . they have to pass over one hundred generals and select a colonel, a captain, or a crammer." Wilkinson criticized Lord Lansdowne, the secretary of state for war, until Roberts wrote from the field that Lansdowne was doing all that could reasonably be expected of him. He also criticized Wolseley, then commander in chief, who in his estimation had erred either in giving bad advice or, if his proposals were solid, in failing to resign as the principal military adviser once he was overruled. "In the crisis of the Nation's fate," Wilkinson concluded, "we are ungoverned and

[18] Wilkinson to the Duke of Devonshire, December 26, 1899 (Wilkinson Papers).
[19] Written November 8, 1899, and reprinted in Wilkinson, *Lessons of the War, Being Comments from Week to Week to the Relief of Ladysmith* (Westminster, 1900), pp. 37, 47.

unled, and to all appearance we are content to be so, and the leader-writers trained in the tradition of respectable formalism interpret the Nation's apathy as fortitude." [20]

The Brain of an Army led ultimately to *The Brain of a Navy* (1895) as Wilkinson grew increasingly concerned over command of an altogether different sort—*The Command of the Sea* (1894). Before 1891 he had not meddled with the navy except in an occasional leader, but when he and Dilke undertook their study of imperial defense he devoured Colomb, Mahan, and everything else about the navy he could lay his hands on. The first result of this inquiry was to convince both men that "the ocean is, in fact, a British possession," and that "the primacy of the Navy" was the master key to imperial defense.[21] A public dispute with Admiral Colomb over the implications of the term "fleet in being" brought the two together and gave Wilkinson fresh confidence in the soundness of his theories, which he explained in *The Command of the Sea*. Written primarily to alert the public to the vital importance of retaining a fleet in the Mediterranean to offset French pressures in Africa, this book led directly to the formation of the Navy League, a non-partisan organization that emerged in the closing months of 1894 "to secure as the primary object of the national policy the command of the sea." The general aims of the League were

1) To spread information showing the vital importance of naval supremacy to the British Empire.
2) To call attention to the enormous demands which war would make upon the Navy and to the fact that the Navy is not at present ready to meet them.
3) To secure the appointment of a single professional adviser, responsible to the Cabinet, upon the maritime defense of the Empire, whose opinion as to the sufficiency of the preparations covered by the Estimates shall be communicated to Parliament.

The hand of Wilkinson is easily detected in this last clause. From his study of the German General Staff he was convinced of the need for some form of corporate brain in the War

[20] Wilkinson, *Lessons of the War,* pp. 92, 100–102, 109–10, 119–20, 152; *War and Policy,* pp. 367–402, *passim.*

[21] Wilkinson to Lord Charles Beresford, October 9, 1894 (Wilkinson Papers). Wilkinson and Dilke, *Imperial Defence,* pp. 34, 50.

Office; Admiral Sir Geoffrey Hornby, possibly taking his cue from *The Brain of an Army*, had recommended in 1890 a general staff for the navy, an idea amplified further in the much publicized joint letter on National Defense and in Wilkinson's *Command of the Sea*, which the League reprinted (10,000 copies) for use as propaganda. Wilkinson next wrote *The Brain of a Navy*, a polemic in which he asserted that "what we have to do is to provide the Cabinet, or make it provide itself, with a naval Moltke." The title itself is somewhat misleading in that Wilkinson, although sincere in his desire to reform the Admiralty, also intended the book as an indirect attack upon the organization of the War Office, where the presence of the Duke of Cambridge still thwarted any frontal assault on reform. The navy appeared to offer riper and more immediate prospects for change.

The problems in both cases were similar. Neither the War Office nor the Admiralty possessed a general staff to make full use of the data supplied by their respective intelligence departments; neither had any man in authority whose duty it was to study and make plans for the next war; and both suffered the curse of anonymity. Wilkinson compared the processes for determining military policy to the preparation of a newspaper leader: one rarely knew the real author, and in both instances the original lines too often were blurred by some less competent individual "and then altered again by a third man who knew less of the subject than either and disagreed with both." Worse still, the military and naval estimates each year were dictated by the wishes of the Treasury and not by professionals familiar with the requirements of imperial defense. The Board of Admiralty was "a legal fiction" that could neither administer the navy nor decide policy; the navy itself was "as absolutely governed by a Cabinet Minister as the Post Office or the Treasury."

Wilkinson did not want to deprive the cabinet of its ultimate responsibility: if there was to be war, the cabinet was the proper body to manage it. But after the reports of Sir James Stephen's Commission in 1887 and the Hartington Commission several years later, it seemed to Wilkinson that no cabinet had performed its primary duty of making the necessary arrangements for the defense of the empire. He wrote *The Brain of a Navy* to apply pressure on the cabinet to get the best professional advice, naval and military, and to consider this advice before submitting the annual estimates. "Knowledge means a man, not a committee." Wilkinson proposed that the first sea lord be elevated to the position of responsible strategical adviser to the civilian minister: he should be a man "selected for his strategical power" and he should be given the assistance of a staff of specialists and relieved of most of his administrative duties. Above all, he should be given the authority to direct the navy in the event of war, for only by giving power "to those who best understand naval war, and who can exercise authority and answer for its right use," could England expect to maintain the standard of naval preparation necessary to secure continued command of the seas.[22]

Although Wilkinson found powerful supporters among the naval hierarchy, men like Sir Geoffrey Hornby, who accepted the presidency of the Navy League because of his desire to see a general staff for the navy, and Admiral Lord Charles Beresford, a personal friend who had resigned his seat upon the Board of Admiralty in 1888 because of cutbacks in the Intelligence Department, he was unsuccessful in his efforts to reorganize the Admiralty. Hornby died shortly after accepting the presidency of the League and the executive committee subsequently decided that the main objective should be to disseminate information and not to upset the Admiralty by probing into questions of a technical, professional, or administrative nature. Accordingly the original clause calling for the appointment of a single professional adviser, which many blamed for the initial failure of the League to win popular support, was replaced by a resolution "to call attention from time to time to such measures as may be requisite to secure adequate preparation for the maritime defence of the Empire." No longer committed to a policy that would create friction with the Admiralty, the League began "to play a conspicuous role in molding public opinion on the needs of the fleet." Wilkinson, however, resigned when he realized that the emphasis was to be upon ships rather than brains. With the unwavering support of Dilke, he continued in his efforts to convince the nation that the Admiralty must be organized for war before the navy could be prepared to fight it, "and that a

[22] Wilkinson, *The Command of the Sea* (Westminster, 1894), pp. 65–69, 101–4, 113–20; *The Brain of a Navy* (2d ed.; London, 1922), pp. 12–16, 22–24, 45–51, 58; *War and Policy*, pp. 315–26.

rightly organized Admiralty should be controlled by the best strategist."

If his proposals were not adopted, Wilkinson was not denied the satisfaction of seeing his writings used as ammunition after the Boer War, when sea power began to receive serious and systematic study with the strengthening of the Naval Intelligence Department in 1902 and the emergence soon afterward of the Committee of Imperial Defence. In 1902 Beresford began to speak out vigorously for the appointment of a "naval Moltke"; three years later Admiral Sir Edmund R. Fremantle publicly indorsed Wilkinson's arguments for a general staff for the navy; and in 1909 Beresford finally pushed home the attack when his charges against the administration of the navy by the first sea lord, Admiral Sir John Fisher, resulted in an investigation by the Committee of Imperial Defence. The report of the subcommittee rejected Beresford's contentions about the organization and disposition of the fleet but recommended "the further development of a Naval War Staff," a measure which already had been projected in the Admiralty before the Beresford hearings to appease the critics, among whom—although he had been eclipsed in the public eye by the popular and overzealous Beresford—was Wilkinson. Another step forward was taken in 1912 with the establishment of an Admiralty War Staff to give advice on matters touching naval strategy and operations. Wilkinson's ideal "brain of a navy" would have been given "authority in matters strategical," but, once again, he recognized that "the standard is one thing; the practical possibilities another." With Winston Churchill the civilian head of the Admiralty and Fisher the guiding spirit in the navy, it was too much to expect such strong personalities willingly to submit to the dictation of a "thinking department," especially when each felt quite competent to serve as his own "naval Moltke." [23]

[23] Wilkinson, *Thirty-Five Years*, pp. 185–97; "Preparation for War," *National Review*, XXXIX (1902), 197–208; Arthur J. Marder, *The Anatomy of British Sea Power: A History of British Naval Policy in the Pre-Dreadnought Era, 1880–1905* (New York, 1940), pp. 48–52, 413–14, 424; Marder, *From the Dreadnought to Scapa Flow: The Royal Navy in the Fisher Era, 1904–1919*. I. *The Road to War, 1904–1914* (London, 1961), pp. 186–204, 247, 265; *The Memoirs of Admiral Lord Charles Beresford* (London, 1914), II, 478–84; Fremantle, "A General Staff for the Navy," *United Service Magazine*, III (1905), 335–42; Beresford to Wilkinson, October 12, 1894; April 7, 1902; February 14, 1908 (Wilkinson Papers).

Wilkinson's efforts to introduce certain features of the German General Staff to both the War Office and the Admiralty represent but one thread in the fabric of his writings. To most contemporaries he was probably more readily identified as a practical authority on matters pertaining to imperial defense. Surprisingly little attention had been given to this subject before Dilke proposed, in 1891, that the two write a popular book on the preparation of the British Empire for war.

The war scare coinciding with the Russo-Turkish War of 1877–78 was perhaps the first occasion since the Napoleonic Wars when British leaders felt compelled to do something about the study of imperial defense: a Colonial Defence Committee was organized to "provide some early and temporary defence in case of any sudden outbreak of hostilities"; MacDougall proposed the formation of a Canadian contingent in what he envisaged as an imperial army, and in 1879 a royal commission was appointed to study "the Defence of British Possessions and Commerce Abroad." But public concern for the defense of the empire died down when it became apparent that there would be no war, and with the return of the Liberals to power in 1880 came the revival of the old idea that "self government begets self-defence." In 1885, however, the Colonial Defence Committee was revived on a permanent basis, and two years later the golden jubilee of Queen Victoria and the appointment of the Hartington Commission led to new efforts to explore areas of common interest and responsibility between Great Britain and the colonies.[24]

Imperial Defence was largely the work of Wilkinson, who wrote the manuscript after the two had thrashed out their ideas. Wilkinson had already won over Dilke to the idea of a responsible strategic adviser for each of the services, and during the preparation of this volume he also gained support for his theories on sea power. Wilkinson's theories evidently were sound, for none other than Admiral Colomb, probably the greatest naval writer in England at the time, wrote to Dilke upon reading the book: "I am inclined to sing 'Nunc dimittis,' for, as far as I can understand the matter, you put forward all the views for which I have contended; and coming thus from

[24] N. H. Gibbs, *The Origins of Imperial Defence* (Oxford, 1955), pp. 3–14; Colonel J. F. C. Fuller, *Imperial Defence 1588–1914* (London, 1926), pp. 38–44.

your hands, I think they will henceforth be current views."
Dilke passed on the letter to Wilkinson with the comment:
"Colomb thinks *he* has converted me. I reply, *he couldn't*. You
did—after he had failed." Previously Dilke had taken the line
that "the concentration of the navy in home waters must
involve the abandonment of the rest of the Empire," but
Wilkinson had convinced him that the command of the sea
would insure the safety of the empire. According to Dilke's
biographer, "This was the turning-point of his studies of
Imperial Defence." [25]

On one subject only—the defense of India—does Dilke
appear to have been the dominant partner, but even here
Wilkinson had already published enough in the *Guardian* to
convince Lord Roberts in India that he was upon the right
track.[26] Roberts therefore felt no compunction about sending
along confidential documents to support the arguments for his
"Forward" policy, for Dilke and Wilkinson agreed that the key
to the defense of India was control of the North West Frontier
during peace and the ability to concentrate sufficient forces in
the borderlands to insure success if it should come to a war.

Imperial Defence was the most significant military book to
appear in England in over a decade. It "attracted wide
attention in both lay and governmental circles"; it was the
first to point out the need of studying imperial defense as one
intricate problem rather than a series of isolated situations;
and it was the most influential naval treatise to follow in the
wake of Colomb and Mahan.[27] One who took exception to the
arguments of Dilke and Wilkinson was Maurice, an outspoken
opponent of the "Forward" policy in India and a champion of
the Triple Alliance. Maurice jumped on Dilke (whom he
considered the sole author of the Indian Frontier chapters) in
the *United Service Magazine* and was answered by Wilkinson,
who refuted the notion that the defense of India was best
accomplished by joining the Triple Alliance. Wilkinson refused to believe that the Central Powers would value an
English alliance so much that they would "increase the risk of
exposing themselves to the agony of a European War, in order
to prevent Russia from taking Herat, or even to save England

[25] Gwynne and Tuckwell, *Dilke*, II, 408–11.
[26] Roberts to Dilke, June 28, 1891 (Wilkinson Papers). *Imperial Defence*, p. 87.
[27] Johnson, *Defence by Committee*, p. 26; Marder, *Anatomy of British
Sea Power*, p. 48.

the comparatively small effort of defending India." No; England's most effective instrument in defending the empire was the absolute mastery of the sea: if she were to tie herself to anyone it should be to her own colonies, where there were broad areas of mutual concern.[28]

The book appeared at a most opportune time for Wilkinson, who was in the uneasy position of having a family to support and no prospects of future employment. His position as leader writer on the *Guardian* had always been tenuous because of his unwillingness to bend his own convictions, particularly in questions of foreign policy, to the line of the Liberals, and he had already received notice that 1892 was to be his last year with the paper. For him it was not merely the question of making a living: presumably he could always fall back on his law practice. But he had found a mission in life, and he could never be satisfied with work that did not absorb all of his interests or at the very least provide time for study "and the possibility of taking my own line." "I should accept with joy," he explained to his father-in-law, Sir Joseph Crowe, "a professorship of tactics or military history; or to be director of a cartographical establishment; or of the intelligence department; or of the small arms and guns factories; or of the Volunteer force." But such positions were, as Wilkinson was fully aware, "Castles in the air." Maurice, who had just purchased the *United Service Magazine,* tried to persuade him to accept the post of editor and under different circumstances Wilkinson might have jumped at the opportunity. But he was anxious to find a way out of journalism, the pay was small, he would have been responsible for all of the bookkeeping, and, above all, he did not relish the prospects of working for his "unpracticable friend" who, "though personally kindly disposed and anxious to do kindnesses," had shown in the recent controversy over *Imperial Defence* "an unparalleled gift of persistent misunderstanding." [29]

The book itself suggested a solution—he would go to India, meet Roberts, visit the North West Frontier, and then hope to

[28] Wilkinson, "England's Policy: Reflections suggested by Colonel Maurice's Criticisms upon "Imperial Defence," *United Service Magazine,* V (1892), 426–34. Dilke to Wilkinson, August 27, 1892 (Wilkinson Papers). Wilkinson to Sir Joseph Crowe, September 25, 1892 (Victoria Wilkinson Papers).

[29] Wilkinson to Sir Joseph Crowe, January 19, 1892; September 25, 1892 (Victoria Wilkinson Papers).

sell articles describing the conditions he found there. The family could live on his savings, his father agreed to finance the trip, and both Dilke and Sir Joseph Crowe encouraged the venture; so in November, 1892, Wilkinson left England for an extended tour of India. Thanks to Roberts' arrangements, he found himself "treated more like a Prince . . . than a pauper journalist out of work." [30] He inspected the North West Frontier, met every general commanding a district between Calcutta and Peshawar, became well acquainted with Roberts' staff and with some of the more experienced administrators in the government, and—most important of all—he became thoroughly familiar with the personality, aims, and methods of Roberts himself.

> For many weeks I had been his close companion, not only living with him as his guest, but accompanying him at all the manoeuvres. I had the privilege of riding with him, the members of his staff keeping at a distance except when sent for, and he encouraged me to criticise freely every operation. I had been a diligent student of war for eighteen years, but I learned more from the weeks I spent with Lord Roberts than could ever be learned from books alone. Little by little I became convinced that he was a great man. . . . Above all, I . . . learned in daily conversations with a great soldier some of the difficulties and . . . secrets of command.[31]

The trip to India produced some articles for the *Times* and the *Nineteenth Century,* but by far the richest reward came from his intimate friendship with Roberts, who kept him informed about military developments in India and elsewhere and always seemed to find time for a frank exchange of views. For his part Roberts was delighted to find someone like Wilkinson to publicize his ideas on national and imperial defense. "Publicize" is an inadequate word, however, for in no sense can Wilkinson be considered "the second pen of Bobs Bahadur." He greatly admired Roberts without succumbing to the partisan sentiments of subordinates such as Ian Hamilton and William Nicholson.[32] He agreed with him on most matters

---

[30] Wilkinson to Sir Joseph Crowe, February 13, 1893 (Victoria Wilkinson Papers).

[31] Wilkinson, *Thirty-Five Years,* pp. 169–70.

[32] Hamilton's views are mentioned above, pp. 182–83. Nicholson's attitude is best revealed in a letter he wrote to Wilkinson two years after they had met in India about pending changes in the War Office. "Of course, it will suit Wolseley, Buller and Co. to obtain a fresh lease of

but did not hesitate to differ over details in War Office organization or the advantages of a volunteer army as opposed to one maintained by compulsory service. A man who will give up his only visible means of support rather than indorse policies he does not believe in and still, after two years' unemployment, assert his independence by writing his father-in-law "I must 'stand or fall' by my own judgment such as it is; and the consequence is that I have done some things which very likely others wouldn't have done. But I am myself and not one of the others" [33]—such a man does not set aside his convictions even for the sake of a friend.

His search ultimately led to the study of foreign relations, which he treated at length in *The Great Alternative* (1894) and *The Nation's Awakening* (1896). In these volumes he refuted the foreign policies of both parties: the Liberals were "a fiction, a mere survival" of outworn ideas; the Conservatives had accepted "all that is Liberal of Liberal doctrines" while following Lord Randolph Churchill's "inane formula" that the business of an Opposition is to oppose. What was needed, Wilkinson asserted, was a return to the spirit of sacrifice and devotion that had built the empire, a forging of policy based upon political and military realities rather than confused creeds, and a general willingness once again to become involved in the affairs of Europe. England must choose between two courses: either she must, through command of the sea, play an active and positive role in maintaining the traditional balance of power in Europe or else, by ignoring Europe and utilizing the sea only to isolate herself from the rest of the world, she must sooner or later become dependent upon a coalition of foreign powers. To persist in a policy of not so splendid isolation, Wilkinson warned, would

---

power and to relegate Lord Roberts to the Irish Command where he will be unable to effect any improvement in our chaotic military system. It has to be remembered, however, that these officers are chiefly responsible for the present state of affairs, and that we shall probably go from bad to worse until someone has the courage to sweep out the Augean Stable that they call the War Office." Later he mentioned that he had seen "a letter from Sir R. Buller in which he remarked that I was exceedingly well qualified for a certain Staff appointment I wanted, had it not been for my intimate association with Lord Roberts" (Nicholson to Wilkinson, June 7, 1894; December 12, 1894 [Wilkinson Papers]).

[33] Wilkinson to Sir Joseph Crowe, October 15, 1894 (Victoria Wilkinson Papers).

mean that the day of challenge—which he was certain would come—would find England alone, powerful enough perhaps to prevent or postpone invasion of the British Isles but almost certainly unable to salvage the Empire. But ships alone would not alter "the unhappy prospect" of foreign domination: Wilkinson called for a "national awakening," a rebirth of "the insight, the courage, and the decision of former times." [34]

Initially he flirted with the idea of a defensive alliance with Germany, if this could be accomplished without jeopardy to "Greater Britain" (e.g., Great Britain, Australia, and Canada).[35] But as a result of German diplomatic interference in South Africa in 1896 and her provocative challenge to British control of the seas, Wilkinson became "completely cured" of the notion, and at one point during the Boer War he was so sure that Germany would intervene that he urged the mobilization of the navy and the volunteers as the only way to avert disaster. While he did not regard a conflict between the two nations as inevitable, from that moment on there was a new note of urgency in Wilkinson's plea for a national policy and the requisite military and naval strength to make it effective, a change that can be measured in the titles of his first and last books on the subject written fifteen years apart—*The Great Alternative* and *Britain at Bay!* [36]

The Boer War marks the end of Wilkinson's formative years, when his horizons were ever widening. Curiosity had brought him to the volunteers; the desire for efficiency had led to the creation of the Manchester Tactical Society; concern for the volunteers had introduced him to problems of leadership at the command level, and his examination of imperial defense had awakened an interest in naval theory, to which Wilkinson had applied his own theories on the functions of a general staff. *Imperial Defence* had embroiled Wilkinson in

[34] Wilkinson, *The Great Alternative: A Plea for a National Policy* (London, 1894), pp. 125–51, 297–314; *War and Policy*, pp. 241–56. *The Nation's Awakening* was essentially a restatement of the views advanced in *The Great Alternative* for popular consumption: it appeared originally as a series of essays in the *Morning Post* (Wilkinson, *Thirty-Five Years*, p. 220).

[35] Wilkinson to Eyre Crowe, July 7, 1891 (Victoria Wilkinson Papers). *Thirty-Five Years*, p. 220.

[36] Wilkinson to Eyre Crowe, July 7, 1891 (Victoria Wilkinson Papers). Wilkinson, *Thirty-Five Years*, pp. 220, 230; *War and Policy*, p. 287; *Lessons of the War*, p. 194; *Britain at Bay* (London, 1909), pp. 71–80.

the controversy over the defense of India, and finally his inquiries had brought him face to face with the basic issues of national policy.

Wilkinson came to grips with most of these problems before the turn of the century, and although he continued to prod his fellow countrymen into a more serious attitude toward the responsibilities of empire, the requirements for defense, and the role of Britain in world affairs, rarely after 1900 did he say anything new.

If his ideas had reached maturity, Wilkinson's influence and sphere of activity continued to grow. He persisted in the fight for military preparedness and a realistic national policy, and because many of his friends had reached positions of high authority he may even have had greater influence than before upon executive circles in government. Roberts, who became commander in chief in 1901, wrote frequently to Wilkinson for advice.[37] Another of his friends from India, Sir William Nicholson, was now director of military intelligence, and the two met regularly to talk over problems. Nicholson, who admired Wilkinson both for his knowledge of the past and his insight into the present,[38] tried to obtain his services as assistant director of military intelligence: the proposal received the sanction of Roberts and the cabinet but fell upon deaf ears at the Treasury once it became apparent that supplementary estimates would be involved. Nicholson subsequently became the first Chief of the Imperial General Staff when the dominions were brought into the defense scheme of the empire in 1909.

Wilkinson's friends in the navy, Beresford and Admiral Sir

[37] Roberts to Wilkinson, November 15, 1901; November 26, 1901; December 30, 1901 (Wilkinson Papers).

[38] Wilkinson, *Thirty-Five Years*, pp. 257–58. Nicholson's esteem for the writings of Wilkinson is recorded in the letter he wrote to support Wilkinson's candidacy for an academic post at Oxford in 1909: "When I first had the pleasure of meeting you in India in 1892, my attention had been drawn to your book, *The Brain of an Army*, and since then I have read with interest and profit most of your other books and a good many of your articles in the Press. . . . I believe that I am not singular in my high appreciation of your military knowledge and research, your clearness of insight, and your lucidity of expression. . . . We may not always see eye to eye on professional subjects, but I know no one who has studied more deeply and investigated more thoroughly not only the history of the past, but the application of the lessons to be derived therefrom to the problems of National Defence as affecting the British Empire at the present time" (Nicholson to Wilkinson, July 23, 1909 [Victoria Wilkinson Papers]).

Reginald Custance, never quite reached the top rung of the ladder: both agreed with his views on the naval general staff and organization of the Admiralty, but as leaders of the anti-Fisher camp they were scarcely in a position to implement their theories and Custance suffered the additional handicap of being known as a bookish sailor. As a member of the "historical" school in a day when the "material" school predominated, his arguments carried little weight with a person like Fisher, who maintained unequivocally that "whatever service the past may be to other professions, it can be categorically stated in regard to the Navy that history is a record of exploded ideas. Every condition of the past is altered." [39]

Wilkinson also had admirers in the government. His brother-in-law, Sir Eyre Crowe, was an influential figure in the Foreign Office and the two usually were of one mind with regard to political as well as military matters; so much so, in fact, that Crowe's famous memorandum of January 1, 1907, on the present state of British relations with France and Germany was in substance a précis of Wilkinson's main arguments in *The Nation's Awakening*.[40] Another personal contact was Arnold-Forster, one of the signatories of the joint letter. Describing himself "as an alert and attentive pupil" of Wilkinson, Arnold Forster was secretary of state for war in 1903–5, and although there is little evidence that they worked actively together, many of Wilkinson's dreams began to materialize during his tenure of office. Arnold-Forster was committed to the doctrine of the primacy of the navy and defense by the command of the sea; he worked to remove the barriers between political and military affairs; and while he

[39] Wilkinson, *Thirty-Five Years*, pp. 278–81. Although Wilkinson agreed with Beresford's views, he did not approve of the way in which he conducted his private war with Fisher in public (Fisher is quoted in Marder, *The Road to War, 1904–1914*, pp. 401–402).

[40] Wilkinson, *Thirty-Five Years*, pp. 220–21, 316–19. Wilkinson was responsible for the military education of Sir Eyre Crowe. The following is typical of their earlier correspondence: "You will perhaps have had time to digest Shaw. I now send you Maurice, French Rapport au Ministre, and Knollys. When you have read these you shouldn't at present read any more tactics, but read Hamley's Operations of War all except Part VI. That will take time, and when you have done it I will send you more. . . . It will take you about a year to know more than any British regular officer. After that about ten years to be up to a first rate German" (Wilkinson to Sir Eyre Crowe, July 7, 1891 [Victoria Wilkinson Papers]).

was at the War Office the Norfolk Commission submitted its report and the recommendations of the Esher Committee took substance in the formation of a general staff and the Army Council. Never popular in the clubs, Arnold-Forster made the mistake of trying to push forward too quickly with his reforms. Wilkinson also had the ear of Haldane, Arnold-Forster's more fortunate successor.[41]

Wilkinson's fame as a writer on war and policy has overshadowed his rather solid achievements in the field of journalism, which was after all his principal vocation. Beginning in 1883 he spent ten years with the *Guardian* as a leader writer. At first he was in sympathy with the Liberal views of the paper, but he lost faith in Gladstone during the 1884 crisis in the Sudan and eventually he had to choose between his Gladstonian principles and his avowed mission to advocate army reform. Since his original purpose in becoming a journalist was to publicize the needs of the army there could be but one outcome to this struggle: when the ex-lawyer was unwilling to plead the best case possible for policies he no longer believed in, particularly in the area of foreign affairs, his services were terminated.

He was a free-lance writer for the next two years, during which he became an authority on the defense of India and produced his articles on sea power, articles which "brought the first few much-needed guineas to an almost starving household." In 1895 he obtained, with Roberts' assistance, the position of drama critic of the *Morning Post* (it happened to be the only vacancy at the time). Wilkinson evidently possessed many hidden talents, for years later none other than George Bernard Shaw wrote to express regret that Wilkinson "had been forced to discard the serious drama of the theatre for the cheap blood and thunder of the war." [42] Although responsible for the dramatic criticism for some sixteen years, Wilkinson soon was writing leaders for the *Post*. At Roberts' instigation he wrote articles on the merits of the forward policy in India [43] and when the crisis ripened in South

[41] Arnold Forster to Wilkinson, October 7, 1903 (Victoria Wilkinson Papers). Glenn and Tuckwell, *Dilke*, II, 441–42; Colonel John K. Dunlop, *The Development of the British Army 1899–1914* (London, 1938), pp. 165–227, *passim*.

[42] G. B. Shaw to Wilkinson, February 17, 1932 (Victoria Wilkinson Papers).

[43] In 1897 Roberts sent Wilkinson a list of questions which he chal-

Africa he reviewed the political and military issues at stake in a series of special articles.

Wilkinson won acclaim in many quarters for his articles on the situation in South Africa. He strongly supported the policies of his friend Lord Milner, high commissioner for South Africa, believing that the only honorable course for Britain to follow was to insist on the acceptance of the Bloemfontein proposals "and to back up that insistence by adequate military preparations." It was not, he emphasized, a party matter: "It is a great national and Imperial issue, involving the welfare of South Africa, the spirit of unity throughout the Empire, and the character of the Nation." British policy had oscillated long enough; English democracy was on trial "to prove its ability to conduct the affairs of an Empire," and success would not come until the politicians had ceased to govern colonies according to catchwords which would bring votes at home.[44]

None of the other papers could boast of a military correspondent with Wilkinson's insight into the problems of modern war. He did not hesitate to criticize a general for faulty strategy or to comment on the need for sound tactics.[45] Friends like Milner, Roberts, and Ian Hamilton kept him well informed about recent developments in their respective areas.

---

lenged opponents of the "Forward Policy" to answer, adding in a postscript: "I know you will treat this letter as strictly private and confidential, and will not make an allusion to me in any articles you may write on the subject. . . ." His next letter began: "I congratulate you heartily on the article on the Indian frontier in the *Morning Post.* . . . It is quite excellent and puts the case in a nutshell" (Roberts to Wilkinson, August 29, 1897; December 3, 1897 [Wilkinson Papers]).

[44] Wilkinson, *British Policy in South Africa* (London, 1899), pp. 101, 107, 112. Shortly before he left for South Africa Milner read *The Nation's Awakening* and wrote to Wilkinson: "I wish I knew what I could do to obtain for it thousands upon thousands of readers. My agreement in its main arguments is so absolute, my sense of the need of a national policy is so strong, that I feel, if I could see my way to giving any effectual help to such ideas, I should just leave everything else and do it.

"Meanwhile I am going on the *'Carthago est delenda'* principle, to introduce into every conversation I have on political questions the categorical imperative 'Read Wilkinson.'

"Please don't answer this letter. What is there to answer? I thought if, like some other people, you sometimes feel a little low that work of such first rate quality and importance does not secure all the public attention it deserves, it might cheer you to know that now and again the seed does not fall on stony ground" (Wilkinson, *Thirty-Five Years,* p. 233).

[45] Wilkinson, *Lessons of the War,* pp. 59, 143–44; *War and Policy,* pp. 406–10.

Hamilton in particular was outspoken in describing the "hideous difficulties" that the army encountered and condemning the generalship of "Sir Reverse" Buller.

> I want you to know, sharp, *Buller is no use.* He is indeed far, far worse than useless. You know that, ever since the big "maneuvers" when Buller funked fighting on every occasion, I have thought him a duffer. . . . Now . . . it is a question of life and death of our own selves here as well as of the empire in general and I write to beg you to use all your influence to get the man recalled before he does more mischief.

Hamilton furnished Wilkinson with official reports and private memoranda about military operations still in progress to the degree that he felt that he was treading "on dangerous ground . . . more suitable to conversation than to black and white"; and more than one letter ended with the statement "You may 'use' this if you care to but of course . . . you will contrive to turn it a little. . . . the actual wording had better not be used." [46]

Needless to say, Hamilton agreed with "about almost everything" that Wilkinson wrote in his columns. He reported that "Lord Bobs was immensely pleased" with Wilkinson's leader on the advance to Pretoria, which "was the only article which he had seen which really understood his position or gave him due credit for his resolute advance despite the fact that we were living from hand to mouth with our only line of communication seriously threatened." Roberts himself was less given to partisan feelings; while generally pleased with the articles in the *Morning Post,* he once took Wilkinson gently to task for criticizing Lord Lansdowne and expressed the hope

> that you will find it possible, after considering what I have said, to abstain from criticizing Lord Lansdowne in future, or if you feel compelled to do so, to recollect what weight with the public is carried by letters which appear under your signature, which may cast reflection on the actions of a minister who is doing his best to fulfill the duties of his office under peculiarly arduous and trying circumstances.[47]

Eyre Crowe reported a conversation he had overheard at his club during which "one of the War Office bosses" had stated

[46] Hamilton to Wilkinson, March 17, 1902; April 19, 1902; May 12, 1902.
[47] Wilkinson, *Thirty-Five Years,* pp. 245–46, 248–51.

that the War Office "entirely shared" the opinions expressed in the military commentaries in the *Morning Post;* and Wolseley at one point wrote to the editor complimenting him on a particular leader (written by Wilkinson) which he had read "with deep interest and much instruction." Whoever he was, Wolseley concluded, the writer deserved to be the next secretary of state for war! [48]

In 1909 Wilkinson embarked upon still another career when he became first Chichele professor of military history at Oxford. For fifteen years he had entertained visions of such a position; now, when the opportunity finally came, he was ripe for a change. Roberts was no longer at the War Office, Beresford was in bad odor at the Admiralty, Dilke was in declining health and nearing the end of his career, and only a few months previously the proprietor of the *Morning Post,* Lord Glenesk, had died. The latter had been a sympathetic friend, a constant supporter, and above all he had appreciated Wilkinson's mission in life; with him gone, the *Morning Post* lost something of its "special character," or so it seemed to Wilkinson. He continued to write for the *Morning Post* until 1914, but his heart was no longer in it.

Wilkinson had another and more positive reason for going to Oxford: he was interested in education, had in fact edited and contributed several chapters to a volume dedicated to educational reform,[49] and had long maintained that military history might be a fruitful field to develop in the universities.[50] He had moreover recently completed a series of thirty lectures on the early campaigns of Napoleon at the University of Manchester, which suggests that already his interests had turned in the direction of military history.

One wonders how much satisfaction Wilkinson did derive from his teaching. He was fond of students and enjoyed working with them, but he had been too long a crusader to

[48] Eyre Crowe to Wilkinson November 1, 1899; Wolseley to Lord Glenesk, January 12, 1901 (Victoria Wilkinson Papers). Some of Wilkinson's other commentaries on the Boer War are reprinted in *War and Policy,* pp. 347–436.

[49] Wilkinson (ed.), *The Nation's Need* (London, 1903). Wilkinson's own chapters are reprinted in Wilkinson, *The Nation's Servants: Three Essays on the Education of Officers* (London, 1916).

[50] See Wilkinson's remarks on a speech by T. Miller Maguire, "The National Study of Military History," *R.U.S.I. Journal,* XLI (1897), 616–18; and his commentary on Lonsdale Hale's "Professional Study of Military History," *ibid.,* p. 719.

understand those who did not share his commitment. According to one colleague, his lectures were better read than heard because his voice was flat, monotonous, "and partially devoured by his beard." Often he was too abstract and detailed for the average student, and he committed the virtuous sin of teaching not for the examination "but as the spirit moved him." [51] Colonel J. M. Scammell, one of his most dedicated and talented students, has left a delightful description of the true apostle at work.

Wilkinson taught military history mainly by guidance and counsel. He and his students were colleagues pursuing knowledge together, the older mind freely placing at the disposal of the younger inquirer the fruits of its experience and the sound judgment that flowed from it. First he probed the limits of the student's knowledge. This probing was a friendly business, often in his "digs" before a glowing hearth, with pipes drawing well, and tea at the appointed time. What have you read on war? Have you read Hamley? You should master Hamley, not for historical accuracy because it isn't accurate, but because Hamley did what he set out to do which was to illustrate the operations of war by concrete examples. "There is only one theory of war—that which is set forth, with some differences of expression and of detail, by Clausewitz, by Jomini, by Mahan." . . . It might be an excursion into the Bodeleian Library or the military library at All Souls, with a running commentary on the titles. . . . One learned to make symbols in the notebook to keep up.

Wilkinson "never ceased to teach and he never ceased to learn," [52] but the lack of many keen students robbed him of some of the pleasures he had anticipated. "You cannot communicate your thought to a block of stone," he complained to the warden of All Souls. The Scammells were few and far between, and Wilkinson also suspected the university had lost sight of its primary function, "the advancement of knowledge." [53] While Wilkinson managed to inspire a few serious students and continue his own investigations,[54] the

[51] Wilkinson obituary, Manchester *Guardian*, February 1, 1937.

[52] J. M. Scammell, "Spenser Wilkinson and the Defense of Britain," *Journal of the American Military Institute* IV (1940), 141–42.

[53] Wilkinson to The Warden, All Souls College, December 2, 1918 (Victoria Wilkinson Papers).

[54] Wilkinson's publications at Oxford include *Hannibal's March through the Alps* (Oxford, 1911); *The Early Life of Moltke* (Oxford, 1913); *The French Army before Napoleon* (Oxford, 1915); *Moltke's Correspondence during the Campaign of 1866* (Oxford, 1915); *Moltke's Military Correspondence 1870–71* (Oxford, 1922); *The Defence of Piedmont* (Oxford, 1927); and *The Rise of General Bonaparte* (Oxford, 1930). He also wrote numerous pamphlets relating to the war.

curious fact remains that neither Wilkinson nor his illustrious successors ever succeeded in founding a vigorous or distinct school of military historians.

The war that burst upon Europe in August, 1914, was a tragic climax to the years Wilkinson had spent trying to educate his fellow countrymen. For at least five years he had been aware that Britain, largely as a result of the naval race, was "drifting unintentionally and half unconsciously into a war." "The dominant fact, the fact that controls all others," he wrote in 1909, "is that from now onwards Great Britain has to face the stern reality of war, immediately by way of preparation and possibly at any moment by way of actual collision." [55] In such a war an invasion of the United Kingdom was unlikely in the face of British naval superiority, but inevitably large-scale military operations would have to be undertaken on the Continent, for in no other way could Germany be defeated. For this reason Wilkinson abandoned the volunteer principle he had championed for thirty-five years and urged the creation of a national army based upon universal service. In place of the present mixed force of regulars, army reserve, special reserves, militia, the territorial force and the officers' training corps (to say nothing of the troops in India), Wilkinson proposed a short-service army in which every man physically fit should serve for a minimum of one year (two years for the cavalry and artillery). Such a "well-trained homogeneous army" would presumably produce sufficient recruits to meet normal commitments overseas. In the political climate that existed before the war this notion was "pure poison," and when the war came Wilkinson hesitated to press for universal service because the necessary machinery was difficult to improvise. But sooner or later, he reasoned, the entire manhood of the nation would be under arms.[56]

[55] Wilkinson, *Britain at Bay*, pp. 2, 12. Lady Bathurst, the proprietor of the *Morning Post* after the death of Lord Glenesk, had refused to print the political chapters in this book when they were submitted originally as articles, although the *Morning Post* did carry Wilkinson's articles dealing with compulsory service (Wilkinson, *Thirty-Five Years*, p. 313). Wilkinson does not say so in his memoirs, but this censorship was probably another factor in his decision to leave the paper for Oxford.

[56] Wilkinson, *Britain at Bay*, pp. 136–86 *passim; August 1914: The Coming of the War* (London, 1914), p. 54. Wilkinson to Asquith, September 18, 1914; Wilkinson to the Editor, the *Daily News and Leader*, November 12, 1914; Roberts to Wilkinson, October 20, 1909; October 23, 1909 (Wilkinson Papers). The conscription issue is treated briefly in Theodore Ropp, "Conscription in Great Britain," *Military Affairs*, XX (1956), 71–76.

He was frustrated, too, by the failure of Britain to organize for the war. "For a whole generation," he complained,

I have been telling you that your army was not ready for war, your navy was not ready, your government was not ready. I tried to tell you what war was like, how armies and navies were made ready for it, above all that it must be conducted by a statesman, and that the statesman's first business was to understand it. . . . I have no faith in any of the politicians. . . . I cannot convince myself that any one of the whole number is fit to lead the nation in this war.

It was ridiculous to believe, as the prime minister had declared, that the war must continue until Prussian militarism has been destroyed. How, Wilkinson wanted to know, can you destroy an -ism by force? One could defeat the German armed forces; would have to, in fact, before there could be peace. But an -ism is something spiritual and must be combated as such. What could the citizen contribute to the victory? He could trust the generals and pray that soon there would be a man at the prime minister's elbow who understood war. Churchill, first lord of the Admiralty, "was not a channel through which the naval judgment could reach the Prime Minister undistorted." Kitchener, secretary of state for war, "had never been a great student of war, and his experience in the field was confined to the African campaigns," so he too was the wrong man to serve as the channel between the prime minister and the military leaders. The Dardanelles expedition, Wilkinson contended, proved his point.[57]

One suspects that the root of Wilkinson's disappointment can be traced to the realization that there was no part in the war for him. No longer was he the foremost military commentator in the press, as he had been during the Boer War. No longer did he have much influence in the War Office. Time after time he volunteered his services only to be informed that "after careful enquiry at the Admiralty and War Office . . . there is at present no opportunity." He submitted a memorandum for expanding the army: his ideas fell on deaf ears. He wrote a booklet to help the new army "learn its work." *First Lessons in War* earned much praise but Wilkinson remained in England, a helpless spectator, while the new

[57] Wilkinson, *Government and the War* (London, 1918), pp. viii–ix, 135–36, 176, 196–202.

armies went to France and disappeared. He lectured to dwindling classes and gave patriotic speeches on the will to win and the way to victory. He lost one boy, an aviator, in France and learned from the other how Jutland appeared to a youth of sixteen. Friends like Field Marshal Sir William Robertson, C.I.G.S., still visited him, but for the one-time drama critic there was only a solitary seat in the back row.[58]

Indeed it is doubtful whether Wilkinson, from where he was seated, could see and hear well enough to measure the significance of what was happening in France and the other military theaters. His primer for the new army represents a look backward rather than ahead: the "first lessons" could just as well have been written ten years before, when it was still expedient to site a trench on a forward slope and possible for cavalry to pounce on a retreating army and make raids far behind enemy lines.[59] Soon after the Battle of the Marne, Wilkinson could feel events eluding his grasp. "In times of trial," he confessed a few weeks before the March offensive at Neuve Chapelle,

a true man falls back upon the resolves deliberately made during the meditations of quiet hours. He abides by the principles which he has previously sought and found. Those of us who during many years of peace have tried to clear our minds about the nature and conditions of war probably do well now to trust rather to such insight as they may have gained in those past efforts than to any of the impulses or new thoughts of the moment.[60]

True to the doctrine of Clausewitz, whose "account of war is the most trustworthy and the most adequate which we possess, and forms the starting point of every fresh inquiry," Wilkinson understood from the first that this was to be a total conflict, one which was apt to last long and which eventually would involve a tremendous national effort to win total victory: "The war that aims at striking down the enemy by the destruction of his forces is that of the successful State; the

[58] Wilkinson to Asquith, August 5, 1914; August 24, 1914; September 18, 1914; September 24, 1914; Asquith to Wilkinson, February 19, 1915; *First Lessons in War* (3d ed.; London, 1914), brought high praise from Nicholson, the late C.I.G.S., Lord Esher, Lieutenant General Sir L. Kiggell, General Sir H. Rawlinson, and others of like stature too numerous to list here.

[59] See, for example, *First Lessons in War*, pp. 68–69, 86–87.

[60] Wilkinson, *Government and the War*, p. 130 (written in January, 1915).

war that tries to limit its aims, and therefore its exertions, is that of the defeated." He criticized both the concept of a second front in the Dardanelles and Ian Hamilton's conduct of operations at Gallipoli. The main enemy, he reminded Asquith in one of his memoranda, was the German army, and the primary objective therefore was to defeat that army where it was strongest—in the West. "If the lives already lost in the vain attempt to storm positions in the Gallipoli peninsula had been sacrificed in northwestern France, would there not have been more to show for the losses endured?" "All the amateurs urge you to dissipate your efforts; all the strategists to concentrate them."

As for his old friend Hamilton, Wilkinson reluctantly decided that Roberts had overestimated Hamilton's ability.[61] Perhaps it was a young man's war. Hamilton had failed, Nicholson was "on the shelf," and the others of his generation also "have passed their prime and have not the force left which is required to rise to the conditions of this war." Remembering that Napoleon's generals in his best days were almost all quite young men, Wilkinson suggested that "in all probability a great improvement would result from a whole-sale removal" of the older generals. Wilkinson too was a victim of a dogmatism which

seriously impaired his understanding of the Great War. His mental arteries had hardened. He resented the new condition. Past campaigns could not supply an answer to the problem how to turn a flankless front. His influence among soldiers had greatly declined. Most of the younger generation fled before his lengthy harangues. Robertson was perhaps the one great figure who heard him gladly.[62]

And Robertson, one is tempted to add, was "short of any boldly creative strategic ideas" and could think of no other way to victory than a war of attrition on the western front.

[61] "I expected Hamilton to be at least Competent. He has plenty of intelligence and is not afraid of responsibility. But if I hear the truth his last attack at Suvla Bay was terribly mismanaged and was a very bloody repulse, as from, what I hear, it deserved to be" (Wilkinson to Lord Kitchener, September 25, 1915 [Wilkinson Papers]). Wilkinson's memorandum on the Dardanelles is dated October 25, 1915.

[62] Wilkinson to Kitchener, September 25, 1915; "Obituary," Manchester Guardian, February 1, 1937; Liddell Hart, Through the Fog of War (London, 1938), p. 114. Ten years after the Passchendaele offensive Wilkinson was still a confirmed "Westerner." See his critique of Liddell Hart's theories in "Killing no Murder: An Examination of Some New Theories of War," Army Quarterly, XV (1927), 14–27.

The First World War closed another chapter in the life of Spenser Wilkinson. *Government and the War,* a compilation of scattered articles, represents his final statement on the nature and conduct of war. The war itself had occurred too late to have a formative influence on his military thought, but it did confirm earlier fears and substantiate many of his basic theories. *Government and the War,* however, is more than a summation of earlier views on organization, administration, and national policy, and it differs sharply from Wilkinson's articles on the Boer War in that he no longer appears to have been primarily interested in military operations. Rather he had become concerned with exploring and understanding intangible factors such as the currents of national energy, the interrelationship of war and society, the nature of duty within the framework of total war and the conditions of national existence. Because his conclusions "did not flow from abstract thinking" but were distilled from a lifelong study of many wars, the book is rich in wisdom and eternal truths and should serve both as an introduction and the concluding chapter to the writings of Spenser Wilkinson.[63]

In the postwar years Wilkinson wrote sparingly about the problems of peace and occasionally reviewed books about the war. Friends who corresponded with him now, however, were more apt to recall past contributions than to agree or take issue with present attitudes. Thus the American Admiral Sims wrote to assure Wilkinson that many of his books "are in constant use at the Naval War College and are widely quoted in naval writings" and that *The Brain of a Navy* in particular was "now in use among the students of the college." And Elihu Root, the American secretary of war when the Army War College and the general staff were established near the turn of the century, recalled "what a great part your little book *The Brain of an Army* played in bringing it to pass that both countries had some sort of an institution of that kind already in existence when the sudden emergency came." [64] What little Wilkinson did publish on current problems after 1918 suggests that the war did not change his basic convictions. The security of Britain, he contended, still depended upon the

[63] The best summary of the views presented in *Government and the War* is found in Scammell, "Spenser Wilkinson and the Defense of Britain," pp. 132–37.

[64] Admiral Sims to Wilkinson, December 24, 1918; December 27, 1918; May 19, 1922; October 19, 1922; March 16, 1923 (Wilkinson Papers). Elihu Root to Wilkinson, October 15, 1919 (Victoria Wilkinson Papers).

Royal Navy, the greatest instrument in history for the establishment of world peace and order.[65]

Most of Wilkinson's writings during this last phase in his career concern the more remote past. In 1922, a year before he retired, he produced *Moltke's Military Correspondence 1870–71*, and he devoted his last years to the completion of a trilogy on Napoleonic warfare. The first volume, *The French Army before Napoleon*, grew out of lectures delivered at Oxford shortly before the war and was published in 1915 in hopes that Englishmen "may derive encouragement and instruction from the records of the like effort successfully made in another age." *The Defence of Piedmont, 1744–1748*, followed in 1927. Subtitled "A Prelude to the Study of Napoleon," it is "more than a review of what the Great Captain owed to his remoter predecessors." It is also a study of "that interdependence of generalship and policy which is after all the first and last lesson of the history of wars." The final volume of the series, *The Rise of General Bonaparte* (1930), had its origins many years before, when Wilkinson furthered his own military education by studying "the way in which Bonaparte had learned his business." [66]

Wilkinson's declining years were greatly saddened by the death of his wife in 1929. For a while he considered writing a biography of his foremost hero, Moltke, but he was eighty years old, handicapped by impaired vision, and the fire within him was nearly gone. A new generation of military critics, impatient men but nonetheless competent, were by this time at work trying to educate the British public about war, and in 1932 Wilkinson officially retired from the struggle when he confided to his foremost successor: "I am getting rather tired of war so I am writing my Recollections and translating Homer. Good Luck." [67] He died in 1937.

Wilkinson once remarked that according to Plato "there were two distinct arts: that of mastering your subject and that of getting paid for your work. He thought they had no connection with one another but were antagonistic." [68] Mani-

[65] Wilkinson, *British Aspects of War and Peace* (London, 1920), pp. 24–25, 45; "Security," *Nineteenth Century*, CI (1927), 465–76.
[66] Scammell, "Wilkinson and the Defense of Britain," pp. 138–39; Wilkinson to J. M. Scammell, November 14, 1930; November 22, 1930 (Scammell Papers).
[67] Wilkinson to Liddell Hart, July 18, 1932 (Liddell Hart Papers).
[68] Scammell, "Wilkinson and the Defense of Britain," p. 129.

festly, Wilkinson thought otherwise, for in his experience the one had followed the other. Once the advocate became a volunteer, the study of war in all of its aspects became the primary motivating force of his life; and his writings, whether in military history, theory, organization, or national policy, reveal one common denominator—a passionate conviction of the need to apply organized knowledge to the problems of national life. Wilkinson was a man blessed with a cause.

As a journalist his careful attention to detail, authoritative sources of information, and his profound knowledge of military history made him the best informed military critic of his day: certainly he was without peer in England until Repington joined the staff of the *Times* and he divided his own time between the classroom and the *Morning Post*. He wrote in a clear, logical style and could plead his case effectively before the public; he could criticize and expose unpleasant truths apparently without giving offense or incurring the reproach that he was meddling "in matters where the professional mind alone could hope to excel." His attachment to Roberts was known but neither man appeared to suffer for it, perhaps because each recognized the duties and special responsibilities of the other. As Roberts once wrote, when Wilkinson had criticized an incident that had occurred at Sandhurst:

I hope you will not think that I resent the criticisms embodied in your leading article. A journalist has his duty to the public, just as an officer has his duty to those placed under his command. My object in writing this letter is to show you that the matter is not quite so simple a one as might appear at first sight, and that there is something to be said in justification of the course I have adopted in regard to it.[69]

Because Wilkinson was well informed and his intense sincerity was never in question, "his words have carried weight while his advice has been regarded with favour."[70] Probably he was never again as influential as he was during the Boer War, and he always cherished the story of a prominent public lecturer who once asked his audience: "What was the cause of the South African war?"

[69] Roberts to Wilkinson, July 18, 1902 (Wilkinson Papers).
[70] *R.U.S.I. Journal*, LXXVII (1933), 451.

The answer? "To give Spenser Wilkinson the chance of showing that he understood war." [71]

As a historian Wilkinson was thorough, original, and scrupulously honest. His work on the German General Staff pleased the Germans; his investigations into the origins of Napoleonic warfare impressed French military writers like General Colin and General Pierron and earned him the Chesney Gold Medal in his own country.[72] Wilkinson was no mere academic historian: he loved to tramp battlefields, he was an expert on maps,[73] and he carried into his books and articles sufficient military knowledge to draw unsolicited praise from the most experienced soldier in the army. "Perhaps you are a soldier," Wolseley once wrote in response to an unsigned review of Moltke's memoirs, "for you certainly know more of what you write about, than most of the soldiers who do write so didactically upon war." [74]

To Spenser Wilkinson,

The military historian is a naturalist. He collects wars as specimens, he dissects them, he compares and classifies them. His laboratory is a collection of documents and maps. He examines the correspondence of governments, to discover the aims with which they made war, the records of armies and navies to find out how they were constituted, the secret dispatches of commanders to understand their motives, the reports they received about the enemy and the orders they issued, which enable him to put himself in their place, to see with their eyes, and to think their thoughts. This kind of inquiry lays bare the secret springs of action.

He would agree with Henderson that the intrinsic value of this approach to military history is "the judgment which it confers upon its devotees. It produces men fit to direct war." [75] But he would disagree with those who asserted that the serving

[71] Wilkinson to Scammell, February 9, 1933 (Scammell Papers).

[72] Captain E. Altham to Wilkinson, February 6, 1936 (Victoria Wilkinson Papers); Le général Pierron to Wilkinson, July 15, 1902 (Wilkinson Papers).

[73] "I was delighted with the leader on the Map question. Gospel truth, every word of it" (Colonel Cooper King [editor of the United Service Magazine] to Wilkinson, September 30, 1890 [Wilkinson Papers]). See also Wilkinson's criticisms of the administrative failure to save the ordnance survey, "The Ordnance Survey," *United Service Magazine*, X (1894–95), 254–65.

[74] Wolseley to (Wilkinson), October 28, 1891 (Victoria Wilkinson Papers).

[75] Wilkinson, *Government and the War*, pp. 152–53, 173.

officer had not time to become a student of more than one or two campaigns. The lawyer who had to master numerous cases himself was "perfectly startled" by this notion, for to him history meant the development of practice and principles, and to understand this it was necessary to understand the meaning of war from the beginning of time to the present. He differed from some military historians in still another respect. Although conceding that a minute scrutiny of the records of a given battle might well suggest methods which would have produced better results, Wilkinson maintained that such conclusions were valuable only insofar as they contributed to the professional knowledge of the officer. They should not be used "as a weapon against those who . . . did their best at the time, and have now passed into eternal silence." [76]

Wilkinson's influence as a reformer is "so pervasive over so long a period that it is not easy to assess or to summarize." [77] His work with the Manchester Tactical Society, his proposals for improvements in the training and organization of the volunteers, his obsession with the idea of a general staff for both army and navy, his early warnings of the potential danger from Germany, his insistence upon absolute command of the seas—in these and many other areas his voice was influential. Perhaps it is not too much to say that if his influence decreased after the Boer War it was only because many of his ideas had already found acceptance. Perhaps the successful military critic is destined to end his days talking mostly to himself. Wilkinson contributed substantially to the efforts in the early years of this century to improve the professional education of officers, and his work "played no small part in setting the intellectual tone of the British staff schools. He was unpedantic, practical and realistic rather than theoretical or dogmatic, and singularly free from the common habit of giving military studies the guise of professional mysteries." [78] If for no other reason he should be remembered as the pioneer of military education in the universities.

Wilkinson's contributions were of least significance in the

[76] Wilkinson's commentary on Lonsdale Hale's "Professional Study of Military History," *R.U.S.I. Journal*, XLI (1898), 717; "Recent German Military Literature," *United Service Magazine*, II (1892), 661.

[77] Liddell Hart, "Critics and the Military Hierarchy," *Army Quarterly*, XXII (1932), 43–44.

[78] *American Historical Review*, XLI (1937), 629.

realm of military theory. His views on tactics generally were progressive and reflected current thinking and his translations of German infantry training manuals were used in the volunteers, but never did he formulate any fresh theories of his own. Also he was careful not to be overly specific in applying the principles of maritime strategy to problems of imperial defense: this was particularly the case after 1895, when certain of his passages in *The Great Alternative* were mistakenly assumed by the German General Staff to signify a shift in British naval policy, with the unfortunate result that the German Naval League soon became far larger and more influential than its English counterpart. Convinced from this experience that his ideas were more apt to be utilized abroad than in England, Wilkinson's real concern was for the establishment of a proper mechanism, a general staff organized upon sound principles, to decide upon questions of tactics and strategy. His was a practical, not a theoretical mind, and "the point of all his work, unusual among Englishmen, was to bid people think consistently and go on thinking until they got to the basis of facts." [79]

Sir John Colomb was right: Spenser Wilkinson was indeed "the great instructor of the public mind." [80]

[79] Wilkinson, *Government and the War*, p. 222; "Preparation for War," *National Review*, XXXIX (1902), 208; *Times* Obituary, February 1, 1937.

[80] Colomb to Wilkinson, April 12, 1909 (Wilkinson Papers).

9

THE VOICE OF THE THUNDERER

Lieutenant Colonel Charles À Court Repington

AMONG the many congratulatory messages sent to Spenser Wilkinson upon his appointment in 1909 as first Chichele professor of military history was a note from another battle-scarred veteran of the press wars. "Oxford is fortunate indeed to have secured your great services," wrote Lieutenant Colonel Charles À Court Repington, formerly of the Rifle Brigade and now the world-famous military correspondent of the *Times*.

> But does this mean your withdrawal from the *Morning Post* and from the buffets of contemporary politics? If it does we are the poorer for a fighter, but I shall envy you, because the calm and serene contemplation of the past offers to my mind, far greater satisfaction and even profit than the dust and the heat of daily life.[1]

For Repington the campaign for adequate military strength was far from over. With his support the army had been reorganized, an expeditionary force created, even an Imperial General Staff established to give unity and direction to defense planning at all levels, but as both men were well aware, much still remained to be done and time was growing short. When the day of battle arrived Repington found himself no less involved than the private in the front lines. His was a more pleasant kind of war—more important, too, for it was Repington's heavy task of trying at once to explain the

[1] Repington to Wilkinson, October 9, 1909 (Victoria Wilkinson Papers).

significance of the most recent military developments on half a dozen different fronts and to instruct the nation in the solemn meaning of total war. In the process he became deeply involved in army and national politics to the extent that he too became a casualty. Repington sacrificed his career to the temptations of the newspaper critic who enjoys power and gossip more than responsibility.

Charles À Court was born in Wiltshire in January, 1858. (Following an established custom he assumed the additional surname of Repington when he inherited the family estate, Amington Hall, in 1903.) His father was Henry Wyndham À Court, a member of Parliament for Wilton, a Peelite in politics and a gentle man who spent "the whole of his life in doing kindnesses for other people." He was, Repington later recalled, "the only man I have ever known who would have died for the Church of England." Family tradition dictated a career in public life (one grandfather had been a general, a great-uncle had become a well-known admiral and another had made his mark as a diplomat) and shaped young Repington's interests and loyalties "unconsciously and without schooling."

> We learnt to believe that the English were the salt of the earth, and England the first and greatest country in the world. Thus England became the real and true love of our lives. Our confidence in her illimitable powers, and our utter disbelief in the possibility of any earthy Power vanquishing her, became a fixed idea which nothing could eradicate and no gloom dispel.[2]

It was a faith that even the terrible days of 1917–18 could not shake.

In 1871 Repington entered Eton, where he spent five years learning subjects that revolted him, particularly mathematics and classics. He would have been happier, he admitted, had he been allowed to study history, geography, modern languages, literature, science, and political economy—all interests which he pursued independently and which in later years were to give depth to his commentaries on the day's military developments. Otherwise he enjoyed Eton, where one event in particular remained engraved in his memory: he was

[2] Lieutenant Colonel Charles À Court Repington, *Vestigia: Reminiscences of Peace and War* (Boston, 1919), pp. 8, 21. Unless otherwise indicated, the facts of Repington's career are taken from this source and the sketch by Brigadier General Sir James E. Edmonds in the *Dictionary of National Biography* (1922–30), pp. 717–18.

there when Wolseley's little army passed in review on its return from Ashanti.

Repington next went to Germany to learn the language and prepare for a career in the army. At the school located, appropriately, at 30 Moltke Strasse and run by "good old Colonel Roberts," Repington "forgot a good deal and learnt very little," but he did have occasion to become acquainted with the German army, then at the height of its prestige from its triumphs five years before, and he did learn to dislike the Germans. His memoirs, which were written while the World War was in progress, probably discolor his impressions of Germany as a young man, but even allowing for this it appears certain that Repington from the first distrusted "the Teutons"; by the 1890's this feeling amounted almost to a phobia.[3]

Soon after his return to England Repington was admitted in 1877 (along with Henderson) to Sandhurst. Free at last from the school subjects that he had found so unattractive, he "plunged into the military lore with the greatest zest and with real enjoyment." From Sandhurst he went to the Indian frontier to join the fourth battalion of the Rifle Brigade, arriving in time to campaign with the Peshawar Valley Field Force in the Second Afghan War. He soon came down with a violent fever, however, and was invalided back to England. For most of the year 1879 he was fit for nothing, and it was late autumn before he was strong enough to join the third battalion in Dublin.

Ireland was a tonic in more ways than one. Repington enjoyed the social life. He also utilized the long winter evenings to read up on his profession, and it was here that he became familiar with the basic French and German treatises on war and the works of Chesney, Home, and Hamley. A trip to Italy prompted him to write a book on the Italian army, a masterly study which he published under an assumed name. Repington's first effort enjoyed "a fair success"—sufficient, at

---

[3] See Brigadier General W. H-H. Waters, *"Secret and Confidential": The Experiences of a Military Attaché* (London, 1926), p. 61. Waters claims that an excess of beer drinking with German officers in 1893, a liquid that did not agree with him, induced Repington "to take a violent dislike to all things German." The truth of the matter probably is that an excess of German beer merely induced Repington to air prejudices that were already firmly ingrained. Repington's comments are found in *Vestigia*, pp. 33–37.

any rate, to attract the attention of the authorities and to encourage him to work for the Staff College, "the best road to success when the royal road of active service was temporarily closed . . . for want of wars."

Repington entered the Staff College in 1887 and spent two profitable years studying under lecturers such as Maurice, exchanging notes with contemporaries who had served in different parts of the world, and absorbing a considerable share of the library's rich holdings in military history and theory. The friends he made there and the knowledge of the other arms of the service that he acquired both were to contribute to his success as a military analyst: significantly he was regarded by all "as the most brilliant man of his year." [4]

Upon passing out of the Staff College Repington returned to regimental duty with the fourth battalion, which was then engaged in partisan fighting following the conquest of Upper Burma. He returned to England late in 1889 to join the Intelligence Department, then under Sir Henry Brackenbury, where he spent the better part of the next five years as a staff captain in the French section, analyzing the military resources and recent developments in that country as well as Italy, Spain, Portugal, Central and South America, and Mexico. In a day when the German General Staff was spending upward of a quarter of a million pounds on intelligence and the Transvaal Republic some £90,000 per annum, the British were paying £11,000 for military intelligence.[5] All that Repington was allotted was one assistant to help cover the field in the French section.

Repington found the work with the intelligence division demanding, congenial, and stimulating: it brought him into contact with foreign officers and justified frequent trips to the Continent, where he visited most of the French Channel ports and attended French army maneuvers regularly. He probably knew more about the French military system and defenses than any man in England at the time. He initiated a new series of publications by the intelligence division with his volume on *The Military Resources of France,* which served as

---

[4] *Ibid.,* pp. 75–77; Edmonds, "Repington," p. 717.

[5] These figures are those of 1899, but the picture was no different at the time Repington was in the intelligence division. See Rayne Kruger, *Good-Bye Dolly Gray: The Story of the Boer War* (Philadelphia, 1960), p. 63.

the model for similar critiques of other armies and represented his own *magnum opus* of this period. Repington had great faith in the French army: in his estimation the graduates of the *École de Guerre* were "nowhere surpassed for professional knowledge," the infantry was "in the very highest state of efficiency," the cavalry was well mounted and reasonably efficient, and the artillery, if slow at maneuvers, was technically competent. "Throughout the whole army," Repington concluded, "there prevails a fine spirit and an undeniable feeling of confidence in the future." Even during his five years in the Intelligence Department he could detect a "marked and continuous progress towards consolidation and increase of offensive power." His knowledge of the German army was more limited, but the officers of the general staff with whom he was acquainted were "rather wooden" and Repington could see "no men of first-class competence among them." [6]

Repington at this time was mildly skeptical of the moral and intellectual qualities of all armies on the Continent maintained by conscription. "More than one of the great Continental armies had reached the zenith of their powers," he asserted, and, although numerically as strong as ever, had begun to decline "as well-tempered weapons of offense." To Repington, whose hand was on the pulse of foreign armies, "the beatings were perceptively more feeble and intermittent." The system of localization that most armies had borrowed from Prussia, together with the gradual disappearance of an officer class with private fortunes ("independent fortunes," Repington observed, "too often go hand in hand with independent thought and bold originality") had not been altogether beneficial. Although more sympathetic to France than to Germany, Repington felt that England had more to fear in the 1890's from the former. He was quite sure that France would not start a war of revenge with Germany—too many forces in French society were working against it—but he suspected that a war with England might be popular. Such

[6] Captain Charles À. Court, *Progress in the French Army in 1893 with Notes on the Reserve Troops, Mobilisation, Supplies, etc.* (London, Printed at the War Office [A282], 1894), pp. 5–7; *Vestigia*, pp. 82–90. Repington also wrote "The Russian Artillery in 1888," *R.U.S.I. Journal*, XXXII (1888–89), 219–304; and "Russian Infantry Tactics," *ibid.*, pp. 957–1001.

a conflict would be colonial in scope, not national, and England obviously was unprepared.[7]

Repington returned to the Rifle Brigade in 1894. In 1897 he was sent to Egypt as a staff officer for the army of occupation. He served under Kitchener in the Atbara campaign and at Omdurman, and he was at Khartoum when French forces under Commandant Marchand appeared at Fashoda, further up the Nile. A clash, perhaps even a war seemed imminent and so Repington, acting on the assumption that he knew more about French military resources "than anybody else," rushed back to London where he might be of valuable service in the crisis. His memoirs allude rather mysteriously to his "strange experiences" during the Fashoda crisis, but all that we know is that soon afterward he was appointed the first military attaché in Belgium and the Netherlands.

Here he continued to prepare reports, mostly of a technical character, for the War Office, and he was at The Hague when the first Peace Conference assembled there in 1899. As a technical delegate Repington came in contact with many of the statesmen and diplomats present: all through the hot summer, he wrote later, "we worked steadily on, making believe that the passions and ambitions of mankind were at an end, and that people who had set their names to agreements would keep them." Again he became suspicious of Germany, whose delegates "scarcely concealed her dislike of the whole of the proceedings"; but Repington himself, it should be noted, professed not to believe in agreements limiting armaments. The Peace Conference had a positive effect upon Repington in one respect, however: it gave him a unique opportunity to study the diplomats present and to get acquainted with the United States naval representative, Admiral Mahan. The two had many long talks on naval matters that obviously shaped Repington's thinking after he had left the army and turned to his pen for a living.[8]

Repington returned to England in September, 1899, and within a matter of weeks he found himself in South Africa, a member of the headquarters staff of the Army corps that had just been assembled for service under Buller in Natal. He participated in the battles at Spion Kop, Vall Krantz, and

[7] Repington, "Pensons y toujours?" United Service Magazine, XIV (1896–97), 210–19.
[8] Repington, Vestigia, pp. 173–89.

Pieter's Hill, but soon after the relieving army entered Ladysmith he came down with enteric fever and this, complicated by jaundice and colitis, caused him to be invalided home. When he became fit for light duty, he was sent to his old post at Brussels and The Hague, remaining there until sometime late in 1901.

It was at this point that Repington's personal life wrecked a most promising military career. While in Egypt he had become involved with Lady Garstin, the wife of a prominent English diplomat. The Foreign Office had insisted as a condition to his appointment as military attaché in the Low countries that he break off the affair, but his good intentions were undermined when Lady Garstin returned from Egypt and settled at Dovercourt, on a direct line between London and The Hague. Sometime, we are not sure exactly when, Repington had signed a document in the presence of two brother officers promising not to see nor communicate with Lady Garstin again: when he went back on his word after being invalided home, the document was circulated among the Army Council and as a consequence he was called upon to resign. Repington's conduct in the matter is not above reproach, but it should be noted that the man who revealed the document to the army authorities was Major (later Field Marshal Sir Henry) Wilson, who likewise had served in the Rifle Brigade, the intelligence division, and on the staff in South Africa. Contemporaries regarded the two as rivals, and in the opinion of one authority, Repington would "certainly have been Chief of the Imperial General Staff" before Wilson. We cannot be sure what motivated Wilson in this affair, but his character as revealed in his published *Life and Diaries* do nothing to remove the suspicion that more than an officer's breach of conduct was at stake. As for Repington, whose army career was ruined by his failure to abide by the agreement and the unfavorable publicity of the divorce trial, Lady Garstin— describing the episode with dignified candor in her memoirs—has written: "This was a terrible blow to Charley. Everything else he could bear and make light of, but the Army, then and always, was the love of his life. All else came second to it." The matter even came to the attention of the King, who understandably refused to intervene.[9]

[9] Notes taken by Liddell Hart in a conversation with General J. E. Edmonds, United Services Club, April 22, 1937. (Edmonds was author

Repington's pen now came to his rescue. Before leaving the army he had already commenced work on the *Times History of the War in South Africa,* but the divorce trial had seriously impaired his usefulness in a project that required him to meet and work with the friends of Sir William Garstin. After his resignation, he wrote a number of "severe strictures on our mismanagement of Army affairs," which brought him into contact with a number of "young Tory dissidents" who opposed the military policies of Mr. St. John Brodrick, the secretary of state for war. These "young Turks" (among whom, characteristically, was Winston Churchill) dreamed of founding a journal to be called *The Gauntlet,* in which they hoped to attack "all and sundry abuses which afflicted the realm." They failed, however, to attract the necessary capital and Repington found a suitable outlet instead in the *Westminster Gazette,* to which he became a regular contributor.

Once established as a journalist, the *Times* again invited Repington to resume work on the history of the Boer War, a task that kept him occupied until the war between Russia and Japan in 1904–5 offered more tempting opportunities. Spenser Wilkinson had already demonstrated by his comprehensive analyses what could be accomplished by remaining at the nerve center in London instead of accompanying one of the columns poised to invade the Orange Free State; and Repington also was quick to discover the advantages of covering a war in London instead of reporting incidents from the field. War had suddenly grown too vast and complex to be covered adequately by the old-style correspondents. In London, however, Repington had access to official sources of information as well as to the various channels maintained by the *Times;* he never was bothered by restrictions of any kind, and his technical knowledge of foreign armies and contemporary military thought often enabled him to penetrate the strategical design of military movements when all that

---

of the sketch on Repington in the *D.N.B.* and, as official historian of British military operations in the First World War, was in a good position to evaluate the professional prospects of both Repington and Sir Henry Wilson.) The personal side of the affair is found in Mary Repington (Lady Garstin), *Thanks for the Memory* (London, 1938), pp. 154–91. Wilson's character is revealed in Major General Sir C. E. Callwell, *Field-Marshal Sir Henry Wilson: His Life and Diaries* (2 vols.; London, 1927).

could be seen by western observers on the spot were the visual details.

From the first Repington looked for a Japanese victory. He admired the superior morale and fighting qualities of the Japanese soldier, and he detected the spiritual successors of Moltke and Roon in the high command. Initially he underestimated the ability of the Japanese to land and maintain an army near Port Arthur before the Russian fleet had been destroyed, but once safely ashore he contended that Japan possessed ample resources for carrying on concurrent operations against the naval base and the Russian field army.

Repington's articles were remarkably accurate, but they are important for still another reason: they reveal the drift of Repington's own ideas on war. They show, for example, the extent to which his assumptions rested on the theories of Clausewitz and Mahan. (The Japanese, he wrote, "have read their Mahan; they must know the pregnant words with which he advises a maritime Power to 'grasp firmly some vital chord of the enemy's communications and so force him to fight there.' ") They indicate a mounting scorn for contemporary German military literature. In Repington's view the German pundits had "been completely at fault from first to last during the war"; German military criticism "had fallen into the hands of men without any practical experience of war," and the great bulk of what they wrote was "very poor stuff." What, Repington wondered, "has become of the great school of Moltke?" [10]

Above all, Repington's articles in the *Times* suggest that the war in the Far East contained instructive lessons for a naval power such as Britain. Conventional naval opinion would have to place greater weight than before on the potentialities of the torpedo, for the "striking success" of the Japanese torpedo flotilla in the outer harbor at Port Arthur on the first night of the war seemed to fulfil the prognostications of the continental theorists who argued that torpedo boats had made the battleship obsolete. If Repington was unable to accept the basic tenets of the *jeune école,* as those who preached the doctrine of torpedo warfare were called, one suspects that he

[10] By the Military Correspondent of the *Times* (Repington), *The War in the Far East 1904–1905* (London, 1905), pp. 20, 97, 235, 292, 328–29, 335, 548.

sympathized with the occasional young lieutenant who claimed—in vain—that he had torpedoed the flagship during maneuvers. At the very least he welcomed the opportunity to strike the balance between the arguments of the torpedo fanatics and their staid opponents. Predicting that "the results of the Japanese blow at Port Arthur will very properly cause torpedo enthusiasts to set to work with redoubled zeal to perfect both the means at their disposal and the methods of its employment in war," Repington halfway suspected that modern science "has outstripped the capacity of certain nations to make intelligent use of the new weapons." [11]

More important still was the lesson that the war offered in the use of amphibious power. "Whatever the decision may be," he wrote six weeks after the Japanese strike at Port Arthur,

there can be no question that the immediate interest of the moment for British onlookers is the recognition of the influence of the threat of invasion from over-sea upon the decisions of a continental enemy. Despite the fact that the main body of the Japanese army has remained at home, and that only the navy and a fraction of the army have been employed, the Russians have radically changed their initial dispositions, and have been . . . groping blindly in the dark and endeavouring to surprise the mysterious secret of the mocking sea, without, as yet, having any certain news of their enemy's plans.

The meaning for Britain was clear—she must continue to maintain a predominant navy and at the same time build an army that "will enable us to execute more than raids" upon the territory of a Continental enemy. The Japanese campaign in Manchuria seemed to confirm what Maurice and Henderson already had deduced from earlier wars, that "the threat of invasion by way of the sea is the most terrible weapon in the armoury of national strategy, if its use is properly understood and the weapon deftly wielded." [12]

The war furnished still another object lesson: it was essential, Repington contended, for England to re-examine the value of modern fortresses and to determine anew what national purpose they were designed to serve. Repington suspected that the American enthusiasm for coast defense rested more on political factors than on strictly military principles, and he looked to the siege of Port Arthur for

[11] *Ibid.*, pp. 55–56, 186.
[12] *Ibid.*, pp. 107, 110, 132, 181.

guidance. Never before had modern artillery using high explosives subjected permanent fortification to the test of serious war. The experience of the Russians persuaded him that

a fortress spells immobility and dispersion. . . . We must not allow ourselves to be led away by the glamour surrounding an heroic defence; we must look to the end, and leave panegyrics to poets. We must . . . regard all fortification as an auxiliary, and nothing more. A fortress, because it is a fortress and because it is ours, is not necessarily an advantage, and may be the reverse.

Port Arthur had served as a "fateful magnet" in drawing a large army to its intended relief; and the lesson it had to teach was clear. Britain must avoid any "noxious contact with such germs of strategic death! For an Imperial race, with the lion for its emblem, a sea-going navy and a mobile field army are everything, and the rest is nothing." [13]

Thus Repington, like most soldiers of his day, warmly embraced the doctrine of the offensive. An army that intrenches, he wrote, "is an army that is lost. War is an affair of activity, initiative, and movement. . . ." In one insupportable passage he even suggested that

every army should have no engineers, but only pioneers; men who can build bridges, blast rocks, make roads, blow open doors, mine the enemy's works, construct railways and telegraphs and work them; do all, in fact, that assists movement, and learn nothing and teach nothing that prevents it.[14]

Repington's view of the Russo-Japanese War, however, extended far beyond the battleground in Manchuria. Of greater concern than the purely military or technical developments in the art of war was the fact that Russia—contrary to what many of the experts had predicted—had managed to assemble and maintain a great army thousands of miles from Europe by means of a single-line railway. And what Russia could accomplish in Manchuria she obviously could do on the borders of Afghanistan. Now, for the first time, England's military planners had a realistic standard to go by, a means of determining whether the army was strong enough to fulfil its

[13] *Ibid.*, pp. 232 ff., 315, 439–43. See also Repington, *Imperial Strategy* (London, 1905), pp. 167–79.
[14] Repington, *War in the Far East*, p. 315.

functions. Repington estimated that Russia could probably assemble an army of half a million on the Afghan frontier within the course of a few months. This in his view was the most important lesson of the war: "the military problem before us is not unlike that which Japan has solved, and solved successfully. It is no light one, but it is not beyond our power if serious statesmen take it in hand with the firm intention and will of succeeding." [15]

For a variety of reasons, then, Repington filed an early plea for a British history of the Russo-Japanese War, a history

written on a national basis, by experts in all branches, the whole edited and harmoniously woven into a single piece by a master of literary eminence, . . . capable of reconciling conflicting views, and of presenting, not a hotch-potch of discursive thought, but a serious, reasoned, and yet readable work, broad in view and treatment, with the necessary balance and sense of proportion maintained from first to last.

No more books like Maurice's official study of the war in South Africa, which deprived the conflict "of half its human and all its political interest"; no history in which each service jealously segregated its own forces; and certainly no "deadly official publication, labelled 'Secret' and read by few." What Repington wanted was the creation of an historical section of the Committee of Imperial Defence, to begin its labors with the first great maritime struggle of modern times—the war in the Far East. Otherwise he feared that the British would continue "to remain ignorant of all the lessons of the past, and then [be forced] to learn them over again, with each succeeding war, at huge and needless cost." Although there is no evidence that Repington's suggestion was directly responsible, the Committee of Imperial Defence, which had been created formally a few months earlier, did in fact organize an historical section, and the first product to appear was an *Official History of the Russo-Japanese War* written very much along the lines urged by Repington. Concerned with all questions relating to imperial strategy, the historical section treated war as an integrated whole rather than a composite of independent military and naval operations; and as a record of what had actually happened, this *Official History* is probably

[15] *Ibid.*, pp. 597–603.

the best account of the war produced by any general staff in Europe.[16]

Repington's wartime articles, written originally on a trial basis, became a regular feature of the *Times* and achieved international fame. Almost overnight he became "the prince of military correspondents." (One journal described him as "the Clausewitz of the occasion and the Mahan of the multitude!"[17]) His articles soon appeared under the heading of "Our Military Correspondent," although his permanent duties in this capacity were not defined until near the end of the war. Repington was not the first writer for the *Times* who specialized on military subjects: frequently Sir George Clarke and Colonel Lonsdale Hale had contributed military articles, and foreign army maneuvers were covered regularly by observers like Colonel G. F. R. Henderson. But with the establishment of the Committee of Imperial Defence and the furor resulting from British failures in the Boer War, the management of the *Times* believed that it was necessary to print regular criticisms of military developments and to find someone "to stimulate thought concerning the art of war" in Printing House Square and in official and political circles. Repington evidently would have preferred to have retained some degree of anonymity and independence, writing as the spirit and financial pressures of the moment moved him, but the opportunity was too golden to pass up. "There is much opening for independent criticism to-day," he confided to the managing editor early in 1905. "The War Office is in a state of chaos, Clarke is fairly despondent, Kitchener cantankerous and the Army generally very ill at ease. Old Bobs [an unfair comment] shirks all serious issues and talks to children, while Wolseley has taken to poultry farming."[18] Army reform still had not made much headway.

Repington remained with the *Times* until January, 1918,

[16] Repington, "A Plea for History," was published originally in the *Times* of September 10, 1904, and is reprinted in a collection of his more important articles entitled *Imperial Strategy*, pp. 211–20. Committee of Imperial Defense, Historical Section, *Official History (Naval and Military) of the Russo-Japanese War* (3 vols.; London, 1910–20), is discussed briefly in Luvaas, "The First British Official Historians," *Military Affairs*, XXVI (Summer, 1962), 53–54.

[17] See the excerpts from reviews reprinted at the end of *Imperial Strategy*.

[18] Repington, *Vestigia*, pp. 253–55; *The History of the Times: The Twentieth Century Test 1884–1912* (London, 1947), pp. 419, 462–63.

when a combination of factors led to his resignation. By and large his association with the *Times* was a happy one. Until the last year of the war he was given a relatively free hand and no one ever suggested either the military policy he should support or the subject of an article. Eventually his contemporaries in the army reached positions of high authority, which enabled him to keep in close touch with developments at the War Office, and throughout the pre-war years he remained relatively free from party interest.[19]

Repington's approach was to study each military question as it arose "and then to state his conclusions without fear and without favour, in the simplest terms, so that the arguments might be comprehensible to the general public."[20] Never before had Britain faced so many perplexing and urgent problems in matters pertaining to defense, the scope and solution of which had already been indicated in the first report of the Esher Committee in January, 1904:

> Our national problems of defence are far more difficult and complex than those of any other Power. They require exhaustive study over a much wider field. The grave danger to which we call attention remains, and demands effective remedy. The British Empire is pre-eminently a great naval, colonial power. There are, nevertheless, no means for co-ordinating defence problems, for dealing with them as a whole, for defining the proper functions of the various elements, and for ensuring that, on the one hand, peace preparations are carried out upon a consistent plan, and, on the other hand, that in time of emergency a definite war policy based upon solid data can be formulated.[21]

The Committee of Imperial Defence had already been established to attack the first problem, that of co-ordination of the military and naval forces of the empire for war, and many of Repington's early articles naturally were devoted to this subject. Perhaps his most fruitful observations concerned India which, from a strictly military point of view, impressed Repington as a "most serious liability." The ugly fact that outweighed all others was that Russia had built up an army of

[19] Repington, *Vestigia*, p. 255.

[20] Repington, *Imperial Strategy*, p. vi.

[21] As quoted in Colonel J. F. C. Fuller, *Imperial Defence, 1885–1914* (London, 1926), pp. 55–56. The recommendations of the Esher Committee are discussed in Franklyn Arthur Johnson, *Defence by Committee: The British Committee of Imperial Defence 1885–1959* (London, 1960), pp. 59–70.

over a million men in east Asia at the close of the war with Japan and that her strategic railways were creeping ever closer to the frontiers of Afghanistan. Repington indorsed the assertion by A. J. Balfour, the prime minister in 1905, that any attempt by Russia to connect her railroads with a railway in Afghanistan should be "considered an act of direct aggression upon this country." For once diplomacy had taken the lead, and England was now fully committed to the defense of Afghanistan as a result of the Anglo-Afghan treaty signed in March, 1905. "Our administrative boundary marks the limits, not of our responsibilities, but of our courage." Repington urged that the British forestall the Russians by securing permission to construct a railroad to Kabul, in the heart of Afghanistan, which would enable them to defend the military frontier of India along a mountain ridge known as the Hindu Kush. He called also for support of Lord Kitchener's proposed reforms of the military administration in India, which was "vicious in theory and inefficient in practice" and, in Repington's judgment, incapable of conducting a successful campaign against the Russians along the North West Frontier.[22]

As fear of Russian encroachment in Persia and along the North West Frontier subsided after the Anglo-Russian entente in 1907 and as England became increasingly involved in European affairs, Repington called for the dominions to shoulder a greater share of the defense burden. After the Imperial Conference in 1907, he wrote that the principles agreed upon—naval superiority, local defense, and mutual support—could not be applied unless the dominions, "in proportion to their relative population and resources, take more effective part in the defence of the Empire by sea and land." They should take over the naval stations and imperial garrisons in their respective spheres. Because the conference of 1907 had not appreciably advanced imperial naval cooperation, Repington urged the development of dominion navies on the ground that the British fleet would have to remain concentrated in home waters to meet the growing threat of German naval power. In his opinion the first prerequisite for imperial defense, the problem to be attacked

[22] Repington, *Imperial Strategy*, pp. ix, 132, 286–306 *passim*, 308–10, 318–35, 341. Repington's views on Indian military policy after the Anglo-Russian entente in 1907 are found in a later volume of his articles entitled *Essays and Criticisms* (London, 1911), pp. 109–42.

before all others, was home defense: "Until we can provide ourselves with ample security against invasion at home . . . it is useless to begin to think of operations over-sea." [23]

Almost from the day he became military correspondent of the *Times* Repington campaigned for a more effective home defense. He contended that the danger of a raid or even an invasion by Germany was real and unceasing: history provided an example, contemporary German doctrine recognized it as a possibility, and the naval expansion of Britain's rising rival served as a forceful storm warning. Repington scoffed at the idea, prevalent in naval circles, that "over-sea invasion is impracticable without the command of the sea." Moltke had been willing to disregard this dogma when, by "absolute secrecy and complete surprise," he had planned to invade Denmark's island defenses in the face of a Danish navy three times the size of the Prussian flotilla in 1864. The suspension of hostilities had interrupted the proposed invasions, but the fact remained that "the first strategist of modern times was prepared, though Prussia was practically without a fleet, to order an army corps to be towed by night across waters he did not and could not hope to command, for the purpose of subjugating an armed and insular State." [24]

Moreover, German theory seemed to support Moltke's belief in the possibility of invasion. Repington quoted Von der Goltz, Germany's foremost military writer, that it was unwise "to consider an invasion of England to be chimerical and unrealizable. The distance is short and can easily be traversed by an enterprising admiral who succeeds, by the excellence of his fleet and by his audacity, in obtaining, for a short time the command of the sea." And Von der Goltz, according to Repington, was but one of many who preached such a doctrine. The new German naval program in 1907 gave added weight to the warnings by Repington and others "that a German invasion attempt, a 'bolt from the blue,' was in the offing." [25]

[23] *Ibid.*, pp. 1–23; Repington, *Imperial Strategy*, p. 124. For the official point of view, see Fuller, *Imperial Defence*, pp. 63–65.

[24] Repington, *The Foundations of Reform* (London, 1908), pp. 13–22.

[25] *Ibid.*, pp. 53–54; Arthur J. Marder, *From the Dreadnought to Scapa Flow: The Royal Navy in the Fisher Era, 1904–1919.* I. *The Road to War, 1904–1914* (London, 1961), pp. 141–45.

Repington opposed the "Blue Water School" or rather the extremists who claimed that command of the sea alone would secure England from invasion. He questioned whether even supremacy at sea would mean absolute security for England and her ocean highways, and he doubted whether naval power alone could profit by its victories and impose peace "unless there stands behind it a national Army ready . . . to complete and confirm the victories won at sea." Such an army, he insisted, could not be obtained as long as the inhabitants of England were lulled into a false sense of security by "the extravagant claims of the Blue Water fanatics." He was in basic agreement with those of the navy who tried to combat the waste of money upon fortifications, but he felt it imperative to support Haldane's plans for a national army. In his judgment the preservation of the empire was not possible unless England was absolutely safe from a surprise attack at home.

Repington, who published these views in the *National Review* and elsewhere because the editorial policy of the *Times* did not concur,[26] joined Roberts, Lord Lovat, and Sir Samuel Scott in forcing the Committee of Imperial Defence to appoint a subcommittee on invasion over the determined opposition of the Admiralty. Roberts and Repington testified on the first day of the inquiry (Roberts' "peroration, delivered with rhetorical emotion, was very well done," Viscount Esher noted in his journal, and Repington's "mass of information, and carefully compiled detail were impressive") and were present during many of the subsequent sessions. According to Lord Hankey, "they rendered invaluable service in pressing home every weak point in the official defence, and thus compelling the Admiralty and War Office to face the problem as they had never faced it before." The subcommittee reported that an army of 70,000 would "ensure an ample margin of safety" for home defense, a figure that represented less than half of the number of men Repington calculated that the Germans could land in England, given the proper circumstances. When Sir John Fisher objected that a naval surprise, which was a necessary condition for any raid or invasion, was "inconceivable," Repington made pointed references to a

[26] *History of the Times, 1884–1912*, p. 843. Repington's key articles on the subject are reprinted in *Foundations of Reform*, pp. 1–80.

similar conviction on the part of the Russians in the days preceding the Japanese strike at Port Arthur.[27]

To avoid trespassing upon the territory of his colleague, the naval correspondent, Repington invented an ally, Colonel von Donner und Blitzen. The accommodating colonel promptly attacked the "Admiralty Notes" of Admiral A. K. Wilson in 1910, in which it was stated "that an invasion on even the modest scale of 70,000 men is practically impossible." Later he wrote in apparent glee of the 1912 and 1913 naval maneuvers, where it had been demonstrated that the east coast of England was indeed vulnerable. The commander in chief, home fleets, conceded in private that "the only proper defence of the country against invasion and raid is by Military Forces, and to make the Navy responsible for this work is a grave strategic error," but the Admiralty managed to keep the results of these maneuvers from the public until Repington's perceptive "friend" asserted, with Teutonic arrogance, that until there was some change in the situation

the protection afforded by your navy is not absolute. . . . Prudence does not permit you to dispense with a national army, good coast defences, and supremacy in the air. All these advantages we [Germans] possess, and they give our High Seas Fleet the liberty of manoeuvre which yours lacks. Just when our wings have grown yours have been clipped by the cowardice of your rulers and the selfishness of your democracy. Each of us, no doubt, will gain his deserts.

Was there ever in history, Von Donner und Blitzen inquired, "a temptation so great as the successful invasion of Albion, the rich, the proud, and the unprepared? *Nein, wahrhaftig nicht.*" [28] As late as 1915 Repington still professed to believe

[27] M. V. Brett (ed.), *Journals and Letters of Viscount Esher* (London, 1934), II, 263. On another day he commented: "Repington was very good, but in the last quarter of an hour (which was excellent) he was put into considerable difficulty" (*ibid.*, p. 278). Repington's testimony is contained in *Vestigia*, pp. 312–40. See also Marder, *From the Dreadnought to Scapa Flow*, pp. 348–50, and Lord Hankey, *The Supreme Command 1914–1918* (London, 1961), pp. 66–69.

[28] Repington, *Vestigia*, pp. 293–94; "The Naval Manoeuvres: Colonel von Donner und Blitzen on Invasion," *Times*, August 27, 1913; "Invasion Theory and Practice," *ibid.*, September 2, September 8, 1913; Lord Sydenham to the editor, the *Times*, September 13, 1913. For the real story of the 1912 and 1913 naval maneuvers, see Marder, *From the Dreadnought to Scapa Flow*, pp. 351–56.

that a German raid or invasion of England was possible, if more remote than at the commencement of the war.[29]

Repington's analysis of the external dangers to the empire and his estimate of the forces necessary to safeguard England against invasion both point to the pressing need for improved military efficiency. If he disagreed with Mr. E. B. (later Viscount) Haldane's view that the navy could protect Great Britain from invasion and at the same time maintain control of the seas wherever British interests were at stake, he gave enthusiastic support to the new war minister's program for army reform. In essence the Haldane reforms of 1906–7 mark a watershed in British military history: they produced a more effective army at less cost, with the creation of a modern striking force capable of intervening in a Continental war, the establishment of a second line organized according to the Cardwell principle of localization, and the organization of reserve forces to feed regular battalions. The new officers' training corps at the universities and schools made possible a steady flow of officers, uniform doctrine was assured by the appearance of the *Field Service Pocket Book* in 1906 and its successor, *Field Service Regulations,* three years later; and more serious attention was paid to collective training and musketry. In 1909 the general staff was expanded into an Imperial General Staff to give unity "to the training, education and war organization of the military forces of the Crown in every part of the Empire." But the special significance of the Haldane reforms, although by no means universally understood at the time, was this: in addition to bringing the army up to date, Haldane's program also signified a shift in emphasis from defense of the empire, particularly in the east, to a more active and positive role in Europe. Maurice, Henderson, and Wilkinson had each pleaded for a national policy in order to determine the functions of the army. Now, with England a member of the Triple Entente—and few people in England in 1907 seemed to appreciate the implications as far as Britain's military forces were concerned—there could be little doubt how or against whom the army was to be used in a future conflict. Instead of tramping over the battlefields of 1870, British officers now began to visit the probable site of collision in the next Franco-German war, a war in which it was postulated that Britain would inter-

[29] Repington, "The War Day by Day," *Times,* September 22, 1915, p. 6.

vene—with an army small by Continental standards but one which, thanks to the efforts of Haldane and his supporters, was "immediately available and highly efficient." [30]

Repington helped to prepare the nation for Haldane's reforms. Occasionally he felt obliged to pander to the opposition—Conservatives who fought abolition of the militia, pacifist Liberals who were against armies on principle, and even followers of Roberts professing to be satisfied with nothing short of conscription—in order to avoid being dubbed a partisan and thus forfeiting the effect of his support, but as he explained to Haldane's mother: "I am convinced that your son is the best Minister of War that we have had in our time, and I only hope that the tail of his party will never compel him to vary by a hairsbreadth from the policy of his Memorandum." [31] He indorsed the plan for the "first line"—the formation of an expeditionary force of six infantry divisions and one cavalry division maintained by reserves, the whole resting on the bedrock of the Cardwell system and in fact even claimed that it was he who had suggested the name of "expeditionary force": "It was first called the Striking Force, and I thought that this would alarm the Radicals unduly." [32]

Similarly, Repington wrote on behalf of the new territorial force, comprising fourteen divisions of the old yeomanry and volunteers. Originally, he was of the opinion that the militia should also be included in the formation of the second line for home defense,[33] but he defended Haldane against charges that

[30] Major D. H. Cole and Major E. C. Priestley, *An Outline of British Military History 1660–1939* (London, 1939), pp. 297–300. Additional information on the reorganization of the army under Haldane is found in Colonel John K. Dunlop, *The Development of the British Army 1899– 1914: From the Eve of the South African War to the Eve of the Great War, with Special Reference to the Territorial Force* (London, 1938), pp. 231–303; J. E. Tyler, *The British Army and the Continent 1904–1914* (London, 1938), pp. 66–73; Sir Charles Harris, "Lord Haldane at the War Office," in Harris *et al. Viscount Haldane of Cloan: The Man and His Work* (London, 1928), pp. 6–18; Haldane, *Richard Burdon Haldane: An Autobiography* (New York, 1929), pp. 180–223.

[31] Repington to Mrs. Haldane, February 27, 1908 (National Library of Scotland, Edinburgh, Haldane Papers).

[32] Repington, *Essays and Criticisms*, pp. 24–34; *The First World War 1914–1918: Personal Experiences of Lieut.-Col. C. à Court Repington* (London, 1920), I, 14; *Foundations of Reform*, pp. 358–71.

[33] The militia fought the scheme to join them to the volunteers and, according to the Territorial and Reserve Forces Act of 1907, formally ceased to exist, although large numbers agreed to transfer to new formations in the special reserve, which fulfilled some of the same functions as the historic militia (Dunlop, *Development of the British Army*, pp. 272–73).

he had created territorial batteries at the sacrifice of the regular artillery, he explained the war minister's intention to create county associations to administer but not to command the territorial force on a county basis, and he applauded the intention to fill the ranks of the territorials by voluntary service. If Roberts and the National Service League were correct in their assertion that voluntary service in the long run would not provide the numbers required for home defense— and Repington was inclined to agree with them—"then the turn of compulsion will come. . . . The hands of the clock move steadily on, but the hour of that change has not yet struck." But for the first line, the regulars and the army and special reserves, Repington insisted that "the voluntary principle is, and always will be, indispensable." An army maintained by conscription could not meet the demand for overseas garrisons.[34]

Repington urged the creation of a modern general staff after "the spirit and not the letter of the German system." He expressed pleasure with the army order of January 6, 1905, establishing the seven military districts in the United Kingdom, but felt that this measure did not go far enough in co-ordinating command and administration. While the work of the great general staff at Berlin has been more or less understood and, according to Repington "rather less than more initiated at headquarters. . . . the functions of the General Staff in the territorialized commands of the German army have completely eluded the War Office understanding."[35] Manifestly, Repington was influenced by Wilkinson's *Brain of an Army* even if the authorities in this instance were not, and his articles on the general staff are little more than Wilkinson's ideas applied to the situation existing in 1905. Repington therefore supported Arnold-Forster's minute of November 11, 1905, in which that minister—who was also familiar with the work of Wilkinson—had made a "serious

[34] Repington, *Foundations of Reform*, pp. 305–11, 343, 344–57; *Essays and Criticisms*, p. 34.

[35] Repington, *Imperial Strategy*, pp. 101, 143. The German General Staff was divided into the Great General Staff (*Grossestab*) in Berlin, where the sections on operations, railway and communications, and intelligence were located; and the Army General Staff (*Truppenstab*), which assisted in the functions of command and administrative control in the various division, corps, and army headquarters. The Army General Staff, therefore, served as the connecting link between the field commands and headquarters in Berlin and is not to be confused with the regular administrative staffs that belonged to the headquarters of the individual commands.

and statesmanlike attempt to graft upon the somewhat rebel British stem the greatest product of the school of Moltke," and he rejoiced to think that

the principles adopted by the Army Council and embodied in the Secretary of State's minute, will tend, if wisely and firmly carried out in practice, to attract to the General Staff the best men in the Army; to create in course of time settled policy and settled doctrines; to prevent the initiation of imprudent and costly experiments, and to provide the country with that aristocracy of talent, independent of birth, influence, or means, which is absolutely indispensable for success in modern war.[36]

Repington naturally approved of the formation of the Imperial General Staff four years later, but he remained unhappy with the work of the general staff in the field. Much could be learned, he insisted, if the authorities "took more trouble to study and profit by the experiences of others," and some of his most original observations concerned the functions of the Napoleonic staff system. Repington maintained that the Napoleonic manner of waging war was still "the fountain-head of military wisdom" and that because Moltke "was practically Commander-in-Chief in the Field" the Napoleonic staff system was more applicable to British wars, since "neither Napoleon nor any British commander could find any use for such an exalted assistant." The guiding principles of Berthier and his assistants could be applied to modern conditions even though "in Napoleon's day the interesting discovery had not been made that a General Staff can direct the movements of an army without knowing how it is administered and fed." [37]

Repington stood firmly behind Haldane for as long as the latter remained at the helm. He had less respect for his successor, Colonel the Rt. Hon. J. E. B. Seely. Within months after Haldane left the War Office in 1912 to become the Lord Chancellor, Repington wrote:

You asked me to let you know how things went on at the War Office and I must tell you that they are going badly in certain respects. . . . The general efficiency of the office has fallen about 50% since it lost you, Lord Nicholson [C.I.G.S.] and Murray [probably General Wolfe Murray]. I like your successor personally and get on with him, but he does nothing and carries no guns.

36 *Ibid*, p. 165.
37 Repington, *Essays and Criticisms*, pp. 169–191.

. . . It would be useless for you to talk to Seely, but the situation is so serious that I think you should ask the Prime Minister to intervene with a firm hand and put matters to rights.[38]

Repington deplored both the policy of drift that characterized military policy after the departure of Haldane and the unwillingness of responsible officials to reveal deficiencies in the Army. Colonel Seely, whom he at first excused as the slave of his political environment, finally provoked Repington into a personal attack upon "that attitude of bland assurance and complacent optimism" which enabled the war minister "to place a gloss upon every defect, and to ignore the fact that since he assumed the reins of office nothing has been done—nothing of any kind—except to allow matters to go from bad to worse unchecked." [39]

Repington's ire was aroused especially by what he considered to be the unwillingness of Britain's political leaders to face up to military realities. Sooner or later, he contended, they would have to decide "whether our first line army of the future shall be designed . . . primarily for the service of the Empire or purely for war in Europe." The British army in 1913 may have been for its size the best in existence, but it was not constructed for a war with a mass army, and Repington argued that "if we have to contemplate such a conflict," then "we must become an armed nation like the rest." He urged a number of reforms for the first line—measures such as increased pay for officers, the creation of a second cavalry division for the expeditionary force, a stronger special reserve, the completion of a mobilization test, rapid rearmament, more progress in aeronautics, and strengthening both the Royal Engineers and the signal service. His proposals for the second line were more revolutionary. Beginning in 1909 he began to speak of the need to adopt some form of national training or compulsion to maintain the territorials at the desired strength and efficiency. "In view of the general position of England in the world, and the stupendous armaments which may be arrayed against her, the basis of her military power is not broad enough, and it can be broadened only by the training to arms of a larger number of the population." Failure to meet

[38] Repington to Haldane, November 27, 1912 (Haldane Papers).
[39] Repington, "The Debate on Defence: A Policy of Procrastination," *Times*, February 12, 1913; "The Army Estimates," *ibid.*, March 21, 1913; "Parliament and the Army," *ibid.*, June 17, 1913.

this situation squarely could mean only that his "friend" Colonel von Donner und Blitzen had been correct two years earlier, when he asserted with what Repington would have regarded as typical Prussian arrogance:

> This, my dear friend, is our century, not yours. You English steadily advert your faces from the facts of the present day. You live in a world which has no real existence. You see what you wish to see, and nothing more. Furbish up, if you please, that champion belt which has so long reposed in John Bull's strongbox, for the hour's at hand when we shall challenge for it.[40]

It should be emphasized that Repington's dissatisfaction was rarely with the army as such, although he was quick to suggest areas of improvement; rather his quarrel was with the politicians and occasionally the nation at large. The empire, he asserted, had been won and managed by the aristocracy, and in 1914 Repington wondered aloud whether a democracy could ever do anything with the British empire "except lose it."[41] Both Germany and France, on the other hand, seemed determined to realize their full military potential, and Repington admired them for their masculine manner even though he saw defects in the German army.

In 1911 Repington attended the German army maneuvers and reported in reassuring terms what he had seen. The German cavalry, he wrote, was adept in fighting dismounted but less mobile than British lancers: "there will be trouble in store for the German cavalry in this matter one of these days." He noted that the Germans continued to retain their fondness for shock, that in reconnaissance they were inferior to the British, and that they had learned from maneuvers the previous year the folly of raiding enemy communications. The infantry were described by Repington as "sullen-looking, half-cowed, and machine-made"—a far cry from the enthusiastic soldiers that had caught the attention of Maurice and Henderson. German infantry tactics were "perfunctory": the troops attacked "in a methodical and plodding manner," they seemed unaware of the value of intrenchments and they

---

[40] Repington, *Essays and Criticisms*, pp. 41–43; "The Higher Policy of Defence," *Times*, February 4, 1911; "Army Estimates, 1912–1913," *ibid.*, March 4, 1912; "Military Policy. I. Principles and Their Application," *ibid.*, February 6, 1913; "Military Policy. II. Revolution or Evolution," *ibid.*, February 7, 1913; "The Case for National Service," *ibid.*, February 25, 1913.
[41] Repington, "The Cost of Failure in War," *Times*, February 13, 1914.

knew little about scouting or mutual fire supports by units in the firing line. Their "great heavy columns offered remunerative targets on countless occasions." German artillery, he reported, was conservative and decidedly behind the French. The Germans were behind also in aviation but were working hard to catch up. Repington concluded that what he had witnessed was a stale army in which there was ample evidence of good drill, discipline, and physique but in which individuality, initiative, and freshness "have been rigorously crushed out." "No other modern army," he concluded, "displays such profound contempt for the effect of modern fire."

Repington's view of the German army as one with a reputation more formidable than it deserved represents wishful thinking rather than objective analysis, for his vision was blurred somewhat by an intense dislike of everything German (the authorities, he complained, had not even provided him with "special facilities" at the maneuvers). Nevertheless, two of his comments merit attention. He mentioned the emphasis that the Germans gave to the machine gun and then warned: "Nations which may have to encounter the German Army must strive to excel in the use of this weapon, which proved its worth in Manchuria." And in his description of the German tactics of envelopment he speculated that such tactics might work in east Prussia but would not be possible on the French frontier, "and we come back once more to the dilemma that either these tactics have no application to a war against France or else that the front of deployment of German armies will not be restricted by the frontiers of neutral states." [42]

Repington found more to emulate in the French army. In his account of the French maneuvers of 1906 he praised the suppleness of the infantry tactics, the power and mobility of the field artillery ("the best in the world"), the discipline of the soldiers on the march, and the training and efficiency of the staff. The cavalry "arouses the enthusiasm" of cavalrymen everywhere, and Repington concluded that the maneuvers "afford fresh evidence that the French army in the field will be thoroughly ready for any effort that may be imposed upon it." Five years later, however, he was more cautious in following

[42] Repington, "The German Army Manoeuvres," *Times*, October 12, 14, 17, 19, 24, 28, 1911. See also his essay, written before the autumn maneuvers, entitled "Tendencies in the German Army," *Essays and Criticisms*, pp. 202–38.

the lead of the French. Even the theories of Foch, "certainly one of the most brilliant of French officers," did not rest upon experience acquired in modern battle. Repington positively shuddered at the writings of those who envisaged massive attacks upon a limited front, tactics which in his judgment should have been "long since dead and buried." [43]

Repington's own views on tactics were orthodox. He wrote always in terms of building up the firing line in the attack and he defended cavalry against critics such as Roberts and Erskine Childers, who were convinced that the *arme blanche* was a thing of the past. Roberts as commander in chief had instructed cavalry to abolish the lance and be prepared to "generally act dismounted." Childers took a more extreme stand, claiming that the Russo-Japanese War had sealed the doom of shock tactics. But by the time Repington joined the staff of the *Times* there had been an official swing back to the sword and lance. In 1906 the new drill book attached less importance to mounted infantry than the *Cavalry Manual* issued two years previously, and the *Manual* for 1907 stated: "The essence of the cavalry spirit lies in holding the balance correctly between fire power and shock action. . . . It must be accepted as a principle that the rifle, effective as it is, cannot replace the effect produced by the speed of the horse, the magnetism of the charge, and the terror of cold steel." [44]

Repington believed that shock tactics still were feasible, that cavalry armed only with the rifle "is a chicken trussed for the spit," and that all cavalry should be armed with the lance, "the best weapon to supplement the rifle." British cavalry doctrine, he insisted, "is sound, the spirit excellent, and the arm efficient mounted and on foot," and he spoke favorably of "the true cavalry spirit which scorns mathematical calculations." As late as 1913, Repington urged the creation of a second cavalry division for the expeditionary force in place of the mounted brigades which contained mounted infantry, "the cavalry of poverty." Even after the trench deadlock he

[43] Repington, *Foundations of Reform*, pp. 87–110; *Essays and Criticisms*, pp. 230–35. Repington acknowledged, but did not editorialize upon, the cult of the offensive then prevalent in the French army, and he did not mention the extreme views of Colonel Grandmaison.

[44] Roberts, "Memorandum by the Commander-in-Chief," *R.U.S.I. Journal*, XLVII (1903) 575–82; David James, *Lord Roberts* (London, 1954), pp. 439–41. The *Manual* for 1907 is quoted in Erskine Childers, *War and the Arme Blanche* (London, 1910), pp. 1–3. See also "German Views on Mounted Infantry," *Cavalry Journal*, II (1907), 347–51.

took comfort in the knowledge th
always be on hand to cross sword:
the time for mounted action return

Adherence to the views of the c:
however, that Repington was con:
tactics or armament. To a remarl
future developments in the use c
submarine, and one cannot rea
exercises and maneuvers withou
evident grasp of the subject at a
from company training to the com
divisions. But his was a practic:
theorist. "Theory," he noted, "do
British officers." Repington was cc
out their own tactical salvation if
be prevailed upon to give them the

Repington became so closely i
fact, that many came to regard hi
man. This was particularly true :
pointed editor of a new general-st
Review. Some interpreted this as a move to reinstate Repington in the army: [47] rival journalists complained that it would
give the military correspondent of the *Times* access to official
information, and many feared that Repington's views would
now be received abroad as official—an alarming thought,
given the sensitive international situation and the fact that
Repington's articles about the Agadir crisis and the Kaiser maneuvers that same year had angered many Germans. (Three
years earlier Repington had been the source of considerable
friction when he had forced publication of the Kaiser's private
letter to the First Lord of the Admiralty in which it was denied
that the German naval bill represented any threat to British su-

[45] Repington, *Essays and Criticisms,* pp. 81–88; "Parliament and the
Army," *Times,* March 24, 1911; "The Mounted Troops of the Expedi-
tionary Force," *ibid.,* February 15, 1912; "The Army Exercises," *ibid.,*
September 30, 1912; "The War Day by Day," *ibid,* November 4, 1914.
For the conflicting views of Haig and Hamilton, see the *Report of His
Majesty's Commissioners to Inquire into the Military Preparations and
Other Matters Connected with the War in South Africa* (London, 1903),
pp. 49–50, 403. A useful summary of the cavalry controversy, written by
one who sympathized with the Haig-French school, is Lieutenant Colonel V. S. Charrington, *Where Cavalry Stands Today* (London, 1927), pp.
17–26.
[46] See Repington, "Company Training," *Times,* May 9, 10, 1911.
[47] See Edmonds, "Repington," p. 717.

premacy of the seas.[48]) Actually Repington was well suited for the position, which called for an editor "of high professional connections but still independent of the service." Haldane was anxious to encourage officers to discuss questions of policy, and it was hoped that the new publication would be able to combine official teaching of doctrine with independent thought. Repington originally had intended to give up the editorship once the *Army Review,* which he "had been largely instrumental in creating," was safely launched, but when the Kaiser pressed for his dismissal following publication of his report on the army maneuvers, he stayed on for an additional six months just to avoid accommodating the Germans.[49]

The French exploited Repington's position by using him as an intermediary in bringing about military conversations with England. Repington's articles during the Moroccan crisis in 1905 revealed that he appreciated the fact that the defense of France and the Low Countries "involved military dispositions of the greatest significance to Britain"; and in December of that year the conversations began unofficially with a private exchange of views between Repington and Major Huguet, the French military attaché. Repington reported the conversation to Sir Edward Grey at the Foreign Office and then, with the encouragement of two highly placed friends, he transmitted to the French government through Huguet a list of questions to determine the official French position on possible joint military action. Within a fortnight the British general staff took up the matter with Huguet, and so began the official negotiations that paved the way for a reversal of England's historic policy and ultimately for "a war effort such as no Englishman had ever conceived." [50] Thereafter Repington worked to condition the army for the test ahead and the nation to accept its responsibilities by supporting France in the event of a war with Germany. He even had some effect

[48] *History of the Times, 1884–1912,* pp. 844–45; "Army Review," *Times,* May 24, 1911; Repington, *Vestigia,* pp. 284–92. Repington's analysis of the 1911 army maneuvers had so angered the German General Staff that British press representatives were not permitted to attend maneuvers the following year (C. E. Callwell, *Stray Recollections* [London, 1923], II, 253).

[49] Repington, *Vestigia,* pp. 303–4; *Times,* July 1, 1911.

[50] *History of the Times, 1884–1912,* p. 464; Liddell Hart, *A History of the World War 1914–1918* (London, 1934), p. 73. Repington's part in the conversations is related in his wartime journal, *The First World War 1914–1918,* I, 1–16; and in Tyler, *British Army and the Continent,* pp. 22, 27, 38–41.

upon opinion in France, where his criticisms of the German army in 1911 found ready acceptance and helped to raise the moral of the army.[51]

As the war clouds darkened and began to drift over Europe in July, 1914, Repington saw clearly what was coming. To readers unaware of the nature of the commitment to France, he uttered a chilling prophecy: "We shall support our friends because we must, and in a very short time after a Russian mobilization is announced it will be a miracle if all Europe is not aflame." England would be dragged in "because we have selfishly refused to make ourselves a nation in arms" and consequently must look for security to the maintenance of the balance of power.[52]

And like many soldiers throughout Europe in the first fateful days of the war, Repington approached his task with a light heart. The first clash would occur on August 14, he predicted the day after England declared war (August 4), and in fact this date marks the beginning of the short-lived French offensive in Lorraine; the first decisive battles would take place no later than August 22—he was one day too early for the British stand at Mons. "Friends on either side who are late at this rendezvous will be late for the fair." On the eve of the battle of Mons, Repington wrote in glowing terms of "glorious country for fighting in, glorious weather, and a glorious cause. What Soldier," he asked exuberantly, "could ask more?" After it became apparent that one battle would not produce victory, Repington then placed undiluted faith in the colossal power of Russia. The obvious strategy for France and Britain, he argued, was to erect a human wall in the west against which the Russian steamroller could crush the Germans. "We are doing very well in Flanders," he reported during the first battle of Ypres (October 30–November 24, 1914). "We have performed the mission that we set out to perform, and are fulfilling the stone-walling *role* to perfection."[53]

It would serve no useful purpose to reconstruct in detail Repington's view of the war. The direction of his thinking is more important than the recording of every turn in the

[51] The effect of Repington's articles in France is reported by the *Times* Paris correspondent in the *Times*, November 3, 1911. See also Repington, *The First World War*, I, 547, for Marshal Petain's reaction.
[52] Repington, "Great Powers and the War," *Times*, July 30, 1914.
[53] Repington, "The War Day by Day," *ibid.*, August 5, 22, 1914: September 2, November 14, 1914.

twisting (some would prefer "serpentine") road that he followed. For the first year and a half Repington did all that could be expected of the military correspondent of the *Times*. He wrote a daily analysis of some aspect of the war, he pointed the way to a more effective national effort, he visited the troops in the front lines and he kept his own lines open to the War Office. More than once he performed valuable service in alerting the nation to unpleasant realities. Russell's angry letters from the Crimea could not have aroused public opinion more effectively than Repington's inspired disclosure in May, 1915, that the B.E.F. was seriously handicapped for want of sufficient quantities of high-explosive shells. Lord Northcliffe, the proprietor of the *Times* and the *Daily Mail*, pounced upon the issue and used it to help tumble the Liberal government from office. A coalition cabinet was formed that included a new ministry of munitons under David Lloyd George.[54] In thus bringing the country face to face with a critical problem Repington made a unique contribution to the war effort.

But by 1916 he was beginning to show signs of fatigue. His articles in the *Times* had become thin fare. He found himself repeating old arguments, plagued more than ever by the censorship and in growing opposition to the editorial policies of the paper. He began to lose perspective and to become overinvolved in politics. His frustrations mounted throughout 1917 until in January the following year he resigned explosively from the *Times* and gave vent to his rancorous, suppressed feelings in Spenser Wilkinson's old paper, the *Morning Post*.[55] His first article began: "I have some things to say to the British public and am going to say them without mincing matters," and almost immediately he and his new

[54] Repington, *The First World War*, I, 34–41; Reginald Pound and Geoffrey Harmsworth, *Northcliffe* (New York, 1959), 473–81; *Lord Riddell's War Diary 1914–1918* (London, 1933), pp. 87, 88.

[55] The story of Repington's resignation from the *Times* is blurred by contradictory evidence which is too lengthy to explain here. He claimed that he did so in protest against a policy he could neither support nor alter, that the *Times* "was misleading the public under the guidance of the politicians" (Mary Repington, *Thanks for the Memory*, pp. 269–70; Repington, *The First World War*, II, 180–88; New York *Times*, January 22, 1918, p. 4). The *Times* charged that Repington had already decided to join the staff of a competitor and for this reason he "was at once relieved of his duties" (*Times*, January 23, 1918). Repington may have committed himself to the *Morning Post* before he severed relations with the *Times*, but his diary does not indicate that he did so and it does reveal that his dissatisfaction with the *Times* had been increasing for many months.

editor were convicted of violating the Defence of the Realm regulations by revealing military secrets in their reckless attacks upon the government. Each was fined £100. At the very least Repington was guilty of bad judgment, indiscretion, and failure to submit the articles for censorship, and his motives in discrediting the leadership of Lloyd George and the war cabinet appear less worthy than had been the case three years earlier when he had alerted the nation to the shell shortages. Lloyd George, on the other hand, probably saw more of a conspiracy against him than in fact existed: he claimed that Repington actually had disclosed "the entire plans of the Allies for the year" and cites evidence in his *Memoirs* to show that the German high command profited thereby. He uses words like "treachery," "treasonable," and "betrayable" in describing Repington's actions, but Repington saw himself as the courageous defender of truth and he continued to wage a personal war with those responsible for the misconduct of the war as well as his old enemy, the Boche. His diary leads one to suspect that he rather enjoyed the thought of becoming a martyr.[56]

Repington's critics have asserted that he often acted as though "fairly stung by a gadfly," that he frequently contradicted himself, that he liked to keep a foot in each camp, was a victim of his own passions, and was guilty of "spurious pretensions, surprising associations, painful efforts to straddle so much." "We defy any one to gain from Colonel Repington's yes-and-no method any coherent view of the present battle and the prospect in France," one outspoken editor complained during the German spring offensives in 1918.

At one time the Boche is said to be deeply chagrined by his checks, hard hit, and licking his wounds. At another time, when it suits the political argument, our army is pictured as jeopardized and almost betrayed under the imbeciles who are trying to conduct the war in London.[57]

---

[56] Repington, *The First World War*, II, 228–36; *War Memoirs of David Lloyd George: 1917–1918* (Boston, 1936), V, 293–302. Repington's article in the *Morning Post*, which unfortunately is not available to the writer, is summarized in the New York *Times*, January 25, 1918.

[57] J. L. Garvin, editor of the London *Observer*, in an article dated May 12, 1918 and reprinted in part in the New York *Times* of the same date. See "Assails Sniping by Army Clique," *ibid.*, p. 2.

Even his friends admit that he had a nose for intrigue, but whether he was the "unprincipled scoundrel" that Lord Milner saw or the "fearlessly honest and independent critic" described in a subsequent review probably depends upon one's point of view toward the ruling circles in London, G.H.Q. in France, and the policies and strategy best calculated to produce victory.[58]

Repington can be pardoned for honest inconsistencies reflecting the news and hopes of the moment, nor is he the first artist to apply somber shades or a dash of bright color to achieve a desired effect. But by the last year of the war he had lost his balance if not his sense of direction. Many would not go so far as J. L. Garvin, who stated in an editorial in the *Observer* that Repington possessed all of the qualities of Caesar's wife, yet if Garvin's facts are correct—and he knew Repington intimately—it would appear that Repington was in fact trying to walk down both sides of the street at the same time and in opposite directions. Citing chapter and verse to support his contention, Garvin pointed out that Repington was writing both for the *Morning Post,* which he described as "reactionary but ultra-patriotic," and for the *Naturalized News,* which "professes to be of extreme democratic tendency." In the former Repington "clamored for Irish conscription"; in the latter, "which is, of course, against it," he "sentimentalizes and hedges." To the writer's knowledge Garvin's charges were never refuted, and Repington, who was intensely suspicious both of democracy and foreigners, whom he associated with pacifists, is strangely silent in his diary about his unlikely bedfellows on a left-wing newspaper edited by a naturalized Austrian and financed by a man who came originally from Holland.[59] If indeed Repington was "the victim of the most personal and violent newspaper attack ever made upon a man in Fleet Street," [60] perhaps it is significant that even the writer of these words refrained from using the adjective "innocent."

Paradoxically, Repington fell from grace ultimately because in certain matters he was unpleasantly consistent. Consider his pre-war career, when he was the legitimate

[58] Pound and Harmsworth, *Northcliffe,* pp. 477, 575, 634; "The First World War," *English Review,* XXXI (1920), 536–41; "An Audacious Military Critic," *Outlook,* CXL (June 10, 1925), 209–10.
[59] Garvin, as quoted in the New York *Times,* May 12, 1918.
[60] "The First World War," *English Review,* XXXI, 537.

prince of all military correspondents, and what do we find? A man who blamed England's lack of military preparedness upon the political rather than the military leaders, a critic almost obsessed with problems of manpower and recruitment, an avowed enemy of Germany and a friend of the French, a thinker who was more orthodox than original, a former officer still closely tied to the army, and above all a journalist who was not content merely to report or to analyse but who, as his role in bringing about military conversations with France and his work with Haldane clearly indicate, was influential in shaping military policy as well.

The war did not alter these traits, or loyalties, or prejudices except to intensify them. The critic who quietly but consistently worked for conscription in 1912–13 found himself screaming a few years later that "numbers alone annihilate, and we must have the numbers" until ultimately he left the *Times* and avoided the censor in order to attack the "procrastination and cowardice" of the cabinet in failing to mobilize all of Britain's available manpower for service in France. His tone had become more strident and his methods, perhaps, more dubious, but his concern to maintain the army at what he considered to be the minimum requisite strength had been evident ever since the days of Haldane.[61]

This was true also of his attitude toward the political leaders. With few exceptions he had never quite trusted them, even before the war: most professional soldiers did not. By 1915 he was openly critical, taking the line that the country was drifting, that the war cabinet "have shown conspicuously an absence of genius for war," and that the most recent fiasco—the Dardanelles expedition—was "from first to last directed from London in the most amateur and scatterbrained fashion." Repington fell back upon Wilkinson's argument "that the responsibility for conducting war shall be vested in one man if a sufficiently competent man can be found," and he called for greater participation by the general staff in determining strategy. Throughout the next two years he grew more impatient still with the "hopeless stupidity of amateurs," the politician who "is forever fuming and fretting and trying

[61] See Repington's articles in the *Times* dated March 13, 1916, May 23, 1916, December 27, 1916, and February 26, 1917; and the following entries in his diary, *The First World War*, I, 43, 185, 471, 474; II, 32, 129, 197.

to interfere and run the campaign in spite of the fact that he had his turn during the early part of the war and plainly made the most appalling bungle of it." The horrors of Passchendaele did not depress him nearly as much as "the shameful poltroonery and strategic incompetence of the War Cabinet." After he left the *Times* his criticisms and impatience reached the level of uncompromising hostility. "There is nothing more that I can do except to watch the inevitable consequences of the War Cabinet's folly during the next few months," he noted bitterly in his diary a few weeks before the German offensive of March, 1918.

> They have starved the Army for men, have dispersed our military resources about the world, and now have to face the consequences of their follies. They have dismissed the safest guide in strategy [Field Marshal Sir William Robertson, until recently the Chief of the Imperial General Staff] after refusing to listen to his warnings, and they have prosecuted me for showing them up. Upon the Army and the country will fall the retribution which Lloyd George and his War Cabinet alone deserve.

"Our good amateurs" of 1915 had grown into deceitful villains! [62]

Repington remained a die-hard "Westerner," adhering to the conviction that "the Front in Flanders is the decisive point for us, and all our resources should be devoted to it. We cannot go wrong if we seek for the enemy's centre of gravity and deal it resounding and pitiless blows, day in, day out, until our aim is achieved." But this had been his view long before the war, for as early as 1905 he predicted:

> the war, if it ever comes, will be fought out, and perhaps decided . . . upon the land frontier. Subsidiary operations . . . will not, in all probability, affect the issue of the first decisive encounters in any material degree. If undertaken by small forces, they are without importance; if by large forces, the less the chance of victory at the decisive point. If victory is not gained at the decisive point, a success elsewhere is barren of results.[63]

Repington was a faithful disciple of Clausewitz, whom he quoted frequently, and he applied many of the German

[62] Repington, "Statecraft and Strategy," *Times*, August 31, September 1, 1915; "The War Day by Day," *ibid.*, October 29, 1915; "The Unity of Fronts," *ibid.*, August 24, 25, 1916; *The First World War*, II, 180, 238.

[63] Repington, "The War Day by Day," *Times*, March 18, 1915; *Imperial Strategy*, p. 262; *Foundations of Reform*, p. 186.

theorist's observations about the "continuity of operations, tensions and rest" to a modern war of attrition. He saw what Clausewitz called the "center of gravity" as the defeat of German armed forces in France; he too stressed absolute war, superiority in numbers, and the value of moral and psychological factors (usually in the absence of advantages more concrete), and he reminded his readers that the doctrines of a man whom a later theorist would label "the Mahdi of Mass" were being abused by "English juveniles, who, with their breezy and practical good sense, abhor theory, and think, as a rule, that they can get on very well without it." [64]

It is understandable, therefore, that Repington should react to the trench deadlock in France in much the same way as the military leaders. With each costly failure to achieve a breakthrough Repington repeated the cry from G.H.Q. for more shells and greater reserves so that the next—and hopefully the last—great offensive might succeed. After the mismanagement at Neuve Chapelle he explained: ". . . the work resembles a siege, and we require not only a large numerical preponderance of infantry, so that we can pour out troops like peas out of a sack, but also means of destruction superior to those of the enemy."

What we are out to do is to kill Germans, and so long as German casualties continue to number 10,000 a day we are doing our work. . . . What we have to avoid are adventures, and particularly the offering to Germany of great strategic successes . . . a wearing war of trenches on parallel fronts is desperately tiresome and the reverse of thrilling. But it must kill Germany in the end if it is continued.[65]

Instead of questioning the causes for failure to break the German lines in the great Somme offensive in 1916, Repington professed satisfaction with the way things were going. The defender was losing more in proportion than the attacking forces, he insisted: German morale was deteriorating rapidly and multitudes of prisoners were being taken. The costly offensive should continue "because our losses of officers and men have been made good, the number of our guns increases daily, and the expenditure of ammunition is exceeded by the supply." Manifestly the objective now was to

[64] Repington, "The War Day by Day," *Times*, March 8, 11, 1915; *The First World War*, I, 375.
[65] Repington, "The War Day by Day," *Times*, April 2, June 17, 1915.

inflict casualties—in a war of attrition this is what counts—through a series of limited attacks in which each position gained was consolidated until artillery could be brought forward in sufficient quantity to pave the way for still another assault.[66]

He warned against an offensive in Flanders the following year because the ground was unsuitable, but he had no quarrel with the tactics employed or the strategy of the campaign. Nor could he believe the "rubbish" he heard about the elasticity of the German defenses, although by 1917 the Germans had evolved an intricate system that enabled them to roll with every punch delivered by the allied armies.[67] Throughout the war Repington's views of tactics and strategy were those of the army leaders in France. In the early months he had described the conflict as "a steeplechase of national impoverishment in which the best staying people win, if winning it can be called." It was drab and dirty; above all it was stupid. He could see no way to restore mobility or exercise initiative: "day after day the butchery of the unknown by the unseen, and events decided by the greatest mass of projectiles hurled simultaneously in the general direction of the enemy." Was there any means for curing "this tactical catalepsy"? Certainly: "fresh troops and plenty of them, with guns, and especially heavy howitzers galore." [68] Repington, like most of his old army friends, adhered to the same formula throughout the war despite the enormous losses, lack of any real success, and the advent of the tank.

The end of the war found him completely committed to the views of the general staff and of G.H.Q. in France and more active than ever with his pen. The encouragement of a sympathetic editor and the arrival of the Americans with fresh problems of organization and command induced him to set aside his memoirs for the moment and concentrate on the war. Once again, for the first time since 1915, he attempted to write something for publication every day. But the climate had changed, and to his disadvantage. Now his

[66] Repington, "German Strategy and Somme Tactics," ibid., October 4, 1916; The First World War, I, 323. See also Robert Blake (ed.), The Private Papers of Douglas Haig 1914–1917 (London, 1952), pp. 157–58.

[67] Repington, "The Flanders Battle," Times, August 3, 1917; The First World War, I, 571; II, 28, 50; "Arras and Messines," Times, June 25, 1917; "The Defensive," ibid., January 10, 1918. An admirable exposition of the new German tactics is Captain G. C. Wynne, If Germany Attacks (London, 1939).

[68] Repington, "The War Day by Day," Times, November 24, 1914.

views were openly challenged in what appear to have been inspired attacks in both England and France; [69] his good friend Robertson had been replaced as C.I.G.S. by his successful rival, Sir Henry Wilson, and his most fertile source of information at the War Office, the son of the late General Maurice, had been supplanted as director of military operations and was in bad odor with the government because of misleading disclosures concerning the numerical strength of the armies in France. [70] Moreover, with victory in sight and the allied forces gathering momentum everywhere, Repington's bitter protests had lost much of their sting.

His postwar career may be passed over lightly. He became military correspondent of the *Daily Telegraph* and remained with this newspaper until he died in May, 1925. Financial considerations evidently were responsible for the decision to publish his memoirs and wartime diaries, and the latter in particular, according to General Edmonds, "had a considerable success but lost him his social position." To some *The First World War* (the ordinal number was deliberate, "in order to prevent the millennium folk from forgetting that the history of the world was the history of war") was "a brave and sincere book"; others probably agreed with the reviewer who predicted that the author "will get plenty of kicks out of his book, and comparatively few halfpence"; and most readers must have felt uncomfortable with the breezy way in which private ("petty" in many cases would be a better word) talk was betrayed. To some it must have come as a shock to learn that the forthright critic who had exposed the shell shortage and fearlessly defended the army against the politicians also had a penchant, when dealing with personalities or side issues, for gnawing on small bones. [71]

[69] In addition to Garvin's devastating attack in the *Observer*, see André Chéradame, "The Fundamentals of the Situation," *Atlantic Monthly*, CXXI (April, 1918), 529–41. Chéradame wrote for the avowed purpose of demonstrating "how far Colonel Repington has gone astray, and what infinite harm his errors have done . . . by reason of the mighty influence of the *Times*," but both he and Garvin were particularly anxious to counteract or discredit Repington's influence in the United States.

[70] See Lloyd George's account of "The Maurice Debate," in his *War Memoirs*, VI, 51–72. Repington naturally supported Maurice.

[71] "The First World War," *English Review*, XXXI, 536; *Spectator*, CXXV (September 25, 1920), 393; *Outlook*, CXXX (March 23, 1922), 472–73. Repington also published his postwar diary dealing with his trip in 1921 to the various European capitals and his experiences during the Washington Conference for the Limitation of Armaments. See *After the War: A Diary* (London, 1922).

Nor is it necessary to give more than passing mention to Repington's last work, a collection of postwar articles entitled *Policy and Arms*. In this book, which contained few fresh ideas and "attracted no attention," [72] he stressed the need for a naval air service and an army at least as strong as the first line in 1914. He also suggested that the territorials be modeled after the United States National Guard and that the American Defense Act of 1920 should serve as the basis for expansion in any national war of the future. He remained an unyielding Westerner and upbraided Winston Churchill for not recognizing, in *The World Crisis*, the folly of seeking a decision anywhere except in France. Such a strategy, however, "was too simple for the politicians, and especially for that little knot of men who persuaded themselves and each other that they were great intellectuals and the soldiers narrow-minded dolts." [73]

How clear the issue seemed now; how remote the hopes and confusions of 1914, when Repington, in one of his more candid moments, had confessed his own inadequacies in comprehending the war.

It transcends all limits of thought, imagination and reason. We little creeping creatures cannot see more than a fraction of it. Even if we climb painfully to the top of the highest ladder of thought we are still pigmies, and the war still towers high above us. We see the raging torrents at our feet, but the high summits are veiled in impenetrable mist. Try as we may to observe a distinct and unbroken view of the scene before us, the clouds of suspicion, prejudice, ignorance, and optimism constantly obscure our vision. We look, gasp, wonder and are dumb. We do not know. Nobody knows. This war, for once, is bigger than anybody. No one dominates it. No one even understands it. Nobody can.[74]

One wonders whether the fog of war ever lifted to give Repington a "distinct and unbroken view," or whether, as he groped his way about executive and military circles, he merely grew accustomed to the horizons of the soldier in France.

Certainly no one can deny that Repington's pen was his sharpest and most effective weapon. Wilkinson considered him the best staff officer in the army before the Boer War, and

[72] Edmonds, "Repington," p. 718.
[73] Repington, *Policy and Arms* (London, 1924), pp. 187, 189, 193–94, 197–206.
[74] Repington, "The War Day by Day," *Times,* December 15, 1914.

once Wilkinson left Fleet Street for Oxford, Repington's technical knowledge, professional experience, wide contacts, and clarity of expression left him in absolute command of the field. People began to look to the military correspondent of the *Times* for an authoritative opinion on military matters. His tone no less than his range of interests was imperial. His influence with the public was enormous: he rendered invaluable service in explaining the needs of the army during peace and analysing its performance in war; he contributed in no small way to acceptance of Haldane's military reforms; his disclosure of the shell shortage in 1915 rocked a ministry and his resignation from the *Times* early in 1918 left some people with the feeling that a cabinet minister had departed.[75] His opinions often were interpreted abroad as representing official views, which led to hostility in Germany before the war and the charge in France that because of the extraordinary influence of the *Times*, Repington had been instrumental "in leading the Allies to commit errors in strategy which have cost millions of men and endangered the issue of the war." [76]

His influence upon policy or individuals in high position is difficult to assess. Many of his suggestions during the Haldane era ultimately were adopted—the history of the Russo-Japanese War prepared under the auspices of the Committee of Imperial Defence would be a case in point—but whether this was due solely or even primarily to Repington's influence would be mere conjecture. During the war he met regularly with French and Robertson (Kitchener forced him to work through a subordinate member of the War Office staff) with whom he usually agreed on problems of manpower and strategy, but there is no evidence to suggest that Repington influenced the C.I.G.S. in his decisions. Possibly the reverse was true, that Robertson and the other generals saw in Repington a powerful vehicle for their own ideas and exploited his willing services for their own ends. Northcliffe's brother observed at the time of the shell controversy that Repington "was desirous of currying favour at all times with the heads of the Army, with whom, privately, he stood in very bad personal odour," [77] and Repington's diaries provide ample evidence of his willingness to carry the views of certain of the

[75] New York *Times*, January 30, 1918, p. 2.
[76] Chéradame, "Fundamentals of the Situation," p. 532.
[77] Pound and Harmsworth, *Northcliffe,* p. 476.

generals to the public. Many generals wrote him in detail of their campaigns in distant theaters, which perhaps worked to the advantage of all parties concerned.

Repington possessed rich sources of information and as a rule was exceptionally well informed, but two traits diminished his stature as a military critic. Often he allowed his emotions to warp his judgment. There were times during the war when he sounded more like a national cheerleader than a distinguished critic, referring contemptuously to the German tribes, the vile hun, and insisting that "the spoilers of churches and of homes" be brought to trial after the war,[78] and frequently he allowed personal loyalties and prejudice to impede his view of what was happening.

Repington also became too deeply involved in intrigue. This was his nature and he could not help it, but it meant that in many instances he approached issues as a partisan rather than a dispassionate critic. Add to this a reputation for indiscretion and it can be seen why, after the war, he himself as well as the army was operating below the efficiency level of 1914. Even his sources of information must have dried up considerably upon publication of his diaries.

Repington frequently commented of others that they suffered from the defects of their qualities. But this is true also of Repington. He was clever: all agree on this point. Perhaps he suffered from being too clever, a trait which, reinforced by his intense partisanship and lack of originality, undermined much of the constructive work he tried to accomplish. Writing in a day when people lived largely on emotions, he was almost bound, sooner or later, to come to grief.

[78] Repington, "The War Day by Day," *Times,* September 18, October 2, 1914.

V REACTION OR REVOLUTION
1919–39

Soon after the end of hostilities in 1918 the army resumed its normal character: the men were demobilized, compulsory service was abolished, and the regular army was reduced to a figure 40,000 below what it had been in 1914. With Germany disarmed, the public war-weary and burdened with ecomonic pressures, the immediate military need was for forces to implement British policy in north Russia and the Near East, to support civil power in Ireland, and to provide garrisons throughout the empire. Once again, as in the pre-Haldane era, the size of the army was hardly equal to its responsibilities.

For the first decade there were cautious and sporadic attempts to modernize the army and assimilate the lessons of the war. The issues centered on the type of war to anticipate in the future, a war of movement or another four years of attrition in trenches; on the size and nature of armies, the nation-in-arms or a small, highly trained professional army; on the capabilities and limitations of air power; and finally, on the use of weapons developed to break the trench deadlock— poison gas and the tank.

The former became a political and moral issue and thus ceased to be strictly a military problem, although none could be sure that it would not reappear when conditions were ripe. As for the tank, which had still been in the experimental stage when the war ended, some soldiers regarded it primarily as an infantry support weapon to transport firepower to the enemy's lines, crush his barbed wire, and cross over his trenches. Others, chief among whom are the subjects of the next two chapters, looked to the tank for a revival of the mobile arm and stressed its capacity for speed, maneuverability, and independent action.

In the British, as in all other armies, the conservatives "were hard to convince," [1] and in their reluctance seriously to experiment with mechanization they found strong support in the Treasury and the forces in India. The great depression in 1929 tightened the pinch on the armed services; the Disarmament Conference in Geneva three years later threatened further reductions.

By the mid-1930's, however, the mood had changed. The rise of Nazi Germany, the expansion of Japan, and Italian aggression in Abyssinia prodded Britain into rearmament, which in essence meant more ships, more planes, a few more soldiers, better equipment and a reconditioned territorial army. This led to fresh debates: must the army be remodeled as well as expanded? Was there a doctrine of war to give direction to rearmament? What was the role of the army in order of priority? How were Britain's forces to be used in the next great war, and what was to be the extent of her involvement?

The civil war in Spain sharpened the differences between Right and Left; appeasement at Munich, which produced new divisions at home and altered the military balance abroad, increased the tempo of rearmament. Now it was no longer a matter of deterring aggressors: now it had become preparation for war. The question was when—and what kind of a war.

The most prolific, controversial and influential military writers produced in Britain or any other country during this period were Fuller and Liddell Hart. Lifelong students of war, they dedicated themselves to the cause of reform and mechanization. They attempted to find order in history to serve as a realistic basis for new theories; they endeavored to develop a reliable method for deducing underlying principles

---

[1] Richard A. Preston, Sydney F. Wise and Herman O. Werner, *Men in Arms: A History of Warfare and its Interrelationships with Western Society* (New York, 1956), p. 280. A convenient summary of Britain's military position between the wars is found in Major D. H. Cole and Major E. C. Priestley, *An Outline of British Military History, 1660–1939* (London, 1939), pp. 389–434.

and for predicting future trends. Carrying their case to the public in a day when the professional soldier was particularly sensitive to criticisms of the conduct of the 1914–18 war, their ideas encountered opposition that at times was reactionary. Between them they developed the concept of the *Blitzkrieg*, which made them true revolutionaries.

10

THE DISCORDANT TRUMPET

Major General J. F. C. Fuller

"FOR IF the trumpet give an uncertain sound, who shall prepare himself to the battle?"

With these challenging words from the First Epistle to the Corinthians as his text, Sir George Milne, chief of the Imperial General Staff, addressed the senior officers of the experimental mechanized force in September, 1927.

It was a momentous occasion, the first in history when component parts of what later would be known as the blitzkrieg method of attack were assembled. It was, moreover, a landmark in the evolution of warfare, although many failed to recognize it as such at the time. For in a series of exercises shortly to be completed on Salisbury Plain, the tank and airplane demonstrated the relative impotence of conventional forces against the new mechanized formations.

To the imaginative architect of armored forces, however, the reverberations from "Uncle George's" trumpet sounded uncomfortably like the parting strains of the *Last Post*. For over a decade Colonel J. F. C. Fuller had been sounding *Reveille* in shrill tones, trying to alert the nation to the need for mechanization. Originally, he was to have commanded the experimental force, but an unfortunate misunderstanding over administrative details and the limits of his responsibilities caused him to relinquish the appointment. Fuller's unique experience later was rejected when he was sent to command a brigade, not of tanks but of infantry—a most unfitting "last post" for the man who, more than any soldier in the history of the British army, had materially altered the shape of future warfare.[1]

John Frederick Charles Fuller was born September 1, 1878, in "that sleepy little city of Chichester." At the age of eight he migrated with his parents to Switzerland, where he attended various schools until returning to England three years later to complete his formal education. Upon leaving Malvern College Fuller passed the Sandhurst entrance examinations, and he spent the year 1897–98 at the Royal Military College. Gazetted to the first battalion of the Oxfordshire Light Infantry, Fuller began his military career in Ireland, where he drilled four hours daily, indulged in occasional sword exercise and shooting, and devoted most of his free time, "like a monk in a Trappist monastery," to reading philosophy. He got along well enough with his fellow officers but he could not share their absorbing interest in foxes, duck, and trout. Already Fuller was an "unconventional soldier." [2]

When war broke out in South Africa the first battalion was sent to the Cape. Fuller himself experienced little fighting because of a near-fatal attack of appendicitis which caused him to miss the Paardeberg campaign, and by the time he was again fit for active duty the last considerable engagement of the war had already been fought. He spent nineteen months in the field trying to overcome space, boredom, and Boer guerrillas, during which time he helped to garrison fortified posts and blockhouse lines, commanded his own scouting detachment, read something like 150 books and saw but one dead British soldier. The impression gained from reading his entertaining recollections of this, *The Last of the Gentlemen's Wars*, is that it was not a particularly unpleasant experience if only because it removed him from the "Brown Bess mentality" he had encountered in the pre-war army: when he rejoined his battalion at the end of the war he "found drill and musketry in full swing, and most that had been learned during the war already forgotten." [3]

---

[1] Captain B. H. Liddell Hart, *The Tanks: The History of the Royal Tank Regiment and Its predecessors Heavy Branch Machine-Gun Corps Tank Corps and Royal Tank Corps 1914–1945* (New York, 1959), I, 221, 241–54.

[2] Fuller, *Memoirs of an Unconventional Soldier* (London, 1936), pp. 1, 6–7. All facts pertaining to Fuller's personal life and military career are taken from this source unless otherwise indicated.

[3] *Ibid.*, p. 16; *The Last of the Gentlemen's Wars: A Subaltern's Journal of the War in South Africa 1899–1902* (London, 1937), *passim.*

In 1903 Fuller accompanied his battalion to India, where he encountered intriguing new religions and philosophies. In 1906 he returned to England on a year's sick leave, and upon his recovery from enteric fever he applied for the adjutancy of the 2d South Middlesex Volunteers. When the battalion was amalgamated with another in the course of the Haldane reforms, Fuller's office became redundant, and he took the lead in organizing a new Middlesex battalion, the tenth. Here he stressed firepower in training to the extent that within a year the tenth had become the top battalion in musketry within the entire territorial force.

As the Manchester volunteers were responsible for Spenser Wilkinson's first efforts as a military critic, so the 10th Middlesex stimulated Fuller to write. He had always been bored with soldiers and soldiering, remaining aloof from his brother officers at the Curragh and enjoying a large degree of independence in South Africa; in fact he had become a volunteer adjutant largely in the hope that he could continue to be "king of all he surveyed." "As a subaltern," he confessed, "I was never what may be called a 'Headquarters' officer'; to be frank, I loathed Headquarters, not because I disliked the officers there, but because I had no show of my own." [4] But he discovered, as had Wilkinson, that work with the volunteers (or in Fuller's case, the territorials) helped to breed fresh ideas and offered challenging opportunities for experimentation. He began seriously to study war, and because he had long nourished a desire for self-expression he began also to publish his views on military training, discipline, and tactics. [5]

Fuller's early writings were based on his experience with the territorials and treat of technical problems that he faced as adjutant. Some of his suggestions, like schemes for overcoming friction in mobilization and simulating combat conditions on the training ground, were the product of his

[4] Fuller, *Memoirs*, pp. 19, 20; *Last of the Gentlemen's Wars*, p. 147.
[5] See Fuller, *Hints on Training Territorial Infantry* (Aldershot, 1911); *Training Soldiers for War* (London, 1914); "The Mobilization of a Territorial Infantry Battalion," *Army Review*, V (July, 1913), 156–86; "The Three Flag System of Instructing Infantry in Fire Tactics," *ibid.*, VI (January, 1914), 119–22; "Notes on the Entrainment of Troops to and from Manoeuvres," *ibid.*, VII (July, 1914), 184–213; "The Procedure of the Infantry Attack: A Synthesis from a Psychological Standpoint, *R.U.S.I. Journal*, LVIII (January, 1914), 63–84; and "The Tactics of Penetration: A Counterblast to German Numerical Superiority," *ibid.*, LIX (November, 1914), 379–89.

own imagination and great practical sense, but for insight into the *moral* training of soldiers Fuller turned to the discoveries of modern psychology. From the writings of men like the French physician and sociologist, Gustave Le Bon, he tried to learn something about habit, the power of suggestion, and the behavior of individuals and of crowds that could be applied to the education of the soldier. "An army," he contended, "is still a crowd, though a highly organized one. It is governed by the same laws . . . and under the stress of war is ever tending to revert to its crowd form. Our object in peace is so to train it that this reversion will become extremely slow." There was more to military training than musketry, drill, and first-class certificates: confidence, discipline, and initiative must also be developed, the fundamental virtues of honor, patriotism, *esprit de corps,* comradeship and duty as well as individual moral qualities systematically cultivated. In other words training "is as much a science as an art," and as such the officer must utilize the behavioral sciences for the wider education of the soldier.[6]

Because war was a science, Fuller asserted that it was governed by fundamental principles that could be discovered through the intelligent study of military history. Turning to the *Correspondence of Napoleon,* Fuller deduced certain fundamental principles which had guided Napoleon and might have universal application. These were:

. . . the principle of the Objective—the true objective being that point at which the enemy may be most decisively defeated; generally this point is to be found along the line of least resistance. The principle of Mass—that is, concentration of strength and effort at the decisive point. The principle of the Offensive, and the principles of Security, Surprise, and Movement (i.e., rapidity).

These principles could not be applied separately, nor were they valid except when considered in relation to conditions of time, space, ground, weather, moral, and supply; but they did, in Fuller's estimation, comprise the essential first step in the formulation of a doctrine of war.[7] The experiences of 1914–18

[6] Fuller, *Training Soldiers for War,* pp. v, 19, 47–86 *passim.* This book was written in 1912–13 and published a few months after war broke out in 1914.
[7] *Ibid.,* pp. 41–43; *The Foundations of the Science of War* (London, 1926), p. 14.

would enable him to test them against modern conditions, and in a "slightly modified" form they would one day creep into the *Field Service Regulations* and stand upright within his own theoretical system.

Many of the ideas expressed by Fuller before the war did in fact form the embryo of his theories. Those familiar with the later writings of this prolific soldier, however, might raise an eyebrow at some of his statements. Obviously influenced by French military writers of the school of Ardant du Picq and Colonel de Grandmaison, Fuller maintained that the will to win was the soul of war: *"to will success* is all but equivalent to victory." Fuller's comments on the offensive spirit smack strongly of the future Marshal Foch, whom he later ridiculed. Even on the defensive, Fuller insisted, "we should teach the men that it is with offensively trained troops that we can defend ourselves the best; for we must never leave a stone unturned to cultivate an offensive spirit." Men were more than "mobile tripods to rest rifles on." The value of the individual soldier was to be found in his will and intellect. "We must teach . . . that the bayonet is the symbol of victory," Fuller asserted, and he supported this theory by pointing to the battle of Liao-yang (1904), where "not one position was captured by the Japanese by fire alone." Fuller later explained that the Japanese bayonet attacks were not assaults at all "but merely occupations of positions from which the enemy had retired or had been driven out by shell fire," but this was not the message he originally conveyed.[8]

When his appointment as adjutant expired in 1912 Fuller set his sights on the Staff College, primarily, he says in his *Memoirs,* to escape routine duty with the regiment. As soon as war was declared he reported to the embarkation commandant at Southampton where, thanks to an earlier article on the entrainment of troops, he was appointed deputy assistant director of railway transport. Transferred in December to the headquarters of the Second Army, Central Force, at Tunbridge Wells, he spent the next seven months itching to get overseas and seeking relief from office routine by writing a manuscript about the training of the new armies during the

[8] Fuller, *Training Soldiers for War,* pp. viii, 94, 118–21; *War and Western Civilization 1823–1932: A Study of War as a Political Instrument and the Expression of Mass Democracy* (London, 1932), pp. 154–64, 179.

war against Napoleon. This work, which he published separately in two volumes after the war,[9] convinced Fuller "that all the mistakes which had been made during the Napoleonic invasion threat were being repeated in detail." It also contributed to his insight into problems of training and discipline, for it is inconceivable that Fuller would have failed himself to observe the spirit of Moore's system. Based on "a close and shrewd study of history," this system was "as fresh" in 1915 as it had been over a century before; and the lectures Fuller gave to the men of the newly formed tank corps on discipline, *moral,* leadership and *esprit de corps* probably owed much to the idle hours at headquarters Second Army, where in desperation he probed the secrets of Moore's success.[10]

In July, 1915, Fuller joined the staff of the VIIth Corps, Third Army, as understudy to the G.S.O.2 (operations), in which capacity he became intimately acquainted with the problems peculiar to trench warfare. In September he completed "The Principles of War with Reference to the Campaigns of 1914–1915," which was published anonymously in the *Journal of the Royal United Service Institution.* To the original six principles expounded in his pre-war writings, Fuller now added two more—economy of force and co-operation; and to the six conditions governing the use of these principles he added three new ones—numbers, communication, and armament, each of which had grown increasingly important in the repeated attempts to break the trench deadlock. Applying these principles to the business at hand, Fuller concluded that the correct plan of action should be:

> To advance against the enemy's main force (objective), with the intention of destroying it (offensive), with the greatest numbers possible (mass and economy of force), with the least friction (co-operation), and in the shortest possible time (movement), so that we may take him unawares (surprise), without undue risks to ourselves (security).

Fuller agreed with Repington that the main objective was the German army in France. "We cannot play fast and loose with the principles of war, and by doing so we have already reaped the punishment we deserved." Three-hundred-thousand more

---

[9] Fuller, *British Light Infantry in the Eighteenth Century* (London, 1925); *Sir John Moore's System of Training* (London, 1924).
[10] *Ibid.,* pp. 114, 218–23; *Memoirs,* pp. 48, 90–91.

soldiers in France, he argued, would have turned the ill-fated Loos offensive into a decisive victory; sea power, from the trenches in France, looked like "a great seducer from the principles of war." [11]

Fuller had not yet witnessed a major battle, so it is perhaps natural that in 1915 he still adhered to the conventional tactical formations. Infantry, he wrote, should attack in a series of single-rank lines which, "wave after wave, each . . . passing the other yet preparing the way for the next, continue until the last trench of the enemy's first line system is pierced." The "maintenance of alignment is of the first importance." When these tactics produced sixty-thousand British casualties during the first day of the great Somme offensive in July, 1916, Fuller quickly became convinced that linear formations "were not suitable to rifle warfare." He now advocated single-file formations—files of ten men, each a pace or two behind the other—which gave the leader more immediate control and at the same time provided a less vulnerable target. [12]

After "a very happy six months" Fuller left VIIth Corps headquarters to help establish the Third Army School for the instruction of officers. He owed this appointment apparently to the small book on training he had written as a territorial adjutant. Later, after he had joined the staff of the 37th Division, he organized the first Commanding Officers Conference. This was almost a one-man operation: Fuller made all of the arrangements, worked out a course of instruction, and gave most of the lectures (two a day for a week) on subjects such as the principles of war, holding a defensive line, and battle drill. After five successful courses the Senior Officers' Course was organized on a permanent basis and transferred to Aldershot, where it continued to thrive after the war as the Senior Officers' School. [13]

These experiences encouraged Fuller to continue his independent studies. He submitted another article, entitled "The

[11] Fuller, "The Principles of War, with Reference to the Campaigns of 1914–1915," *R.U.S.I. Journal,* LXI (February, 1916), 3–5, 10.

[12] *Ibid.,* pp. 34–36; *Memoirs,* pp. 82, 152. "Battalions attacked in four or eight waves, not more than a hundred yards apart, the men in each almost shoulder to shoulder, in a symmetrical well-dressed alignment, and taught to advance steadily upright at a slow walk with their rifles held aslant in front of them, bayonets upwards" (Liddell Hart, *A History of the World War 1914–1918* [London, 1934], p. 315).

[13] Fuller, *Memoirs,* pp. 56–57, 61–62.

Principles of Defence as Applied to Trench Warfare," which was not published because the War Office thought that it might be of value to the enemy. In this study Fuller attempted to devise a rational scheme to replace the myriad of fire and communication trenches (on the six-mile front occupied by the VIIth Corps alone he had identified over 500 separate trenches) that meandered some four- to five-hundred miles from Switzerland to the Belgian coast without any apparent purpose, general plan, or unity of design. Applying his principles of war to the construction of trenches, Fuller proposed a system that would reduce the numbers required for protective duties to an absolute minimum and thus free more manpower for offensive action; he suggested measures by which greater security might be achieved, and he urged a single-system to replace the patchwork that represented "an endless string of changing ideas . . . and a colossal wastage in personnel and material."

In one word, *organise*. Look upon the trenches as defended barracks, to and from which units will come and go without altering rules, structure or accommodation; and not as mere camping-ground where each man selects his own pitch. This will lead to co-operation in its highest sense, for not only will all know what they have to do, but all will know that, as they are part of one system, those on their flanks will equally know it, and that all will act together accordingly on one plan and not on a hundred and one, irrespective of reliefs, irrespective of changes.[14]

But Fuller soon switched his attention to a revolutionary new weapon designed to puncture the German defense lines. In December, 1916, he left Third Army headquarters—which he had joined in September after the Somme offensive had destroyed the 37th Division—to become senior general staff officer at the headquarters of the heavy branch of the machine gun corps, as the future tank corps was then known. Once again Fuller's initial reaction to a new situation bordered on the conventional: when he arrived at his new post at Bermicourt he was "caustically sceptical" about the possibilities of tanks, which he regarded as "an adjunct to the infantry and not an arm of their own." Not until after he had had some ex-

14 Excerpts from this still-born article are published in *ibid.*, pp. 62–69.

perience could Fuller appreciate the potential of the new weapon.[15]

There is a graphic description of Fuller as he appeared to other members of the tank corps headquarters.

A little man, with a bald head, and a sharp face and a nose of a Napoleonic cast, his general appearance, stature, and feature earning him the title of Boney. He stood out at once as a totally unconventional soldier, prolific in ideas, fluent in expression, at daggers drawn with received opinion, authority, and tradition. In the mess his attacks on the red-tabbed hierarchy were viewed in the spirit of a rat hunt; a spirit he responded to with much vivacity, and no little wit. But he could talk amusingly and paradoxically on any subject. His specialities were Eastern religions, about which he could be bewildering, spiritualism, occultism, military history and the theory of war. His knowledge of literature was wide enough to enable him to condemn most of what was good; on the other hand he was a great reader of Shakespeare, whom he admired and understood from an angle of his own, and had dabbled in philosophy, of which he could handle a few elementary statements to the complete confounding and obfuscation of the mess. He was an inexhaustible writer, and from his office issued reams on reams about training, plans of campaign, organisation, and schemes for the use of tanks. He was an invaluable element both from a military and social point of view, but his brains would have been better utilised at G.H.Q. galvanising that conservative centre with advanced ideas.

Nothing disturbed him or put him out of countenance. He never took the military view that minor mistakes were cardinal sins and capital offenses, but retained a sense of proportion, put irrelevant things in their place, and dismissed trivialities. He was neither an administrator nor probably a good commander, but just what a staff officer ought to be, evolving sound ideas and leaving their execution to others. He was well up in Napoleonic lore, and had all the maxims at his finger ends.[16]

Once familiar with conditions in the tank corps, Fuller "metaphorically burnt *The King's Regulations*" and set about training the men, instructing the officers, and devising schemes for the new force to achieve maximum tactical power. He wrote the first manual, "Training Note No. 16," and

[15] Lieutenant General Sir G. le Q. Martel, as quoted in Liddell Hart, *The Tanks*, I, 94; Liddell Hart to J. R. Lester, March 21, 1942 (Liddell Hart Papers).
[16] As quoted in Liddell Hart, *The Tanks*, I, 120–21.

most of the subsequent notes on tank training and tactics; he examined all available information after each battle to test his theories, which he then recast in a series of brilliant and far-sighted papers on the mechanics of tank warfare; finally he produced his revolutionary "Plan 1919," a prophetic paper that embodied many of the concepts later developed in the German blitzkrieg. By the end of the war Fuller had been brought back to the War Office, where he was in a strong position to give material assistance to the tank corps in France and at the same time win powerful friends for his proposed plan of attack in 1919.[17]

Fuller remained within "the tower of Babel," as he called the War Office, until 1922. Throughout these four "chaotic" years he fought to preserve the tank corps and waged an imaginative war upon red tape and the Treasury. Here indeed was a man with a mission: in the face of public apathy, hasty demobilization, prejudice, and vested interests he labored to convince public opinion and the War Office alike of the need to create a new model army based upon mechanization. He lectured, he wrote, he neglected no opportunity to preach the gospel, but unlike St. Paul, who made a point of becoming "all things to all men" for the sake of the good word, this modern apostle developed a quite different technique. Christ, he reminded his friends,

taught in parables [yet] how many Christians are there today, and how many have cut each others' throats concerning their meaning. Nothing could be more intelligible than "sell all and give to the poor"—look at Russia. I have never attempted to make an appeal to the people in order to gain a following. It amuses me to state what I believe to be true, but whether my audience under-

[17] Fuller's tactical studies in 1917–18 include "Projected Bases for the Tactical Employment of Tanks in 1918" (June, 1917), "Minor Tank and Infantry Operations against Strong Points" (August, 1917), "Tank Raids" (August, 1917), "Tank and Infantry Operations without Methodical Artillery Preparation" (November, 1917), "Training in Co-operation between Infantry and Tanks" (December, 1917), "Anti-Tank Defence" (December, 1917), "Defensive and Offensive Use of Tanks" (January, 1918), "Tank Operations Decisive and Preparatory, 1918–1919" (January, 1918), and of course "Plan 1919," which appeared originally as "The Tactics of the Attack as Affected by the Speed and Circuit of the Medium D Tank" (May, 1918). Excerpts from most of these papers are contained in Fuller, *Memoirs*, pp. 122–30, 153–54, 172–74, 194–96, 227–32, 235–37, 322–36.

stands or not I do not much care, because truth in the end wins through.[18]

At the risk of appearing "a vulgar self-advertizing fellow" and cultivating enemies well intrenched in high places, Fuller became an intellectual bully to help explode "deep-rooted absurdities." In 1919, much to the discomfort of his superiors, he won the Gold Medal Prize essay awarded by the Royal United Service Institution for his entry entitled "The Application of Recent Developments in Mechanics and Other Scientific Knowledge to Preparation and Training for Future War on Land"; and in 1921 he violated custom by competing for a similar prize for the best essay on "Future Naval Tactics." Uncertain whether to refer to a ship as "it" or "she," he nonetheless managed to conceal the fact that his entry did not come from the pen of a sailor. The naval authorities were astounded when the winner was identified as an army colonel and outraged when they learned that Fuller had actually written his article over a weekend and submitted it as a leg-pull. He received the money award, but his was the only prize essay never published in the *Journal*.[19]

In 1922 Fuller was named chief instructor at the Staff College. "After four years at the War Office it was a delight to get away from its hair-splitting arguments, and once again to be free from the everlasting financial quibblings of men who no more understood the needs of the soldier than they did the ways of the ornithorhynchus." Given free rein by the commandant, Major General (later General) Sir Edmund Ironside, Fuller worked to transform the Staff College, which he claimed was being run like a school, into a university. "The

[18] Fuller to Liddell Hart, March 27, 1923 (Liddell Hart Papers).

[19] Fuller, *Memoirs*, pp. 391–94; Lieutenant General Sir Giffard Martel, *An Outspoken Soldier: His Views and Memoirs* (London, 1949), pp. 35–36. Fuller's prize essay, "The Application of Recent Developments in Mechanics and Other Scientific Knowledge to Preparation and Training for Future War on Land," was published in the *R.U.S.I. Journal*, LXV (1920), 239–74. The writer was unable to consult the issue of *Naval Review* (1922) containing Fuller's essay entitled "What Changes Are Suggested in Naval Construction and Tactics as a Result of (*a*) The Experiences of the War? (*b*) The Development of Submarine and Aerial Warfare in the Future?" His basic views on naval warfare probably are those expressed in "The Purpose and Nature of a Fleet," *Nineteenth Century*, XC (1921), 699–714.

ideal I intend to aim at," he announced on the occasion of his first lecture,

is that we shall teach each other; first, because we all have a vast amount of war experience behind us, and secondly, because . . . it is only through free criticism of each other's ideas that truth can be thrashed out. Mere swallowing of either food or opinions does not of necessity carry with it digestion, and without digestion swallowing is but labour lost and food wasted . . . until you learn how to teach yourselves, you will never be taught by others.[20]

Fuller was a born teacher. His lectures occasionally may have overshot their mark, but he was an articulate, witty, enthusiastic, and colorful performer, and he packed more original thought into his teaching than any of his predecessors, including Henderson. He was also highly unorthodox: on one occasion, when an exceptionally bright officer applied for entrance to the Staff College, Fuller awarded him a perfect score of 1,000 on his examination and explained to the bewildered authorities that, on second thought, he ought to have graded the paper 2,000 inasmuch as the answer was 100 per cent better than he himself could have done on his own questions.[21]

The years spent at the War Office and the Staff College represent the most creative period in the development of Fuller's military thought. His theories on mechanization had yet to be refined, but in the early 1920's his concept of armored warfare and his philosophy of war had both emerged in visible form. And it was also at the Staff College that Fuller made his most significant contribution to the study of the science of war.

From the first Fuller had contended that war was both a science and an art—a science in that it comprised certain elements governed by fixed laws or principles, and an art when it came to applying these principles to the fluctuating conditions that prevailed in the field. He also contended that

[20] Fuller, *Memoirs*, pp. 416, 419–20.
[21] Fuller to Liddell Hart, May 20, 1943 (Liddell Hart Papers). The young officer was (later) Major General Eric Dorman-Smith, deputy chief of the general staff, Middle East, who was credited by his commander in chief "for the tactical and organisational ideas that saved Egypt at First Alamein: the fluid, mobile defence . . . the concentration of the armour," etc. See the sketch in Correlli Barnett, *The Desert Generals* (London, 1960), pp. 305–9.

war must be investigated as a science "before, as an art, its forces can be correctly expended." [22] In 1912 he had endeavored to apply the techniques of the behavioral sciences to military training and also to define the fundamental principles of war. In France a few years later he had occasion to test these principles empirically, which led to the inclusion of two new principles. In 1918 his article, "The Principles of War with Reference to the Campaigns of 1914–15," was used as a text in the Commanding Officers' School in Aldershot, and in 1921 Fuller's principles became official when they were incorporated into the new edition of the *Field Service Regulations*.[23] He revised these principles again after the war.

In his Gold Medal essay for 1919, which won first prize, Fuller asserted that military history to be meaningful must be supplemented by a knowledge of the physical and moral sciences. Instead of following the "old unscientific methods of 1914," when soldiers had wrangled about rifle trajectories and counted strength in bayonets and sabers, Britain must develop a new model army based upon tanks and the cross-country tracked vehicle. What was needed was fighting power, not numbers of men, and Fuller looked to the day when the present army, "a monster carrying with it all kinds of rudimentary organs and ever sprouting new horns," was replaced by a revolutionary organization "of educated men, of formidable weapons and of astonishing movement, an army led by scientists and fought by mechanics—a true machine of war." And to serve as the nerve center of this new model army Fuller proposed the creation of a ministry of defense embodying representatives from all of the services and including "thinking sections" staffed with researchers and designers.[24]

His next step in expounding the science of war was a polemic intended primarily for civilians. In a book hastily compiled from previous writings (the basic manuscript was written in less than a month, working only an hour or two in the evenings and during weekends) and described by the author himself as a potboiler,[25] Fuller assailed the conven-

[22] Fuller, *Foundations of the Science of War*, p. 324.

[23] *Ibid.*, pp. 13–14; Fuller, *Memoirs*, pp. 388–89; Fuller to Liddell Hart, April 11, 1949 (Liddell Hart Papers).

[24] Fuller, "The Application of Recent Developments in Mechanics and Other Scientific Knowledge to Preparation and Training for Future War on Land," pp. 240–41, 252–56, 263.

[25] Fuller to Liddell Hart, September 15, 1922; March 27, 1923 (Liddell Hart Papers).

tional mentality responsible for the tragic miscalculations during the First World War and the failure rationally to appraise the probable conditions of the next. Machine power, he stressed with forceful repetition, and not manpower wins wars; and no war is truly won if in the process it destroys so much life and property that no basis remains for a durable peace. The old notion of winning wars by destroying the enemy must yield to a new military ideal, "the imposition of will at the least possible general loss"; and this could be accomplished through the scientific use of those weapons devised to master the conditions of trench warfare—gas, the airplane, and the tank. Because the next war was apt to be directed against civilians as much as the army, because "national reform" must precede military reform, the civilian must realize that gas was a humane weapon that could demoralize without necessarily killing, that command of the air offered new means of waging war, and that the tank would make the foot soldier obsolete. It was imperative that the nation learn to think seriously about war and study military problems logically according to the facts. And this, Fuller insisted, was impossible as long as "our minds are shackled by our sentiments or stamped by our emotions." [26]

The brazen tone of *The Reformation of War* is perhaps to be expected of any book written, as this was, "in about a dozen hotels each with a jazzband," but it was adopted deliberately in order to stir up controversy and focus attention on the need for a new model army. Fuller himself was not wholly satisfied with the volume, but it did accomplish one important objective: it created sufficient interest to induce his publisher to accept a much more profound and instructive, yet abstruse and sophisticated manuscript in which Fuller explored the foundations of the science of war. [27]

One reason why Fuller was dissatisfied with *The Reformation of War* was that it appeared to destroy more than it created: he had exposed the fallacies of the military scholastics but had not succeeded in establishing an enduring basis for reform. In contrast his next book, *The Foundations of the Science of War*, represents an ambitious attempt to

[26] Fuller, *The Reformation of War* (London, 1923), pp. ix, xiii, xv, 101–19, 141–49, 168, 229.

[27] Fuller to Liddell Hart, September 15, 1922; March 27, 1923 (Liddell Hart Papers).

develop some method by which certain knowledge of war could be systematically acquired. Fuller sought to replace the authority of a previous epoch with an authoritative method for arriving at truth; he discovered—or at least thought that he had discovered—fundamental laws that could be applied universally; and he believed that it was possible to establish a foundation of knowledge "so universal that it may be considered axiomatic to knowledge in all its forms." [28]

The essential first step in laying the foundations for a science of war was to achieve agreement on method, to devise some "workable piece of mental machinery which will enable the student of war to sort out military values." If war was a science, as Fuller believed, then truth could be discovered by observing the methods of science based upon analysis, synthesis, and hypothesis. And by applying the scientific method to the study of war, rational man might reasonably expect to determine the conditions and therefore the requirements of war in the future.[29]

Fuller based his system upon "the threefold order." Obviously influenced by the German idealistic philosophers, principally Hegel, Fuller maintained that all knowledge was relational in character and based upon the relationship or differences between things. In other words knowledge represented a threefold order comprising the person, the object, and the relationship between the two. Like Hegel, Fuller saw the universe and everything in it as an intricate pattern of innumerable triads: earth, water, and air; solids, liquids, and gases; mind, body, and soul, and so on. While he did not claim that the threefold order was the *only* system, he did insist upon the necessity for *some* system to "discover the true meaning of events and experiences," and the threefold order offered "the key to the understanding of all things"—including war.[30]

Fuller proceeded to analyze man to discover universal principles governing the human element in war. Man too, he discovered, is organized on a threefold order. The body possesses *structure*, in which the skeleton provides the stable base, the muscles give power of action, and the ligaments link the two in close co-operation. The body likewise possesses

---

[28] Fuller, *Foundations of the Science of War*, p. 48.
[29] *Ibid.*, pp. 33–47, 324.
[30] *Ibid.*, pp. 48–54.

control, in which the senses provide the stable base, the brain furnishes power of action, and the nerves make possible co-operation. Finally the body possesses *maintenance,* in which the stomach serves as the stable base, the repair organs give power of action, and the blood links the stomach to all parts of the body in close co-operation.[31]

Assuming all knowledge to be based upon "the universal inference of a threefold order," Fuller treated human society as an extension of the organization, nature, and activity of man "in a higher and more complex form." Thus the military instrument, representing the army, navy, and air force, is built upon the same structural lines as the human organism, namely stability, activity, and co-operation. When two un-armed men fight, Fuller reflected, each "protects himself with one arm and hits out with the other." Similarly the military commander fights with two forces—a stable force to resist pressure, and an active force to provide striking power. The two combined "constitute the foundations of tactical power," and the threefold order is complete with the introduction of a mobile arm. In the case of man this is supplied by footwork; with armies it was provided traditionally by cavalry and, more recently, by the tank. The 1914–18 war, according to Fuller, represents a period of "tactical mediocrity" because of the immobility of artillery, the defensive strength of infantry, and the offensive weakness of cavalry.[32]

Like the human body, the military instrument also pos-sessed maintenance and control. By *maintenance* Fuller meant the "link between fighting force and national power" based upon a "correlation between military demand and national supply." This would involve the services of supply, repair, and transportation. By *control* he had in mind both the machinery necessary for efficient information, decision, and communication within each of the fighting services and, on a higher level, the establishment of an advisory council to consider basic questions of national or imperial defense. Fuller would vest the power of control in one man, a generalissimo, for only in this way did he believe it possible to attain complete unity of command.[33] His reasoning in this instance provides a clue to his future political deviation.

[31] *Ibid.,* pp. 55–62.
[32] *Ibid.,* pp. 81–85, 171.
[33] *Ibid.,* pp. 85–92.

Fuller next considered the threefold nature of war itself. In a penetrating chapter on its mental sphere he argued that the decisive point in modern war is not the body of the hostile army or nation so much as the will of the enemy commander. Mental destruction, he contended, was more effective than physical destruction. Fuller divided the physical sphere of war into three elements—movement, weapons, and protection— and his discussion of the physical aspect was devoted largely to the strategical and tactical formations best calculated to unite these elements. To restore the balance to tactics, Fuller reasoned that "artillery must be endowed with a higher power of movement. Infantry must be endowed with higher offensive power, and cavalry must be more highly protected." [34] In brief, the obvious solution lay in the development of armored formations.

Fuller also raised the question whether there was any general law of causation as true of war as of the physical sciences. From Herbert Spencer's *First Principles* came the answer—one supreme law, the economy of force. This necessitated a revision of Fuller's original principles to comply with this basic law,[35] but the details need not concern us here. The point is that Fuller by 1925 already had improved upon his own principles as they had appeared in the 1924 edition of *Field Service Regulations*.

This brief and oversimplified résumé, however inadequate, of Fuller's complex system is sufficient to introduce a new element to British military thought. Previously, soldiers who wished to understand the course of modern war had looked to history for guidance, and while writers such as Henderson frequently spoke of a "science of war" the method they used was historical rather than scientific. But not Fuller. He studied the science of war with the tools of science, and if his treatise contains frequent historical references it is because military history provided helpful illustrations and at the same time offered empirical proof of a sort. Fuller utilized military history to teach, but he himself learned by other methods.

Fuller's system is not beyond criticism. Not every manifestation of his threefold order can be tested empirically, and there is a lingering suspicion that what he has done on occasion is to elevate certain predilections into metaphysical prin-

---

[34] *Ibid.*, pp. 93–174.
[35] *Ibid.*, pp. 16, 195–207, 324–27.

ciples. The reader is not always sure what is meant by various terms and his logic at times is difficult to follow. One can imagine how the conventional soldier received the book, if ever he bothered to read it. (One of Fuller's most constant critics confessed "I have not read Fuller's book! And I don't expect I ever shall. It would only annoy me." [36]) Some undoubtedly dismissed it as a presumptuous bit of mysticism and nonsense; others may have taken it literally; and probably most who made an effort to read it failed to appreciate what Fuller was really saying. In his *Memoirs* Fuller records that the book provoked personal abuse ("he who can, does; he who cannot, teaches") rather than constructive criticisms.[37]

Fuller did not claim infallibility for his particular system; he only insisted upon the practical necessity for devising some method or system for the study of war. In a scientific age it seemed imperative that armies should be organized and constructed along scientific lines. Most of the soldiers in 1914 had failed altogether to anticipate the nature and conditions of the First World War—even a thoughtful student such as Wilkinson and a clever critic like Repington had been baffled by the turn of events. Convinced that a new epoch of war had arrived, Fuller wished to find some method for extracting what was valuable and instructive from experience and also for examining and testing new theories and weapons.

Fuller's main thesis is valid therefore with or without the threefold order, which is not a necessary condition for the acceptance of either his general principles or his case that war must be treated as a science. All that he wanted really was to force soldiers to think in terms of the present and future as well as the past. The war had introduced new weapons, chief among which were the tank, airplane, and poison gas, and the question of the day was whether these weapons were to be tied to the armies of 1914–18 and used as they had been during the war, or whether they were to provide the means with which to change the very nature of armies and give a new dimension to warfare. Fuller was especially interested in what happened to the tank: would it continue to serve as an

[36] Lieutenant General (later Field Marshal) Sir Archibald Montgomery-Massingberd to Captain B. H. Liddell Hart, April 27, 1926 (Liddell Hart Papers).

[37] Liddell Hart to Lieutenant Colonel Sir Cuthbert Headlam (editor of *Army Quarterly*), April 7, 1926 (Liddell Hart Papers); Fuller, *Memoirs*, p. 458.

infantry support weapon, or could it be developed to provide a radically new and independent arm, the armored division. Applying his system to the study of this problem, Fuller offered perhaps his most original contribution to the development of military thought.

During the war Fuller's job had been to devise tactics, establish the general procedure of attack, and to analyze recent operations where tanks had been employed. But unlike most soldiers in France, Fuller—to borrow a phrase from Repington—did not let the war transcend "all limits of thought, imagination, and reason," all of which are present to a striking degree in his novel "Plan 1919." Fuller's plan was aimed at the moral deterioration of the German high command. First the Germans must be persuaded to mass reserves in a given sector, which could be done easily enough through visible preparations for another great offensive. Then, operating on a frontage of ninety miles, Fuller suggested a surprise stroke of medium tanks instead of the usual frontal assault based on a preponderance of material. This "Disorganizing Force" would puncture the German front lines and head straight for the respective army, corps, and divisional headquarters located some twenty miles to the rear. In a modern army disorganization spells paralysis, and with the enemy headquarters captured or dispersed and the reserves disorganized, the front-line troops would become confused and susceptible to panic. He would then launch a carefully mounted tank, infantry, and artillery attack against the enemy lines on a frontage of fifty miles, followed by a pursuit force of medium tanks and infantry carried in trucks. Fuller calculated that roughly five thousand heavy and medium tanks would be required for the disorganizing, breaking, and pursuing forces, and he would have the Royal Air Force provide tactical assistance and reconnaissance and also to drop several hundred tons of explosives upon the German western G.H.Q.: "that, at least, will neutralize clear thinking." [38] The war ended before this revolutionary plan to disorganize the enemy's command before assaulting his front could be put into effect, but it did win acceptance in high quarters and of course it provided the basis for Fuller's later theories on mechanized warfare.

[38] Plan 1919 is printed in Fuller, *Memoirs*, pp. 322–36, and is condensed in Fuller, *On Future Warfare* (London, 1928), pp. 83–105.

While at the War Office Fuller campaigned vigorously on behalf of the tank corps. In collaboration with a colleague he produced *Weekly Tank Notes,* a propaganda leaflet that ran to 78 numbers, attained a circulation of better than four hundred, and ultimately, at the suggestion of Winston Churchill, the secretary of state for war, was printed in four quarterly volumes "for confidential use." Even His Majesty expressed an interest in receiving an "undiluted copy" each week.[39]

Fuller also wrote on behalf of those outside the "400 Club." In 1919 he refashioned many of his articles for the *Weekly Tank Notes* into a volume entitled *Tanks in the Great War.* The tank, he insisted,

has come not only to stay, but to revolutionize, and I for one . . . do not for a minute doubt that my wildest dreams about its future will not only be realised but surpassed, and that from its clumsy endeavours in the Great War will arise a completely new direction in the art of warfare itself.

At no time during the war, Fuller asserted, had a "well-planned extensive tank attack . . . failed"; once a cross-country tractor was developed to maintain communications, the possibilities of mechanized forces would become un-limited.[40] In his Gold Medal essay for 1919 he outlined the steps to be taken in the evolution of an all-mechanized army, and the following year he wrote at length upon the role of cavalry during the immediate years of transition ahead. In the most hidebound military organ of its day, *The Cavalry Journal,* Fuller proclaimed to a hostile audience that the cavalry cycle that had begun in the sixteenth century was nearly over, and that "either the Cavalryman had to be rendered impervious to bullets or a new weapon had to be invented which would prevent bullets being thrown against him." Fuller conceded that until the tank was perfected there still was a place for the horse, but never again, he argued, could cavalry expect to deliver the knockout blow in a major battle and it might soon find itself replaced by the airplane as a means of reconnaissance. Fast disappearing in the com-mercial world, he could see no valid reason why the horse

[39] Fuller, *Memoirs,* pp. 343–45.
[40] Fuller, *Tanks in the Great War 1914–1918* (London, 1920), pp. xvii–xix, 79–80, 177.

should expect to find refuge in the military establishment. "The horse," Fuller warned, "is doomed; it is no longer an argument of fire-arms *versus* the *arme blanche*, but of a change in the element of movement itself." Cavalry leaders had a choice: either they could adapt the cavalry "idea" of annihilating the enemy to the new equipment or else "they may become the interesting counterparts of the Yeoman of the Guard." Fuller urged his readers to rejuvenate the mounted arm by making the best of mechanization. Remember, he cautioned, "to establish a new invention is like establishing a new religion—it usually demands the conversion or destruction of an entire priesthood." [41]

The cavalry hit back with the thunder and fury of old. The Palestine campaign of 1917 proved, it was contended, that the *arme blanche* was superior even to dismounted attacks. Another writer asserted that battles were largely a matter of chance, and that therefore much of Fuller's historical argument "must apparently be characterized as invalid." Experience "will generally temper criticism." A third (who evidently was not familiar with Fuller's other writings) claimed that Fuller overlooked "the all-important human element" and fixed his thoughts on the machine rather than the man who works it, and still another wrote that the cost of keeping things like tanks and airplanes up to date "would be prohibitive." Replace the horse with a tank?—Why, "you might as well attempt to replace our railway system by lines of airships.[42]

For the next decade Fuller advanced his theories on mechanization in the lecture hall and service journals. Sometimes he tailored his arguments to the special interests of the audience. In the *Journal of the Royal Artillery*, for instance, he stressed his belief that artillery would be "the principal arm of the future"—that is, artillery "mechanically-

[41] Fuller, "Application of Recent Developments in Mechanics and Other Scientific Knowledge to Preparation and Training for Future War on Land," p. 263; "The Influence of Tanks on Cavalry Tactics (A Study in the Evolution of Mobility in Warfare)," *Cavalry Journal*, X (1920), 128–30, 313, 320–23, 526, 530.

[42] Lieutenant Colonel R. G. H. Howard-Vyse, "A Defence of the Arme Blanche," *ibid.*, pp. 323–30; Major General W. D. Bird, "Years versus Ideas," *ibid.*, pp. 331–33; Brigadier General G. A. Weir, "Some Critics of Cavalry and the Palestine Campaign," *ibid.*, pp. 531–41; Colonel Commandant Neil Haig, "Substance or Shadow," *R.U.S.I. Journal*, LXVI (1921), 117–19.

propelled" or mounted in tanks.[43] On other occasions he forecast a radically different kind of war.

On Future Warfare, published in 1928, contains the first detailed picture of mechanized war as Fuller envisaged it. Although the work itself is a compilation of previous articles, it stands nevertheless as a bold attempt to bridge the gap between an army that was only partially motorized and completely armored forces. Fuller despaired that the army in his time was in essence the army of 1914—"masses of men who cannot face fire, but who can deliver it in such overwhelming strength that the art of war expires in slaughter and universal ruin." The armies of 1914–18 had been reduced to the position of human cattle who "browsed behind their fences and on occasion snorted and bellowed at each other," yet the only means of avoiding a repetition of this hopeless situation were being discounted or ignored. Artillery and tanks had been drastically cut down, gas was outlawed, and aircraft reduced in number. Such of the new weapons that had been retained were grafted on to the antiquated prewar system in place of being allowed to revolutionize the methods of waging war. Fuller believed that man's inventive powers could be stimulated during peace as well as in war, and he insisted that the army which fails to keep pace with the march of technology "is but a phantom force for war." [44]

The present, he emphasized, was a period of transition during which infantry remained the decisive arm until the army became sufficiently mechanized to overcome the advantages modern weapons gave to the defense. He preached a doctrine of evolution, convinced that in time the tank, by increasing mobility, security, and offensive power must introduce a new era in tactics. Infantry then would be useless on terrain suitable for tanks, armies consequently would become smaller in size and more highly trained, "and conscription will be relegated to the troops of the second line . . . which will occupy the enemy's country after his mechanised forces have been defeated." Thus the army of the future would depend upon quality rather than quantity, superior means of production instead of manpower.

But before the nation could develop the ideal army of the machine age a certain amount of mental retooling was

[43] Fuller, *On Future Warfare,* pp. 366–67.
[44] *Ibid.,* pp. v, 29–30, 91, 96, 106–71.

necessary. "We must," Fuller insisted, "get the present form of war out of our heads" and learn to think in terms of tactical functions rather than the conventional arms. Improved weapons and new inventions should not be distributed to the old-style infantry, artillery, and cavalry, but instead should be used to perform roughly the same functions as these arms had in the wars of Frederick or Napoleon. Tanks, motorized field and medium artillery, and motorized infantry eventually would replace conventional infantry as close combat troops; motorized heavy guns and infantry pioneers would provide the protection formerly offered by artillery; and cavalry (as long as the horse was useful) would join fast, lightly armored tanks, scout tanks, and airplanes to pursue after battle. Wellington, Fuller observed, "did not think in terms of archers, pikemen and knights," and his own contemporaries must likewise cease to think in terms of the old.[45]

Had Fuller at this juncture received official recognition and encouragement for his theories on mechanized war, the subsequent course of history in all probability would have been altered greatly to Britain's advantage. But although Fuller had returned to the War Office in 1926 as military assistant to the C.I.G.S., his unique experience with tanks was never utilized. When the army displayed its new mechanized equipment at Camberley in November, ending the demonstration with an exercise that "embraced all the elements of the blitzkrieg method of attack," Fuller was conspicuously absent. A month earlier he had been sent to India to investigate general questions of defense and military policy. His report, he later confided, "so terrified the C.I.G.S. that he at once got rid of me." In fact there were not many soldiers prepared to accept his assertion that the East could benefit from mechanization as much as the West and that the British forces at home and in India must "agree upon a definite policy of mechanisation which will suit both European and Oriental tactical and administrative requirements." [46]

When he returned from India, Fuller learned that he was to

[45] *Ibid.*, pp. 31, 92, 104, 230, 300–302. See also Fuller, "One Hundred Problems on Mechanization," *Army Quarterly,* XIX (1929–30), 14–25, 256–69.

[46] Liddell Hart, *The Tanks,* I, 242–43; Fuller to Liddell Hart, September 3, 1926; July 26, 1929 (Liddell Hart Papers); Fuller, *Memoirs,* pp. 432–34.

command an experimental force to be assembled on Salisbury Plain during the 1927 maneuvers. His initial joy at the prospects of working once again with tanks soon turned to dismay, however, when he discovered that the so-called mechanized force was really the 7th Infantry Brigade, to which "certain mechanised units were from time to time to be allotted." Moreover, he was not to be relieved of any of his regular duties as garrison commander nor given an adequate staff to assist with the experiment. Convinced that under the circumstances it would be extremely difficult, if not impossible, to sell the experimental force to the rest of the army (to Fuller it was "a first day of Creation show" only he was "not in a position to emulate the Almighty"), Fuller repeatedly requested sufficient staff and time, and, when neither was forthcoming, he resigned from the army. He withdrew his resignation after the C.I.G.S. assured him of his intent to modernize the army, but the command of the experimental mechanized force, reconstituted to include greater numbers of tanks and motorized units as a result of outside pressure,[47] went to an infantryman with "no experience of mechanized troops"—and the foremost apostle of mechanization went to the 2d Division as a staff officer. In 1929 Fuller accepted command of an infantry brigade; in 1930 he was promoted to Major General and placed on half pay, and in 1933 he was retired.

It was just as well that Fuller left the army when he did. For the last few years he had been "very tired of soldiering" and "looking forward to freedom and usefulness" in civil life, and any chance he might have had further to stimulate the development of armored formations was ruined when General Sir Archibald Montgomery-Massingberd became C.I.G.S. in 1933. The latter was lukewarm about tanks ("they cannot be relied on as the backbone of an attack") and had a low boiling point where Fuller's writings were concerned. There were two types of people for whom Montgomery-Massingberd had no stomach—"those who run down and crab every one about them and those who think that because they have read a little Military History, everyone else is an ignoramus." In his view Fuller stood conspicuously near to the top in both categories.[48]

[47] See below, pp. 385–86.
[48] Fuller, *Memoirs,* pp. 434–49; Fuller to Liddell Hart, January 7, 1927;

Although Fuller never again after 1927 was given an opportunity to work with tanks, he persisted in his fight for mechanization. Even his lively little volume of commentary on the official infantry training manual entitled *Lectures on F.S.R. II*, which he wrote in the brief space of two weeks while commanding the 13th Infantry Brigade in 1930, was mostly about tanks—tanks in strategical reconnaissance, amphibious assault craft for landing operations, tanks replacing artillery as an anti-machine gun weapon, tanks escorting infantry, tanks on the North West Frontier, and so on. The effect of the volume was to accentuate the weakness of infantry as a separate arm and to demolish the arguments for cavalry altogether: as Fuller told his officers in the fourth lecture, he could not swallow official doctrine on cavalry in the attack "without grave risks of acute mental indigestion." [49]

When placed on half pay Fuller shifted his attention from the present period of transition to future possibilities. Hitherto he had illustrated arguments for mechanization with mental pictures of future battles that bordered on the lurid and fantastic, but in *Lectures on F.S.R. III*, which appeared in 1932, his concepts were expressed in more concrete and convincing terms. In this, by far his most detailed and methodical book on armored warfare, he worked out to a startling degree the strategy and to an even greater extent the tactics of what, ten years later, was described as the blitzkrieg.

One need not become immersed in technical detail to appreciate Fuller's clairvoyance in his unofficial manual of operations between mechanized forces. He correctly predicted the revival of guerrilla warfare, the comparative decline in the value of conscript armies vis-à-vis highly trained professional forces (less than half of the Polish army, it should be noted, managed even to reach the concentration areas in 1939), and the utilization of a strategy aimed at the destruction of enemy morale, civil as well as military, rather than the physical annihilation that determined the pattern of the offensives of 1914–18. Linear warfare would be replaced by area warfare,

July 29, 1929; August (?), 1929; June 9, 1931; Montgomery-Massingberd to Liddell Hart, April 27, 1926; June 18, 1926 (Liddell Hart Papers).
[49] Fuller to Liddell Hart, June 9, 1931 (Liddell Hart Papers); Fuller, *Lectures on F.S.R. II* (London, 1931), p. 98.

now that the tank made possible the penetration of an intrenched front under conditions that permitted a continuous advance and a widening of the initial breakthrough; the decisive point of attack would be the rear of the enemy's army; battles would become fluid, fronts might be anywhere.

Following the same line of reasoning developed in *The Foundations of the Science of War,* Fuller maintained that the mechanized force of the future must consist of a stable force to resist pressure and an active force to provide striking power. The former would comprise "transportable anti-tank weapons" and would provide a "wagon laager" defended by guns, antitank machine guns, mine fields, and field fortifications both to shelter auxiliary troops and serve as a base for the striking force. The tank force which was to provide the offensive punch would include special reconnaissance tanks, scout tanks, artillery tanks, destroyer tanks, and combat tanks. It would be supplied in part by cross-country tractors and would work in close harmony with aircraft. Because armies in the future would be increasingly exposed to flank and rear attacks, Fuller anticipated that "a reversion is likely to take place to the supply system which held good during the seventeenth and eighteenth centuries—namely, defended field depots with convoys working in between." [50]

From the antitank fortress, which from the standpoint of logistics served as a strategical base and at the same time provided a tactical harbor when the tanks were operating in the immediate neighborhood, the tank force would emerge to give battle in formations sufficiently small and compact for the commanders to lead their troops into action. "Normally, the attack is likely to progress through the following stages":

1) Movement forward from the anti-tank base.
2) Manoeuvring for position, and distracting attacks to force the enemy to change his plan and draw on his reserves.
3) Driving the enemy into a corner from which he will have to fight under a disadvantage, or succumb to petrol starvation.
4) Movement forward of the anti-tank base and the handing over of the conquered area to the army of occupation.

Taking every advantage of the terrain the tanks would occupy

[50] Fuller, *Armoured Warfare: An Annotated Edition of Fifteen Lectures on Operations between Mechanized Forces* (London, 1943), pp. 8–40, 51. This book was first published in 1932 under the title *Lectures on F.S.R. III.*

positions and open fire *"at the halt."* Battles thus "will largely consist in establishing movable strong points from which carefully directed fire can be brought to bear on the enemy's machines, whilst other forces of moving machines drive him towards them." If on the other hand the next war should see the reappearance of trench warfare, then Fuller recommended assault tactics along the suggested lines of "Plan 1919." Should this attack fail, then,

it is certain that offensive operations will be translated to the air, every effort being made to demoralize the enemy by attacking his cities, industrial centres and civil population. Whereas mobile warfare means the attack on armed forces, static warfare can lead to but one end—attack on the civil will.[51]

In stressing the possibilities of armored forces in the attack Fuller did not slight the defense, for in his view the secret in mobile warfare was to be found in the interaction of the two. "Let us never forget," he cautioned, "that a judicious defensive is the foundation of victory," by which he meant that a well-prepared defensive position can either stop or delay the enemy's movement, giving time to organize and mount a counterthrust elsewhere, while in the field the antitank "laager" provided a base for offensive action. Fuller thought of defense in terms of zones rather than lines, with antitank works (mine fields, ditches, and concrete strongholds) supported by "a mobile counterattacking force, generally kept well in rear and towards the most exposed flank, so that should the enemy attempt to turn the works, he can be attacked in flank or rear." Paradoxically, he believed that mobile warfare inevitably would lead to some form of static warfare, wherein movement would be confined by antitank zones behind which a secure air base might be established to carry the offensive to the enemy's industrial centers and the "civil foundations of the contending armies."[52]

Anyone familiar with the German conquest of France in 1940 or the subsequent campaigns in the North African desert can appreciate the accuracy of Fuller's forecast. He saw

[51] *Ibid.,* pp. 94, 101, 115–18. This was confirmed by events in 1940.
[52] *Ibid.,* pp. 120–33. For a concise description of the nature of the next war, written a decade before Hitler's invasion of Poland and in phrases that might have been incorporated without alteration into a history of the 1940 battle of France, see Fuller's article on "Tactics," in the *Encyclopaedia Britannica* (14th ed.; New York, 1929), XXI, 750.

clearly the inherent weakness in static defense positions such as the Maginot Line and urged instead a defense in depth combined with a mechanized reserve: had such a defense system existed at the time of the German offensive, the Panzer divisions most certainly would have been stopped. And Fuller's idea that a mechanized force should consist of both a tank and an antitank wing was amply confirmed by the experience of the *Afrika Korps:* as one of Rommel's staff officers, an authority on panzer tactics, later explained:

To my mind, our victories depended on three factors—the superior quality of our anti-tank guns, our systematic practice of the Principle of *Co-operation-of-Arms*, and . . . our tactical methods. While the British restricted their 3.7 inch anti-aircraft gun . . . to an anti-aircraft role, we employed our 88-mm gun to shoot at tanks as well as aeroplanes. . . . Moving in close touch with our panzers these guns did terrific execution among the British tanks. Moreover, our high-velocity 50mm anti-tank . . . guns always accompanied our tanks in action. Our field artillery, also, was trained to co-operate with the panzers. In short, a German panzer division was a highly flexible formation of all arms, which always relied on artillery in attack or defence. In contrast the British regarded the anti-tank gun as a defensive weapon, and they failed to make adequate use of their powerful field artillery.[53]

The Germans, it was officially noted in the British Eighth Army, refused to be drawn into a tank versus tank battle but instead co-ordinated the action of artillery, tanks, and infantry on the defense and also in "pushing forward a mixed force and then fighting defensively on the ground occupied." Even something resembling the mechanized "laager" became a reality: in the Gazala battles "heavily fortified boxes" such as those at Knightsbridge and El Adem prolonged the British defense once the original position had been penetrated and turned.[54]

Fuller did not anticipate every development in mechanized warfare, of course, nor did all of his predictions materialize. His comments on aircraft suggest that he thought of the plane more as an aid to reconnaissance than a weapon providing close tactical support, although he does speak of the need "to

[53] Major General F. W. von Mellenthin, *Panzer Battles 1939–1945: A Study of the Employment of Armour in the Second World War* (London, 1956), pp. 52–53.
[54] Barnett, *Desert Generals*, pp. 104–5, 147–52; Liddell Hart, *The Tanks*, II, 147–80.

gain local command of the air." Similarly he apparently underrated the role of motorized infantry in a future war. Except for what he termed "field pioneers" to accompany the antitank wing, Fuller asserted that infantry would be of value only in occupying conquered territory or operating in areas "unsuited to tank movement." [55] Perhaps this is to be expected in a manual devoted primarily to operations between mechanized forces (and as such it stressed tactical rather than the strategical aspects of the subject). Tank armor later was strengthened beyond his expectations; reconnaissance tanks and cross-country transport were never developed to the extent he had anticipated; the antitank base was utilized only occasionally (but enough to indicate that the concept was fundamentally sound); and the advent of the dive bomber and the increased ranges of aircraft eventually outdated Fuller's views on the nature of air-ground co-operation and the need to develop a protracted defense within fairly close range of enemy industrial centers; but in most respects Fuller's prognostications accurately foreshadowed technical and tactical developments in World War II. In his Foreword to the 1943 edition Lieutenant Colonel S. L. A. Marshall, the American military critic, claimed that Fuller's original appraisal of mechanized warfare was "nigh faultless" and that only his collateral ideas had to be re-examined, while Fuller himself, in a fresh study of the subject published that same year, concluded that the experiences of the war to date seemed to confirm most of his theories expounded in *Lectures on F.S.R. III*.[56]

Fuller never rewrote his lectures. As long as he could not detect fundamental changes in tactics or equipment it seemed pointless to do so, and it was unlikely that those who had resisted his arguments for mechanization while he remained a serving officer would be won over once he had retired— certainly not with Montgomery-Massingberd at the helm. Besides, his interests had changed. It is characteristic of Fuller that his pen would reflect his military activities.

[55] Fuller, *Armoured Warfare*, pp. 28–29, 95, 107.
[56] S. L. A. Marshall in the Foreword to the American edition of *Armored Warfare* (Harrisburg, Pa., 1943), p. ix; Fuller, *Machine Warfare: An Inquiry into the Influence of Mechanics on the Art of War* (Washington, 1943), pp. 113–204 *passim*. Marshall's own views, which show clearly the influence of Fuller's writings, are found in his book *Blitzkrieg: Armies on Wheels* (Washington, 1943).

Free now to travel and to devote his leisure time to books, Fuller turned to the study of international politics and to what he called "the natural history of war." In 1931 Fuller wrote *The Dragon's Teeth,* a "kind of witches' cauldron" in which he stirred his underlying ideas on war, politics, and economics. The next year *War and Western Civilization* was published. In this book Fuller documented his thesis that war as an expression of mass democracy was becoming increasingly emotional and brutal while at the same time science had "delivered into the hands of the masses more and more deadly means of destruction"—two mighty streams which by 1914 had merged to overwhelm the dikes of traditional warfare. In 1934 appeared *Empire Unity and Defence,* a rational attempt to overhaul the defense machinery of an empire. Much of the present world chaos, Fuller asserted, was due to the fact that the British Empire had become "utterly unstable." Britain must put her own house in order and then, with the solid support of a united empire, work as a neutral third force to establish a strong and stable Europe. The prospects, Fuller conceded, were not encouraging:

not because what I suggest is impossible, but because the states-men who muddle our destiny are incapable. They are old and out of date. . . . They are afraid of the people, and what we call public opinion; consequently, they have no authority. Each crisis startles them, each lull is proclaimed the doorstep to the millen-nium. They argue and they talk; they split hairs and then stick them together again. They are half-measure men who live in a shadow-land of unreality—the Empire cannot be run by wind-bags and ghosts.[57]

Lacking respect for the palsied leadership in the Western democracies, despairing an "insane world where the highest statesmanship depends upon the vocal unthinking masses," [58] convinced that civilization was in an advanced state of decay and that even the race was deteriorating, Fuller felt an acute need for national discipline and new ideals. Although he opposed communism he admired Russia for the pursuit of a revolutionary ideal, and he saw in fascism and the corporate

[57] Fuller, *Empire Unity and Defence* (London, 1934), pp. 293–94. For similar criticisms of British military leadership, see Fuller, *Generalship: Its Diseases and Their Cure: A Study of the Personal Factor in Command* (London, 1933), *passim.*

[58] Fuller, *The Dragon's Teeth: A Study of War and Peace* (London, 1932), p. 181.

state a well-meaning attempt to seek higher economic, political, and cultural freedom through co-ordinated knowledge,
order, and authority.[59] If fascism on the Continent had
assumed "temporary" attitudes that were undesirable, Fuller
believed that British Fascism would develop along constitutional lines. He supported Sir Oswald Mosley, the leader of the
English Fascist movement, and attacked the so-called international conspiracy of the Jews; [60] he talked with Hitler and
Mussolini and was struck by the contrast between the virile
spirit in their countries and the decadent materialism domi-
nating England and France; he scorned the League of Nations
as the eunuch of the French "international harem" and the
pawn of Soviet expansionism; and he predicted that the day
would come when "the Western democratic nations will be
rapidly paralysed, and . . . the decisive war will be waged
between Germany and the U.S.S.R." When it came Armageddon would be a clash between civilizations rather than
nations, with communism emerging as the climax of the
democratic system and fascism constituting the reaction
against it.[61]

Fuller's political views seriously damaged his reputation as
a military writer: there is, as R. H. S. Crossman has justly
observed, "a natural tendency to write off authors who belong
to the wrong side." But his loyalty to England should never
have been in doubt, and if—like Hobbes or Carlyle—he
preferred to place his trust in an authoritarian government or
the leadership of great men rather than in the disorderly,
illiterate, and irrational masses, many of his observations on
the modern state were no less original or valuable than his
analysis of modern war. In 1932 he foresaw that economic
unity would of necessity be the first step to political federali-
zation in Europe and perceived that "an elaborate and ever-
increasing system of pensions, poor reliefs and doles, are

[59] Fuller, *The First of the League Wars: Its Lessons and Omens*
(London, 1936), pp. 285–301.
[60] *Ibid.*, pp. 151, 159. Fuller's article on "The Cancer of Europe" in the
first number of the *Fascist Quarterly* alienated the proprietors of the
Daily Telegraph and lost him the opportunity of succeeding Liddell Hart
as military correspondent of that paper in 1935 (private information).
[61] Fuller, *First of the League Wars*, pp. 7, 12, 120, 194; *Towards
Armageddon: The Defence Problem and Its Solution* (London, 1937),
pp. 227, 236. Fuller's political views during this period are treated more
extensively in David H. Zook, "John Frederick Charles Fuller Military
Historian," *Military Affairs*, XXIII (1959–60), 190–91.

rapidly transferring individual initiative to the State." Asia, he predicted, would soon be forced through overpopulation either to "burst her geographic bonds or reduce her numbers by civil war." Armed with modern weapons "it is scarcely to be doubted which course she will adopt." [62] And behind Russia he could detect China, possessing "an essential unity which is totally wanting in India" and driven by a particularly virile form of communism. According to Fuller, the supreme military problem was the consolidation of Europe to meet Asia, for the Russian ideal was "essentially an Asiatic impulse" and Russia clearly was mobilizing for a tremendous struggle," in which force, as he later pointed out, "cannot annihilate ideas." [63]

More to the point is Fuller's insight into what he called totalitarian warfare—the rationalization of Clausewitz, the psychology of the moral attack, the organization and discipline of the modern war state, and the concentration of all powers, political and military, in the hands of what was in effect a generalissimo. In contrast to the muddle in defense planning in England,[64] the totalitarian nations had developed a new concept of war incorporating the dynamic forces at work in their societies and reflecting the philosophy of the corporate state. Fuller himself had witnessed the birth of totalitarian tactics in Abyssinia, where he had accompanied the Italian army as a special correspondent to the *Daily Mail*. The serious threat of an oil embargo had "forced" the Italians to place the war upon a totalitarian footing by employing air power and gas "to scatter fear and death" throughout the more densely populated areas behind enemy lines. "From a military point of view, this was the only thing he [Mussolini] could do," and Fuller warned that any nation with its back to the wall could be expected to react similarly.

As there can be no doubt that totalitarian tactics have come to stay . . . more and more will war become, not so much a

[62] R. H. S. Crossman, *The Charm of Politics and Other Essays in Political Criticism* (New York, 1958), p. 209; Fuller, *Dragon's Teeth*, pp. 176, 180–81, 183–86. In his writings Fuller frequently quotes Carlyle, and his view of the nature of government is essentially that of Hobbes' Leviathan. Governments, Fuller maintained, "are established for two main purposes—namely, the maintenance of law and order and protection against foreign invasion" (*ibid.*, p. 164).

[63] Fuller, *First of the League Wars*, p. 93.

[64] "What is wanted is not to lay war under interdict but under examination" (Fuller, *Dragon's Teeth*, p. 273; *Towards Armageddon*, p. 29).

continuation of national policy as its mainspring and foundation. Not only will generals prepare for it, but dictators also. More and more will the heads of totalitarian States become involved in the war problem until it becomes their one absorbing study.[65]

The war of the future would probably commence with "a bolt from the blue of a cloudless sky instead of a declaration preceded by political thunder" and would be shaped by instruments of terror rather than those of slaughter or destruction. The problem, therefore, was how to achieve national discipline, for with a disciplined nation it would be as easy to hold war in check as it was to launch it, and only a disciplined people could withstand the terrors of repeated air attacks.[66]

As the Second World War approached Fuller attached still greater importance to air power, declaring that the primary object of land forces was to establish a protected base for air action, that the battleship would soon give way to the aircraft carrier, and that eventually rockets would even replace manned aircraft. In considering the military potential of the British Empire Fuller advanced essentially the same argument that is often heard nowadays for the continued maintenance of air and missile bases throughout the world. The great dominions, he pointed out, were at present beyond the range of European air attack, and if the empire were to create a mighty air force, which it could easily do with its industrial potential, what power would be foolish enough to bomb London out of existence if it meant that "the whole aerial might of the Empire would be turned against it in an overwhelming reprisal?" An empire thus based on air power could become the real arbiter of peace: Fuller had little faith in the principle of collective security, which, in a typical epigram, he interpreted to mean: "security when needed has to be collected." [67]

There remains Fuller the military historian, for of the forty-odd books that he has written no less than a dozen would be catalogued under the headings "history" and "biography." At first Fuller dabbled in military history; during the early days of the First World War it offered a relief from boredom;

[65] Fuller, *First of the League Wars*, pp. 80–89.
[66] *Ibid.*, pp. 174, 176; *Towards Armageddon*, p. 53.
[67] *Ibid.*, pp. 134, 149, 181, 196, 214; *First of the League Wars*, pp. 193 n., 203, 213.

but not until he was an instructor at the Staff College did he become seriously interested in the history of war. He contributed articles on various phases of military history to the *Encyclopaedia Britannica*, and in 1929 he produced *The Generalship of Ulysses S. Grant*, followed three years later by *Grant and Lee*. Most of his writings in the 1930's are philosophical rather than historical, polemics with historical illustrations. Fuller tended to arrange the past into patterns that supported his own point of view, writing what one critic has described as "dogmatic and wayward history." [68]

Fuller's philosophy of history is developed in *The Foundations of the Science of War*. The function of military history was to uncover what is of permanent value in war by examining the origin and objectives of a particular conflict, studying the military instruments available, and applying the principles of war to each campaign, which he viewed in three dimensions—how the situation appeared at the time to the rival commanders and also how it looked to the disinterested critic. It made no difference, Fuller contended, whether the persons involved were aware of the principles of war or not: These principles, "as truths, nevertheless existed, and . . . their unconscious application or violation resulted in success and failure, even if [the] reasons . . . were not apparent at the time." It was also the task of the military historian to project all deductions into the future and "consider their values with reference to the most probable conditions in which the next war will be fought."

In many respects Fuller's approach to history did not differ

[68] Crossman, *Charm of Politics*, p. 211. A case in point is Fuller's treatment of the economic causes of war in which he states that the United States went to war with Spain in 1898 "in order to seize the Philippine Islands, and so gain a naval base in the China Seas" (Fuller, *Dragon's Teeth*, p. 170). This fits neatly into Fuller's thesis and perhaps reflects the strategical thinking of Mahan, but the fact remains that prior to the outbreak of hostilities the United States had no designs on the Philippines. President McKinley later confessed: "The truth is I didn't want the Philippines, and . . . I did not know what to do with them." "I could not have told where those durned islands were within 20,000 miles." Even the perceptive Mr. Dooley was not altogether sure "whether they were islands or canned goods" (as quoted in Robert H. Ferrell, *American Diplomacy: A History* [New York, 1959], p. 206; and Robert A. Goldwin [ed.], *Readings in American Foreign Policy* [New York, 1959], pp. 102–3). It is also pertinent to note that Fuller's article on "War" was rejected by the *Encyclopaedia Britannica* because it "contained many generalizations contrary to the verdict of historians" (Fuller to J. L. Garvin, March 12, 1928 [Liddell Hart Papers]).

substantially from that of Henderson, although the latter was more conventional and far less addicted to method. Both were interested in the instructive value of history; both occasionally read their own thoughts into the minds of the subject. But it is a far cry from the manner in which Fuller had been taught history at the Staff College where, thanks largely to Henderson, Fuller and his fellow students had

set out, not for the Elysian fields, but straight for the Shenandoah Valley, never dreaming that a far more important war, namely the next war . . . was ever going to be fought. To the Shenandoah Valley we went without really going there, and we carried with us an immense number of brain-sacks and a huge shovel. And what did we do when we got there? . . . We shovelled facts and fictions into those sacks, pell-mell, to bursting point, and then we came home and played golf! [69]

Fuller professed skepticism about facts. A little speculation "even if it is not immediately related to facts, is sometimes more illuminating" than a straight narrative based upon accepted historical evidence, and in *The Generalship of Ulysses S. Grant* Fuller sought to endow the dead facts of history "with a little life" by applying his own system to the armies, methods, and conditions of 1861–65.[70] If his writings on the Civil War did not yield any new factual information they did go far to rehabilitate the reputation of Grant and also to provide fresh insight into the personalities and military conditions that dominated this, "the first of the modern wars."

When Britain went to war in 1939 Fuller had turned his thoughts from tanks and politics to military history. In June of that year he had put the finishing touches on a weighty manuscript entitled *Decisive Battles: Their Influence upon History and Civilization*, and the following year, when the great tank battles were beginning in Africa, Fuller confessed to an American correspondent: "You may imagine how far my thoughts are from such matters when I tell you that I am now writing a paper on Chief Pontiac's attack on . . . Detroit." [71] In 1942 he published *Decisive Battles of the U.S.A.*, followed

[69] Fuller, *Foundations of the Science of War*, pp. 327–34.
[70] Fuller to Liddell Hart, June 14, 1929 (Liddell Hart Papers). *The Generalship of Ulysses S. Grant* (London, 1929), pp. viii, 10–15. See Captain Liddell Hart's review of *The Generalship of Ulysses S. Grant* in the *Daily Telegraph*, December 24, 1929.
[71] Marshall, "Foreword," in Fuller, *Armored Warfare*, p. ix.

after the war by *Armament and History* (1946), *The Second World War* (1948), and an extensively revised edition of *Decisive Battles*.

The new and enlarged *Decisive Battles of the Western World* is Fuller's magnum opus and marks his coming of age as a military historian. Gone are the ideological overtones that marred most of his writings in the 1930's, his tendency to use history as a base for special pleading (*Grant*, he once admitted to Liddell Hart, "has enabled me to hinge on a good deal which is not directly connected with him" [72]), and his discernible impatience to polish off one book in order to get on with another. His mind had been too restless, his interests too varied, his personal life too disrupted by travel to enable him to linger long in writing a book or to spend endless hours in research among archives. Most of his early efforts at history, like his other books, represent a creative idea grafted to intensive (but not necessarily exhaustive or methodical) reading; if the underlying concept had been a while in gestation, the book itself was often delivered in haste.

In contrast, Fuller spent a decade rewriting the military history of the Western world. "There is no money in it," he once wrote, "but it is interesting and at the same time one learns a lot." [73] Written on a broader scale and with greater care than its predecessor, this monumental three-volume history stands as a unique contribution to military literature. Together with *The Generalship of Alexander the Great* (1958), which had been conceived while Fuller was still at the Staff College, it establishes this original and influential student of war as a military historian of major importance.

Similarly, Fuller's latest work, *The Conduct of War* (1961), contains his mature reflections on war and policy. Examining the impact of the French, Industrial, and Russian revolutions upon warfare, Fuller found a unifying theme in Clausewitz's famous dictum: "War is only a continuation of State policy by other means." Here he refined his earlier theories, softened many of his political views, and used the Marxian theory of class conflict to introduce the special problems of the Cold War. If some would challenge Fuller's views on the conduct of World War II, particularly with regard to mass bombing and grand strategy, none can deny his assertion that Hitler and

[72] Fuller to Liddell Hart, June 6, 1929 (Liddell Hart Papers).
[73] Fuller to Liddell Hart, April 8, 1948 (Liddell Hart Papers).

Stalin possessed a surer grasp of what Clausewitz meant by
war than did the leaders of the Western democracies. Churchill and Roosevelt may have won the war; Fuller's point is that
they failed to win the peace. *The Conduct of War*, therefore, is
written for the statesman as well as the soldier; it concerns
the diplomatic, economic, and psychological aspects of war in
addition to the military, and as such it offers thoughtful
instruction for the present as well as a fascinating interpretation of the recent past.

Yet these volumes represent only a final chapter: they do
not show the unconventional staff officer wrestling with the
principles of war or searching out solutions to military
problems aggravated by industrialization. They do not trace
his steps to comprehend the universal meaning of war as a
scientist, social scientist, philosopher, and historian. They do
not communicate his early enthusiasm and prophetic visions,
nor do they catch the trenchant criticisms and political
iconoclasm that gave a sting to his writings in the 1930's.
They do not document the evolution of a theory or reveal the
impact of a new idea.[74] In brief, Fuller's writings have a basic
integrity that transcends the worth—or the weakness—of any
single book.

Like the proverbial prophet Fuller has lived most of his life
unhonored in his own country. In part this has been due to the
prevailing political winds—the impulse to retrench after
World War I, "the growing strength of pacifist sentiment
among the politicians and the lack of funds for Army
expansion and modernization." This was barren ground for
the growth of a revolutionary idea based upon new weapons,
but it does not explain the unyielding resistance to Fuller
among those who comprised the military establishment. After
all, the decision in 1935 to rearm did increase the army
estimates (counting the supplement) by 28 per cent for the
following year, and still mechanization made no important
headway. The British army continued to spend over three
times as much for forage as for petrol![75]

Reasons for the antagonism within the army to Fuller and

[74] See, for example, the influence of Lewis Mumford's *Technics and
Civilization* on Fuller's *First of the League Wars*.

[75] See Walter H. Butler, "A Case in Preparedness," *Armor* (November–
December, 1951), pp. 33–35; Captain J. R. Kennedy, *Modern War and
Defence Reconstruction* (London, 1936), pp. 14–16, 113; Liddell Hart,
The Tanks, I, 338.

his theories are more easily explained than justified. There is a psychiatric basis for Major General John Mitchell's assertions a century earlier that the professional soldier was temperamentally conservative and dreaded innovation. Remembering that when Mitchell and Fuller wrote, England in each case had just emerged victorious from a great war, the following comments by an eminent psychiatrist are enlightening.

In the past, the outcome of the struggle between man's need to see and his need to hide his eyes, between his need to change and his need to stand pat, has always been determined somewhat unexpectedly by the consequences of prosperity and power. The civilization which had both has always refused to face reality. . . . The extraordinary technological advances which have marked the last half century of Man's history accentuate the fact that man himself drags his feet—man and also the institutions which man creates. . . . That which is rigid and unchanging in human nature tends to entrench itself in institutions which are themselves firmly entrenched. . . . The result is that at any prospect of change, individual anxiety increases the rigidity of old compulsions. . . . So we face the paradox: Progress requires change, which in turn triggers every neurotic defense which opposes change. This is why it is hard to change not only individuals, but also those institutions in which individual neuroses are invested.[76]

Fuller himself pointed this out, and with such zest that he only created additional friction and hostility. When his essay on *Generalship* was published, his friend Liddell Hart received so many letters of protest "from more senior people" that he wrote Fuller: "I am afraid the real truth is that they now suffer a sort of prickly affection of the skin whenever a book of yours appears in sight. It's rather depressing." And when *The Army in My Time* appeared the following year, Sir Ernest Swinton conceded that although it contained "a great deal, a very great deal of truth," it was "put in a way to exasperate and cause doubts as to the author's motives and judicial sense." There is much truth in Liddell Hart's explanation: "If you say to Smith, 'Mrs. Brown has a pimple on her nose', he simply takes it as a statement of fact: but if you say it to Mrs. Brown she takes it as an insult." [77]

Fuller courted antagonism in other ways. One suspects that occasionally he paid a price for being too clever, particularly in his biting epigrams and heavy use of ridicule—weapons which he chose deliberately to combat "the combined ignorance and stupidity of our army." Then, too, he never attempted to conceal his impatience with those of mediocre ability or his scorn for the unthinking masses. At the Staff College he aimed his lectures at "the two or three flyers out of my 55 students," claiming that he would be content to produce one good one out of the lot. "I hate Soviets and bottle feeding. . . . What an army wants is a handful of supermen and not cart loads of clever men." When asked to make "some tiny alteration" in his account of Alexander's victory at Guagamela (Arbela), Fuller replied to the military editor of the *Encyclopaedia Britannica:* "don't bother. . . . The ordinary reader will never read it. The Extraordinary reader will know." [78] Convinced from the reception of his more serious works that the reading public was not interested in heavy fare, Fuller began to produce an occasional "spiritual potboiler" better calculated to win readers among the lowbrows (he did after all contribute to the *Daily Mail*) than disciples within the military hierarchy, many of whom found his politics offensive. In justice to Fuller, however, it should be emphasized that while he would tailor his style to suit the audience, he refused to compromise his convictions. "A book," Lichtenberg once observed, "is a mirror: when a monkey looks in, no apostle can look out." [79] The phrase and the sentiment are both worthy of Fuller; the statement could apply to more than one of his critics.

But those who were irritated by the tone of Fuller's writings and his "presumption" in lecturing superiors on the art of war, or who questioned his motives and accused him of being wise

[77] Fuller to Liddell Hart, January 27, 1932; Liddell Hart to Fuller, February 21, 1933; Swinton to Liddell Hart, March 16, 1935; Liddell Hart to Lieutenant Colonel H. G. de Watteville (ed. the *R.U.S.I. Journal*), April 26, 1933 (Liddell Hart Papers).

[78] Fuller to Liddell Hart, September 17, 1929; March 2, 1923; April 25, 1928 (Liddell Hart Papers).

[79] Franc H. Mautner and Henry Hatfield (translators and editors), *The Lichtenberg Reader: Selected Writings of Georg Christoph Lichtenberg* (Boston, 1959), p. 64.

after the event, would have done well to have pondered the wisdom of his searching observations. "In the next war," Fuller wrote in 1925, "if we do not realize the influence of new forms of movement on weapons and protection, the war, in place of being in nature static, will be dynamic in the extreme; we shall be swept into the sea." [80]

They nearly were, and by the very methods that Fuller had foreseen and fought consistently to have introduced into his own army. Unfortunately for Britain, his ideas were better received in Germany than at home. One has only to scan the memoirs of German generals to see how Fuller's ideas influenced the development of the blitzkrieg method of attack that overran Poland, brought France to her knees, and enabled the Germans with greatly inferior forces to come close to victory in North Africa.[81] The Russians too were familiar with Fuller's theories. A large number of his books—we do not know how many—were sold in Russia, and Marshal Timoshenko is reported to have ordered that *Lectures on F.S.R. III* "be made a 'table book' for the Red Army—to be kept at every officer's elbow and used for constant reference" along with Clausewitz' *On War* and Douhet's *Command of the Air*. In the United States Fuller attracted a handful of followers, but some indication of the general impact of his theories on mechanization may be seen in the fact that his most famous work on the subject was received by the *Infantry Journal* but never reviewed.[82] He was probably better known in America as the author of a book on Grant.

Today Fuller, the first British military theorist "who ever made the heads of Continental armies look to England for

[80] Fuller, *Foundations of the Science of War*, p. 258. Fuller also predicted before the war that the Maginot Line would be "The Tombstone of France." No editor, unfortunately, would publish this article, although Fuller's views on the subject are a matter of record. See Fuller, *Machine Warfare*, pp. 44–45 n.

[81] For the testimony of the foremost German exponent of armored warfare, see General Heinz Guderian, *Panzer Leader* (London, 1952), p. 20.

[82] Liddell Hart to Fuller, October 5, 1949 (Liddell Hart Papers). Marshall, "Foreword," in Fuller, *Armored Warfare*, pp. x, xiii–xiv. S. L. A. Marshall is one of Fuller's American disciples; Hoffman Nickerson, author of *The Armed Horde 1793–1939* (New York, 1942), is another. But Marshall has recorded that from 1932 until 1939, not more than half a dozen officers had checked out Fuller's *Lectures on F.S.R. III* from the library at the Infantry School.

professional guidance," [83] has at last won public recognition in his own country. His authoritarian views have been modified to the extent that they no longer damage his reputation as a military thinker,[84] the campaigns of the Second World War have strikingly fulfilled many of his earlier prophesies, and the improved historical quality of his latest writings has added immeasurably to his stature. Friends and admirers of Sir Winston Churchill undoubtedly resent his treatment of Britain's wartime leader as something of a mountebank and disagree with his slashing indictment of mass bombing and unconditional surrender; [85] career soldiers may still show irritability at charges of mismanagement in the First World War and blind conservatism afterward, but history—and in more than one sense—has come to Fuller's rescue.

Fuller's tone has mellowed considerably over the years. At eighty-five he retains much of his vitality and the strength of his convictions and no one can deny that his mind is still as sharp as his pen, but the theme of his recent writings permits a more pleasing sound. Today Fuller looks more to the past than into the future, hence there is little need to resort to discord for effect. In music discord produces tension, provokes attention, sustains interest, and demands resolution—all effects that Fuller tried to achieve through his writings. But it is no longer Fuller's function to blow *Reveille*, which of necessity is impatient, authoritative, and usually displeasing.

[83] Liddell Hart places Fuller above even Napoleon and Clausewitz in imaginative powers and mental range. "There were flaws in his logic and gaps in his vision," but neither Napoleon nor Clausewitz "matched him in progressiveness and far-sightedness" (*The Tanks*, I, 221).

[84] For Fuller's current assessment of fascism, see *The Generalship of Alexander the Great* (London, 1958), pp. 308–12; *The Conduct of War, 1789–1961* (London, 1961), pp. 248–49; Zook, "Fuller," p. 191.

[85] See Fuller, *Conduct of War*, pp. 248–49. Fuller's criticisms of Churchill in this volume are restrained, perhaps for the sake of his publisher.

11

THE CAPTAIN WHO TEACHES GENERALS

Captain B. H. Liddell Hart

" 'Tis the good reader that makes the good book."
If Emerson's observation is allowed as a criterion, then
Liddell Hart, particularly in German translation, must be
considered one of the most successful writers of modern
times. A brilliant and prolific journalist, an imaginative,
far-sighted theorist, an unselfish and aggressive advocate of
army reform and an historian of commanding stature and
integrity, Liddell Hart has often despaired of ever teaching
anybody anything. Yet history and the testimony of his more
successful pupils offer convincing proof of his influence. The
walls of his study, which may strike the irreverent visitor as
the nest of a monstrous magpie, are adorned with photo-
graphs of readers who found something of value in what the
controversial Captain had to say. Heads of state are represented by Mussolini, Lloyd George, and John F. Kennedy; the
British tank pioneers are there to a man; so, too, are many of
the leading generals of the Second World War. But the
photograph with the most appropriate inscription comes from
the youthful commander of Israeli forces on the southern
front against Egypt in 1948. General Yigal Allon wrote
simply: "To Basil, the Captain who teaches Generals."
The statement is not accurate—it would be more to the
point to say that the Captain had much that he could have
taught. Certainly "the good reader," concerned over some
problem in tactics, strategy, or organization, could "nearly
always find some sudden and brilliant illumination" from the

pages of Liddell Hart,[1] who continues to meditate on military and defense problems and to bombard friends in high circles with his latest thoughts on the cold war and the road to peace.

Basil Henry Liddell Hart was born October 31, 1895, in Paris, where his father was serving as pastor.[2] He attended Edgeborough and Willington Preparatory schools and later St. Paul's, where he slighted ordinary studies in favor of history and geography and learned much about life, if not the classics, from a celebrated master named Elam. This eccentric clergyman [3] forced Liddell Hart to question conventional ideas. In 1913, Liddell Hart left St. Paul's for Corpus Christi College, Cambridge, where he began seriously to study military history and tactics (which were not part of his curriculum) and to write letters to the daily and technical papers on sports, principally tennis, a subject on which he was "almost a walking encyclopedia."

When Liddell Hart returned to Cambridge for the fall term Britain was at war. He promptly joined the Officers Training Corps; in December he was gazetted second lieutenant in the King's Own Yorkshire Light Infantry and was sent to France in September, 1915. In the great Somme offensive the following summer his battalion was destroyed. At one point Liddell Hart, twenty-one years of age and a lieutenant, found himself temporarily in command of the battalion. In the July 14 attack on the German second-line position, his company, which had been reinforced, acted as immediate brigade reserve. Relieved four days later, they were in the process of withdrawing when the Germans opened their first gas-shell bombardment, and Liddell Hart became a stretcher case when he reported to a dressing station next morning to have a hand wound looked after. He was sent immediately to a hospital in England, where he kept himself occupied writing his impressions of the Somme battle.

From his later books one would deduce that Liddell Hart's harsh indictment of the leadership in France grew out of his

[1] R. H. S. Crossman, *The Charm of Politics and Other Essays in Political Criticism* (New York, 1958), p. 224.

[2] Facts pertaining to Liddell Hart's life and career are derived from his files and correspondence preserved at States House, Medmenham, Marlow, Buckinghamshire, unless otherwise indicated.

[3] Elam is depicted by Compton Mackenzie in *Sinister Street* and Ernest Raymond in *Mr. Olim.*

own experiences in 1915–16, but in fact his diary and early letters make it plain that as a young officer he liked the army, respected the generals, and had every intention of remaining a career soldier: his account of the Somme written while on sick leave is far more generous with the British high command than any of his subsequent studies. Although the book was stillborn, since the War Office would not sanction publication, it brought Liddell Hart to the attention of John Buchan, then with G.H.Q. in France. It also encouraged him, since he was now condemned to "light duty in an office only," to take up the pen. He wrote an occasional article on the war for the *Daily Express* and the *Saturday Review*, and after becoming adjutant of a volunteer regiment he began to produce pamphlets on discipline, training, and tactics. Like Wilkinson and Fuller, Liddell Hart began his career as a military critic and theorist with the volunteers.

His first accomplishment with the volunteers was to develop "battle drill," a new and simplified drill designed to facilitate movement and to exercise formations that could be applied both in battle and on the barrack square. Other volunteer battalions and some of the (regular) officer cadet battalions took up the new drill, but it was not adopted officially at the time. Liddell Hart next incorporated "battle drill" into a new training manual, which in turn provided a springboard to his postwar analysis of infantry tactics.[4]

After the war Liddell Hart served in various capacities as education officer organizing educational work in hospitals, helping to rehabilitate disabled veterans in civil life, and teaching military history to officers studying for their promotion examinations. He sought an appointment to the historical section, Committee of Imperial Defence, but was turned down because the economy-minded financial branch would not allow an officer to go to a government department on pay from army funds. He applied for a commission in the newly formed Army Educational Corps but was rejected by the medical board, and when friends in high quarters intervened to have him declared physically fit, the best the selection board would offer was a regular commission as lieutenant. He thought for awhile of returning to the infantry but was dissuaded by

[4] See Liddell Hart, *Battle Drill or Attack Formations Simplified* (Cambridge, 1918); *New Methods of Infantry Training* (Cambridge, 1918).

Lieutenant General Sir Ivor Maxse, who had taken an interest in the young officer's tactical ideas and training methods and therefore wished him to remain on the 10th Infantry Brigade staff where he might perform special duties in accordance with his talents. At Maxse's initiative he was appointed to the staff of Brigadier General (later Major General Sir) Winston Dugan to help compile the first postwar *Infantry Training* manual. Liddell Hart wrote the vital sections and incorporated the first part of his battle drill into the manual issued in 1921–22. The second part, the "attack drills," were included in *Small Arms Training,* 1924, which he himself edited. An attempt to transfer to the tank corps after he had become interested in mechanization also failed, and in 1924 Liddell Hart was placed on half pay, retiring three years later. Although he himself later assumed that his retirement was "the result of war injuries, not personal opposition," Fuller took a characteristically different view. "I am most sorry to hear of your fate," he wrote. "Personally I consider it inevitable. The pretext is your health, the cause is that you are a writer. . . . You are being decapitated. I am being slowly strangled. I do not know who is to be envied most." [5]

By this time Liddell Hart had already made a name for himself for his tactical theories, which he had propounded in lectures before various military audiences, exposed to the readers of the *National Review,* and published separately in *The Framework of a Science of Infantry Tactics.*

In this booklet, first published in 1921, Liddell Hart attempted to do for tactics what Fuller was trying to accomplish for the whole science of war. Beginning, like Fuller, with individual man, Liddell Hart deduced what he considered to be "the correct principles of action which a man seeking to attack an enemy in the dark would naturally adopt." Assuming that any man so engaged would first seek out his enemy, next grope for some vulnerable spot, then hold his adversary firmly at arm's length while striking with his other fist at some unguarded point, and finally follow up any initial advantage by taking whatever steps necessary to render his opponent powerless, Liddell Hart deduced five principles which could be applied to infantry tactics—protective formation, reconnais-

[5] Liddell Hart to the Editor of the *Times,* March 9, 1951; Liddell Hart to the Editor of the Melbourne *Herald,* May 3, 1937; Fuller to Liddell Hart, June 3, 1924 (Liddell Hart Papers).

sance, fixing, decisive maneuver, and exploitation. Since the man in the dark is concerned primarily with guarding and hitting, the successful application of these basic battle principles depends upon the proper distribution of the advanced guard and what Liddell Hart called the maneuver body, and this in turn is governed by two supreme principles—security and economy of force. Together the principles inherent in the man-in-the-dark theory provided a flexible framework of tactical action to guide every small unit even in a large-scale battle.

To meet the problem of breaking through a defense distributed in depth such as the German trench system of 1916,[6] Liddell Hart developed the "expanding torrent" system of attack. The proper antidote to a defense in depth, he reasoned, was not the broad frontal assault of 1916, with the firing line reinforced uniformly at every point and the dead piled up in front of enemy strong points. Instead, each unit should advance with a "forward body—the outstretched arm—pushed out in the probable direction of the enemy, whilst the main, or manoeuvre body, follows in rear," each moving alternately under covering fire of the other. Comparing an attack to the actions of a torrent against an earthen dam, he recommended that the first subunit (in principle it made little difference whether it was a battalion, company, or even a platoon) to penetrate a breach in the enemy line "should go through and push straight ahead so long as it is backed up by the manoeuvre body of the unit." Flanking units meanwhile should rush their maneuver bodies towards the gap to attack the enemy in flank and widen the breach and additional units as they arrived were to flow through the breach, deploy, and continue the advance. In this way momentum could be maintained and speed combined with security as progressive steps were taken to widen the breach in proportion to the depth of penetration. Conversely the ideal defense, according to Liddell Hart, is also based upon the same five battle principles, with the maneuver bodies in each unit forming "a gradually contracting funnel raked by fire" in such a way that "the further the attacker penetrates the more

[6] For a masterly analysis of the German defensive theories in World War I, see Captain G. C. Wynne, *If Germany Attacks: The Battle in Depth in the West* (London, 1940).

resistance he encounters and the more confined becomes the space in which he can manoeuvre." [7]

The keynote to Liddell Hart's system of infantry tactics is simplicity. The basic principles should govern units of every size in all forms of action. Liddell Hart stressed dispersion: modern battle had become "a mosaic of momentary opportunities" in which the best chance for success was to be found in an "automatic process that works successively from the platoon upwards." [8] Like Fuller, Liddell Hart thought essentially in terms of tactical functions ("forward" and "maneuver" bodies) rather than traditional arms; he too anticipated the replacement of linear by an elastic defense in depth. The main difference between them at this stage was that Fuller already was convinced that the tank alone made possible the sustained exploitation of a breach in an intrenched front while Liddell Hart believed still in the capability of infantry once it had developed new tactical methods based upon "the intelligent manoeuvre of fire power." [9]

The two first met in June, 1920, a few weeks after Liddell Hart had submitted his articles in the *National Review* to Fuller for comment. They began to exchange views by correspondence on tactics. Fuller insisted that Liddell Hart's system applied to infantry against infantry only: "If the enemy produces tanks your infantry tactics will prove useless, for it is impossible to pit infantry against machines." Liddell Hart, on the other hand, never contended that infantry alone were a match for machines but sought initially to utilize the tank as an infantry weapon by integrating a section of tanks into each infantry combat unit. He did not look upon the tank exclusively as an infantry support weapon, however: from the first he maintained that the tank corps was the logical arm to provide advanced guards and a mobile pursuit force. [10]

Liddell Hart soon became a zealous advocate of mechanization. When Maxse asked him in 1921 to write for the *Encyclopaedia Britannica* that portion of the article on

[7] Liddell Hart, *The Framework of a Science of Infantry Tactics* (London, 1921), pp. 5–27 *passim*.

[8] Liddell Hart, *Thoughts on War* (London, 1944), p. 271.

[9] Liddell Hart, *Framework of a Science of Infantry Tactics*, p. 10.

[10] Fuller to Liddell Hart, August 26, 1922; Liddell Hart, "Suggestions on the Future Development of the Combat Unit: The Tank as a Weapon of Infantry," *R.U.S.I. Journal*, LXIV (1919), 666–69.

"Infantry" dealing with the role and characteristics of the arm in modern war, Liddell Hart exposed his case for the foot soldier to the sweeping criticisms of Fuller. Even as he prepared the article, however, he began to suspect that infantry "is more likely to endure because of conservatism, financial and official, than its own inherent merits." Fuller's arguments convinced him that "to uphold infantry against the inroads of mechanical warfare is impossible." If only he could be satisfied about one or two technical details, he confessed to Fuller, he was prepared to enter the tank corps and "become a disciple." [11] He was not long in becoming a full partner.

In 1922, three years after Fuller had received the Royal United Service Institution Gold Medal for his essay on the impact of technology and science on war, Liddell Hart submitted his entry entitled "The Development of the 'New Model' Army." Once again Fuller was prophetic: "I am afraid you will not win the essay," he predicted; "you should have proved that men on donkeys armed with bow and arrows will win the next war." The judges awarded the prize to a "cautiously progressive" essay which stressed the limitations of the new arms and emphasized the continued need for cavalry. Ironically, it was the Germans who paid closest attention to Liddell Hart's proposals; when his essay was published in the *Army Quarterly* a year or two later it was translated into German and circulated for study in the *Reichswehr*, where it fed the interest of progressive young officers like Guderian in the possibilities of armored warfare.[12]

Like Fuller, Liddell Hart looked to the day when a new model army based on mechanization would be created. Viewing the present as a period of transition, Liddell Hart was more specific than Fuller in his recommendations. He advocated progress by stages, each bringing an improvement in mobility and power of concentration, as the army groped its way toward complete mechanization. First divisional transport was to be mechanized, followed as soon as it was financially possible by the mechanization of battalion transport and field artillery and the acquisition of armored cater-

[11] Liddell Hart to Fuller, January 16, 1922; January 31, 1922.

[12] Fuller to Liddell Hart, December 18, 1922. Liddell Hart, *The Tanks: The History of the Royal Tank Regiment and Its Predecessors Heavy Branch Machine-Gun Corps, Tank Corps, and Royal Tank Corps 1914–1945* (New York, 1959), I, 224.

pillar carriers for all infantry. The goal to be achieved by the end of this first or evolutionary stage was a new-model division which, in Liddell Hart's judgment, should consist of three strong composite brigades, each to comprise one heavy and one medium tank battalion, three infantry battalions mounted in armored carriers, one brigade of mechanized artillery, and motorized transport, signal, and service troops. Such a division, he contended, would require only 60 per cent of the personnel of the present infantry division but would be significantly more compact, mobile, and hard-hitting. Ultimately there would be a complete revolution in tactics when the tank swallowed the conventional arms. Thus as early as 1922 Liddell Hart envisaged an army "composed principally of tanks and aircraft, with a small force of siege artillery, for the reduction and defence of the fortified tank and aircraft bases and of mechanical-borne infantry for use as land-marines." He anticipated that the new-model division probably would comprise one battalion of scout tanks, two brigades of cruiser tanks, one brigade of battle tanks, a train of supply tanks, and several squadrons of airplanes. But this lay far in the future: technology as well as the military mind had a long way to go before the new-model army could be realized.[13]

The year 1924 marks the first of several watersheds in Liddell Hart's versatile career. His days as an active soldier now were behind him: ahead lay the solid achievements that were to be his as theorist, historian, military correspondent, and army reformer. Already he had established a framework for his infantry tactics, and his article on the new-model army was an important contribution to the theory of mechanized warfare. Also in 1924 he published his analysis of the campaigns of Jenghiz Khan,[14] which served as an entering wedge for future articles and books on military history. On half pay, it became necessary for Liddell Hart in 1924 to find other means of support. Again Sir Ivor Maxse came to the rescue. Long impressed with the tactical views of his protégé, the former trainer of the British armies in France had done

[13] Liddell Hart, "The Development of the 'New Model' Army: Suggestions on a Progressive, but Gradual Mechanicalization," *Army Quarterly,* IX (1924), 37–50.

[14] Liddell Hart, "Two Great Captains: Jenghiz Khan and Sabutai," *Blackwoods,* CCXV (1924), 644–59, reprinted in Liddell Hart, *Great Captains Unveiled* (Boston, 1927), chap. i.

what he could to find a definite place in the army for a man of Liddell Hart's "particular gifts"; indeed it was Maxse who was primarily responsible for providing the *Infantry Training* manual, the *Encyclopaedia Britannica,* and the *National Review* [15] as outlets for Liddell Hart's theories on infantry tactics and training and as a director of the *Morning Post,* he now used his influence to have Liddell Hart sent to cover the coming annual maneuvers.

The results amply confirmed his judgment: utilizing the experience acquired from writing occasional articles during the war and from covering the Wimbledon and Davis Cup matches simultaneously for five different papers or journals, Liddell Hart admirably fulfilled the assignment. "Nothing better," Maxse reported after the maneuvers, "than your stuff has appeared in any daily paper since the Great War." [16] Others evidently shared this view, for when Repington died the following spring Liddell Hart was selected over a number of better-known applicants to succeed him on the staff of the *Daily Telegraph.*

As the only fulltime military correspondent then in Britain, Liddell Hart was an immediate success. He had an uncanny ability of being able to grasp the essentials of any new development and present the issues to the reading public with clarity and imagination. He was also exceptionally well informed. He kept in close touch with his old army friends, while those who believed in his doctrines of reform and mechanization gladly fed him information. He also had many contacts at the War Office enabling him to keep his fingers on the military pulse. Liddell Hart's rapid rise to the top of his profession is perhaps best reflected in a letter he received in 1927 from Fuller, who wrote: "People are jealous of you. Look at your position 1922 and 1927—5 years. In 1922 you had to say 'Yes Sir' and 'No Sir' to a twopenny halfpenny Captain; now you can put wind up the Army Council." [17]

Unfortunately, Liddell Hart had alienated not a few of the senior and more conservative officers in the process, among them the chief of the Imperial General Staff. Soon after he joined the *Daily Telegraph* the Captain received a letter from

[15] Leo Maxse, the General's brother, was editor of the *National Review.*
[16] Sir Ivor Maxse to Liddell Hart, October 16, 1924. For an indication of what he might have achieved as a sports commentator, see Liddell Hart, *The Lawn Tennis Masters Unveiled* (London, 1926).
[17] Fuller to Liddell Hart, December 5, 1927.

the man just appointed the next C.I.G.S. Pointing out "that without the support of the Press . . . it is quite impossible for the Army to carry out many reforms," General Sir George Milne emphasized the need to educate popular opinion. "You know as well as I do," he wrote,

that I dislike advertisement, but self-advertisement and propaganda for a good cause are two quite different things. I hope therefore that we may be able to work together during the next few years for the purpose of achieving the end which I am certain we both have in view.[18]

But Liddell Hart was too independent of mind and critical in outlook to serve the army as publicist. Careful always to protect the identity of his sources, his knowledge of what went on in the War Office often frustrated the generals, who were content to use his position with the press as a lever whenever it suited their interests or those of a particular branch of the service, but who often were—as Maxse had warned—"more sensitive than *prima donnas*" and resented criticism from an "outsider."

The boiling point in his relations with the War Office came in 1927, when Liddell Hart used the columns of the *Daily Telegraph* to expose the muddle over the experimental armored force that had caused Fuller to tender his resignation that year in despair. In several pungent articles, Liddell Hart called attention to the contrast between the initial statement about a force to be "composed of completely mechanized units" and the makeshift aggregation that actually was offered to Fuller. "Has the scheme broken down," he demanded to know, "or was the formation of such a force no more than a figure of speech."

"You have the knack of putting your finger on the sore spots," Swinton wrote a short time later, and from the resulting furor it is apparent that the military correspondent had touched tender nerves. His revelations caused embarrassing questions to be asked of the secretary of state in Parliament. The latter in turn complained that his military advisers had made him look foolish, and a workable mechanized force was hastily formed.[19]

[18] Field Marshal Sir George Milne to Liddell Hart, July 8, 1925.

[19] Liddell Hart, *The Tanks*, I, 246–47; E. W. Swinton to Liddell Hart, May 23, 1927; Liddell Hart to Dr. E. Wingfield-Stratford, April 12, 1942. Fuller's role in this episode is mentioned above, pp. 357–58.

It was, however, a costly victory. Fuller was not to command the experimental armored force and Liddell Hart had sacrificed his privileged position with the War Office. A high ranking officer bluntly told him: "You have lost the valuable position of the 'most favoured nation' at the War Office and also, I happen to know, the opinion of several officers who took a great interest in your writings." [20] There were other sources of friction as well, but it was Liddell Hart's exposure of the lack of any significant progress in mechanization that caused the real row with the War Office.

In self-defense Liddell Hart protested that on such issues he never criticized individuals, only a state of affairs, but the damage done by the disclosures in 1927 was never fully repaired. From this time on he was mistrusted by many of the army's leaders, including Milne and his successor, Field Marshal Sir Archibald Montgomery-Massingberd. Although the former expressed the hope that the two might be able to return to the "former pleasant relations" that had existed between them, friends reported to Liddell Hart that there remained "a certain amount of prejudice against you in War Office circles." Milne himself complained of "a distinct tone of hostility to the regular officer, as compared with the non-regular" in Liddell Hart's writings, an attitude that "does not help to encourage a devotion of service to country in the hard-worked and under-paid professional officer." [21]

The new C.I.G.S. likewise attempted to "protect" the army from Liddell Hart's influence. Critical of Liddell Hart in 1927, Montgomery-Massingberd became openly hostile two years later when the military correspondent suggested in a "demoralizing" article on territorial training that the citizen soldiers could afford to devote less time to drill and less attention to off-parade restrictions without any appreciable loss in efficiency. But Liddell Hart's worst fears were not for himself. Upon learning late in 1932 who was to succeed Milne, he wrote privately of his acute foreboding.

. . . I anticipate that he will not favour, still less initiate, steps towards the necessary reorganization of the Army; that he will be antipathetic to the extended use of tanks, and also of aircraft; that he will discourage, if not penalize, independence of

[20] Lieutenant General Sir Archibald Montgomery-Massingberd to Liddell Hart, May 16, 1927; May 22, 1927.
[21] John Buchan to Liddell Hart, April 22, 1932; Field Marshal Sir George Milne to Liddell Hart, May 30, 1927; September 2, 1930.

view and freedom of speech among the younger officers; that he will endeavour to check critical examination of the history of the war. . . . What I fear most is that his regime will lead to influential posts being increasingly filled with officers who are either unprogressive or skilled in hiding their opinions at the expense of the more constructive-minded. . . . I shall be pleasantly surprised if Fuller is not squeezed out of the Army without further employment.[22]

Within a year Fuller *was* placed on the retired list, and Liddell Hart's own relations with the War Office continued to deteriorate.

In contrast, the air ministry welcomed Liddell Hart as a friendly critic who "shows a most masterly grip of the essentials." Both marshal of the Royal Air Force Lord Trenchard and Sir Christopher Bullock, principal private secretary to the secretary of state for air, recognized his immense value as a publicist and kept him well informed. His dealings with Lord Trenchard were kept quiet lest the rival services accuse the air ministry of propagandizing through the press, but his friend Bullock willingly fed him the information—some of it confidential—that he needed. Liddell Hart also enjoyed the confidence of the Right Honorable Sir Samual Hoare, the secretary of state, who frequently solicited his views about defense questions.[23]

Liddell Hart remained with the *Daily Telegraph* until 1935, when he joined the *Times* to become the first permanent military correspondent of that paper since Repington's resignation in 1918. He was ripe for the move. A change in the ownership of the *Daily Telegraph* in 1927 had produced greater demands for news-gathering, and had not the *Times* provided him with an opportunity to give up the relentless pursuit of hot facts and devote his energies to commenting on current affairs and advising the paper on defense problems, it is likely that Liddell Hart would have left the field of journalism altogether in favor of writing history. For by 1935, a year that constitutes another significant turning point in his career, he was also firmly established as an historian.

His first work of an historical nature, *A Greater than*

[22] Liddell Hart to Sir Maurice Hankey (secretary to both the Committee of Imperial Defence and the cabinet), December 2, 1932.
[23] Sir Samual Hoare to Liddell Hart, March 10, 1930; March 20, 1930; March 3, 1936; Sir Christopher Bullock to Liddell Hart, May 15, 1930; September 15, 1930; December 21, 1934; December 27, 1934; Liddell Hart to Field Marshal Sir C. J. Deverell, November 1, 1935.

Napoleon, was published in 1926. A vital and instructive biography of Scipio Africanus based upon the ancient sources, this is perhaps one of his best books from a literary point of view although Liddell Hart himself later questioned whether it is not too "coherent and convincing." Scipio served as an admirable vehicle for Liddell Hart's own military views, but the material, he confessed to a friend, was "hardly adequate as a basis for an analysis" or "a scientific study of a personality." [24] This book was followed in the next year by *Great Captains Unveiled,* a compilation of articles about Jenghiz Khan, Saxe, Gustavus Adolphus, Wallenstein, and Wolfe published originally in *Blackwood's.* Both books reveal a careful reading of the primary sources, a trim and lucid style, and a tendency to view the past in terms of the present. Using modern phrases to explain the thoughts and actions of the "great captains," Liddell Hart encouraged his subjects to speak out on questions of tactics, strategy, and organization for the benefit of contemporaries. Jenghiz Khan and Sabutai, he took pleasure in pointing out, had lived in a day when "merit and not seniority was the key to advancement." Under their leadership the Mongols had become pioneers in "artillery preparation," being in a sense the first to employ fire systematically "to pave the way for the assault." Responding to the same spirit in the writings of Saxe that had caught the attention of Mitchell, Liddell Hart observed that the French marshal's "idea of leaving intervals between units in a general attack had to wait until the last year of the World War for official acceptance," while his use of redoubts "bears a distinct resemblance to the 'pill-boxes' and strong points which so hampered our advance at Ypres in 1917." Scipio emerges as a distinctly modern general, a profound strategist and an imaginative tactician who, in developing cavalry as "a superior mobile arm of decision," had fundamentally altered the character of an army which hitherto had been built around the legionary infantry. Scipio's vision, Liddell Hart pointedly observed,

is an object-lesson to modern general staffs, shivering on the brink of mechanicalisation, fearful of the plunge despite the proved ineffectiveness of the older arms in their present form,

[24] Liddell Hart to J. M. Scammell, May 31, 1937 (Scammell Papers).

for no military tradition has been a tithe so enduring and so resplendent as that of the legion.[25]

In his capacity as editor of the military and military history section of the fourteenth edition of the *Encyclopaedia Britannica,* Liddell Hart contributed several of the most important articles and was responsible for reseeding the entire field. If he intrusted the conventional subjects to established military historians, he assigned the significant topics to progressive soldiers like Fuller, Major (later Lieutenant General Sir) Giffard le Q. Martel, and Colonel (later Field Marshal Sir) Archibald Wavell. He got Fuller, of all people, to write the article on "cavalry," and one has only to glance through the volume containing articles on "strategy," "tactics," and "tanks" to appreciate the way in which he and others who were similarly "enlightened" attempted to propagate the spirit of mechanization.[26]

This is not to say, however, that history in Liddell Hart's hands was primarily a sounding board. Admittedly some of his analogies seem a little contrived ("I enjoyed 'Jenghiz Khan,'" his patron Maxse had written, "and especially the masterly infiltration into it of our 'platoon training' effort!"[27]), but he was careful to avoid abusing history in his efforts to use it for constructive purposes.

Indeed, in his varied writings on the First World War Liddell Hart made a distinctive contribution to our knowledge

[25] Liddell Hart, *Great Captains Unveiled,* pp. 8, 11–12, 28, 58, 63–64; *A Greater than Napoleon: Scipio Africanus* (Edinburgh, 1930), pp. 96–97.

[26] See Liddell Hart, "Strategy," Fuller, "Tactics," and Martel, "Tanks," in *Encyclopaedia Britannica* (14th ed.; New York, 1929), XXI, 452–59, 739–50, 786–92.

[27] Maxse to Liddell Hart, October 3, 1927. For an example of such "infiltration" tactics, compare Liddell Hart's comments in *Battle Drill,* where he recommended control by a system of signals as a means of "avoiding the ever-present risk of confusion and . . . achieving that speed of execution which is one of the chief aids to victory," with his exposition of Mongol tactics, which "were indeed built up on a definite framework of tactical moves, so that they resembled an applied battle drill. The analogy is further heightened by the fact that the different manoeuvres were directed by signals, so that the delays and upsets caused by orders and messages were obviated. The result of these battle drill tactics was seen in an amazing perfection and rapidity of execution. The Mongol force was a machine which worked like clockwork, and this very mobility made it irresistible to troops far more strongly armed and numerous" (*Battle Drill,* p. 2; *Great Captains Unveiled,* pp. 9–10).

of that titanic and often shapeless conflict. In 1928 he produced *Reputations,* a preliminary assessment of the generalship of ten not-so-great captains in 1914–18. Two years later he completed *The Real War,* which he revised and expanded in 1934, after having in the meantime written comprehensive biographies of Foch and T. E. Lawrence.[28] Behind each of these volumes lies conscientious research among the documents, diaries, and memoirs, lengthy conversations with the actors, and voluminous correspondence with those in a position to shed fuller light on the men and events under examination. Aside from the Lawrence biography, which demanded special research in a limited sphere, each book, each article, each obituary even, served as a steppingstone to the next history or biography as Liddell Hart labored to remain on top of the deluge of evidence that poured in from all sides. In this manner he was able gradually "to fit each fresh bit of evidence into an expanding frame" [29] and to explain the war effectively to soldier and civilian alike.

The reaction among soldiers varied. There were many among the younger generation of officers who hoped that *The Real War* might do something to avoid recreating "those mental attitudes produced by preconceived ideas combined with insufficient education and imagination," a reason no doubt that led to its selection as a text at Sandhurst and other military institutions in the dominions. "I cannot imagine anyone looking on *The Real War* . . . as an attack on the higher command," wrote a senior officer. "Criticism certainly —and lots of it . . . but criticism such as yours can only stimulate discussion and must in the end do nothing but good." "At the same time much of it is terribly sad reading," wrote another, "and I fear that the attitude of mind that led to the results that make it sad reading, is by no means extinct." [30]

Nor was it. Sir George Milne, the C.I.G.S., was so upset by

---

[28] See Liddell Hart, *Reputations* (London, 1928); *The Real War 1914–1918* (London, 1930); *Foch the Man of Orleans* (Boston, 1932); *T. E. Lawrence in Arabia and After* (London, 1934); and *A History of the World War 1914–1918* (London, 1934).

[29] Liddell Hart, *History of the World War,* p. 11.

[30] Major General J. C. Harding-Newman to Liddell Hart, June 19, 1930; Major General (later Lieutenant General Sir) B. D. Fisher to Liddell Hart, July 7, 1933; Brigadier General (later Major General) G. M. Lindsay to Liddell Hart, October 14, 1930.

the thought that some of the criticisms "may shake the confidence of impressionable youths in their superiors" that he exerted influence to have the book discontinued as a military text, despite the desire of the instructors at Sandhurst to retain it. (It was reinstated a few years later.) Similarly Montgomery-Massingberd, once he became C.I.G.S., changed the subject of the military history section of the promotion examinations from the American Civil War to the Gallipoli campaign to avoid using Liddell Hart's *Sherman* and Fuller's *Grant and Lee* as texts. Even *Foch* was "more or less banned" in France when the publisher, "apparently under pressure from some higher quarter," broke the contract on the ground that "the book is too different" from the prevailing French view of the national hero.[31]

Official opposition to Liddell Hart mounted as he grew increasingly critical of the performance of the higher command in 1914–18. By 1927, after he had been in touch with many of the chief military leaders themselves—none other than Montgomery-Massingberd asked him to collaborate on a volume on the lessons of the war [32]—he had adjusted the reputations to fit new facts revealed by published records and private revelations. The scale of judgment began to weigh more heavily against those responsible for the conduct of the war, a change in attitude that is transparent in Liddell Hart's personal correspondence. In 1922, for example, commenting upon the murder of Field Marshal Sir Henry Wilson in London, Liddell Hart claimed that Repington's old antagonist was, "with Henderson . . . the only real military genius thrown up by us for the past century." A decade later, explaining his treatment of Wilson in *Foch*, he wrote to the same friend: "The condemnation of Henry Wilson is entirely supplied by his own diaries [published in 1927], when fitted into the evidence available now in documents from other sources. Never has any man so condemned himself." Wilson's diaries, he wrote elsewhere, exploded his reputation and "stamped him as of third-rate judgment." [33]

[31] Liddell Hart diary, July 25, 1932; August 3, 1932; Liddell Hart to Captain J. Swire, December 26, 1941; Major D. H. Cole to Liddell Hart, April 15, 1935; Liddell Hart to J. M. Scammell, October 10,1933; Liddell Hart to Donald Russell, November 28, 1931.

[32] Liddell Hart, "Some More Personal Reminiscences," July 20, 1961 (manuscript in the Liddell Hart Papers).

[33] Liddell Hart to J. M. Scammell, June 24, 1922; March 22, 1932; Liddell Hart, *Through the Fog of War* (London, 1938), p. 175.

A similar metamorphosis can be seen in his treatment of Field Marshal Sir Douglas Haig and the Passchendaele offensive in 1917. In *Reputations* he pointed to the unsuitable terrain, which had been converted into a quagmire by the prolonged preparatory bombardment, blamed Haig gently for failing to provide the necessary reserves in the Cambrai attack, and capped his analysis with a summary which, on balance, is more favorable to Haig than otherwise. In *The Real War* he holds Haig somewhat more strictly to account, blaming him for ignoring the lessons of history, recent experience, and material facts in selecting the wrong time and an impossible site, for "having wasted the summer and his strength in the mud, where tanks foundered and infantry floundered," and for needlessly prolonging the "pitiful tragedy." In 1935 Liddell Hart re-examined the facts and ripped into Haig for misleading the cabinet in order to gain approval for his own plans at Passchendaele.

> Haig was an honourable man according to his lights. . . . But he was not honest enough by true standards. And the real troubles of Passchendaele arose from his deception of the Cabinet, which may have been partly deliberate . . . but was also doubtless a combination of the effect of (i) his tendency to deceive himself; (ii) his tendency, therefore, to encourage subordinates to . . . tell him what he wanted to hear; (iii) their tendency—strong enough even when unassisted—to tell a superior what was likely to coincide with his wishes.

If the real villain was the system that prevented the men concerned "from hearing the truth or their subordinates from frankly expressing it," Liddell Hart could find little consolation in the realization that although "the men have gone; the system remains." He is still fighting the historic battle.[34]

It is not generally realized that in his indictment of the higher command Liddell Hart received assistance and to a certain point support from a very curious source, the director of the historical section of the Committee of Imperial Defence. In preparing the official history, Brigadier General J. E. Edmonds had set out "to discover what actually happened, in

---

[34] Liddell Hart, *Reputations*, pp. 110–14, 123; *The Real War*, pp. 361–67; *Thoughts on War*, pp. 149–50; *The War in Outline 1914–1918* (New York, 1936), pp. 184–99; *Through the Fog of War*, pp. 39–57; "The Basic Truths of Passchendaele," *R.U.S.I. Journal*, CIV (1959), 1–7. See also Duff Cooper's autobiography, *Old Men Forget* (London, 1953), pp. 185–86.

order that there may be material for study, and that lessons for future guidance may be deduced." [35] Sometimes, however, "Archimedes," as he was called by a younger generation, declined to tell "what actually happened," admitting to Liddell Hart in confidence:

I want the young of the Army who are to occupy the high places later on to see the mistakes of their predecessors, yet without telling the public too much. What one cannot hint—except very occasionally—is that the great ones resented suggestions and ideas, fearing perhaps that if they encouraged such things they might in the end lose their jobs.

"I have to write of Haig with my tongue in my cheek," he confessed to Liddell Hart the year *The Real War* was published. "One can't tell the truth. He was really above the average—or rather below the average—in stupidity. He could not grasp things at conferences, particularly anything technical." [36] Unable to express such thoughts in print and feeling a need, as he once admitted, for "some outlet for his suppressed bile," Edmonds willingly passed on information with the stipulation: "You can use what I enclose provided you don't quote me." He read and approved many of Liddell Hart's chapters in manuscript and then, remembering that he was after all the official historian, he occasionally took an impish delight in pouncing upon the unsparing critic in public for deductions drawn from facts he himself had provided. As the years passed, however, and as civilian criticism of the higher command increased, Edmonds began to close ranks with his old comrades and he became much more defensive.

I see the divergence between our views increasing as we grow older. I become more and more inclined to lay weight on the difficulties of the fighting soldier's task and sympathize with them, whilst you are becoming more and more critical and see their blunders larger than their achievements. . . . Many of your points passed through my mind, but I had always space and the views of my comrades to consider.[37]

[35] Edmonds, *Military Operations, France and Belgium, 1915,* II (London, 1936), viii. A critique of the official history may be found in the writer's paper, "The First British Official Historians," *Military Affairs,* XXVI (Summer, 1962), 54–58.

[36] Edmonds to Liddell Hart, February 8, 1932; notes on a conversation with Edmonds, December 8, 1930; October 27, 1933 (Liddell Hart Papers).

[37] Edmonds to Liddell Hart, April 18, 1927; January 5, 1934; November 9, 1934; April 3, 1938.

The two continued to enjoy friendly relations until publication of the official account of Passchendaele in 1948, by which time they had walked past each other to the point where communication was no longer possible.

Liddell Hart's basic criticisms also were verified in the unpublished report of the War Office committee appointed in 1932 to examine the lessons of the war. According to this report, which never was released, the instructive lessons of the war "are largely the mistakes of Command." "Are we going the right way about producing self-reliant Commanders of initiative and imagination. The whole terrible story of these battles is a story of the lack of them." The report stated categorically: "There was absolutely no need for a large number of the casualties if troops had been properly handled with battle wise Commanders." [38] Many of the military judgments of Liddell Hart on the importance of surprise, the desirability of an indirect approach, the solution of maintaining the momentum of the attack, the advantages of night operations, the need to recreate a tactically mobile arm, and the power of defense over attack likewise were confirmed by this outspoken, yet silent report. [39]

As others drew lessons from Liddell Hart, he in turn looked to history for guidance because of its practical and philosophical value. It transcends the limitations of personal experience, and it provides greater depth and variety in every aspect of military activity. If it does nothing more, such "indirect experience" ought to teach the intelligent reader what mistakes to avoid; even the *Official History* of military operations in France and Belgium, as the report of the War Office committee clearly demonstrates, was rich in examples of how *not* to fight a war. Liddell Hart underlined his frequent references to the negative lessons of history by applying Bismarck's saying, "Fools say that they learn from their own experience. I have always contrived to get my experience at the expense of others." [40]

[38] Lessons of the War Committee, *France and Belgium 1915: Somme 1916* (typescript copy in the Liddell Hart Papers). See also Liddell Hart, "Night Action—and Its Development," *Army Quarterly* LXVI (1954), 4–6.

[39] This is particularly true of that portion of the report written by Major General B. D. Fisher entitled "General Notes with Special Reference to the Mesopotamian Campaign, Vols. I and II" (copy in Liddell Hart Papers). Fisher corresponded frequently with Liddell Hart and was in basic agreement with many of his views.

[40] Liddell Hart, *Thoughts on War*, pp. 97, 120, 127–28. For a fuller exposition of Liddell Hart's philosophy of history, see his provocative booklet entitled *Why Don't We Learn from History* (London, 1944).

But history does more than simply teach "how to traverse the rugged and slippery surface of world politics [and military situations] without bruises or broken bones." History serves also as a scientific basis for theory. Whereas Fuller, who was in many respects an intuitive man of vision, used history to teach what his own quick mind had already grasped by other methods, many of Liddell Hart's theories—particularly his views on strategy—were born of a searching examination of history. In the beginning he, too, formulated his "man-in-the-dark" and "expanding torrent" theories by a process of inductive reasoning, but once converted to the tank he turned increasingly to history for signposts to the revival of mobile warfare. The battle of Adrianople in August, A.D. 378, had introduced the age of cavalry which lasted until the supremacy of the horseman was ended by the longbow and pike a thousand years later; the tank attack at Amiens on August 8, 1918, struck Liddell Hart as an event of similar significance, and if modern battle conditions prohibited a reincarnation of the mounted horseman certainly the functions of cavalry in its heyday might be appropriated by the tank. History seemed to confirm what Fuller and Liddell Hart's own theories already assumed to be true, namely that "the action of cavalry was vital to the functioning of the body military, and when it ceased to work, warfare became stagnant." [41]

This reference to the previous accomplishments of cavalry was more than an analogy, for it indicated the paths to be explored in determining the proper role of the tank. From his study of the Mongol campaigns of the thirteenth century Liddell Hart learned to appreciate that quality was more important to success than quantity and that "superior general mobility when allied with hitting-power is both a more powerful and a more secure tool than the mere loco-mobility and defensive power of an army founded on infantry." Compare his description of Mongol tactics with the tactics he later suggested for the mechanized warfare of the future. In his article on Jenghiz Khan he wrote:

The battle formation was comprised of five ranks, the squadrons being separated by wide intervals. The troops in the two front ranks wore complete armour, with sword and lance, and their horses also were armoured. The three rear ranks wore no armour, and their weapons were the bow and the javelin. From

[41] Liddell Hart, *The Remaking of Modern Armies* (London, 1927), pp. 38–60, 173.

these latter were thrown out mounted skirmishers or light troops, who harassed the enemy as he advanced. Later, as the two forces drew near each other, the rear ranks advanced through the intervals in the front ranks, and poured a deadly hail of arrows and javelins on the enemy. Then, when they had disorganised the enemy ranks, they retired into the intervals, and the front ranks charged to deliver the decisive blow. It was a perfect combination of fire and shock tactics.

Adapting Mongol tactics to mechanized warfare, Liddell Hart recommended that

The actual tank attack should be made by combined units of heavy and light tanks. The light tanks would lead, to pave the way by drawing the enemy's fire and testing his defence. If found to be weak, they would go through it "all out," with the battle-tanks on their heels. If strong, they would halt on any suitable close-up fire-position, thus turning themselves into a screen of minute pill-boxes, stationary to ensure aimed fire, yet capable of instant change of position at need.

Through this screen the heavier tanks would sweep, and the position of every anti-tank gun which opened against them would be smothered with a thick spray of aimed machine-gunfire from the light tanks. . . . Once the battle-tanks were through the first layer of anti-tank defence, the light tanks would race ahead, pass through them and repeat the process against any further layers.

Thus the tank attack would be an alternating process of movement and a compound process of fire. According to the hostile fire and the circumstances, the light tanks might either make direct for a chosen fire-position, or, like the Mongol horse-archers, race closer to the enemy before wheeling about and retiring a short distance to their covering fire-position.[42]

Even the sketch maps illustrating the campaigns of Jenghiz Khan and Sabutai bear a striking resemblance to the fluid arrows used to indicate the paths of armored columns in more

---

[42] Liddell Hart, *Great Captains Unveiled*, p. 10; *Thoughts on War*, pp. 132, 267. Liddell Hart, a tidy keeper of files, for years has been in the habit of writing down each thought, dating it, and filing it away for future reference. These were collated in *Thoughts on War*, making it possible to trace the development of his theories by observing the date of each entry. His suggestion for a pattern of mechanized warfare based upon the Mongol campaigns is dated September, 1927.

recent studies of the German operations in the Second World War.[43]

But it was in the realm of strategy that Liddell Hart learned most from his study of history. Driven by the desire, amounting almost to a passion, to avoid repetition of the pointless slaughter of 1914–18, Liddell Hart formulated in the late 1920's his well-known "strategy of the indirect approach." The purpose of strategy, he contended, "is to diminish the possibility of resistance . . . by exploiting the elements of movement and surprise." Movement could be achieved through mechanization ("Without mobility an army is but a corpse— awaiting burial in a trench" [44]); surprise by following the line of least resistance or expectation. In place of the frontal attacks of the First World War, colossal assaults that had merely pushed the enemy back a short distance upon his reserves and secondary defenses, Liddell Hart advocated a deep movement behind the enemy's flank or a deep penetration of his lines by independent armored columns, indirect thrusts aimed at cutting the enemy's communications and causing what Fuller similarly had hoped to achieve in his "Plan 1919"—"the paralysis of the opposing command." History convinced Liddell Hart that a direct approach to the objective along the line of natural expectation "has ever tended to negative results." The truly decisive victories have come rather from the strategy of indirect approach aimed at dislocating the enemy's moral, mental, or material balance before attempting to overthrow him on the field of battle.

Flexibility and deception obviously were essential to the success of a strategy of indirect approach, for even a stroke against the enemy's flank or rear, "by the very directness of its progress," became a direct approach once the opposing commander changed fronts to meet it. Hence it was necessary to pursue "alternative objectives," to threaten two or more points simultaneously in order to force the enemy either to abandon one in defense of the other or else to become

---

[43] Compare the maps in *Great Captains Unveiled*, pp. 11, 22, with those found in S. L. A. Marshall, *Blitzkrieg: Armies on Wheels* (Washington, 1943), pp. 20, 119, 139; Field Marshall Erich von Manstein, *Lost Victories* (Chicago, 1958), *passim;* or Major General F. W. von Mellenthin, *Panzer Battles 1939–1945: A Study of the Employment of Armour in the Second World War* (London, 1955), *passim.*

[44] Liddell Hart, *Remaking of Modern Armies*, p. x.

overextended in an effort to defend both—a move similar to the fork play in chess. To achieve flexibility in execution, Liddell Hart suggested an advance in a wide, loosely grouped formation "like the waving tentacles of an octopus," which would distract the enemy and conceal until the last moment the true objective of the campaign. This appeared to constitute a violation of the principle of concentration, but Liddell Hart maintained that effective concentration was possible only when the enemy was dispersed, "and usually, in order to ensure this, one's own forces must be widely distributed." A premature concentration against the enemy's main army too often resulted in a direct, frontal attack with the advantages resting solidly on the side of the defensive—a repetition of 1914–18 which Liddell Hart desperately wanted to avoid. Respecting the "great and growing superiority" of the defensive, Liddell Hart also developed what he called the "baited gambit," which in essence was offensive strategy combined with defensive tactics. "By rapidity of advance and mobility of manoeuvre," he explained,

you may be able to seize points which the enemy, sensitive to the threat, will be constrained to attack. Thus you will invite him to a repulse which in turn may be exploited by a riposte. Such a counterstroke, against an exhausted attacker, is much less difficult than the attack on a defended position.[45]

Liddell Hart never claimed to have invented the strategy of indirect approach; "alternative objectives," the "strategic net," and the "baited gambit" simply were his terms for stratagems that had been used before in history. (MacDougall had suggested a combination of defensive-offensive tactics similar to the "baited gambit," and even Napier had sensed possibilities in "organized dispersion."[46]) But he did organize and blend these lessons gleaned from past wars into an elevated doctrine adaptable to mechanized war, and many of his theories were successfully employed in the blitzkrieg of a later day.

Sherman occupied a unique position among Liddell Hart's tutors. First introduced to the Civil War by Henderson's *Stonewall Jackson,* Liddell Hart at once appreciated the

[45] The strategy of the indirect approach is woven into the fabric of most of Liddell Hart's writings after 1927. Quotations used here come from *Thoughts on War*, pp. 231, 238, 241; *The British Way in Warfare* (London, 1932), p. 107.

[46] See above, pp. 33, 114.

surprise, mobility, "unexpected thrusts and skilful strategic combinations" evident in the American campaigns. Although engaged at the time in research on the First World War, he developed an interest in the ways in which a somewhat similar trench deadlock had been overcome during the Civil War, and in his fertile mind Sherman's campaigns in the west pointed the way to a revival of mobile warfare. In 1928, when Liddell Hart commenced work on a biography of Sherman, the strategy of indirect approach had just emerged from the shadows of history, and in fact he elected to write about Sherman in preference to Lee because of the former's successful adherence to a strategy of indirect approach that minimized fighting by upsetting the opponent both mentally and physically and by substituting mobility and deception for force.[47]

In the Atlanta campaign, Sherman had devised a new technique. Although committed to a direct line of advance because he was dependent for supplies upon a single railroad line, he had nevertheless managed to maneuver his wary opponent out of successive defensive positions by advancing "in a wide loose grouping or net" which was pliable yet at the same time sufficiently cohesive to prevent the Confederates from attacking and defeating isolated columns in detail. Here the concept of the "strategic net," which Sherman later used to good advantage in his march to the sea and in the subsequent sweep northward through the Carolinas, first enters the thought of Liddell Hart.[48]

Sherman also taught him the potentialities of the "baited gambit" and of "alternative objectives." During the Atlanta campaign he had maneuvered "so skilfully as to lure the Confederates time after time into vain attacks, their repulse being ensured by the skill of his troops in rapid entrenching after gaining a vantage point." The lessons for an armored force were clear:

[47] Liddell Hart, *Reputations*, p. 272. In November, 1927, Liddell Hart wrote: "In exploring the field of military history certain deductions have emerged, and are now sufficiently clear in my mind as to justify an attempt to formulate them. Among them is the theory of what may be termed 'the Strategy of Indirect Approach' " (*Thoughts on War*, p. 238).

[48] Liddell Hart, *Sherman: Soldier, Realist, American* (New York, 1929), pp. 242, 253, 369. See also the Introduction by Liddell Hart in William T. Sherman, *From Atlanta to the Sea* (London, 1961), pp. 13–14.

It is advantageous . . . to seek the enemy's rear before seeking battle. Thereby it may even draw the enemy into attacking it to gain relief—and the power of an armoured force to crumple up such an attack, for which it has schemed, has potentialities not yet exploited.[49]

In his celebrated march to the sea Sherman, no longer forced to adhere to a single objective like Atlanta, advanced along a line that threatened several objectives simultaneously, always keeping the Confederates in doubt as to his ultimate destination. Macon or Augusta, Augusta or Savannah, Charlotte or Fayetteville?—the Confederates never knew for certain whither Sherman was bound until it was too late to take effective means to stop him. "Sherman had sought and found a solution in variability, or elasticity—the choice of a line leading to alternative objectives with the power to vary his course to gain whichever the enemy left open." Henceforth "alternative objectives" was an integral part of the strategy of indirect approach, which in its mature form became the philosophical basis for an interpretative survey of *The Decisive Wars of History*.[50]

While serving as fulltime journalist, writing books—many of them based upon original research—on military history and biography, and evolving in the process his own tactical and strategical theories, Liddell Hart also wrote widely in the field of military science. Although many of his views are no longer of interest because they have fallen by the wayside in the forced march of scientific progress and recent history, his contributions in this area are significant and creative.

Liddell Hart was an early advocate of air power, which he predicted would transcend the auxiliary role of 1914–18 to become the dominant factor in the next war. Once the air weapon reached maturity it might within hours paralyze the nerve centers of an enemy nation, destroying communica-

[49] Liddell Hart, *Thoughts on War*, pp. 241–42.

[50] *Ibid.*, pp. 58–59, 242–43; *Sherman*, pp. 315, 383. Liddell Hart, *The Decisive Wars of History: A Study in Strategy* (London, 1929). A new and revised edition, incorporating further examples from the early stages of the Second World War, was published under the unvarnished title *The Strategy of Indirect Approach* (London, 1941). The latest edition includes an account by Fuller's former pupil at the Staff College, Major General Eric Dorman-Smith, on "The Strategy of Indirect Approach in the North African Campaign, 1940–42," and also General Yadin's strategical analysis of the Arab-Israel War. See *Strategy: The Indirect Approach* (London, 1954), pp. 373–404.

tions and if need be whole cities, although Liddell Hart objected to the wanton destruction of population centers because "to inflict widespread death and destruction is to damage one's own future prosperity, and, by sowing the seeds of revenge, to jeopardize one's future security." Better to use a non-lethal gas to overcome hostile resistance and spread panic; it was more humane and also more effective. Anticipating that supremacy in any future war would go to the nation with the greatest industrial resources, Liddell Hart cautioned against "a sudden and overwhelming blow from the air": specifically the United States, he wrote in 1925, would do well to remember that the Japanese were familiar with the axiom of Clausewitz that a smaller state, if it considers war inevitable and sees its own relative position deteriorating with the passage of time, should "seize the time when the situation is furthest from the worst" and attack. "It was on this principle that Japan declared war on Russia [in 1904], and *for the United States the next decade is the danger period.*" [51]

Liddell Hart offered a number of practical suggestions to help modernize the army. Every infantry section should have as its basic weapon a light automatic such as the Browning, with the ultimate goal being an automatic rifle for every foot soldier; close-order drill should be remodeled and adapted to tactical battle drill; training for territorials should be intensified and greater attention paid to winter instruction. Liddell Hart's reports of the annual maneuvers pointed to the need for greater mobility and a reappraisal of the individual arms; [52] his analysis of the postwar doctrines of Germany and France in the early 1920's revealed that while the former emphasized mobility, maneuver, and surprise, the latter was obsessed with "the dominance and development of fire-power." [53] Meanwhile he continued to exert an influence upon the shaping of British

[51] Liddell Hart, *Paris or the Future of War* (London, 1925), pp. 43–59; *British Way in Warfare*, pp. 139–61. Trenchard was so pleased with the former that he presented copies to the other members of the chiefs of staff committee (Liddell Hart to Sir Maurice Hankey, December 29, 1933). Another air marshal wrote that *Paris, or the Future of War*, "is practically what is taught at the R.A.F. Staff College" (Sir A. Brooke-Popham, to Liddell Hart, July 17, 1925).
[52] Liddell Hart, "Army Manoeuvres, 1925" *R.U.S.I. Journal*, LXV (1925), 647–55; "The Army Exercises of 1930," *ibid.*, LXXV (1930), 683–90; *British Way in Warfare*, pp. 239–58.
[53] Liddell Hart, *Remaking of Modern Armies*, pp. 115–68, 211–34, 241–77.

infantry doctrine. The 1926 revision of the *Infantry Training* manual was intrusted to Colonel the Viscount Gort, a personal friend who happened also to be in close agreement with Liddell Hart's basic tactical theories. Gort asked Liddell Hart to suggest points that ought to be included and reported his criticisms "very valuable." The following year another friend solicited his views on an advance copy of *Artillery Training,* Volume III, found them "illuminating," and in 1931 many of his ideas were incorporated into the new edition of *Infantry Training* written by Lieutenant Colonel (later Field Marshal) B. L. Montgomery. By this time, however, the exposition of Liddell Hart's theories dealing with deep penetration and rapid exploitation had been watered down, even though Montgomery a few years earlier had indicated almost complete agreement with Liddell Hart's writings on drill and infantry tactics.[54]

His most important contribution, however, was in the fight for mechanization. The *Daily Telegraph* provided a rostrum from which he could preach the new gospel and at the same time publicize the efforts of Fuller, Martel, Major (later Major General) G. M. Lindsay, Lieutenant Colonel (later Major General Sir) Percy Hobart, Lieutenant Colonel (later Lieutenant General Sir) Charles Broad, Lieutenant Colonel (later General Sir) Frederick Pile, and others of that devoted band of tank enthusiasts who improvised, experimented, planned, exchanged views and information, and fought by whatever means available to overcome the Treasury, conservatism, and apathy in order to create the armored force of their dreams. Liddell Hart's theories on armored warfare have tended to overshadow his importance to this effort as publicist, but as the military correspondent of one of the leading newspapers in the country, he brought the case squarely before the public and on occasion even managed to bring pressure to bear on the authorities themselves. His books and articles were an essential factor in the decision to form an experimental armored force in 1927.[55]

[54] Colonel the Viscount Gort to Liddell Hart, September 7, 1920; February 2, 1921; September 27, 1922; April 14, 1924; (later Major General Sir) J. N. Kennedy, April 8, 1927; May 9, 1927; Lieutenant Colonel B. L. Montgomery to Liddell Hart, July 24, 1924; August 2, 1925; September 5, 1930; Brigadier General (later Lieutenant General Sir) B. D. Fisher to Liddell Hart, September 7, 1930; Liddell Hart, "Brief Analysis of *Infantry Training,* Vol. II, 1931," Liddell Hart Papers.

[55] Liddell Hart, "The Army of Tomorrow," *Daily Telegraph,* September 30, 1925. This article, the last in a series of three on the lessons of the

He provided many of the ideas as well as the impetus, sharing with Fuller the vision of fast-moving, armored forces and devising new theories of his own. There is no need to discuss his theory of mechanized warfare in detail: in most respects he agreed with Fuller, and his idea of what should constitute a "new model" army and the formulation of his strategy of indirect approach indicate the nature of the instrument, as he conceived it, and the way in which he thought it should be used.

He did, however, incorporate several new concepts of fundamental importance into the emerging British doctrine of mechanized warfare. He placed greater emphasis than Fuller on the combination of tanks and aircraft. "Tanks move so fast," he wrote in 1926,

that the difficulty of normal artillery co-operation is intensified, and for this reason . . . "offensive" support must come, and can only come effectively, from an even more mobile auxiliary moving immediately alongside. For this purpose the close co-operation of low-flying aircraft is essential. Such a combined assault would seem almost irresistible.

Almost as though he had attended a sneak preview of the action of the Stuka dive bombers against the French artillery in the battle of the Meuse in 1940, when by their own admission the French gunners "stopped firing and went to ground" and the infantry "cowered in their trenches, dazed by the crash of the bombs and the shriek of the dive bombers," [56] Liddell Hart described the moral effects of such an attack well over a decade before the event itself. To diminish the hazard of a direct assault by an armored force, he suggested that the charging troops should be protected,

. . . not only by armour plate and smoke, but by guardian angels overhead—in other words, by simultaneous air attack.

The so-called "practical man" may argue that a diving airplane

---

1925 maneuvers, brought many letters of approval from high-ranking army officers including, curiously enough, Montgomery-Massingberd (Montgomery-Massingberd to Liddell Hart, November 19, 1925). Martel in his *Memoirs* reveals how Liddell Hart's views on armored warfare as expressed in *Paris or the Future of War* influenced Sir George Milne, the C.I.G.S. (Martel, *An Outspoken Soldier; His Views and Memoirs* [London, 1949], p. 52).

[56] Colonel A. Goutard, *The Battle of France, 1940* (London, 1958), p. 133. Goutard pointed out that while "bombing by the Stukas caused relatively little damage" in the physical sense, the moral effect "was enormous."

might easily miss such a small target as an anti-tank gun. But the man who has had personal experience of being machine-gunned or bombed from low-flying aircraft knows that it is so unnerving that few men could be trusted to aim coolly at the tanks —and such disturbance, rather than destruction, fulfills the object of this combined air attack.

But such a combination did not, in Liddell Hart's estimation, serve as an alternative to art; rather it was "a means to make the art of generalship more effective." If it reduced the risk of a frontal assault, still more did it insure a successful indirect thrust against the enemy's rear—as in the Ardennes a few years later.[57]

Liddell Hart also differed from Fuller in his appraisal of infantry in armored warfare. In his pregnant *Lectures on F.R.S. III* Fuller had stated that "in battles between armoured machines infantry can play no part worth their risk." Their usefulness would be limited to holding territory overrun by the tanks, operating in mountainous and forested areas unsuited to tank movement, and serving as field pioneers in establishing the defenses of the field army. Liddell Hart, on the other hand, assigned infantry a more important role. In 1919 he had advocated training infantry together with tanks as integral parts of the same combat unit, while at the same time developing a separate tank force to fulfil the old cavalry role of probing and exploitation. In 1922 he wrote of a new-model division comprising three mixed brigades, each to comprise three infantry battalions mounted in armored carriers during the initial stages of the evolution of the army of the future and "mechanical-borne infantry for use as land-marines" when the final goal was achieved. In *The Remaking of Modern Armies*, published in 1927, he suggested converting all infantry to mounted infantry by reducing the number of battalions by one third and mounting the rest in the new one-man tankette invented by Martel. Four years later, in a lecture to the officers of the Southern Command, Liddell Hart proposed the creation of an infantry *corps d'élite* for mobile operations, with each battalion consisting of one "light-car skirmisher company," one company of "mechanized supporting weapons," and a "motorised reserve company."

In all of his writings Liddell Hart pressed for the develop-

[57] Liddell Hart, *Thoughts on War*, pp. 159, 172; *British Way in Warfare*, pp. 200–201.

ment of armored infantry as part of the strategic armored forces,[58] an argument that failed to win many converts either among the traditional infantry or from the "all-tank" school that believed, along with Fuller, that infantry had no permanent place among the combat elements of an armored force. The latter view prevailed in British tank circles throughout the 1920's and early 1930's, and consequently it was the Germans who, led by men like Guderian, actually found a way to blend motorized infantry with tanks without diminishing the strategic and tactical potentialities of armored forces. The war establishment of the First Panzer Division in 1935 contained two battalions of motorized infantry and one motorcycle battalion plus other infantry elements: in May, 1940, an additional battalion of motorized infantry was added, and it was this "balanced force of all arms" that was to provide the precision instrument that made possible the conquest of France. "Although we attached the greatest importance to armour," a successful Panzer general testified later, "we realized that tanks cannot operate without the close support of motorized infantry and artillery. . . . that was a lesson which the British did not learn until well into 1942." [59]

Liddell Hart correctly anticipated still another feature of the 1940 campaign in France, for although he did not often mention *deep* strategic penetration as such, the concept is implicit in his strategy of indirect approach and easily identified in his analysis of the Mongol campaigns and Sherman's march to the sea. In 1935, as a direct outgrowth of a discussion with Wavell, the future field marshal, Liddell Hart made a special study of Civil War cavalry operations in

[58] Fuller, *Armoured Warfare: An Annotated Edition of Fifteen Lectures on Operations between Mechanized Forces* (rev. ed.; London, 1943), pp. 21, 97. Liddell Hart, *Remaking of Modern Armies*, pp. 61–79; *British Way in Warfare*, pp. 218–25; *The Future of Infantry* (London, 1933), pp. 35 ff.; *When Britain Goes to War: Adaptability and Mobility* (London, 1936), pp. 261, 264–65. See also Liddell Hart, *Thoughts on War*, pp. 160, 211, 257–61.

[59] Mellenthin, *Panzer Battles*, p. 24; Guderian, *Panzer Leader*, pp. 30–46, 518–20; Guderian, "Armored Forces," in Colonel Joseph I. Greene (ed.), *The Infantry Journal Reader* (New York, 1944), pp. 469–73; Liddell Hart, *The Tanks*, I, 269–70. It would appear that the Germans later went too far in the direction of motorized infantry, for in 1941 they diluted their armored division still more by reducing the tank units to three and increasing the infantry battalions to four, a "fatal disproportion" according to the testimony of some of the German generals after the war. See Liddell Hart, *Defence of the West: Some Riddles of War and Peace* (London, 1950), pp. 267–89.

the western theater in order to determine whether a stroke against enemy communications should be directed against the immediate rear of the field army, or further back. Like Burgoyne, who had refuted Jomini's axiom that a march against the rear of an opposing force could produce grand results only if it occurred immediately behind the enemy's line while the best to be expected of deep thrust was "ephemeral successes," [60] Liddell Hart discovered that as a general rule, "the nearer to the force that the cut is made, the *more immediate* the effect; the nearer to the base, the *greater* the effect." While the results of this study were never published in book form until the year after Guderian's breakthrough in the Ardennes and subsequent dash for the Channel coast,[61] its contents were communicated informally to Wavell and Hobart at a time when the latter, as commander of the First Tank Brigade, had already begun to experiment with the possibilities of an armored force operating independently against enemy objectives many miles behind the battle zone. Thus the Mongols had first drawn Liddell Hart's attention to the possibilities of deep strategic penetration; Sherman's campaigns indicated "its deadly reaction upon the opposing army"; the tank brigade exercises of 1934 offered solid evidence that such a march was still possible with armored forces, and fresh insight into its current application and potentialities came from his historical analysis of Civil War cavalry operations: with the application of Liddell Hart's "expanding torrent" method of attack, devised originally for infantry in 1920, to the strategic advance of armored columns, all of the ingredients of the *blitzkrieg* were present.[62] By this time, however, Liddell Hart himself had become deeply involved with other and more pressing problems, and time did not permit a final synthesis of his views on armored warfare. His own horizons and the limits of his responsibilities had suddenly expanded.

When Liddell Hart joined the *Times* in March, 1935, he appeared to be riding the crest of a great wave. The new

[60] See above, p. 71.
[61] Liddell Hart, *Strategy of Indirect Approach*, pp. 199–200. The complete "Analysis of Cavalry Operations in the American Civil War, with Special Reference to Raids on Communications," is reprinted as Appendix B in Luvaas, *Military Legacy of the Civil War*, pp. 237–44.
[62] Liddell Hart, *When Britain Goes to War*, pp. 254–63, 280–96; *Thoughts on War*, p. 200; *The Tanks*, I, 304–31 *passim*.

position enlarged the scope of his activities from military affairs to defense questions in general, giving him "a channel where what one says tends to have a much bigger effect—and effect," Liddell Hart confided to a friend, "is what matters most." [63] The outlook became brighter still in 1936, when Field Marshal Sir C. J. Deverell replaced Montgomery-Massingberd as C.I.G.S. to the obvious relief of progressive soldiers throughout the army. "We shall have no more of the wretched clique which have ruled the Army for more than 10 years," General Sir Edmund Ironside announced when he heard the welcome news. Later he confessed that finding the Milne-Massingberd regime gone "was like being relieved of a ton-weight. I went into the War Office for the first time for 10 years and I felt the atmosphere quite different." [64]

Liddell Hart also rejoiced. Now the cordial relations he had maintained with some of the younger officers in the War Office could include the new C.I.G.S. himself. With the prestige of the *Times* behind him, a new and more progressive regime in the War Office, and what one high-ranking officer described as "the renaissance of interest in defence measures" [65] that followed the recent decision to rearm, Liddell Hart had fertile ground in which to sow the seeds of reform. He intensified his press campaign for mechanization and mobile forces for the Middle East; he made practical suggestions for more comfortable clothing and living conditions for the soldier; he urged the adoption of modernized drill throughout the army and higher standards in the territorial army; he tried to awaken an interest in the need to improve antiaircraft defenses, reorganize the army, and co-ordinate defense.[66] He even became actively involved in shaping defense policies.

His opportunity to play a more active role came when Duff Cooper, the war minister, invited him to lunch late in 1935. Duff Cooper wanted Liddell Hart to feel free to pass on criticisms or suggestions. He would be grateful for these, he said, because he was shut off from unofficial advice and he

---

[63] Liddell Hart to Major W. Lloyd Jones, March 6, 1936.

[64] General Sir Edmund Ironside to Liddell Hart, November 17, 1935; May 1, 1936.

[65] Major General the Viscount Gort to Liddell Hart, March 31, 1936.

[66] Many of Liddell Hart's proposals during these eleventh-hour reforms are contained in his books *Europe in Arms* (London, 1937), and *The Defence of Britain* (New York, 1939).

was afraid that his judgment might someday suffer as a consequence. Because soldiers were apt to resent ideas coming from the outside, it was agreed that there would be no publicity given to their informal conversations.[67]

When Duff Cooper left the War Office for the Admiralty in May, 1937, he arranged for Liddell Hart to meet his successor, Leslie Hore-Belisha, thinking it "would be for everybody's benefit if you made friends." [68] Several days later Liddell Hart sent the new war minister a memorandum on "Measures To Improve the Officers' Situation in the Army." This led to a further discussion, and by August Liddell Hart was being asked to draft notes on other military problems. The creation of a research department of the general staff; extra pay for special qualifications; the best arguments for reducing the garrison of India; a suitable announcement for the press about providing scope for younger men as generals; recommendations of officers of outstanding promise—Liddell Hart submitted his considered views on these and many kindred subjects. Before long, things were buzzing at the War Office; friends reported that Hore-Belisha had "set the General Staff a holiday task to work out details much on the lines of your suggestions." But it was also apparent that the new proposals were encountering opposition. Aside from Duff Cooper's earlier warnings that the senior generals often were "absurdly sensitive to criticism," there was another reason for the breakers ahead. According to one friend well placed at the War Office, "the greatest hindrance is that the people at the top don't want to face any big reorganisation." [69]

"You and I are going to make history together," promised the war minister during one of their frequent meetings in the fall of 1937. "I owe everything to your advice, which I have followed at every step." Liddell Hart by this time had become

[67] Liddell Hart's notes of a talk with Duff Cooper, December 14, 1935 (Liddell Hart Papers).

[68] Duff Cooper to Liddell Hart, May 28, 1937.

[69] Martel to Liddell Hart, August 14, 1937; Liddell Hart's notes on a talk with Hobart, August 17, 1937 (Liddell Hart Papers). Liddell Hart kept meticulous records of his conversations and communications with Hore-Belisha and, unless otherwise specified, the following account of their "partnership" is based upon these transcripts. Rather surprisingly, R. J. Minney pays slight attention to the influence of Liddell Hart upon Hore-Belisha's administration at the War Office in 1937–38, although one of the documents he reproduces clearly indicates the realities of their relationship. See Minney, *The Private Papers of Hore-Belisha* (London, 1960), pp. 183–84.

indispensable to Hore-Belisha, whose political background had scarcely equipped him for his present task. Feeling a need for information and advice and lacking sympathy from his own staff, Hore-Belisha naturally turned to the most imaginative and best-informed man on defense matters available. In Liddell Hart he found a man who had spent fifteen years scrutinizing the army and its problems, who was in close contact with progressive officers of the type he wished to seek out and promote, and whose position with the *Times* seemed to assure the support of that powerful organ for the coming reforms. For his part Liddell Hart was equally pleased with the "partnership." For years he had been urging reform and reorganization; now at last he had an opportunity to test his ideas and help modernize, if not fully mechanize, the British army. His own work with the *Times* had to continue, but somehow Liddell Hart found time for the lengthy daily telephone conversations, the frequent luncheon and dinner meetings, and the long hours spent preparing memoranda on details of the proposed reforms.

The senior army officers naturally resented the influence of an outsider. Many in the War Office never had been in sympathy with Liddell Hart's basic views on mechanization; others had been alienated over the years by his outspoken commentary on maneuvers and appointments; a few, according to Hobart, were indignant at the thought that any civilian "should dare to criticize, much more advise the Army." [70] One suspects that the officers were particularly touchy on the question of promotion, since Liddell Hart's recommendations in this area could easily affect an individual's career.

By September, 1937, the general staff was already growing uneasy. Deverell went out of his way to caution Liddell Hart against any radical changes and once went so far as to grab some papers from under the latter's arm, pretending half-jokingly that they were memoranda for the war minister. Possibly his suspicions were allayed for the moment when he found himself holding the Aldershot Command exercise papers,[71] but had he known what the two were spending most of their time discussing, he would have had good cause for concern. For Liddell Hart had been searching the army list for

[70] Major General P. C. S. Hobart to Liddell Hart, July 24, 1937.
[71] The incident is related in Minney, *Private Papers of Hore-Belisha,* pp. 55–56.

names of prominent officers of recognized ability and imagination: a shake-up in the higher command was pending.

Many of the major appointments soon to be made were influenced by Liddell Hart, yet his recommendations were not accepted in two crucial areas. Hore-Belisha wanted Deverell replaced by a younger man who would be more receptive to change. Liddell Hart suggested Wavell, a man of marked originality whose intelligence and opinions he had learned to respect. Hore-Belisha, however, preferred Gort, another friend of long standing, and the latter ultimately received the appointment.

Liddell Hart fought harder for a suitable commander of the mobile division, which in his judgment had been badly led during recent maneuvers. He urged the war minister to appoint someone with "adequate experience in handling a mechanised unit" who had also studied the problems of mechanized operations, someone with the qualifications of Hobart, Pile, or Broad, and not to yield to the desire of the C.I.G.S. by selecting a cavalryman "of late employed in training riding instructors." In the end the appointment went to Major General Alan Brooke (later Field Marshal the Viscount Alanbrooke), a most capable artillery expert in Liddell Hart's estimation, but deliberate in his tactical methods and not at his best in handling mobile forces. Hobart, who had spent three years as commander of the First Tank Brigade, became director of military training; Pile, a dashing tank commander, already had been placed in command of the first antiaircraft division, and Broad's valuable experience was similarly wasted when he was given "a purely administrative post mainly concerned with barracks and the Aldershot Tattoo!" [72]

By the spring of 1938 strains in the "partnership" were in evidence. Although willing to continue, Liddell Hart discovered that his association with the war minister made it awkward to criticize details or the tempo of pending reforms in the *Times*. He began to talk about "regaining my old freedom as a critic," and to press for some sort of official recognition such as adviser on military research that would make it easier for him to communicate directly with others in

[72] Liddell Hart to Hore-Belisha, October 7, 1937; October 19, 1937; October 23, 1937. See also Liddell Hart, *Dynamic Defence* (London, 1940), pp. 36–37.

the War Office. Hore-Belisha, however, followed the suggestion of Gort and his deputy, Lieutenant General Sir Ronald
Adam, by appointing a panel of military scientists to serve as
consultants. He began also to take childish measures to conceal the relationship, mentioning casually to others at the
War Office, "Oh, I see Liddell Hart occasionally, not often,"
and pretending on social occasions that he was unfamiliar
with Liddell Hart's books and unlikely in any case to solicit
the opinions of a writer.[73]

They split openly over what Liddell Hart regarded as "the
utterly inadequate state of our anti-aircraft defense preparations." Claiming that Hore-Belisha had tried to conceal from
him the true state of affairs, a damaging blow as far as the
"partnership" was concerned and a futile attempt to mislead a
man who already was in possession of the vital facts, Liddell
Hart became convinced that the time had come for him to
resume the role of a helpful but independent critic, which he
had been during Duff Cooper's regime at the War Office. He
had to feel free to criticize government policies in the *Times;*
to remain silent any longer would, in his view, "have been a
crime against the country's security." By July the partnership
was finally dissolved, although for many months yet the
public and even close friends continued to believe that Liddell
Hart was still at the elbow of the war minister.[74]

It is not necessary to discuss the constructive efforts by
Hore-Belisha to reorganize and reform the army or even to
develop Liddell Hart's role in this urgent endeavor: the
subject would require a separate volume and is in any case too
intricate and technical to be treated here. Suffice it to say that
Liddell Hart provided the inspiration and momentum for
many of the reforms pushed through during the first two years
Hore-Belisha was in office. He would have preferred to have
moved at a slower pace, but the international situation and
the military requirements of Britain did not permit this and

[73] Liddell Hart to Hore-Belisha, March 29, 1938; March 31, 1938; notes
on a talk with Hore-Belisha, April 5, 1938; notes, June 2, 1938.

[74] Liddell Hart, "Notes for Hore-Belisha," June 27, 1938; June 28,
1938. Another factor inducing Liddell Hart to cut his ties with Hore-
Belisha was a divergence of views over the treatment of Mr. Duncan
Sandys, whose questions in Parliament regarding deficiencies in Britain's air defenses revealed sources of information that suggested "a
serious breach of the Official Secrets Act." The story is told in Minney,
Private Papers of Hore-Belisha, pp. 122–30.

his own temperament in any case would have made it difficult.[75]

What is pertinent, however, is the impact that the brief association with Hore-Belisha had on Liddell Hart's subsequent career. For he discovered that men whom he had considered close friends were working against his influence in order to protect vested interests at the same time that they paid lip service to his ideas. Gort suddenly lost his reforming zeal and a month after becoming C.I.G.S. warned: "We must go slow for a time. We must not upset the people in the clubs." And Adam, who owed his appointment as deputy C.I.G.S. to Liddell Hart's recommendation, soon grew distant and aloof. Strained relationships with other friends prompted Liddell Hart to write in May, 1938:

> I am coming to feel that from a long-term point of view, the most damaging step I've ever taken was to go in with . . . Hore-Belisha. Previous to that I was in an unassailable position, standing apart, yet on good terms with most of the rising generation of soldiers. I put forward my ideas in print and could keep up the pressure . . . until they were adopted. Now, every suggestion which I put up, through Hore-Belisha, is resisted. And the people I have helped to put in power are trying to cut off my influence. Worse still, they know who are the other men of whom I had a high opinion, and are trying to keep them out. Thus it is becoming dangerous to be, and to be known to be, a friend of mine.[76]

It is also possible that each of the partners inadvertently injured the other. Sir John Kennedy, who worked closely with Hore-Belisha in the War Office, claims that one of the army's objections to the secretary of state was his association with Liddell Hart, whose theories "were anathema to many professional soldiers." [77] On the other hand, the following letter from a forthright friend reveals how the "partnership" worked also to the detriment of Liddell Hart. "For many years," wrote an old campaigner in the fight for mechanization,

[75] Liddell Hart's own views have been placed on record in his book, *Defence of Britain*, pp. 163–87, 255–436.

[76] Liddell Hart, "Notes for Hore-Belisha," May 31, 1938; "Note on a talk with Hobart," January 12, 1938; "Note on a talk with Gort," January 21, 1938 (Liddell Hart Papers). Gort also told Pile that the army had to be run by soldiers again, "and not by newspaper men" (Liddell Hart, "Note on a talk with Pile," January 14, 1938).

[77] Major General Sir John Kennedy, *The Business of War* (New York, 1958), p. 14.

you and I have talked most freely—neither of us has ever abused the confidence of the other. I hope my friendship has been some help to you and I know to what great lengths you have gone to help me. I want that intimacy to continue. I will still keep you as fully au fait with matters I have knowledge of as before, but . . . I do not want to give Hore-Belisha sticks to beat the Army Council with. I think they are out to do what they think just for the Army and I fear Hore-Belisha is only out for Hore-Belisha. . . . I could come and discuss this with you but it clears my own mind to put it on paper and I have a hope that it may tend to strengthen your own views. And that you may resume the role of impartial critic. This must be not only pleasanter for you but better for the defence of our country, and infinitely safer from your personal point of view.[78]

Within a year of the dissolution of the partnership Liddell Hart felt it necessary also to resign from the *Times*. That paper had been growing increasingly reluctant to print criticisms of weaknesses in the nation's defenses. "Close observation has made me increasingly conscious of the serious inefficiency of our forces," Liddell Hart protested to Geoffrey Dawson, the editor, in August, 1938.

. . . if I am unable to do anything effective towards correcting the faults, I have no mind or heart to continue writing about the military preparations that are likely to prove futile. If I were to . . . write mere half-truths, I should be more guilty of misleading the public than those who lack the knowledge that I have acquired.

There was in addition a fundamental disagreement over editorial policies. In 1935 Liddell Hart had urged the editor to press for effective economic sanctions against Italy; in 1936 he had wanted a stronger line taken against the Fascist countries in Spain; in 1938 he attacked the *Times*' support of appeasement at Munich, and in 1939 he questioned the wisdom of the Polish Guaranty, which represented a complete and sudden reversal of British policy and, according to Liddell Hart, was impossible to fulfil without the active assistance of Russia. As for the Polish army, Liddell Hart reminded the assistant editor of Wellington's comments about several of his own subordinates: "My God, I only hope that they frighten the enemy as much as they frighten me." [79]

[78] Sir Frederick Pile to Liddell Hart, July 5, 1938.
[79] Liddell Hart to Geoffrey Dawson, August 10, 1938; April 30, 1937; October 5, 1938; Liddell Hart to Robert M. Barrington-Ward (assistant editor, the *Times*), March 24, 1938; March 29, 1938; September 20, 1938; January 2, 1939; January 7, 1939; May 9, 1939.

Out of step with the *Times* on foreign affairs and opposed to the current "whoop for compulsory service" on the grounds that a small, mobile, professional force was inherently superior to a mass army based upon conscription, Liddell Hart tried in various ways to carry his case to the public. Beginning in January, 1939, he published an occasional article in evening and Sunday papers not in direct competition with the *Times;* he also threw together in a month's time a book compiled from previous articles and hitherto unpublished memoranda. Then in June, just as he was finishing the proofs to *The Defence of Britain,* he was stricken with a heart attack. He tried to see the *Times* through the maneuver season before finally severing his connection, but the task was too much for him and he collapsed again from exhaustion. Thus when the war came Liddell Hart was no longer associated with either the War Office or the *Times,* nor had he fully recovered from his physical breakdown during the summer and the strain of a marital crisis.[80]

More than Liddell Hart's health suffered in this final effort to warn the nation of the inadequacy of Britain's defenses: his reputation as a military critic and theorist also was severely, though not permanently injured. For largely on the basis of recommendations advocated in *The Defence of Britain* for measures best calculated to meet the specific military and political situation that existed in 1939, Liddell Hart became identified in the public mind and also in the minds of many soldiers with defensive policies that seemed at the time to lead directly to Dunkirk.[81] In the disillusionment that followed, many accused him of being a false prophet and his defensive doctrines often were distorted and ridiculed. It was even rumored abroad that his physical collapse was in some way connected with the collapse of his favorite theories, an erroneous impression that may have gained some credence from the fact that he no longer was associated with the *Times.*

[80] Liddell Hart, diary notes, March 22, 1939; Liddell Hart to Cyril Lakin, November 30, 1939; Liddell Hart to J. M. Scammell, August 7, 1940.

[81] For an assessment of his influence based upon what appeared in print at the time, see Irving M. Gibson, "Maginot and Liddell Hart: The Doctrine of Defense," in Edward Mead Earle (ed.), *Makers of Modern Strategy: Military Thought from Machiavelli to Hitler* (Princeton, N.J., 1943), pp. 375–87. Gibson's account reveals as much about the mood and misconception at the time as it does about Liddell Hart, who is viewed here largely through the eyes of his critics.

His occasional articles in papers like the *News Chronicle* and the *Evening Standard* and his periodical commentaries that appeared in the *Daily Mail* after March, 1941, were obviously much less known outside of England than what he had written previously for the *Times*.

To what extent are these criticisms justified? Certainly the general impression gained from a casual reading of his writings immediately prior to the war, particularly *Europe in Arms* and *The Defence of Britain,* do indeed make him chief counsel for the defense. Isolated phrases like "on the whole, in a modern war of peoples a new truth is becoming apparent— that defence is the best attack," and "in sum, the soldier's dream of the 'lightning war' has a decreasing prospect of fulfillment" [82] could easily have conveyed the notion in 1941–42 that what Liddell Hart advocated was essentially what Britain and France had attempted during the so-called "phoney war" or "sitzkrieg" that preceded the German conquest of France. As a result Liddell Hart himself was placed on the defensive, and in defending his theories he frequently was as reluctant as the generals of 1914–18 to give up familiar ground. There was a difference, he explained to one critic, between what he felt and what the policy of the *Times* and the tense political situation allowed him to write: one must therefore be sophisticated enough to read between the lines and familiar enough with his earlier books to see what he had really meant. But this approach is too indirect to be appreciated by the average reader: even an able student of military affairs like S. L. A. Marshall claimed "that several of the major premises" of Liddell Hart's doctrine "have been proved absurdly wrong by the passage of events. False doctrine is never so dangerous as when it is forcefully presented by a brilliant logician." [83]

In judging what one political commentator has labeled "the strange case of Liddell Hart," [84] it is necessary to look at the entire structure of his theories in the 1930's rather than the last-minute attempt to adjust these to the facts of geography and politics and to the military capabilities of the Western

[82] Liddell Hart, *Defence of Britain*, pp. 42, 125.
[83] Marshall, *Blitzkrieg: Armies on Wheels* (Washington, 1943), p. 59 n.
[84] Crossman, *Charm of Politics*, pp. 223–24. See also Colonel Robert J. Icks, "Liddell Hart: One View," *Armor* (November–December 1952), pp. 25–27.

democracies in 1939. For the curious fact is that his recommendations for the defense of Britain were suddenly discredited when the Germans brilliantly executed his strategy of indirect approach and achieved a deep strategic penetration through the Ardennes to the Channel by the use of armored forces organized as he had suggested years before and led by an acknowledged disciple.

It should be kept in mind that Liddell Hart's pre-war writings emphasized the inherent superiority of the defense under the conditions that prevailed in 1914–18—a verdict that was reinforced by the War Office committee that studied the official histories. Convinced that the offensive could succeed only through the development of new weapons and techniques—armored mobility, night attacks, a strategy of indirect approach—he became a proponent of mechanization. Then, aware of the progress of the totalitarian powers, particularly Germany and Russia, in creating new-style armored formations, seeing in the Abyssinian campaign fresh evidence that mass manpower was no match for machines, and deducing from the war in Spain "that the ultimate general effect of mechanization will be towards enhancing the power of defence," [85] Liddell Hart suggested the course for Britain to follow in the "second Great War," which he contended already had begun with the involvement of Germany and Italy in the Spanish Civil War. If he leaned "rather far on the defensive side," to borrow a phrase from Martel, he never advocated the defensive as a constant policy: he was concerned primarily with the situation facing Britain in 1939.[86]

The crucial problem that concerned Liddell Hart was how to avoid a repetition of the sequence of events that had led to Passchendaele and "national exhaustion"—"strategic entanglement, illimitable expansion, mass conscription, futile sacrifice." The first he would seek to avoid by a return to the traditional British strategy "based on economic pressure exercised through sea-power" and embracing "sea-borne expeditions against the enemy's vulnerable extremities" and the dispatch of one or two mechanized divisions to France. Even after Munich, when the altered balance of forces made

---

[85] Liddell Hart, *Europe in Arms*, pp. 21–39, 302–18.
[86] Liddell Hart, *Defence of Britain*, p. 65; Martel to Liddell Hart, April 1, 1943.

it appear probable that substantial British reinforcements would have to go to France, Liddell Hart urged that the British contribution consist essentially of air and sea support *and mechanized forces.* The latter would be in harmony with Britain's historic strategy, it would have the additional advantage of representing a more controllable commitment than the B.E.F. that was sucked into the vortex in 1914, and above all it would provide the type of reinforcements France most critically needed.

Liddell Hart's critics have overlooked his qualification of the growing superiority of the defense. The offensive "is likely to succeed," he still maintained in 1939, "in a campaign where the defender has no effective counter-weapons to nullify the offensive instruments such as aircraft and tanks." An expeditionary force of three armored divisions would, therefore, greatly strengthen the defense of France by providing "exceptional power and mobility of counterstroke": used as a strategic reserve behind the French lines, it would constitute the ideal counterweapon to German Panzer divisions. Liddell Hart argued against adopting the offensive in 1939 because, convinced from his studies of the last war that a superiority "approaching three to one in weapon-power is necessary for the offensive to succeed," he could see no logical grounds for assuming that Britain and France "would enjoy such favorable odds," qualitatively or even quantitatively, against Germany. Therefore he recommended a strategy of "active and mobile defence" and emphasized the counteroffensive "after the enemy has overstrained himself" as a means of combining "the immediate advantages of the defence and the ultimate advantages of the attack." [87]

It may be argued, as it was vehemently when Liddell Hart's controversial "Attack and Defence" articles first appeared in October, 1937,[88] that such a strategy does not win wars, or at least cannot produce total victory, and that it was politically impossible, however desirable it might be from a military point of view, to leave France to bear the main weight of the burden. With regard to the first criticism, it should be pointed

[87] Liddell Hart, *British Way in Warfare*, pp. 13–41; *Defence of Britain*, pp. 100–125, 209–10; "The Defense of the Empire," *Fortnightly Review*, CXLIII, N.S. (1938), 20–31.

[88] For the case against Liddell Hart's theories, see Gibson's chapter in Earle, *Makers of Modern Strategy*, pp. 375–87.

out that Liddell Hart questioned both the possibility of victory in a war where one side did not enjoy a substantial edge in armament and resources, and the common assumption "that war inevitably means a fight to a finish." The ultimate victory of the united nations, chief among which were Russia and the United States—neither of them certain allies and one a potential enemy in 1939—does not disprove the validity of Liddell Hart's evaluation of the situation as it existed in 1939; [89] nor, in view of more recent attacks upon the policy of "unconditional surrender" announced in 1943 at Casablanca, does he deserve to be ridiculed for questioning the advisability of such a doctrine: the issue is not nearly as clear today as it appears to have been during the war, when Liddell Hart's stock had declined.

As for the view that his recommendations would, if followed, have left a disproportionate share of fighting to the French, it is only fair to point out that while the thought bothered many British officers, there were at the time well-informed soldiers in France who indorsed *The Defence of Britain*. The semiofficial *Revue militaire générale francaise* defended his point of view, and no less an authority than General Chassin has since asserted that Liddell Hart was proved "painfully right" by the events of 1940.[90] Goutard's frank history of the Allied collapse and lost opportunities in the battle of France also makes it clear that time and again the German Panzer corridor that stretched 125 miles from the Meuse to the Channel might have been severed and Guderian's armored spearhead stopped by a strategic mobile reserve, had there been one,[91] in which case Liddell Hart could

[89] In August, 1939, Liddell Hart predicted that "the most probable result of prolonged efforts to restore Poland's territory would be the mutual exhaustion of all the warring countries, with the consequent establishment of Russia's supremacy in Europe" (Liddell Hart, *The Current of War* [London, 1941], p. 146). And in March of the following year an official of the ministry of information wrote informing him "that our critics in the United States are spreading the view that the Allies cannot win the war and that they are citing in support of this view alleged statements by you." Would Liddell Hart be willing to help the war effort by writing something for publication in America which would "come down strongly in favour of the continuation of the war and . . . of the thesis that the Allies can . . . achieve their object of restoring Poland and Czechoslovakia and guaranteeing Europe against a recurrence of German aggression" (D. to Liddell Hart, March 18, 1940).

[90] Général L. M. Chassin, "Un grand penseur militaire britannique: B. H. Liddell Hart," *Revue de défense nationale* (October, 1950), p. 338.

[91] Goutard, *Battle of France*, 1940, pp. 78, 89, 180–223.

just as easily have been discredited for being overoptimistic about the potentialities of the tank and unrealistic in thinking that the deep strategic penetration of the Mongols was possible in modern warfare! As it was, his theories were among the reasons advanced for what happened in 1940, even though the allies did not follow his suggested antidote to his own conception of armored warfare.

Liddell Hart's career after 1940 lies beyond the scope of this work. To describe his personal activities during the past twenty-five years would be a formidable task even for the biographer; to analyze his published wartime commentaries and his confidential proposals for surmounting military problems[92] would be pointless without an accompanying chapter on the war itself; while to evaluate his military and strategic thinking since 1945 would necessitate a detailed examination of a new and radically different set of problems involving nuclear weapons, missiles, NATO, Berlin, and Cuba—all of which have occupied his attention in recent years. But this account of Liddell Hart's writings during the interwar period should offer ample proof that his views on the present world scene merit close attention.[93]

This is not to suggest that Liddell Hart has always been correct. Like Fuller, he was wrong in his belief that gas would play an important part in the next war; he now concedes that he "went too far in arguing the advantages of the air stroke at civil objectives," and that he overemphasized the importance of rivers and canals as serious obstacles to mechanized forces. His prophecy that a future war would be decided by small mechanized armies was unfulfilled because at no time in 1939–45 was there a small mechanized army—the war was fought with large, conventional forces using armored divisions for spearheads.[94]

Critics have found fault with his theories on other grounds. Wavell, who considered him "the most stimulating and thoughtful military writer, by far, that we have," chided him gently for searching for "the military philosopher's stone" in

---

[92] Many of these are found in Liddell Hart, *Dynamic Defence* (London 1940), *The Current of War*, and *This Expanding War* (London, 1943).

[93] See Liddell Hart, *The Revolution in Warfare* (London, 1946); *Defence of the West: Some Riddles of War and Peace* (London, 1950); and *Deterrent or Defense: A Fresh Look at the West's Military Position* (New York, 1960).

[94] Liddell Hart, *Strategy: The Indirect Approach*, p. 363.

"hoping to find some formula to win wars without fighting." Field Marshal Sir Philip Chetwode accused him of succumbing to the "unscrupulous" propaganda of the air ministry: "You know perfectly well," this prominent soldier declared a scant six years before the sinking of the "Prince of Wales" and the "Repulse" by Japanese aircraft, "that the Navy laughs at the Air now. They have got protected decks, and with their blisters and multiple machine guns and . . . antiaircraft guns, they don't fear them in the slightest." Liddell Hart also was exposed to the same cross fire from old-line infantry and cavalry officers that Fuller had encountered in advancing his theories: there were many, even in the 1930's, who remained contemptuous of the "garage school" of military thought.[95]

One suspects that Liddell Hart's critics often were more irritated by the way in which he expressed his ideas than by any specific theories or proposals for reform, for even his friends felt occasionally that he failed "to make allowance for the Regular's point of view." Wavell called attention to passages "which I can assure you do irritate and annoy unnecessarily . . . it is a pity and detracts from the value of your writings." Another suggested that by trying "to make capital out of running down the Higher Command" and "your rather pontifical and contemptuous way" of referring to a past with which the senior commanders are closely identified, Liddell Hart was alienating unnecessarily the very people who were in a position to "help the cause"—"a pity, because resentment prevents them from grasping and appreciating what you have to say." An American officer explained to Liddell Hart that although he was impressed by his "ability to see more than the usual historian" and fully in agreement with his strategical principles, he felt it necessary to write a critical review of a recent book because

[95] Wavell to Liddell Hart, March 15, 1934; June 16, 1936; Field Marshal Sir Philip Chetwode to Liddell Hart, July 28, 1935; "The 'Garage' School of Thought," *Army Quarterly*, XXI (1931), 380–83. For the detailed views of one of the more extreme opponents of the Fuller-Liddell Hart theory of mechanized warfare, see Victor Wallace Germains, *The Mechanization of War* (London, 1937), and "Mirage and Mechanization,"*Edinburgh Review*, CCL (1929), 128–38. Germains attempted to demonstrate that the tank had not been a formidable weapon in the First World War and that therefore the claims of Fuller and Liddell Hart rested upon a shaky foundation. While recognizing the limited value of the tank as an adjunct to infantry, Germains contended that future war would be dominated by armies which had attained a superiority in conventional weapons.

. . . the intelligentsia . . . are only too happy to take a fall out of the military. I rather resented the gloating of the civilians over here over your criticism of the military mind. I know too well how much warrant there is for your conclusions and I fear my class consciousness got somewhat the better of my judgment. I wrote as I did for a very particular audience. Had I written for a military periodical I should not have felt the same urge to defend the military mind.[96]

Others questioned the historical basis for his theories. Spenser Wilkinson challenged his interpretation of some of the doctrines of Clausewitz, accused him of being doctrinaire rather than historical in presenting his case for a strategy of indirect approach, and was inclined to think that the Captain "writes too much and is in a hurry." [97] Colonel E. H. Beadon attacked Liddell Hart for slanting history to support his theories, a point that some who were far more sympathetic also have conceded. Wavell, who voiced the doubts of many British soldiers in wondering whether there is "any true 'theory' of war," once slyly suggested to Liddell Hart that "with your knowledge and brains and command of the pen, you could have written just as convincing a book called the Strategy of the Direct Approach." [98]

Such criticism is not without foundation, especially in the case of *The Decisive Wars of History* and its lineal descendants. Having spent years seeking, defining, and testing principles, it is perhaps to be expected that Liddell Hart should be attracted to patterns in history (he believed also that Fuller's "three-fold law holds the germ of a great and far-reaching truth" [99]); and in looking to past wars for con-

[96] Wavell to Liddell Hart, March 15, 1934; General Sir John Burnett-Stuart to Liddell Hart, September 14, 1932; November 7, 1936; Lieutenant Colonel A. to Liddell Hart, January 27, 1937.

[97] "The right way to get there (wherever he is going) is to go quietly, slow and sure" (Spenser Wilkinson to J. M. Scammell, January 18, 1928 [Scammell Papers]); Wilkinson to Liddell Hart, June 14, 1924; "Comments on Liddell Hart's Article 'Strategy' for the Encyclopaedia Britannica" (Liddell Hart Papers). See also Wilkinson, "Killing No Murder: An Examination of Some New Theories of War," *Army Quarterly*, XV (1927), 14–27.

[98] Sir Ivor Maxse to Liddell Hart, September 4, 1932; Beadon, "Some Strategical Theories of Captain Liddell Hart," *R.U.S.I. Journal*, LXXXI (1936), 747–60; Wavell to Liddell Hart, January 5, 1935; January 23, 1942. For a reiteration of the view that "the weakness of Captain Liddell Hart rested upon a shaky foundation. While recognizing the limited has led him to try to prove too much," see Gordon Harrison, "Master of Indirect Approach," *Saturday Review* (August 28, 1954), pp. 11–12.

[99] Liddell Hart to Scammell, February 5, 1924 (Scammell Papers).

firmation of theories deduced principally from the campaigns of the Mongols and of Sherman, it is scarcely surprising that the indirect approach would crop up again and again in italics, sometimes in sharper focus than a close look at the facts would allow and occasionally to the exclusion of other factors. Similarly, by resorting to catch phrases—which he created initially to make his concepts more graphic—to explain military movements, he has been guilty at times of oversimplification. What may appear to have been a successful example of the "baited gambit" or of "alternative objectives" may in fact have been a far more intricate or confused situation than the term itself would imply.

If these criticisms are true of those works on the conduct of war in which history provides the vehicle or confirmation of Liddell Hart's theories, they do not apply to his major works on history. *Sherman, Foch, Lawrence,* and *A History of the World War* have weathered the storms remarkably well: they represent sound and original research, careful, objective analysis, and a genuine desire to get at the truth. In editing *The Letters of Private Wheeler* and *The Rommel Papers* Liddell Hart has demonstrated meticulous scholarship, and his latest work of history, *The Tanks,* is a masterpiece that may become a military classic. In describing the fight for mechanization Liddell Hart has been almost as careful as Thucydides to conceal his own efforts and treat the opposition impartially. If the theorist dominated the historical examination of the strategy of indirect approach, in *The Tanks* it is the historian who prevails.

In a work of this scope one can only suggest the nature and extent of Liddell Hart's influence. In the 1920's his views on training and tactics were incorporated into his own *Infantry Training* manual, retained to some degree by Gort and Montgomery in subsequent revisions, and supported by influential soldiers such as Maxse and Lieutenant General Sir David Campbell. Three of his works—*Paris, or the Future of War, Great Captains Unveiled,* and *A Greater than Napoleon* —were among the twelve books officially recommended in 1927 for the theoretical preparation for the experimental mechanized force,[100] and the first British official manuals on armored forces reflected many of his ideas. *Mechanized and*

Armoured Formations (1929) was written by Broad, and if it advanced Fuller's view that such formations should be composed purely of tanks it also incorporates many of the ideas (even some of the phrases) of Liddell Hart. The revised manual issued in 1931 under the title *Modern Formations* likewise contains many of Liddell Hart's theories and indorses his basic philosophy that "without mobility, decisions could be sought only by a process of attrition. So costly is this process that its repetition would end our present civilization." [101]

In the decade of the 1930's Liddell Hart's influence upon the infantry training manuals declined, although his drill system for movement and deployment under fire was successfully practiced in the Eastern Command in 1937 [102] and later was adopted by the War Office. But his writings on mechanization—largely because Fuller began to cultivate other fields upon retirement, his own friends in the tank corps had reached positions where they often could implement his theories, and his prestige had continued to rise—carried if anything still greater weight than before. In the general area of defense policies Liddell Hart now found his views solicited by M.P.'s and other public officials, and his rapport with Duff Cooper and "partnership" with Hore-Belisha gave him an unusual opportunity to translate ideas into action. Advancing on a broad front Liddell Hart used his books, the *Times*, and his personal influence to arouse the nation and the nation's leaders to the need for preparedness.

Liddell Hart's influence upon individuals is much more difficult to assess. He had a strong following among the younger, more progressive officers, many of whom appear to have accepted nearly everything that he wrote. Then there were others, men like Montgomery, Gort, and Wavell, who found much food for reflection in his writings if they did not agree with him in every detail: Wavell once referred to *The Ghost of Napoleon* as "an excellent mental irritant." [103] Even those who spoke of Liddell Hart "in the most damnatory terms" occasionally found themselves in agreement with some

[101] *Modern Formations* (1931 Provisional), pp. 10, 14.
[102] Lieutenant General C. G. Liddell to Liddell Hart, June 5, 1937; Liddell Hart to C. S. Forester, March 15, 1937.
[103] Wavell to Liddell Hart, January 5, 1935. Montgomery also admitted that "in many cases the inspiration has come from your writings, which I always read with no small benefit" (Montgomery to Liddell Hart, September 7, 1937).

particular article or proposal.[104] In his efforts to prevent
Britain from returning to the unlimited policy in land
commitments that had dictated British strategy in the First
World War and from building up a large conventional army
for intervention on the Continent, Liddell Hart probably did
not influence British policy so much as he articulated the
feelings of those who could not get the experiences of
1914–18 out of their systems.[105] His conception of mechanized
warfare, on the other hand, was a vital part of a co-operative
process conceived and developed in Britain but finding its
greatest practitioners among the Germans, a surprisingly
large number of whom have publicly acknowledged their debt
to the coauthor of the *Blitzkrieg*. Even in England his
influence was probably more real than apparent. According to
Sir Christopher Bullock, who spent many years "in close and
continuous touch with the Whitehall Defence Machine,"

. . . no single individual outside Whitehall exercised so far reaching and beneficial an influence on successive generations of the
General and Air Staffs. If his ruthless logic was sometimes un-
palatable to those who lived unduly in the past to the neglect of
the present and the future, it was salutary—and most helpful to
those of us who were striving for reform from within—that someone outside should have the courage and independence of mind to
apply a long overdue stimulus." [106]

Looking at his creative contributions as theorist, military
correspondent, historian, and reformer, and especially in view
of the impact that his work has had upon the twentieth-
century revolution in warfare, surely the time has come to
recognize the greatness of Liddell Hart.

[104] The first chapter in *Europe in Arms* "has made one notable convert,
Sir Philip Chetwode. He usually speaks of you in the most damnatory
terms, but he thought that chapter fine" (Lieutenant Colonel R. M.
Raynsford to Liddell Hart, April 23, 1937).
[105] "I broached the subject . . . at a lunch Club of Dons. . . . Nearly
all served in the War. . . . There was a consensus . . . that you had
written just what we all wanted to say, and a chorus of appreciation of
your articles. I think it is epoch-making stuff. *You have done a good
deed, my boy.*" E. W. Swinton to Liddell Hart (1937). Liddell Hart's
files contain dozens of letters from prominent Englishmen expressing
similar sentiments.
[106] Sir Christopher Bullock to Liddell Hart, March 30, 1946.

12

EPILOGUE

THIS study of eleven personalities, scattered as they are over more than a century and selected initially to satisfy my own curiosity about individuals overlooked or misunderstood by history, can hardly constitute a sound basis for generalized conclusions. A comprehensive survey of British military thought would probably be a more reliable guide to trends in tactics and strategy, the impact of technology upon military theory and practice, and the influence of political considerations at home and of theorists abroad. Yet one is tempted to offer a few observations on what would appear to be trends in British military thinking and on the course and effect of ideas upon the evolution of the modern British army.

Manifestly, there are different ways in which a military man can make his mark with the pen. Military history is perhaps the most obvious or common medium, and in this field the British writers have made significant and enduring contributions. Napier, Henderson, Wilkinson, Fuller, and Liddell Hart must rank among the world's foremost military historians, and *The War in the Crimea* suggests that Hamley too could have marched in the front ranks had he not succumbed to an interest in literature. These historians all paid scrupulous attention to accuracy; each cultivated a distinct and highly readable style. *History of the War in the Peninsula,* for all its faults, remains a noble classic; *Stonewall Jackson and the American Civil War* has yet to be replaced; Wilkinson became an important pioneer in *The Brain of an Army, The Rise of General Bonaparte,* and *The Defence of Piedmont.* Fuller explored some unknown eighteenth-century theorists and wrote thought-provoking books on the Civil War: his *Decisive Battles of the Western World* will long remain a landmark in military literature. Liddell Hart's exposition of Sherman's strategy and his exposé of the generalship in World War I have weathered the recent flood of books in the one field and the stormy debates still aroused by the other. *The Tanks* alone would establish him as an eminent historian.

Some of these writers influenced the study of military history in another sense. MacDougall and Hamley were both instrumental in establishing the subject as part of the course of study at the Staff College; Maurice and Henderson were the men most responsible for its popularity at that institution; and Wilkinson introduced the study of war to the British universities.

These writers also show the many facets to military history. To Napier, history meant narrative within the framework of accepted military maxims, and he drew upon the latter to explain some maneuver or to pass judgment upon the individual commanders. Mitchell on the other hand found history useful in examining the validity of cherished notions on armament and tactics: his method of proving the rule by citing the exception was no more historical than it was scientific, but he did regard history as a helpful guide to the future.

Burgoyne never wrote history. MacDougall and Hamley used historical examples to illustrate the views of Continental theorists. MacDougall especially appreciated the didactic value of history and in this respect he was a forerunner of Maurice and Henderson, whose historical studies of the American Civil War and the German wars for unification suggested that the proper tactical lessons of both conflicts were being overlooked. Henderson also developed a novel use for military history in employing campaign studies as a means for self-instruction or evaluation in tactics and command.

Beginning with Maurice military history also served to provide answers to current questions of policy and organization. In documenting the army's case against the proposed Channel tunnel, Maurice made some rather surprising discoveries about the frequency of undeclared wars. Similarly, Repington searched the plans of Moltke and the treatises of German theorists to demonstrate the possibilities of invasion, and Wilkinson analyzed the nature and functions of the Prussian general staff to learn what ought to be transplanted in English soil. At the same time, however, Wilkinson urged the study of many wars, rather than the excessive concentration upon a few campaigns, in order to discover features common to all wars and to understand the complex nature of war itself.

Maurice and to a lesser extent Henderson reveal something of the plight of the official historian. Established writers at the time they assumed their official duties, and honest in their intention to get at the facts, each found it difficult to expose mistakes in high quarters and Maurice especially was aware of the problem of public reactions. Neither man, however, was a captive of the general staff, which so often was the case upon the Continent, nor did official history in England ever serve merely to illustrate army doctrine. On the other hand, Liddell Hart's relations with Edmonds and the findings of the War Office committee appointed in 1932 to examine the lessons of World War I suggest that the official history of that conflict, if utilized properly, might have had a constructive influence upon British doctrine prior to 1939.

Finally, with Fuller and Liddell Hart military history became important in still another sense—as a basis for new theories. Fuller originally deduced his principles of war from Napoleon's *Correspondence,* and many of Liddell Hart's tank theories and the essential ingredients of his strategy of indirect approach owe their inspiration to his study of Mongol warfare and the campaigns of Sherman. However, it should be pointed out that not all of their historical works served as foundation for theory. Both men were as anxious to teach as they were to learn, and sometimes they regarded history as a platform for their own ideas.

British military writers have often found an outlet in journalism. Mitchell and Hamley frequently contributed to the literary journals, and Maurice acted as special correspondent for the *Daily News* during the Ashanti campaign, he revived the *United Service Magazine,* and in 1904–5 he analyzed military developments in Manchuria for the *Daily Telegraph.* Henderson represented the *Times* at foreign military maneuvers. Fuller covered the Abyssinian campaign as special correspondent to the *Daily Mail* and wrote commentaries on the military operations of World War II.

But the most creative accomplishments in the field of journalism was the work, not of soldiers who went abroad, but rather of civilian critics who remained at home—the military correspondents. For over half a century there was a Wilkinson, a Repington, or Liddell Hart to interpret military maneuvers, explain the latest development in military science, expose military weaknesses and public fallacies, and fight for reforms in organization and training. Each had the backing of a powerful newspaper; each had access to friends in high places; each enjoyed an immense public following; and each advanced the cause of reform. No other country has produced military commentators to match their accomplishments or to rival them in influence.

With the exception of Napier, who declined an invitation to write a general treatise on war, these soldiers wrote widely on various topics touching military art and science. Mitchell exposed the fundamental weakness in Napoleonic tactics and the shortcomings in the British system, although it may be questioned whether his particular solutions were practical in the 1830's. Burgoyne tackled a score of subjects, but his primary concern was to see that the experience of contemporary wars and recent improvements in weapons and technology were not overlooked. He seems clearly to have understood the military trends of his day. MacDougall and Hamley popularized the theories of Continental writers. In evaluating the tactical lessons of 1861–65 and 1870–71, MacDougall found compelling reasons why Britain should not attempt to imitate the Germans either in tactics or in organization. Lacking the sophistication and literary style of Hamley, he had a keener appreciation of the impact of modern firepower upon tactics. Maurice wrote on nearly every phase of war: as a member of the Wolseley Ring he knew what was going on in the War Office and he could speak with authority on problems of colonial warfare. Henderson applied his knowledge of tactics, which he had acquired from the intelligent study of military history, to the recent campaigns in South Africa and to the changing role of the three arms in modern battle. He also became increasingly absorbed with the study of strategy and its teaching. Wilkinson wrote extensively on doctrine and training, and Repington analyzed changes in the doctrines and armament of the great Continental armies.

But these writers were critics and analysts, not theorists. None ever constructed an original system of his own, and if several correctly indicated the drift of modern war, their approach was pragmatic rather than theoretical. Not until Fuller and Liddell Hart, in fact, did any British soldier advance a new theory that ultimately would change the course of warfare. These foremost architects of the blitzkrieg had many disciples abroad and their influence upon the military world probably was as pronounced—and incalculable—as that of Jomini and Clausewitz a century before. De Gaulle's admirers would have us believe that he was the main creator of mechanized warfare, but this assertion collapses upon reading his book *Vers l'armée de métier*, which was published in 1934. While modern in outlook and presenting a good case for mechanization, De Gaulle said nothing that had not been worked out more systematically and in greater detail by English theorists in the previous decade.

Yet Fuller and Liddell Hart were prophets without honor in their own army, a fact that might be attributed to their aggressive, critical attitudes were it not for the existence of other factors that had discouraged the growth of military theory in an earlier age—the size and distribution of the army and its unique functions during the heyday of empire and years of "splendid isolation," an aristocratic or indifferent officer corps, and a national, perhaps even a natural preference for the man of action, the practitioner. Not until science had forced a revolution in warfare did any British writer seriously approach the study of war with the tools of science, even though lip service had been paid to the idea for over a century.

The writings of these eleven personalities are too varied to be compressed into a single theme. Most of them were concerned about the training and capabilities of the reserve forces; most worked to improve the education of the British officer and to stimulate greater professional interest. As politics became more responsive to public opinion, most of these soldiers wrote also with an eye to instructing the electorate. In varying degrees most of them considered England's position as somehow special, recognizing by the end of the nineteenth century that "much as Clausewitz and Foch have to teach us . . . neither mentions the sea." [1] Of the eleven, Hamley, Repington, and Fuller were probably the most continental in outlook; Maurice, Henderson, Wilkinson, and Liddell Hart seem to have been more concerned than the others to uncover "the British way in warfare."

On specific issues these writers often were sharply divided. Mitchell and Napier took a different view of practically everything; Hamley and Maurice represented opposite schools of strategy with regard to the defense of India; and Wilkinson and Repington did not always see eye to eye. Fuller and Liddell Hart usually stood together, although on minor points (such as the relative merits of Grant and Sherman) even they would disagree. More often than not, however, they found themselves standing side by side—and often alone.

The careers of these writers seem to indicate a general pattern in the evolution of British military thought. They show, for example, that there was very little interest in tactics and none in strategy prior to the Crimean War, and that very little attention initially was devoted to the military literature of other countries. Promotion by purchase, the use of flogging to maintain discipline, and the fear in the 1840's of a possible invasion by the French provided the main themes for those who took up the pen in the years following Waterloo.

The Crimean War and the introduction of improved firearms, together with the German campaigns and those of the American Civil War, created an interest in tactics and encouraged soldiers like MacDougall and Hamley to popularize the theories of prominent writers on the Continent and to apply their knowledge to contemporary war. The mismanagement in the Crimea, followed by the Indian Mutiny and the impressive Prussian victories over France also made imperative a reorganization of the British army. In this fight the pen became a useful weapon, and for the next twenty years British soldiers refought the battles of 1870 in an effort to add proper seasoning to their experiences in colonial warfare.

Beginning in the 1880's a new interest in strategy became apparent. Soldiers began to ponder questions relating to the North West Frontier, the role of an expeditionary force, and the influence of seapower upon Britain's strategic situation. By this time it had also become apparent that wars were too

[1] Major General Sir Frederick Maurice, *British Strategy: A Study of the Application of the Principles of War* (London, 1938), p. 49.

complex to trust to improvisation, and thinking soldiers called for a reorganization of the War Office or at the very least a redistribution of duties that would enable those responsible for the efficiency of the army to prepare adequately during peace and to co-ordinate more effectively in war: the initial defeats in South Africa further strengthened the hands of those pressing for the creation of a modern general staff.

In the years preceding the outbreak of war in 1914, British soldiers wrote profusely on a wide variety of subjects— reform, foreign armies, tactical trends, the role of the expeditionary force, the territorial force, home defense. Every issue had its partisans; every journal had its stable of military experts. By this time most writers seemed content to leave the subject of tactics to those compiling the manuals as they battled the Royal Navy for a larger place in the public estimation—and in the annual estimates. The basic problem after World War I was what kind of conflict to anticipate in the future. Those who expected a repetition of the stalemate on the western front continued to think in terms of the conventional force that had been sent to France in 1914. Those on the other hand who believed that new weapons would make it possible to restore mobility to warfare claimed that a new model army was required, and the debate continued even after Hitler invaded Poland in 1939.

Some of these writers have raised questions that deserve to be asked again. What has been the influence of colonial warfare on the development of British tactics? To what extent has the situation in Canada or India helped to shape the organization of the British army? What role did military considerations have upon the formulation of national policy? How did the members of Parliament who happened also to hold commissions in the army influence legislation? Were Maurice and Henderson correct in their appraisal of the flexibility of Prussian leadership on the battlefield, or was Repington more accurate in describing the German soldier as an automaton? Possibly both points of view were correct at the time they were expressed, which leads one to inquire when the character of the Prussian army changed.

Others in advancing their ideas have encountered barriers that may contain lessons for today. To Mitchell the enemy was the innate conservatism of the military mind—an oversimplification, to be sure, but a real obstacle nonetheless to Wolseley in his dealings with the Duke of Cambridge and also to the able exponents of mechanization. Burgoyne had to contend with public apathy and a reluctant Treasury, which may explain his use of the shock treatment in disclosing the defenseless state of Great Britain in the event of invasion. Hamley pitted an abrasive personality against the Wolseley Ring and lost; personality clashes also helped to undermine the influence of Fuller and Liddell Hart in their own army. Henderson claimed that the army was drifting largely because of a failure in political leadership: the prime minister and the cabinet officials responsible for the armed forces had neglected to establish the policies and priorities essential for intelligent military planning. Wilkinson went further, contending that the major defect in the British military system was that authority usually was intrusted to men lacking knowledge and experience in war. "Victory cannot be won by a government of amateurs." [2]

Another obstacle, one especially troublesome to the civilian analysts, was the tendency among soldiers to resist ideas coming from outsiders. This is evident in Hamley's reaction to Russell's letters from the Crimea, Burgoyne's defense of the regimental officers in that campaign, and Maurice's account of the 1882 campaign in Egypt. It also explains much of the opposition within the War Office to various proposals advanced by Wilkinson and Liddell Hart, neither of whom, it might be pointed out, was given any opportunity in time of war to put his specialized knowledge to work for the government. Wilkinson was ignored by the War Office both in the Boer War and throughout World War I; Liddell Hart's contacts with the War Office during World War II were indirect, and usually he took the initiative.

Yet today the British and still more the United States army are drawing upon the findings of such joint research organizations as The RAND Corporation, the Historical Evaluation and Research Organization, the Institute for Strategic Studies, and similar institutes or seminars established in universities. In a very real sense these collective brains have been developed to do what Wilkinson, Fuller, and Liddell Hart each tried to accomplish on a far more modest scale. Wilkinson compared his studies to that of a naturalist who "collects wars as specimens . . . dissects them . . . compares and classifies them." Nothing would have brought him greater happiness and satisfaction than the opportunity to investigate military problems for a "thinking department" in the general staff. Fuller would go further in establishing research sections within each department of the general staff to deduce lessons from the past and to analyze present trends in technology, economics, and politics, especially as they relate to war. Liddell Hart, too, campaigned for the creation of a department for scientific and operational research. During the interwar years he made a number of statistical analyses on problems such as the age of commanders, the scale of artillery concentration for infantry attacks, the ratio of force to space and the relative effect of cutting an opponent's communications near to the front lines or to his base. [3]

[2] Spenser Wilkinson, *Government and the War* (London, 1918), p. 268.

[3] *Ibid.*, pp. 152–53; Colonel J. F. C. Fuller, *The Reformation of War* (London, 1923), pp. 229–40; Liddell Hart, *Thoughts on War* (London, 1944), pp. 104, 125, 164.

In various ways and in varying degrees these eleven soldiers who took up the pen helped to shape policy and doctrine. Their individual roles have been developed in each chapter; the ultimate result of their collective efforts has been to provide many of the standards and suggestions, and much of the inspiration and momentum for the emergence of the British army from the backward and conservative force of the 1830's to the progressive army of our own era. The establishment of the Staff College, improvements in the living conditions and training of the British soldier, the application of new weapons to tactics, the reorganization of the army under Cardwell, the creation of a general staff, the reforms following the Boer War, the first faltering steps toward mechanization —these are only a few of the areas where the pen has promoted the interests of the army more effectively than the sword. In their specific proposals on these and similar problems, in their influence upon individuals more directly involved in determining policy, and in their contributions to the public discussion of military issues, most of these writers played an important part in the development of the British army.

They were not always successful; they have not always been recognized. Their ideas were of uneven merit and not always the best of these took root. Some of these individuals were only of temporary significance; a few left monumental works behind.

But at one time or another each had the satisfaction of seeing his work bear some good fruit, and a few had a marked effect upon the course of British military thought. For them, at least, the pen was mightier than the sword.

SELECTED BIBLIOGRAPHY

This bibliography indicates the most helpful sources that relate to the history of the British army and military thought from 1815 to 1940. It also includes the basic sources for the careers of the individual subjects and suggests the most typical or significant books written by each.

A complete bibliography of works consulted would contain well over one thousand items, among which would be many anonymous articles and reviews and a number of redundant titles of material published in two or more places. In the interest of saving space, therefore, and with the hope that this distilled list will encourage the reader to become personally acquainted with the major works of some of these personalities, I gladly leave the bulk of my bibliography buried harmlessly in the footnotes and cite here only those works which in my judgment will be the most interesting or significant to read today.

MANUSCRIPT SOURCES

BLACKWOOD PAPERS. National Library of Scotland, Edinburgh.

> Among this very large quantity of letters received by the publishing firm of William Blackwood and Sons Ltd. from its beginnings up to the year 1900 are a number of letters from Hamley, MacDougall, and Maurice.

BURGOYNE, JOHN FOX. Correspondence and Miscellaneous Papers. Royal Engineers Museum, Chatham.

> Most of the correspondence in this collection is published in Wrottesley's *Life and Correspondence of Field Marshal Sir John Fox Burgoyne*, but there is some fresh material on Burgoyne's intellectual activities during the Peninsular War. Of special interest is the thirty-nine page foolscap manuscript analysis of Jomini, which to the writer's knowledge has never appeared in print.

HALDANE, RICHARD BURDON. Correspondence. National Library of Scotland, Edinburgh.

> This important collection includes fifteen letters of Charles À Court Repington.

LIDDELL HART, B. H. Correspondence and Miscellaneous Papers. States House, Medmenham, Marlow, Buckinghamshire.

> A vast collection of letters, notes, manuscripts, and memoranda that reveals the innumerable activities and diversified interests of this historian, journalist, and theorist. Included also are a large number of letters from Major General J. F. C. Fuller. The Liddell Hart Papers ultimately will go to the University of London.

SCAMMELL, J. MARIUS. Correspondence. In the possession of Miss Nancy Scammell, San Mateo, California.

Scammell was an intimate friend of Liddell Hart and a devoted pupil of Spenser Wilkinson: his papers contain many early letters from the former and some of the last correspondence of Wilkinson. Copies of a portion of the Scammell Papers have been deposited in the Duke University Library, Durham, North Carolina.

WILKINSON, SPENSER. Correspondence. Army Museums Ogilby Trust, the War Office, London.

Most of the correspondence preserved by the Ogilby Trust are letters to Wilkinson by his military friends and associates. The Manchester Tactical Society minutes are found in the War Office Library.

Letters to Wilkinson of a more private nature, including those of his brother-in-law and friend, Sir Eyre Crowe, remain in the possession of his daughter, Miss Victoria Wilkinson, London.

WOLSELEY, GARNET JOSEPH, VISCOUNT. Correspondence. Royal United Service Institution, Whitehall.

The great majority of the letters in this collection between Lord and Lady Wolseley have been published, but the editor, Sir George Arthur, was too much the proper Victorian to include the more revealing portions, particularly if these diminished the reputation of a person in the public eye. The Wolseley Papers also contain a few letters from friends intriguing to have Wolseley appointed commander in chief in 1895.

BIOGRAPHIES AND MEMOIRS

All but the more recent writers are included in *The Dictionary of National Biography*. Captain Liddell Hart's memoirs will be published shortly. The most important published sources available for the others are:

BRUCE, H. A. (ed.). *Life of General Sir William Napier, K.C.B., Author of "History of the Peninsular War."* 2 vols. London, 1864.

FULLER, J. F. C. *Memoirs of an Unconventional Soldier.* London, 1936.

MAURICE, FREDERICK. *Sir Frederick Maurice: A Record of His Work and Opinions, with Eight Essays on Discipline and National Efficiency.* London, 1913.

REPINGTON, CHARLES À COURT. *The First World War 1914–1918: Personal Experiences of Lieut.-Col. C. à Court Repington.* 2 vols. London, 1920.

———. *Vestigia: Reminiscences of Peace and War.* Boston, 1919.

REPINGTON, MARY. *Thanks for the Memory.* London, 1938.

ROBERTS, EARL. "Memoir," in NEILL MALCOLM (ed.) *The Science of War: A Collection of Essays and Lectures 1891–1903 by the late Colonel G. F. R. Henderson, C.B.* London, 1906.

SHAND, ALEXANDER INNIS. *The Life of General Sir Edward Bruce Hamley.* 2 vols. Edinburgh, 1895.

WILKINSON, SPENSER. *Thirty-Five Years, 1874–1909.* London, 1933.

WROTTESLEY, GEORGE. *Life and Correspondence of Field Marshal Sir John Burgoyne, Bart.* 2 vols. London, 1873.

THE BRITISH ARMY, 1815–1940

Army Quarterly. 1920–1940.

Army Review. 1911–1914.

ARTHUR, GEORGE. *From Wellington to Wavell.* London, 1942.

COLE, D. H., and E. C. PRIESTLY. *An Outline of British Military History 1660–1939.* London, 1939.

DUNLOP, JOHN K. *The Development of the British Army 1899–1914: From the Eve of the South African War to the Eve of the Great War, with Special Reference to the Territorial Force.* London, 1938.

FORTESCUE, J. W. *A History of the British Army.* 13 vols. London, 1899–1930. Vols. XI–XIII deal with the period in question.

GODWIN-AUSTEN, A. R. *The Staff and the Staff College.* London, 1927.

GOODENOUGH W. H., and J. C. DALTON. *The Army Book for the British Empire: A Record of the Development and Present Composition of the Military Forces and Their Duties in Peace and War.* London, 1893.

JOHNSON, FRANKLYN ARTHUR. *Defence by Committee: The British Committee of Imperial Defence 1885–1959.* London, 1960.

Journal of the Royal United Service Institution. 1857–1940.

OMOND, J. S. *Parliament and the Army 1642–1904.* Cambridge, 1933.

TYLER, J. E. *The British Army and the Continent 1904–1914.* London, 1938.

United Service Magazine. 1829–1914. The title of this important journal varies from 1841 to 1890, when Maurice became the proprietor and editor.

WHEELER, OWEN. *The War Office Past and Present.* London, 1914.

SUGGESTED READINGS

(BURGOYNE.) WROTTESLEY, GEORGE (ed.). *The Military Opinions of General Sir John Fox Burgoyne.* Part I. *National Defences.* II. *The War in the Baltic and Crimea.* III. *Military Maxims, Etc.* London, 1859.

Compiled by his son-in-law at a time when Burgoyne's reputation in the army was at low ebb, this volume contains the essential thoughts of the famous engineer.

FULLER, J. F. C. *The Foundations of the Science of War.* London, 1926.

This is not an easy book to read, and it is more difficult still to understand. It is included here because it represents a new approach to the study of war and because Fuller for at least a decade considered it his most important book. His later view that it was too mechanical and ambitious and should be rewritten does not necessarily detract from its significance as a milestone in military theory.

————. *On Future Warfare.* London, 1928.

An uneven collection of previous articles, this book more than any other imparts the spirit of Fuller's inquiries in the

1920's, when he was struggling to formulate a theory and at the same time induce the army to catch up with the march of the budding technical civilization.

————. *The Army in My Time.* London, 1935.

In some respects a potboiler, this book perhaps better than any other shows the author's irreverent attitude toward many of the army's institutions and leaders.

————. *Armoured Warfare: An Annotated Edition of Fifteen Lectures on Operations between Mechanized Forces.* London, 1943.

Fuller's most important work on mechanization. The reader should remember, however, that this was originally written in 1932 and that improvements were made in both tanks and aircraft by the time of World War II.

————. *The Decisive Battles of the Western World and Their Influence upon History.* 3 vols. London, 1957.

Fuller's magnum opus; his most significant contribution to military history.

————. *The Generalship of Alexander the Great.* London, 1958.

Fuller has been intrigued with this subject ever since his days as instructor at the Staff College.

————. *The Conduct of War, 1789–1961.* London, 1961.

Most of Fuller's constructive ideas are contained in this volume, which may be regarded as a final summation of his ideas on the theory and history of modern war.

HAMLEY, EDWARD BRUCE. *The War in the Crimea.* London, 1891.

This remains one of the best and most enjoyable accounts of the Crimean War. Hamley's experience in the war is supplemented by careful research, his judgment is mature, and his style is superb.

————. *The Operations of War Explained and Illustrated* (6th ed.). Edinburgh and London, 1907.

Published after the death of Hamley, this edition does not include his original section on tactics. This is an unimportant omission, however, since the reputation of Hamley's text rests exclusively on his treatment of strategy.

(HENDERSON, G. F. R.) NEILL MALCOLM (ed.). *The Science of War.* London, 1906.

Henderson's most important contribution to military science.

————. *Stonewall Jackson and the American Civil War.* 2 vols. London, 1906.

A military classic, embodying Henderson's own views on tactics and command and representing an imaginative approach to the study of strategy.

————. *The Civil War: A Soldier's View.* Edited with an Introduction by JAY LUVAAS. Chicago, 1958.

Contains Henderson's classic "Campaign of Fredericksburg" and five articles interpreting military aspects of the Civil War.

LIDDELL HART, B. H. *Great Captains Unveiled.* London, 1927.

In addition to providing a fascinating glimpse of the actions and thoughts of Jenghiz Khan, Saxe, Gustavus Adolphus, Wallenstein, and Wolfe, this book also illustrates the use of historical analogies in the evolution of armored warfare. This scarce work deserves to be reprinted.

———. *The British Way in Warfare.* London, 1932.

Like many of Liddell Hart's books, this is largely a compilation of previous articles and reviews. This work is perhaps the most complete exposition of Liddell Hart's thoughts on tactics and strategy before he joined the staff of the *Times*, when he was compelled to expand his activities and to apply his theories to a crumbling military and political situation on the Continent.

———. *Foch: The Man of Orleans.* Boston, 1932.

This is perhaps Liddell Hart's best biography, although his biography of T. E. Lawrence is better known. Lawrence wrote of this book: "You demolish him thoroughly as a soldier: as a politician he needed no other evidence than his own to discredit him. But as a human being he came out well and honourably in what you wrote."

———. *Thoughts on War.* London, 1944.

A collection of reflections on nearly every aspect of war, arranged to enable the general reader to trace the evolution of Liddell Hart's theories. Indispensable to the student who wishes to become familiar with the views of this prolific critic.

———. *Strategy: The Indirect Approach.* London, 1954.

The most recent edition of *The Decisive Wars of History*, which Liddell Hart wrote originally in 1929 to furnish historical proof of the validity of his strategical theories. The approach therefore is philosophical more than historical.

———. *Sherman: Soldier, Realist, American.* New York, 1958.

One of the best biographies of Sherman and important in the development of Liddell Hart's military thought.

———. *The Tanks: The History of the Royal Tank Regiment and Its Predecessors, Heavy Branch Machine-Gun Corps, Tank Corps, and Royal Tank Corps 1914–1945.* 2 vols. London, 1959.

A superb history of the evolution of the tank, the development of a theory of mechanized warfare, and the role of the Royal Tank Corps in World War II.

———. *Deterrent or Defense: A Fresh Look at the West's Military Position.* New York, 1960.

Liddell Hart's most recent analysis of the cold war and of the problems facing the West.

MacDougall, Patrick. *The Campaigns of Hannibal Arranged and Critically Considered Expressly for the Use of Students of Military History.* London, 1858.

Illustrates the author's method of teaching the theory of war by historical examples. It is also a respectable study of Hannibal's generalship.

———. *Modern Warfare as Influenced by Modern Artillery.* London, 1864.

One of the first attempts to learn from the Civil War what impact the breech-loader and rifled artillery would have upon tactics.

MAURICE, FREDERICK. *The System of Field Manoeuvres Best Adapted for Enabling Our Troops To Meet a Continental Army.* Edinburgh, 1872.

Despite the formidable title, this is an interesting and readable analysis of Prussian tactics by one who was not blinded by the victories over France. The book that brought Maurice his opportunity.

————. *War: Reproduced with Amendments from the Article in the Last Edition of the "Encyclopaedia Britannica" to which is added an Essay on Military Literature and a List of Books with Brief Comments.* London, 1891.

One of the most famous works on the subject of war published in England during the nineteenth century. The annotated bibliography is a helpful introduction to the general military literature of the period.

MITCHELL, JOHN. *The Life of Wallenstein, Duke of Friedland.* London, 1837.

The most objective of Mitchell's historical studies and still a useful book on Wallenstein.

————. *Thoughts on Tactics and Military Organization: Together with an Enquiry into the Power and Position of Russia.* London, 1838.

Contains Mitchell's most fertile thoughts on training and tactics and reveals many of the weaknesses in the British army later brought to light in the Crimean War.

NAPIER, WILLIAM. *English Battles and Sieges in the Peninsula.* London, 1906.

A one-volume edition containing the most stirring passages from the *History of the War in the Peninsula.*

REPINGTON, CHARLES À COURT. *Imperial Strategy.* London, 1906.

Miscellaneous essays on strategy, organization, and administration as they relate to the defense of the British Empire.

————. *Foundations of Reform.* London, 1908.

Contains many of Repington's key articles from the *Times* and elsewhere on home defense and the Haldane reforms.

WILKINSON, SPENCER. *The Brain of an Army: A Popular Account of the German General Staff.* London, 1890.

Another military gem. It says something for Wilkinson that, despite the didactic nature of this volume, it is still a delight to read and remains a standard source for the history of the German army during this period.

————. *Imperial Defence* (rev. ed.)., Westminster, 1897.

Written in collaboration with Sir Charles Dilke, this is one of Wilkinson's best books and one of the most influential in its day. It is especially interesting for Wilkinson's ideas on naval power.

————. *War and Policy.* New York, 1900.

A collection of essays on military history, the art of war, national policy and defense, and the South African war representing Wilkinson at his best.

————. *Government and the War.* London, 1918.

Wilkinson the patriot and Wilkinson the military analyst combine forces in this wartime volume of essays. It is essential for an understanding of Wilkinson.

———. *The Defence of Piedmont*. Oxford, 1927.

This is probably the best—certainly it is the most difficult to acquire—of Wilkinson's books dealing with the origins of Napoleonic warfare.

INDEX

The names of persons not directly related to the development of British military thought, as well as merely casual references, are not included in the Index.

Halifax, 218
Hamilton, General Sir Ian, 167, 182–83, 190 n., 271, 277–78, 284
Hamley, Major General Sir E. B., 99, 126, 128, 174, 175–76, 181, 185, 187, 192, 195, 203, 217, 225, 242, 254, 275 n., 280, 293, 425–31
William George, 131–32
Hankey, Colonel Lord, 307
Hannibal, 105–6, 126, 127, 141
 see also Campaigns of Hannibal
Head, Sir Francis, 77
Hegel, 349
Henderson, Colonel G. F. R., 110 n., 150–51, 165, 171, 188, 189, 209, 210, 249, 257, 288, 293, 300, 303, 309, 314, 346, 369, 398, 425–30
Herat, 269
HERO, 431
Hildyard, Colonel H. T. H., 224
Hindu Kush, 305
History of General Sir Charles Napier's Administration of Scinde (Napier), 30
History of the Sudan Campaign, 189
History of the War in the Peninsula (Napier), 13–28, 48, 102, 109, 127, 199, 425
History of the War in South Africa (Maurice and others), 188–90, 211, 302
History of the World War, A (Liddell Hart), 422
Hitler, Adolph, 370, 430
Hoare, Rt. Hon. Sir Samual, secretary of state for air, 387
Hobart, Major General Sir Percy, 402, 409, 410
Hobbes, Thomas, 365
Hohenlohe-Ingelfingen, Prince Kraft zu, 245
Home, Colonel Robert, 169, 182, 183, 293
Home Defense, 31–32, 73–77, 98, 161, 170, 204, 306
Hore-Belisha, Rt. Hon. Leslie, secretary of state for war, 408–13, 423
Hornby, Admiral Sir Geoffry, 195, 204 n., 265–66
Horse Guards, 13, 17, 31, 36, 44, 56

Hostilities without Declaration of War (Maurice), 184, 210
Huguet, Major, 318
Hume, Joseph, 56
Hythe, school of musketry, 98

Imperial Conference of 1907, 300
Imperial Defence (Wilkinson), 268–70, 273–74
Imperial Defense, 98, 161–62, 183, 268–72, 304–505
India, 8, 29–30, 37, 60, 200, 203, 218, 269–71, 274, 276, 281, 332, 357, 366, 430
India Board, 96, 182
Indian Mutiny (1857), 97, 99, 175, 429
Infantry Drill Book, 245
Infantry Journal, The, 374
Infantry Training
 1905, 249
 1921, 379, 384, 422
 1926, 402
Institute for Strategic Studies, 431
Intelligence Department, War Office, 121, 184, 266, 294
Invasion of the Crimea, The (Kinglake), 85
Invasion Panic of 1859, 94, 97, 258
Ireland, 4, 8, 32, 73, 218
 Board of Public Works of, 72
Irish Command, 272 n.
 Home Rule, 163
 Relief Commission, 75
Ironside, General Sir Edmund, 345, 407
Irving, Washington, 14 n.
Isandlhwana, Battle of (1879), 125, 200
Ismailia, 156
Italy, 205–7, 293, 294, 332
 army of, 293–94
 see also Abyssinia
Italian War of 1759, 62, 97

Jackson, Lieutenant General T. J. "Stonewall," 150, 173, 225–26, 229, 237, 241, 243, 247
 see also Stonewall Jackson and the American Civil War
Japan, 196, 332, 401
 army of, 299–300
Jena, Battle of (1806), 3
Jenghiz Khan, 383, 388, 389, 395–96